Book Two

Shattered
People Series:

Journeys to Love
- Revised

Pastor Michael E. Chalberg

SCP
Shepherds Care Publishing

SHATTERED PEOPLE SERIES:
Journeys to Love - Revised
By Pastor Michael E. Chalberg

Printed in the USA & Internationally by LSI & Ingram
Library of Congress Control Number: 2003099165
Paperback edition - ISBN 0-974646-43-1   2005
Hardback edition - ISBN 0-974646-44-X   2005
Revised PB edition – ISBN 978-1-7349703-95 December 2020
Ebook edition – ISBN 97809746464-73 January 2021

Unless otherwise indicated, Bible quotations are taken from the New Open Bible, Study Edition, Copyright © 1990 by Thomas Nelson, Inc; The Message, New Testament with Psalms and Proverbs, Copyright © 1993, 1994, 1995 by Eugene Peterson, and NAVPRESS.

Shepherds Care Publishing
An Outreach of Shepherd's Care Counseling Ministries.
2473 S. Higley Road Suite 104 PMB 210
Gilbert, AZ 85295

Web: *www.shepherdscareministries.org*
Order: *scpublishing2020@gmail.com*
Email: *pastormike@shepherdscareministries.org*

Dedication

To the ministry of
Hope, Healing, & Love that is
Jesus Christ our Lord.
May He be glorified in
The fulfillment of these
Scriptures in our lives:

"The Spirit of the Lord God is upon me,
Because the Lord has anointed me
To bring good news to the afflicted;
He has sent me to bind up the broken-hearted,
To proclaim liberty to captives,
And freedom to prisoners;
To proclaim the favorable year of the Lord."
Isaiah 61: 1 – 2

Acknowledgments

The author wishes to thank these people for their love & support.

David Beskeen
Ed & Marilyn Chalberg
Bruce & Tone Ferry
Bruce Fielding
Elizabeth Ray
SCM Board
The System

And most importantly
My wife, Carol
Whose Love, Dedication,
And Sacrifices for me
Allowed for the completion
Of this book.

Table of Contents

Note:
Definitions of terms like Multiple Personality Disorder (MPD), Dissociative Identity Disorder (DID), integration, blending, and shadowing; as well as a detailed structure map of the System and brief individual histories of each member of the System as shown in the beginning of the *Shattered People Series*: *Journeys to Joy*. Numerous details there set the stage chronologically for the events of the following books. Several reference works are also footnoted there.

Forward

You are about to embark on a journey which will likely challenge how you think about abuse and the abused, about healing, and about God's commitment to wholeness. It tells the story of how one multiple sought God's healing, and how God responded to all of them. I hope and pray that, if you are one who has been abused, this book will provide support for you in your healing. And if you are a family member, therapist, minister or friend, it will support you as you help those who have been abused.

You should understand before you start reading that this is not primarily a book about Dissociative Identity Disorder (DID) or Multiple Personality Disorder (MPD), nor about a person who suffers from either. Neither is this primarily a book about treatment methods, the necessity of a support system for multiples, or the difficulty multiples have in reconciling what has happened to them with a loving God. All of these issues are touched on, but they are not the core of the book.

Ultimately this book, and the others in this series, is about the personal commitment that God makes to each of our lives to bring healing, to bring fulfillment and to bring redemption; and about the incredible struggle and journey of one group of people who responded to God's commitment.

When Maria first came to my office, there was no hint of either her history or of her vast resolve to recover; nor was there any hint of the community of souls who lived with her. She was a scared, broken individual, hardly able to look me in the eyes; yet behind that fear and fragility laid an incredible reserve of courage and strength, and an amazing ability to take risks in order to find a better life. Ultimately, Pastor Mike and I discovered a level of faith and trust that was, and is, truly humbling. And God met Maria and her system's willingness to take risks and trust (sometimes kicking and screaming) and brought vast and beautiful healing.

And here's the good news: every multiple, every adult victim of childhood trauma, indeed every victim of trauma can find the same strength inside themselves and the same healing response from God. I have seen the same journey embarked on by many victims, most with the joyous result of healing and wholeness.

If you are multiple, or if you are a victim of trauma, you will find much in these pages to encourage you and challenge you to hope again, to seek healing from God and support from others. It will not be easy, but it is more rewarding than you can ever imagine.

If you are a therapist, you will see a view of the mind and the psychological functioning of a multiple that may be foreign to you. This should challenge you to think differently about those we diagnose as DID and give you a fresh perspective on how to support them in their recovery.

If you are a family member, you will be challenged to provide a higher level of support for the multiple in your life and will gain a greater understanding of what goes on in their very private, very interior life.

And if you are a pastor or church worker, you are in for a bumpy ride. This book is unflinching in its analysis of the modern day church and its attitude and reaction to both those with psychiatric problems and those who are oppressed. It is unforgiving in its view of the local church as nearly incapable of effectively supporting those who are attempting to recover from childhood trauma, and of its focus on doctrine rather than individuals. As someone who lives in both places (helping individuals recover from trauma and working within a local church), I see the struggles of both parties from both sides. This book should, however, challenge you to reexamine how we can recapture Jesus' commitment to those who are most in need of His love and redemption.

Finally, if you are Roman Catholic, you will find that this book is most scathing of a church organization that has, either by intentionality, inaction, or both, allowed horrible abuses within its ranks. It is my hope and prayer that by reading this book you will challenge your leaders or superiors to take responsibility for the reforms and healing that are desperately needed. Meanwhile, we Protestants can view this as a warning: such abuse doesn't occur only in the Catholic Church, and we need to be on guard against the same abuses within our groups.

One more warning: The language that is used in this book will be offensive to some. Please understand that, for a lot of people, cussing is the language of the marketplace, and is evidence of their rage, passion and depth of feeling. If, as you read these pages, you get so hung up on the language that you can't see the message, then you have missed the entire point of Jesus' willingness to live with and minister to those who were labeled "sinners" by the Pharisees.

But as I said at the beginning, these are all secondary issues to the message of hope, healing and redemption...may you find all of these in this book.

Bruce Fielding
Licensed Marriage & Family Counselor

Preface

A friend commented on how these books are as much about redemption as they are about healing from trauma and severe abuse. What is presented here are true stories of healing of the human heart, soul, mind and spirit with God Almighty, our creator. It is the continuing saga of my clients and friends known as the System, whose journeys of healing are literally an open book for other lives shattered by abuse to learn and grow with them in their quest for God's unconditional love.

An important amount of information is shared in book one of the ***Shattered People Series*** revised November 2020 entitled ***Journeys to Joy***, to inform my readers of how their sixteen-year journey of healing began. They write their personal autobiographies about the abuse they suffered from infancy all the way to their diagnosis of having multiple personality disorder **(MPD),** as adults trying to survive in mainstream society. The first book supplies brief histories and definitions of terms used to clarify how the System exists. Details of the types of abuses put on them by others in control over them are given, to remove the veil of fear that blocks our sensitivity to the pain and suffering, which too many people have endured without any compassionate help to survive. A **Content Warning** is given before difficult sections.

This book follows the second leg of our journey together and follows their struggles to understand and discover God's plan for their lives. Some have entered into a relationship with Jesus Christ, while others are still seeking to establish their own self-awareness and identity before making that choice. They are learning that survivors of severe abuse continue to live with the knowledge of their loss of innocence before God…but not without hope.

Come with them as they build relationships, start careers, learn the joy of playing with their Dragonslayer, their Lord Jesus Christ, and the truth about God; as they endure hardship, trauma, mental and emotional abuse, and the abuses of evil within our world. Discover with them the renewal of life in the kingdom of God here on earth and revel in the joy of His presence.

Pastor Michael E. Chalberg

PROLOGUE

"Remembering the Journey"

**"For I know the plans I have for you,' declares the Lord,
'plans for welfare and not calamity
to give you a future and a hope..."
Jeremiah 29:11**

As I watched the ball come down in Times Square, I pondered what the Lord had planned for all of us in this new Millennium and more specifically, the next few days. Maria had left us only the day before to go home and prepare for what seemed like the biggest hurdle of her life. She would be telling a group of people the truth about her life for the first time, with the hope that they would accept her unconditionally. Outside of a dozen or so who knew her, the 50 people remaining could potentially destroy much of the preceding 5 years of therapy in one brief evening. Maria was not alone in her fears about taking this risk. Experience screamed out from the past telling her how the world was not ready to accept a 'Multiple.' Yet, what choice did she have? It was Jesus who had taken her this far and now telling both of us that He wanted this to happen.

Ann had repeatedly stated her position against it happening at all, both the week there and every time it was brought up as a possibility the month before we went to Lake Tahoe. She had no doubts that we were all crazy and at the very least insensitive to her, for planning something that could cost her not only her job, but also her very life if Maria's father found out.

Liz was placing bets on the high probability that these Suburban Christians would repeat what they had done so many times before and reject someone quite different from themselves. She too had no doubt over the odds being in her favor, yet she wasn't completely at ease with how Jesus had told all of them "it was time." The last thing she wanted was to have her hopes smashed again by Christians.

Circle Council was nervous but remained obedient. They were remembering something Lindsay had said some 3 years earlier after our first surgery together. *"Growth doesn't come without change…change doesn't come without loss…loss doesn't come without pain."* "How much pain, loss and change,' they asked, 'must one person endure in order to be accepted as a person, and especially among one's Christian peers?" Jesus wasn't telling any of us what the outcome was going to be ahead of time, only that they needed to trust in the plans He had for them. It was difficult for all of the men of Circle Council to set aside Ann's logic in arguing against the coming event. What if Ann was correct and her predictions of doom did take the entire System down? Could they maintain enough control to survive? What if this was simply one more test of their trust in Jesus as Lord?

All week long in the cabin I was asked, *"Are you certain this is what Jesus wants?"* Even my wife questioned the wisdom and logic of it at this time of change for all of us. The risks were abundantly real and difficult. Yet, Jesus had just reminded us of how He had carried all of us through many trials over the last 5 years, at Christmas when He instituted a new tradition for us with Mariann. The night after the System arrived we decorated the tree as we had in previous years with ornaments that had specific memories of our time together since our first Christmas in 1995. While we did this to remember the good times, there was a need to also remember the difficult times when our total dependence was on Jesus to get us through it. For His purposes of remembering, Jesus had Mariann pick out a tree on Christmas Eve while we played in the snow. Actually, she picked out a small dead branch that might have just as easily become a burning bush…and in many ways it did.

Carol brought some strips of colored paper the size of bookmarkers and ribbon; to tie each one on the 'tree' after every person had a chance to write on them. We wrote about the times that God was faithful in fulfilling His promises to heal us, of His protection in times of spiritual warfare, and how He was always there to renew us, when all we had left to give was obedience. While most of the branches of this tree weren't any bigger than spaghetti, not one of them sagged under the weight of about 50 notes from everyone. This tree glowed with the reminders of new resurrected lives, because of Jesus' strength and healing power.

Tears of thanks filled our eyes as we read the memories out loud, sometimes with bursts of laughter and sometimes with prayers, of never wanting to go through that kind of trial again. The spirit of hope was rekindled about where Jesus was going to lead us in the future. It felt safe that Christmas Eve to say, *"Jesus, our Dragonslayer, is in control. I'm ready to go anywhere you say Lord."* Yet, as often happens after pinnacles of spiritual blessings, the sober reality of what He was asking from Maria and the System caused a somber mood to cover the rest of our stay there.

I could offer no guarantees to anyone that it wasn't going to end up being another painful rejection, or that their trust would carry them through the pain of having their greatest desire shattered. None of us could have expected, or foreseen, just how the following events were going to be played out and the necessity of this new Christmas tradition in our lives. This same tradition of remembering our journey happens not only at Christmas now, but also throughout the year, whenever we're asked to take another difficult step on God's path.

When the Lord told me it was time to write this second book in the series and have it ready by the end of 2004, I had to set aside time to remember again all of the miraculous events He had accomplished to bring us to this destination. I knew the timeline for *Shattered People Series: Journeys to Love* would pick up our stories following the first cancer surgery in August of 1996 and take them through Easter of 1999. Maria's testimony the following January will cause me to focus on the events of this book, that inspire the possibility of her testimony ever happening at all. That is why I wanted to offer to my readers as accurate an account of this time period as possible for a number of reasons.

Book One, *Shattered People Series: Journeys to Joy* only opens the door to the miraculous healing power of Jesus, in the telling of the events of the first two years of their journey. Telling the details of their past lives and all of the severe abuse they suffered from family, the Church, and people with power over them, wasn't as hard as telling this second stage of their healing process. They had just begun a 'new journey' essentially, as a new creation in Christ filled with great expectations of 'wholeness' and

3

healing waiting for them just out of sight. However, this new relationship with Jesus brought with it a new awareness, one that many of us would rather avoid than risk what it means to integrate it into our lives, to understand all that it means to call oneself a Christian.

"When people realize it is the living God you are presenting and not some idol that makes them feel good, they are going to turn on you, even people in your own family. There is a great irony here: proclaiming so much love, experiencing so much hate! But don't quit. Don't cave in. It is all worth it in the end. It is not success you are after in such times but survival. Be survivors! Before you've run out of options, the Son of Man will have arrived...

If you find the godless world hates you, remember it got its start hating me. If you lived on the world's terms, the world would love you as one of its own. But since I picked you to live on God's terms and no longer on the world's terms, the world is going to hate you."

Matt. 10 & John 15 - The Message

Survival of Maria and the System becomes the focus for all of the parts during this period. But the difficulty of this becomes all too clear, as they try to integrate themselves as individual Christians into the traditional Christian world. Even to approach a pastor and say, *"I'm a person with multiple personalities, some of whom are Christian, and I would like to attend your church,"* becomes a real test of courage and faith for all who are challenged by it. Their quest for acceptance is about to lead them into a reality about our human nature...our never-ending communal struggle to speak with the Almighty God, but in our own individual way. It is this particular flaw in our nature that has created the various divisions in the Church, both Catholic and Protestant, and outside of it with every individual who seeks to understand God.

As the System begins to become a cohesive group that functions as one person, they will discover very quickly how the Christians around them can't function as one Church together under God's rule. Many times in their search for truth, they will become perplexed and overwhelmed. They will often ask me, *"How is it possible that Christian pastors can have opposing answers to our questions about the one God we all serve? Why is it their answers aren't the same ones that Jesus says to us?"* These questions will cause many debates on Council and in the Land of Preservation during the time period of these books.

As in the first part of this series, *Journeys to Joy,* I will present a list of people continuing with their journeys to find the truth about God and His unconditional love. You will be able to find more detailed information on each individual and their personal history in the Prologue of book one. There are also a number of questions that are raised throughout that book about these people and the two worlds they live in. Then, as now, you'll have to draw your own conclusions as to whether or not the answers they find are the ones that resonate in you. One reader of the first book asked me for a direct answer to one question raised early on; *"Does each personality of a multiple have their own soul before God, or is integration of the personalities into one soul the only way they are acceptable to God?"* I gave her a direct answer that she didn't want to hear, because she wasn't prepared for that possible conclusion. I suggested that she contact me again after she read some Scriptural references and was able to tell me in her own understanding...*how does God define a human soul?*

As of late August 1996, the System was preparing for the first day of chemotherapy following the cancer surgery and recovery at our house detailed in the epilogue of book one. They consisted of the people on Level One:

Circle Council:
Helper
Paladin
Keeper of Functions
King of the Lights
Daniel
Lion
(Tolip will join Council in a few months.)

The Women:
Maria
Louise
Ann
Liz

Ruth
Raquel – Quiet Walker (+ Eagle Clan – 4)
Elizabeth Ray
Jennifer
Mari
Marie
House of Prayer (7)

The Children:
Mariann
Tabitha
Penny
Anna
Angelina
Hopi (Peace-be-still)
Lilah – Otosis
The Little Ones (2)

Those Who Are Core on Level Two:
Tolip
Pod Alpha (5)
Pod Mu (5)
Egar
Pod Omega (5)
(Hopi & Lilah were still under the care of Core)

The System was still under the care of their primary therapist Bruce, as they were quickly turning to Carol and I to fill the greater need for love in their lives. Some blending (the process of having two or more personalities or parts integrate into one) had occurred in the Clan of Argus into Daniel, Labyrinth into Paladin and Elysian Fields into King of the Lights. More blending occurs in the next few years, but at a much slower rate. The statement of Jesus to them of, **"You shall remain a multiple for My purposes and you shall bring Me glory by your testimonies"** will continue to have deepening implications for all, as they heal and move out of the darkness of the past. (See System map, pages 26-27, Book One -Rev.)

Consider what one reviewer of *Journeys to Joy* wrote, *"Chalberg...had a definite purpose in writing this book. He intends to suggest ways in which we can find the real God for ourselves by exposing the inadequate conceptions of God, which prevent us from seeing Him."* The reviewer felt I had accomplished that in writing about these people in that book. I hope so. But I also know how difficult it is for anyone to overcome their preconceived concepts of a God they don't know or at the very least…think they know, so I'll continue to challenge these concepts throughout all of the books for one reason, to test the truth of it. In fact, one pastor thought the detailed descriptions of God's interactions with the System was miraculous and stretched him spiritually to a new awareness of God. I wanted him to be prepared for this book and Book Three because they will push those boundaries even further, as the System draws closer to God and God draws closer to them removing the boundaries. All boundaries that is except one, our free will to choose to accept His will, His love and His plan.

These three points (His will, His love and His plan) are why I have set the three subtitles in the order they are; *"Journeys to Joy…Journeys to Love…Living With Jesus Each Day"*. When a life has been shattered or broken by another human being, it becomes a real journey to crawl back to the point of believing that your life is a part of God's will. There can be a true joy in finding there is purpose for enduring suffering that to us has no reason. Accepting God's will for our lives is the hardest part of the journey because it gets you moving again in God's direction.

To accept God's will for our lives without understanding it is by all accounts a leap of faith. The first step that carries with it a belief that God is the navigator of the journey and we are not alone. To be in God's will is to be in the joy of His presence. *Journeys to Joy* tells the stories of how the System learned that God had never abandoned them and there was great joy in this truth, because now they knew the path to freedom.

**"And you shall know the truth,
and the truth shall make you free."
John 8:32**

The next three years for the System will bring with it new definitions of the terms: rejection, trust, obedience, endurance, love and suffering, as they strive to understand God's love. They would experience a new kind of distancing from family and 'friends', simply because they were changing from victims to survivors. They would respond to a new kind of love that would carry them through great peril and pain, but without real understanding of it for several more years. Like many new Christians, they will learn how the cost of discipleship will test the limits of their perception of God's plans for them in this life. Living on God's terms will have them testing the boundaries of people's capacity to love in 'spirit and truth', while discovering the limitless possibilities of how the truth of Jesus' love can be tested through them.

"Love seeketh not itself to please,
Nor for itself have any care,
But for another gives its ease,
And builds a Heaven in Hell's despair."
William Blake, *Songs of Experience* (1794)

The central theme of *Journeys to Love* is the journey, or the process itself. All of the System will reach points along the way where they begin to understand the difference between human love and God's love. They will search for the truth of it in each other, as well as in those with whom they develop a relationship. For those parts most severely abused, and those who felt alone or abandoned most of their life, it will become as important for them to believe in the reality of unconditional love existing in this life, as it will be for them to receive it from God. They needed examples of real love in action from others outside, not just within the System, in order to establish a solid foundation for knowing what love is. My old friend Aristotle said this in his *Metaphysics*:

"All human beings by nature have an urge to know."

Most philosophers think he was only talking about objective truth, but what good is truth without love? It is the urge to know both truth and love that will drive the System on into the next part of their journey. It will be a modern-day philosopher/artist that will capture their hopes and fears upon this journey in his song. Though he has never met them, you wouldn't know it by his lyrics.

"The River of Dreams" by Billy Joel

In the middle of the night
I go walking in my sleep
From the mountains of faith
To a river so deep
I must be looking for something
Something sacred I lost
But the river is wide
And it's too hard to cross

And even though I know the river is wide
I walk down every evening and I stand on the shore
And try to cross to the opposite side
So I can finally find out what I've been looking for

In the middle of the night
I go walking in my sleep
Through the valley of fear
To a river so deep
And I've been searching for something
Taken out of my soul
Something I would never lose
Something somebody stole

I don't know why I go walking at night
But now I'm tired and I don't want to walk anymore
I hope it doesn't take the rest of my life
Until I find what it is that I'm looking for

In the middle of the night
I go walking in my sleep
Through the jungle of doubt
To a river so deep
I know I'm searching for something
Something so undefined

That it can only be seen
By the eyes of the blind
In the middle of the night
I'm not sure about a life after this
God knows I've never been a spiritual man
Baptized by the fire, I wade into the river
That runs into the promised land

In the middle of the night
I go walking in my sleep
Through the desert of truth
To the river so deep
We all end in the ocean
We all start in the streams
We're all carried along
By the river of dreams
In the middle of the night.

The System begins the second leg of their journey in search of the truth about God's love. Will it turn out to be only an illusion, a dream started so long ago to fill the void that replaced their innocence? Or will this 'Truth' turn dreams into visions that foresee reality?

"To die, to sleep;
To sleep: perchance to dream: aye, there's the rub;
For in that sleep of death what dreams may come
when we have shuffled off this mortal coil,
must give us pause."
William Shakespeare, *Hamlet, III*

"...Then you will call upon Me and come and pray to Me,
And you will seek Me and find Me, when you search for
Me with all of your heart. And I will be found by you,'
Declares the Lord..."
Jeremiah 29:12 – 14

Chapter One

"Devastation or Resurrection"

"Because of the devastation of the afflicted,
Because of the groaning of the needy,
Now I will arise," says the Lord; "I will set
them in the safety for which they long."
The words of the Lord are pure words;
As silver tried in a furnace on the earth,
refined seven times. Thou, O Lord,
will keep them;"
Psalm 12: 5-7

*"REMEMBER THE WAYS OF THE ANCIENT ONES
REMEMBER THE PROMISE OF THE GREAT SPIRIT
REMEMBER WHO WE ARE
WE ARE LIKE THE PHOENIX AND
WE SHALL RISE OUT OF THE ASHES
CANCER CAN NOT CONTROL US
IT CANNOT DESTROY THE LOVE WE HAVE FOUND
IT CANNOT DISSOLVE OUR FAITH
IT CANNOT SMASH OUR HOPE
OR SHATTER OUR PEACE
CANCER HAS NOT THE POWER TO INVADE OUR
SPIRIT OR ROB US OF ETERNAL LIFE
WE SHALL OVERCOME AND THE
LAND OF PRESERVATION SHALL BE RESTORED
REMAIN FAITHFUL
HOLD ON TO COURAGE
REMEMBER THE WAYS OF THE ANCIENT ONES
REMEMBER THE PROMISE OF THE GREAT SPIRIT"*
- QUIET WALKER

I remember when Raquel gave me this letter to read to Maria on the first day of chemotherapy in August of '96. Nobody truly knew what was about to happen on the inside in Preservation and to all of the inhabitants there. In the decree of Circle Council the week before, they warned of imminent danger coming with the chemo and the necessity for everyone to prepare for some level of devastation to their world. I used the three weeks between recovery and chemo to learn as much as I could about their reality inside. During the previous year and a half, the System described a 'Garden of Eden' existing on the inside that was their 'other' world reality. There wasn't any real scientific way to test that reality of their stated existence being anything more than a spiritual realm, or metaphysical reality, until the chemotherapy was given.

We were all put into a state of trust, or faith if you will, that what Jesus had created…He was now allowing to be destroyed, while He was promising to restore it in time. So many questions began to flood my mind. If the inside were a spiritual reality only, why would He allow the physical reality of this world and CAF to destroy it? Why would He allow the System, who had suffered so much in this physical world, have to go through more of it in the only world that had been their refuge? Could the natural laws that the Lord had created to govern our world, somehow have a direct relationship in the spiritual dimension as an indication of how our two worlds are connected? Or was this simply an isolated case where the Lord was going to teach and test His disciples about His power over both worlds and the power available to us through faith in Him? Maybe these questions are unimportant to some of you, but I've wanted to know how and why the spiritual realm works as it does, if as a Christian I'm to be a sojourner in this world while trying to live as a citizen of God's kingdom.

"For our citizenship is in heaven, from which also we eagerly wait for a Savior, the Lord Jesus Christ; who will transform the body of our humble state into conformity with the body of His glory."
Philippians 3:20-21

"I do not ask Thee to take them out of the world, but to keep them from the evil one. They are not of the world, even as I am not of the world. Sanctify them in the truth; Thy word is truth."
John 17: 15-17

Yes, the chemotherapy was an opportunity to learn more about our spiritual relationships and how faith operates in two worlds at the same time. I'm sure that everyone who has read the following Scripture verse has wondered about its implications for any person who is a follower of Jesus. Is it to be understood metaphorically or as a real possibility in our physical world?

"Have faith in God. Truly I say to you, whoever says to this mountain, 'Be taken up and cast into the sea,' and does not doubt in his heart, but believes what he says is going to happen, it shall be granted him."
Mark 11: 22-23

When I've been asked as a pastor about the meaning of this verse in context to our physical world, I've stated how the focal point is the power of God through faith and not our own power. If God wishes to reveal His power through the faith of an individual to accomplish His plan, He'll do it! When people of faith begin to take credit for wondrous works that only God can do, they begin to remove themselves from God's plan. In the case of the System's chemotherapy changing the Land of Preservation, it was going to be God allowing His creation to be changed, but without altering or destroying the spiritual life forms living there. Why? What was He trying to teach us?

By the time we started chemotherapy, the System was mutually aware of the existence of almost every other part that lived within the body. But being aware of their existence didn't mean they possessed knowledge of the other's memories and experiences that gave each one an identity of 'self'. This was learned in the same way as anyone else might acquire it as a sentient being, by living out a measure of existence in this physical world. I don't know when each one became aware of their inside world as distinct from the outside world, but I would guess it wasn't much different than how a child might learn of the greater world existing around them as they experience it. I do know that Preservation pre-existed the emergence or splitting off of Elizabeth Ray and Maria from the birth child Maria Ann.

God had prepared this place for them before they existed so that they might find a refuge from all of the abuse they received in the outside world. He made it beautiful and simple and filled it with a variety of living things. As each part emerges, there is a home provided for their time there. There is order and peace in this realm, perhaps like the world as it existed for Adam and Eve. And just like in our world, evil exists inside their world, but manifesting itself within their reality as a conquered enemy in the kingdom of God. Apparently the boundaries of evil's activity were the same in both worlds and, as described in the New Testament, it could have no authority over the inhabitants of Preservation other than what they gave to it or accepted over them.

I will go into greater detail about evil's reality in both worlds and the System's battles with it as more is revealed to us in the ongoing issues of their healing. In this and the third book the battle lines are drawn more distinctively as each in the System accepts Jesus. It was already clear that whenever someone called on His name for help, even if they hadn't accepted Him yet, evil would not stay in the vicinity. Like Mariann says, *"They run like chickens when Dragonslayer comes!"* However, most of the parts at this stage do not yet have the strength that Mariann has for coping with these attacks of evil, or even aware of evil's existence inside.

I wanted to discover if the chemo was going to affect evil in any way, because I didn't expect it to, beyond giving evil the source for more lies, which it did. Even before we entered chemo evil ones began telling the children and Maria that it was in their power to destroy Preservation and they would, because Maria and Louise had accepted Jesus. It used what Jesus had revealed previously about the immediate results of chemo on Preservation to intimidate the System into thinking everything was in its power and had moderate success with certain parts believing it. Evil tried to reinforce the brainwashing that had occurred in the early abuses of the child parts. It was a simple method to raise fears quickly.

What evil wasn't prepared for was Jesus initiating a pre-emptive defense for the children of the System. He explained to Mariann in detail how He was going to fight the 'cancer monsters' within the chemotherapy and had her put together a book with drawings and a description in her own interpretation of the events. She received help from Raquel to put it together and began sharing it with everyone she met the moment we arrived in the treatment room. Mariann's little booklet will be published at the same time

14

as this second book and the title is of course, _The Cancer Monster by Mariann._ It is our hope that this booklet will help other children facing cancer.

Circle Council had spent a considerable amount of time before chemo in preparation for the effects it would have on Preservation. In their decree issued the week before the chemo, they spoke of 3 caves or dwelling places on Sacred Mountain that were stocked with food and water for them to last the length of the chemo. CORE was provided with titanium shelters for its inhabitants. Holding pens and an aquarium were built to protect the animals, birds, and aquatic life in Preservation. A trumpet would sound to alert every part to enter the shelters and would sound again when it was safe to leave the shelters following each treatment.

Obviously Council expected devastation from fire and pollution to the waterways and air to some degree. It didn't look promising and seemed to confirm Jennifer's dire prediction, yet Council encouraged the parts to have hope and work out their differences as they would be spending a lot of time together in close quarters. People had to plan on who they wanted to be sealed inside a cave with for a yet to be determined amount of time. It may sound easy but you have to remember, each person had their fears and resentment about having to go through this change at all. Not every part perceived the treatment as necessary, or that it wouldn't alter the body as they knew it. No one wanted to lose their hair, have hot flashes, become weak enough where they couldn't defend themselves, be forced into entering menopause or worst of all, be dependent upon others to take care of them. Their trust of doctors was nil, except for their oncologist who quickly proved herself worthy of their trust by the way she accepted them individually for who they are, a rare quality in a doctor.

Mariann had been chosen to receive the IV injection at the beginning of each treatment. This was due to her trust in me to protect her and more importantly in Dragonslayer to walk with her through this. She was the only one that I knew would follow my instructions, so we could get through the preliminary bloodwork and into the treatment room. We were both calling on Dragonslayer often to make it through each encounter. Maria would trade places with her from her cave, as soon as the CAF was starting to be injected. We would often discuss the changes

15

occurring on the inside as it was happening, as well as how Jesus might fulfill His promises of healing and restoration to Preservation.

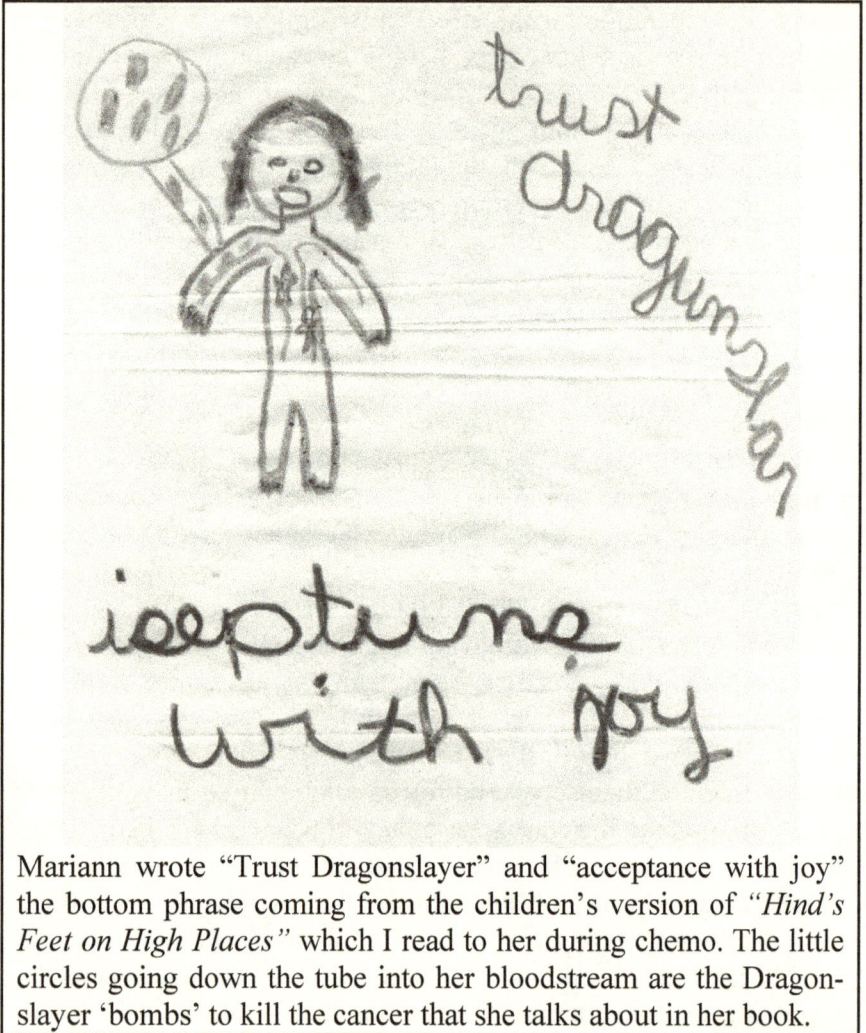

Mariann wrote "Trust Dragonslayer" and "acceptance with joy" the bottom phrase coming from the children's version of *"Hind's Feet on High Places"* which I read to her during chemo. The little circles going down the tube into her bloodstream are the Dragonslayer 'bombs' to kill the cancer that she talks about in her book.

Plate # 1

On August 26th I arrived early at their home to take them to the hospital. As anticipated, it took some effort to get them into my car with all of the switching going on. Some parts did **not** want to go through the treatment, primarily because they thought the doctors were going to use this second chance to kill them. Ruth had to come out long enough to get inside the hospital. From that point forward it would be Mariann, who was **not** going to let go of my hand for any reason. It was difficult when she cried over the pain of the nurses screwing up the blood draws in her already bruised arms. Circumstances required a lot of trust in me on her part, to be telling her the truth about how this was necessary. She recovered enough strength shortly after that however, to present her booklet to the nurses preparing her for the CAF injection. If I could give an award to the nurses in oncology for their responses to Mariann, I would. They were wonderfully gracious and kind.

As the CAF was injected, I had to have Mariann go inside and Maria come out, because the chemical that was injected first was blood red in color and caused the body to heat up quickly as though it were on fire. This condition was an immediate trigger for some of the severely abused child parts. Maria didn't look at it and stayed focused on what we discussed. As the chemical entered the bloodstream, she described how earthquakes and trembling had begun in Preservation and were being felt by the last stragglers entering the caves.

They looked back over the Land of Preservation to witness the devastation beginning. Red fire was flowing like lava and burning up the meadows, burning up the trees and destroying vegetation. A hot rain fell on the land, as the wind rose stirring up the fires and carrying the sounds of trees exploding all the way up into the caves on Sacred Mountain. They knew that all of their homes were being destroyed as they waited in fear in the sealed caves. Preservation was becoming a wasteland where nothing was left that gave any sign of life. Several parts thought their death was imminent.

The second injection was a clear substance that had the opposite effect inside. It was very cold going in and caused Preservation to start snowing again, covering everything in a blanket of ice. This process continued with each session of chemotherapy that followed but became less intense after the first one destroyed everything, as there was nothing left to burn up or freeze that wasn't already protected.

Within a few days, Preservation would find its balance to where the lower elevations had a warm/hot climate, and the high elevations held a constant ice cap. Some of the more hyper parts would come out to walk in what was now a desert. They would return to the caves when they became thirsty or hungry, and before the next treatment when climatic changes hit. There was some migration by parts in the 3 caves following the first treatment. They had fought hard in the beginning to have their own dwelling and not be forced to live in the same house. Now, some resorted to pitching tents on the cliffs for privacy. Ruth wrote us (Bruce and I) about her observations following the chemo.

The system as a whole is doing okay with the side effects of the chemotherapy. Liz is one least affected by the drugs. Unfortunately Liz is also the one who gets bored easily and wants to take off. Ann seems to fare the second best and is still demanding a lot out of the rest of us. We won't need any physical therapy for our arm or chest muscles because of Ann.

The rest of us become tired easily and deal with digestive problems and an overall blah feeling. Maria, Louise and Angelina seem to be affected the most. Mariann complains about her 'tummy hurting', but other than that we are holding our own. Ann is concerned about the system becoming anemic. Ann took HRT until the cancer to control excessive bleeding. Studies indicate that HRT might spark breast cancer and since Ann is estrogen positive, she has taken us off HRT. We're waiting now for the chemo to start our menopause like the books indicated, but it is not going the way they said. The bleeding is no longer controlled by HRT, so Ann is feeding Maria iron pills and waiting to see what happens after the next dose. Council is monitoring it all and is aware of Ann's concerns. However, they also know that the system will not go in for another surgery, especially surgery in the area of the most trauma. They will not even consider reconstructive breast surgery. They want to get away from doctors as soon as possible.

Council has noticed how the children are showing signs of changing in their development. Anna and Tabitha are together almost all of the time now and both are advancing rapidly in vocabulary and speech. Tabitha is using more English and is becoming more assertive towards Mariann. Both girls play a lot in the caves with the Pollyanna children. Marie is usually in charge of the kids and gets exhausted at their never-ending energy to explore the mountain. I try to help, but they run faster and never seem to get tired. They crawl through places that I can't fit. I can't

18

wait for the valley to be restored again to have a safe environment for them to play in. I have more appreciation for what parents must go through raising kids.

Council is puzzled as to why Mariann is not advancing and seems to be regressing. They wonder if it is because of the cancer and her part in the treatment. Are Hopi and the CORE children pulling her down? Angelina seems to be frozen in time. She is held continually by Jesus in a type of cloth sling that is tied over His shoulder. She never cries when she is with Him and seems to identify with Him very closely. We have no idea if she has any understanding of what's happening to the body.

The system still does not trust doctors or hospitals. It took a lot for the system to get through surgery. If it had not been for Pastor Chalberg's constant surveillance, parts would have switched out and walked away from the hospital. Even in chemo it's a struggle. There is a lot of switching just before he picks us up. When he has control of her, Council can relax and focus on comforting the anxious ones on the inside. Unless there is a trigger to push another part out, he is able to keep Maria and Mariann out at the hospital, while constantly on alert for others.

At times I get frustrated at the amount of resistance to chemo, but Helper reminds me that I'm not volunteering to take Maria's place. He can be very stern with me about my judging Maria's weaknesses, and he's right. I haven't walked in her shoes and God knows how I do with pain. I can't even imagine what it must be like for her. I have to remember to be patient.

(Ruth went on in this rather lengthy letter to discuss parenting issues facing the System in the family with Claudia, Rosalinda, Jose and marital problems with Sergio. She concluded her letter on the issue of marriage counseling.)

Council has decided that I'm to tell Sergio that we desire marriage counseling as soon as possible. They are aware that he has no money to spare for this, so we will come in three times a month for therapy and Sergio will come in with Maria once a month for counseling with the chosen therapist. This is important as Council can not afford to have another bad experience with a counselor and Sergio, or they fear that he will never walk into another office again. They are going to hold him to his promise

19

that he made, "If you fight to live through cancer, I'll go to counseling with you."

Council wants Sergio to be treated fairly by you or whoever does the counseling and hopes he can learn the skills that will help the system emotionally. They believe that if Sergio can learn to nurture the female parts, they will respond to him in a positive fashion. They would appreciate a quick response from you about these issues on counseling. See you at the next chemo, Ruth.

As I continued to research the effects of chemo on the Land of Preservation and the inhabitants therein, I quickly became aware of the psychological and spiritual affects of the devastation upon several parts both on the inside world and the outside. For those parts that had only accepted Jesus within the last year, trusting His promises to them to renew Preservation in the future became the only real hope they had. They had watched their world that had been their known existence for over 40 years, become a wasteland within a couple of days. Their living environment had been badly shaken and reduced to living out of a cave. Whoever was the person on the surface in this world...well nothing much had changed or improved on the outside for encouragement. The house was still torn up in remodel and the 'Christian' contractor was making everyone even angrier by his poor workmanship, lying and gross failure to fulfill his contract.

Maria's family wasn't equipped to really support her during this time, as they hadn't yet been able to come to grips with her condition of multiplicity. She was still expected to do everything that she had done before the cancer surgery, as she was going through chemo. There was no one from her church, other than Lindsay, offering to help her out in any way. The attitude of her parents and extended family was to tell her either home remedies in lieu of chemo, or "get prepared to die." They would direct their sympathy toward Sergio for what he must be enduring, while chastising Maria for causing him this trouble. This extended attitude may have contributed to the fears of Sergio and the kids to the point where they were not able to try and understand all that was happening to Maria. And both Maria and Louise didn't want them to understand because they were convinced that the family would reject them if anyone knew the truth.

Mix this all together with what had just happened inside and you can begin to understand why their trust in the future was becoming strained at the very least. Yet, hope persisted even in the confines of the caves. The subsequent chemo treatments couldn't destroy what was already gone. The side effects were mostly external in appearance with the loss of hair, weakness and general nausea. However, some of the parts began to discover truths about themselves and the circumstances surrounding them. Liz wrote the following letter to God shortly after the first chemotherapy.

Well here it is the end of chemo day one. Maria is a mess. And me, well God, you know me. Can't keep a wild girl down. I gotta tell you God, when I heard the baby coffin story, I could sure identify with the dad. Man do you remember how many times I've shaken my fist at you and yelled damn you God? And that pizza oven...in the beginning I could handle the heat. I figured I don't want him to see me sweat. But then you turned it up so high that I had to escape and let the others have it. I hate heat...it cramps my style you know.

I really have been pissed at you for a very long time. And all that crap about you seeing the big picture. Well when I'm being fried in the pizza oven, I say screw the big picture. I just want out. Incidentally, I've been able to adjust my heat regulator...I can handle level three now. But I ain't bragging so don't go looking for more heat.

Before all of this happened...before Maria's kid's illness... and before the cancer, I always looked at myself as just a sandpaper kind of person. People that hung around me knew I was rough and real...no wimps stayed around too long. I was rough because it was the only way I knew how to survive...kind of scare them off before they do damage to me. It worked, but it's been a shitty way to live all of my life. I've always had to watch over my shoulders to see who was going to try to take me down. I've always had to be alert and one step ahead of them and trust no one, nothing, nada... because if I did then I'd be taken down and destroyed. Yes I learned real good from my childhood...real good. But inside I was always a time bomb ready to go off. Anybody do shit to me and I'd crucify them. You know all of my shit...the cat food in the salsa...getting the john's high and stealing their money...lying

21

through my teeth like a pro. Yeah, I've hung around with some real rough sandpaper people, but now I've got a different perspective.

I ain't going to be one of those flowery Christians who talks like an airhead, "God really spoke to me in this situation and I've been blessed..." Shit, you zapped my car and got down on me and turned up the heat on high. I've been through shit and it has not been a picnic, but I gotta admit that you haven't taken off and left me hangin'. You've stayed here and you're helping me through it. Yeah I'm sure you got a message in there somewhere for me and I'm sure there is a blessing somewhere. But man when the heat's on high and my buns are roasting...I ain't looking for no message, just a way out. And I know now the way out...right straight through it with you.

So God I've been giving this sandpaper thing a lot of thought. I will never make real good chiffon paper...make Ruth chiffon paper. I'm Liz, remember? What you see is what you get. I mean there's got to be some use for sandpaper. Mariann told me she was talking to you (that kid is always doing that) and you told her that sandpaper has a very important use. The carpenter takes the sandpaper at just the right grade and uses it to smooth out the roughness in the wood. The sandpaper has to bend and be torn in order for the carpenter to make maximum use of it. Without the sandpaper, the work the carpenter is creating would not have the finishing touch that would make it a quality work. Sandpaper is used to smooth out the edges that need to fit together more securely. It is used to remove unwanted blemishes and flaws. It has many benefits for a carpenter.

So God, you are the carpenter and I'm the sandpaper. And I suppose that Suburban Christians are the work? I think there is a lot in what Mariann told me, like the carpenter picks out the grade. If you have the wrong grade, you could do permanent damage to the work. So don't be too hard ...Liz. Let you determine the degree, the words and the method. God knows the grade! Man, Chalberg should write a sermon on the benefits of having sandpaper people in the church.

Boy what a relief. I'd die if I had to be chiffon paper. Oh and by the way...thanks for not letting the chemo affect me. Somebody in the system has to stay alert and eat. I've kept my promise so I hope you are noticing!!!

Later, Liz

(Mike, I found this on the computer. It really encouraged me and I hope it does you. Do I really look like chiffon paper?
Take care, Ruth)

The Saturday after the chemo I attended the men's prayer time at Menlo Park Presbyterian Church and asked the 100+ men to pray for Maria's healing. It was their practice to send a card signed by those in attendance to whoever was lifted up in prayer. It was a simple thing really, but I was surprised by Maria's response to receiving the card. She wrote back to the group and I read her letter to them a couple of weeks later.

To MPPC – Sat. morning men's prayer group,
My name is Maria and Pastor Chalberg told me that you prayed for us. When we get prayed for, it helps us be Dragonslayer strong like Mariann says. Before we met Pastor Chalberg, we never had anyone pray for us and now all of these people are praying to Jesus to help us. Jesus is helping us a lot, but we've got to keep trusting in Him all of the time.
Ruth tells me it is hardest to trust when things are real bad, but that is when we can have our faith tested cuz it is easy to trust when everything is good. Quiet Walker says remember your trust bag Maria. Louise and I got baptized on April 6th and Jesus is teaching us about how He wants us to live for Him. He wants us to be kind to people and not think we are better than others, or not think more about having things than Him. He wants us to say only true things and to obey and trust Him. He wants us to do true things and tell people that He loves them. We got a lot of bad things that we learned and got to get out of us, so that Jesus can pour in the true things so we can do what He wants. He tells us we got to be with Him all of the time to really get to know Him good.
Before we knew about the real Jesus, we thought that love always hurt and God thought we were so evil that He didn't want to be around us. We got real mixed up because we got told things about Jesus that made us scared of Him. Lots of bad things happened to us and we just wanted to die. But then Bruce and Pastor Chalberg were nice to us and didn't hurt us and told us

23

Jesus loved us. It took us a long time to trust them, cuz when we trusted before we got hurt. The real Jesus you trust and He is safe.

Jesus told us that He didn't leave us when we got hurt, but He let us make parts so we could live and that He loves us. Jesus is our best friend and we want to get better so that we can work for Him. We got cancer now and it has been hard cuz we don't like hospitals and cuttings and things that go in us. But Pastor Chalberg takes us to the hospital and goes into surgery with us and makes sure no one hurts us. He works for the real Jesus and he is safe.

We don't know why we got cancer, but Jesus tells us that He is not going to leave us and He is going to help us not be afraid of the chemotherapy and stuff. When we get afraid, He tells us things like He told us not to give up and be strong in Him and His great power. Then He told us about our garden. We love to hear stories. Louise loves gardens and plants little things that grow beautifully in her garden. Jesus said just as Louise's garden is dormant in the darkness of winter, it begins to grow and flourish in the spring, so shall He heal our soul and it will bloom and grow.

The darkness will be overtaken by the light and the warmth of His love will break through the cracks of pain and hopelessness, and it will melt away our sadness. Then He said that the garden of our soul will prosper and the bouquet of our heart will bring beauty for all who see. Then He said He will say to us, "Look! The winter is past and the rains are over and gone. The blossoms appear through all of the Land of Preservation. The time has come to sing. The cooing of the doves is heard in our land. There are young figs on the fig trees and the blossoms on the vines smell sweet. Get up My child, take My hand and together we shall walk through life."

We still get scared and sad, but Jesus talks a lot to us. We now have His umbrella of love and we try to hold on to Him real tight. When the twisters hit us, we try not to give up so they don't kill us.

Pastor Chalberg said you all put your names on a card for us. We are going to look at your names on that card real good and ask Jesus to help you hold on to Him real tight too. He can change your sadness into happiness and give you comfort and joy like He helps us. We just sometimes forget to hold on to Him and then the bad ones start telling us the terrible things again.

We wish there were churches of people who could help people like us hold on to Jesus better. Bruce told Ann that there is only one in California that helps people like us. I guess it is because it takes lots of time to help us and churches don't have the time. I hope someday there are lots of people like Pastor Chalberg to help people like us, cuz people like us got to know more about real love and the real Jesus so we can get better. Thank you so much for praying for us.

With everything that was going on in her life at that point, it was encouraging to read how Maria was going to find time to pray for each of those names. She would ask me about some of them as the Lord brought that man to her thoughts for prayer. We would pray for them together when she was receiving an injection in chemo.

There would be an occasional communiqué from Tolip about the status of CORE during the chemotherapy. The courier was usually Quiet Walker as she was the only one outside of Jesus that was welcome in their territory. I had hoped for more details about what the chemo was doing to the area where CORE resided, but alas it was not to be so. I remembered the details of what happened when Jesus entered there to begin the healing of Hopi and the pod children, but apparently they were deep enough to receive only minimal impact from the CAF.

Communiqué from Tolip to the leaders of Circle Council

Greetings from Those Who Are Core. Quiet Walker has delivered your message. Thank you for the offer of assistance. Our pods are holding and there has been minimal effect from the poisonings above. Much has changed since the one known as Dragonslayer entered our camp. The boy, Hopi, has told us many strange and interesting stories of visions in the place called Sacred Mountain. We have spent much time conversing with Quiet Walker about these strange phenomena and speakings.

Quiet Walker is well respected among the ranks. Our command has seen past her shell and into her heart. Her words are authentic for they come in action and truth. We have seen how she surrounded Hopi with warmth and treated him with patience while being alert to protect him from harm. She has been compassionately present to all of us, willing to serve us without question and always encouraging us.

It is with this trust and respect for Quiet Walker that she was invited to the strategic planning meeting and asked to speak on that which has happened to the pod children. She told us of her journey towards understanding and that she had no answers as to why our children were hurt. But she told us of the wisdom that she has learned from the one called Dragonslayer. Her words are cause for much thought and discussion. We were very interested in the moment when Quiet Walker said, "I have learned that what I desire most cannot be achieved without going through the process to acquire it. To be refined, purified and perfected takes much time and much heat. Only through this process can the result be of lasting value."

We questioned Quiet Walker as to what it is that she desires most and her answer was that "my acceptance of the truth that I follow will be genuine. I follow the truth of the Great Spirit. I have learned that I shall be sorrowed by many sufferings, but that is necessary so that the genuineness of my trust will be honorable to the Great Spirit. For the Great Spirit knows the paths I walk and he has walked my grief and sorrow with me. He will take my suffering and change it into a witness for him and I shall come forth as gold. I do not focus on what is behind my path, but I look forward to that which lies ahead and the call of the Great Spirit. It is in this hope that I walk on with confidence."

These are strong words that Quiet Walker has shared with us. We have asked her to return soon to teach us more of her wisdom.

Quiet Walker was gradually touching the lives of everyone in Preservation and on the outside world as new relationships were started. One relationship that began the week of the first chemo was with my daughter Britta. She knew of some of the stories of the System from Carol and I over the previous summer and had recently begun a course on Native American Culture & History. When she heard about what happened in the recovery at our house following the cancer surgery, she was determined to meet Quiet Walker and learn something, she just didn't know what. I warned her that Quiet Walker rarely comes out for strangers unless prompted to do so by the Great Spirit. Britta wasn't prepared for what she received after their first meeting, as Quiet Walker began to talk about hidden questions residing in Britta's heart in a letter. It began with giving her a Native American name:

One Who Searches For Trust,

On Sacred Mountain is where I do my private work, where I learn survival wisdoms and the meaning of harmony and balance. One must travel one's journey along the quiet, balanced path away from the spinning, swirling world. Do you have your trust bag yet?

In my journey I have studied the web of my life. At the center of my web is the core of my design...all life is interconnected and sacred. From the core each strand reaches out to form my shape. I have learned that wisdom does not change. Each strand from the core unfolds that wisdom and is given in different designs for each life web. At the center is the Sacred Law of the Sacred Circle. The Sacred Law is taking and giving back with respect. This is the law of respect and if not cared for, the life web will not be.

I have written much of the tribe of greed, who do not understand the Sacred Law. They do not understand the concept of harmony, but only understand dominance. The tribe of greed is killing its own and they are so foolish, they do not see what they are doing. They do not see the land as our mother, but rather as something to be owned, controlled, used and consumed. Oh men of the tribe of greed, how do you own the eagle or the wind? They do not understand the strand of wisdom of connectedness. They do not consider all things connected, but as objects to be controlled and owned. They do not understand the truth that to disconnect with all things is to die.

I will not follow any principle that breaks my spirit and invades my life web balance, for balance is key. Imbalance, lack of respect and harmony, can destroy one's life web and affect all relationships.

I travel the path of Sacred Mountain on my journey of understanding the strands of my web. I go to Sacred Mountain for healing. Here the broken strands in my web can be repaired by the Great Spirit and returned to balance, but I must carry my trust bag. Without my trust bag, I would not have the strength to go back to the original untruth, correct it and reweave from there.

I must travel the path of healing, for if I do not, the imbalance of my life web will invade my spirit, then my mind, then my words and then the core of my life web. If it reaches the core, the poison will kill. Thus to survive, I must travel. I must remember the wisdom given to me by the Great Spirit. The venom is entering, be vigilant. Seek out truth and wisdom. Correct and repair the broken strands before the design is destroyed. Travel the path.

As I walk my path up Sacred Mountain, I walk the path of strength, respect, balance, adaptability, cooperation and unity in diversity. I learn that hope strengthens my will to survive and determination and work make my survival possible. I have made the choice to survive...to reconnect my life web and mend the broken strands of my life. Do you, One Who Searches For Trust, remember the words of Red Clay?

"We have survived
We thank the Great Spirit
We shall renew our strength
We shall mount up with wings"

I have chosen to walk the path up Sacred Mountain and mount up with wings like Brave Eagle. It is a difficult path to journey...one that requires much endurance. As I travel the path, like the seed, I protect myself. I live deep in my spirit and I listen to the wisdom within where the Great Spirit speaks to me. I watch with spirit eyes and I hear with spirit ears. And I am still.

The journey up Sacred Mountain is well charted...for all journeys must have shape and fixed bearings. Here, I am the spirit walker. Here, I journey. Here, I am connected. I walk barefoot, to feel the joy and know reality. For barefoot cannot hide and must endure the pain.

In the belly of your life web, you will find meaning. As you travel your journey path, if you seek truth and wisdom and are diligent, you will find it. For you also have a life web in need of reweaving and mending of broken strands but remember... you must first carry your trust bag.

-Quiet Walker

Britta is still analyzing much of what she has learned from Quiet Walker over the years, as are many of us. Many within the System would take time as well to reflect on the meaning of their individual lives while going through the chemo over the next 12 weeks. Even for those like Liz and Ann who were least affected by it, each took time to contemplate their purpose, if only to find strength to challenge the other's purpose. Ann wrote to Bruce for help with Liz:

To: Bruce
From: Ann
Re: Liz

Do not encourage her! Council has grounded her for one hour for drag racing a guy in town. The car does not belong to Liz. I had to take Claudia's van in for maintenance. They give customers a free rental to use while repairing the owner's car. And wouldn't it be my luck that they had no cars left but a silver Camero convertible. Needless to say, I have not driven it yet. Liz got her hands on that car, jacked up Wild 107 and figured it was a free gift from God for her. The car goes back soon! But in the meantime, if she shows up at your office again, do not encourage her!

Ann would not be aware of all that happened to Liz in this 'gift from God' for several more months and even then she won't believe it. Liz called my wife that afternoon and told her she was leaving town in a car she just stole and wanted to stop by to say so long. When I came home and heard the story I began to laugh, telling Carol that Liz was only tweaking her to get a rise out of her. She arrived in the silver convertible to take us out for burgers and beer at the Alpine Inn. When she began telling us about almost getting stopped down the street in a murder investigation, I had to stop her from proceeding with what I thought was bullshit. It turns out that there was a murder scene a few blocks away, which Liz just happened up on coming to our place. The irony here is that had she been stopped and questioned for identification; she probably would have been prevented from moving on as she was driving without a license. In her excitement of driving this car she had left it home. This would have been another instance where Liz escaped inside and had Ann or Ruth switch out to take the heat, as she did when she was pulled over for speeding. The end results are never good for Liz and embarrassing to whoever receives the ticket. After all, what could they say, "Officer, I wasn't driving the car!"

Liz had something else on her mind this evening. After dinner she wanted me to go cruisin' with her to talk. Carol had enough excitement for one day and stayed home, while I took Liz on a cruise to the parking lot of our church, as I knew it would be a quiet reminder in the background. On the drive there she asked me several questions about my life before I had accepted Jesus and what changed for me afterward. I sensed this was leading up to something and I needed to give her enough time to tell me about what was troubling her. The next letter tells what happened next.

Hey Buddy,

Remember your promise to me – that you'll kick my butt if I ever start looking even a little like a Suburban Christian. I don't want to be a Suburban Christian...fate worse than death. Last night was great, thanks for cruisin' with me. I took some time after leaving you just to feel the cool night breeze. I had to put the top down because I hate being boxed in. You know me...I like my space.

I have my identification mark figured out now. I AM A CHRISTIAN ACCORDING TO JESUS. I like that because it identifies where I stand. As I parked the car to absorb all that happened to me, I had an interesting conversation with Jesus. He said,

"Why do you keep taking the library back Liz? I died on the cross for all of your sins not just some of them. And if you keep taking them back then I died in vain."

Whoa! That hit me like a ton of bricks. "You mean, knowing all the lies, manipulating, cheating, stealing, drugs, sex, alcohol, slandering, violence, abuse to men and everything else I could pack in my life that is rotten, you want it all and you are just going to forget it because I told you I was sorry and asked you to forgive me?"

He said yes, so I gave him not only the library, but the foundation, the flagpole and even the termites. Man do I feel good. It's like getting to start over. I mean I get to start all over again. You were right, Buddy, more freedom than I can absorb, especially for someone like me who has always had to fight for any freedom I could get. Jesus really has me figured out. I guess that's okay because he doesn't seem to be using it to trap me like I thought. He isn't telling me what my future holds in detail. He has told me that our multiplicity will not be a hindrance, but an asset. We will work together in reaching people for him.

Then he told me something weird. He said some of the people who are distanced the most from him are the ones I call the Suburban Christians. I thought he was kidding. He was dead serious. Then I heard this:

"Do not ever be ashamed to testify about me Liz. Die to self-will. Be patient and endure, looking to me for strength. You are a part of my heavenly kingdom now, don't deny me. Remember that you will make mistakes and blow it, but I will remain faithful. Remember the truth and warn those in the church about arguing about little differences that don't matter. Do your best to always correctly preach my truth.

Liz, leave the past desires and pursue righteousness, faith and love. And as you speak to Suburban Christians as you call them, remember this: Do not have anything to do with foolish and stupid arguments. They serve no purpose and lead to quarrels. Liz, as my servant, you must be kind to everyone including the Suburban Christians so that you can gently teach the knowledge of truth to them, and they will come to an understanding and turn from the trap of the evil one.

I am sending you into the battlefield, so remember this: You will be pressed on all sides by people who love themselves, who love money, who are arrogant, abusive, ungrateful, unholy, without love, conceited, lamps without oil. YOU ARE NOT ONE OF THESE PEOPLE ANYMORE LIZ. Do not follow their ways. See to it that they don't take you captive through hollow and deceptive philosophy rooted in principles of this world, rather than in me. They worm their way into my church and cause much division and confusion. They don't listen to sound doctrine. They gather teachers around them who say what their itching ears want to hear. They turn their minds away from truth.

31

But Liz, I want you to keep listening to the truth, endure the hardship and do the work of an evangelist and prophet. Stand firm and do not be afraid in any way by those who will oppose you. These are your instructions Liz: Preach the truth. Guard the truth. Live the truth. Be prepared at all times to correct, rebuke and encourage. But do it with great patience and careful instruction. In order to do that Liz, you need to know my word like you know how to breathe.

I realized that after listening to him, I better start reading his word. I am just not sure how much truth I know. I know that God created everything and everything he created was good. He made man and woman and gave them instructions that they could enjoy everything, but the tree of good and evil they were not to touch. At that time God was very close to man and they walked and talked together. There was no sin, no death, no aging and no decay. Then man blew it. He had the choice to obey God's commandment about the tree or not. He chose to eat the fruit of the tree. So sin, death, aging and decay were the result of his disobedience.

God could not just ignore his sin because God can't condone sin. He is sinless and that would be a compromise of who he is. OK so over the years man got further and further away from God and things kept getting worse…Sodom, Noah's Ark stuff. The world was a mess. But God loved his creation so much that he made a way for us. Now he couldn't just say no consequences, so he let his son die on the cross as the consequences for our sins so that we could be free of them and live. In other words, Jesus took our punishment so we wouldn't have to die. Now, if we believe that and accept Jesus' sacrifice for us, admit that we are sinners, we are saved because of Jesus. Then, because of God's grace, we have life forever and we are clean. God didn't give three options for us to get out of our mess, he gave only one…his son. So accepting Jesus as Lord and Savior is the only way we can have life. If we don't accept the truth of what Jesus has done for us, then we can't live. Once we truly understand the awesomeness of his sacrifice and his love for us, we can't help but want to love him, learn more about him, and serve him. And that is all I know about truth.

Well, it's about time I get in the Camero for one last fling. Bill is taking me to Max's, so I am cruisin' to San Ramon. But before I end I want to say something to you buddy and don't go thinkin' I'm getting mushy because I'm not!

Thanks! Thanks for hanging in there with me. Thanks for accepting me and not belittling me. You know I shadowed more than you know and I have watched you closely. I mean real closely. I saw something in you that I never saw in anyone else. I watched you be the voice for Mariann when she could not speak. I watched you be strong when she was weak. I watched you have faith in us to endure. I listened to you encourage Maria when she was sad and discouraged. I saw how you gave up your quality time to help us. That week at your house was probably the turning point for me. I saw. I saw and I saw more. And inside I just knew you understood us...not in your mind, but in your heart. You cared in a way the world doesn't care. And I knew you had something that I wanted and now I know that what I was seeing was Jesus in you. I remember in the car when I asked you, "well Chalberg, any regrets? I mean do you miss your old life?" And do you remember your answer? I'll never forget it.

Thanks for being there for me. I AM FREE!

A Christian According to Jesus = Liz

There were many things I said that night to Liz and what I said to her question isn't really of much importance to anyone else. I was there in that parking lot primarily as a referee in Liz's ongoing battle with the Holy Spirit who was pursuing her. Before that night, the major roadblock keeping Liz from accepting Jesus was her own definition of what it means to become 'Christian'. All I asked her to do was take a risk, a 'leap of faith', and let Jesus define for her what being a Christian is. That meant simply to open the door to your heart and let Him enter. He'll teach you all you need to know from there, as you are willing to accept it. When she finally put the words together in her own rebel fashion, and asked Him to enter her life, she began to cry and became embarrassed. When I told her there was no need to be embarrassed over accepting Jesus, she said that it was because of what He said on entering:

"I've been knocking for a long time! Why did you wait so long to open your heart and let Me love you?"

33

All of her fears about rules restricting her from being herself, of being labeled a hypocrite for not being real, of being accepted into an institution she saw closing its doors to those who are different and in such great need that they do nothing of lasting value...all of these and more were removed that night. Based on what she said in her letter, I felt she had a pretty good grasp of the truth.

"Behold, I stand at the door and knock; if anyone hears My voice and opens the door, I will come into him, and will dine with him, and he with Me."
Revelation 4:20

The common MO of the System during chemotherapy was to watch one another as they encountered Jesus in both the outside world and inside, and then try to learn from the other's experience. Several parts observed the risk taken by Liz, while it was totally missed by Ann. Maria wrote me to share her thoughts about what Liz's new title meant for her:

Hi Pastor Chalberg,

I am trying to get used to Jose's new computer. It's scary cuz it's all new now and I got to not break it. I have been thinking lots about being a Christian according to Jesus. Liz tells me that there are a lot of packages being sold in churches and she tells me I got to know the real thing. So I have been thinking about it lots and asking Jesus to help me understand.

I think to be a Christian according to Jesus means to be what Jesus says a follower of him is to be like. So first I got to know what Jesus says a Christian is supposed to be. He tells me Maria, you got to have your mind connected to your heart and you got to have a Jesus heart, not a world heart. You got to let the Holy Spirit lead your heart and mind, not the world. I think that means I got to be stiller and talk to Jesus more and learn how he acted when he was in the world. Jesus always thanked his Father for whatever he had. He didn't complain about not having enough stuff. He knew it all belonged to his Father and that whatever he was given was a gift

34

from his dad. Stuff wasn't important to him. People were important to him.

In the world stuff is important, not people. I saw on a car one time, the one with the most toys wins, but I think that is wrong. People will say bad things about other people. They will say they did something when someone else did it, just to make themselves look important to the boss. People will do lots of bad stuff to get success and money. But I think that being a Christian according to Jesus means not loving stuff but loving people and sharing whatever you have with other people like Jesus did. Jesus has a heart that's got peace and love in it. He showed us that he loves everyone, even people that are different.

He always looked for the chance to be with people that no one else cared about and didn't want to be around, cuz they were dirty or looked different or came from a different place. I liked it when Jesus was at the well with the Samaritan woman. The big church leaders wouldn't be around her cuz she was different and not worth the time, but Jesus valued her and wanted her to know him. I think that if we all got a chance to be sent to Hell for one hour and then came back, we would want like Jesus that no one perishes.

I remember once in San Francisco I was at Fisherman's Wharf and there was this homeless man sitting next to where they get tickets for the boats. I watched the people walk... way out of their way so they wouldn't get near him. His hair was dirty and he looked sad. I had no money but I had my lunch and a drink left so I asked him if he wanted it. He said yes and took it behind some bushes to eat it. I think being a Christian according to Jesus means loving people who are different like Jesus does, even if it is uncomfortable at first. Jesus never stayed only with people that were like him and easy.

He said he didn't come cuz of the ones who are well, but he came to save the lost and heal the sick. To be a Christian according to Jesus means getting out of the church building and being around people who need to see Jesus love. We don't do that lots. We don't

35

go around people much just to love them. We seem to be around people cuz we want something from them.

Jesus wants us to obey and worship him and bring him glory. I think it makes him very happy when he sees us share his hope with people who don't have none, cuz it means that if we sacrifice our TV time and shopping time to do it, we know it is important. Jesus brought me people to teach me about love. They helped me when I had to go to surgery and chemotherapy. They didn't leave me alone scared. They stayed in surgery and took me to their home and I stayed a whole week. They cleaned the cuts and drained the stuff, fed and hugged me, and kept me warm. Jesus was very happy cuz they were showing me his love for me and that my life was important to him. When my friend took off work to be with me in chemotherapy, I learned that I was more important than stuff.

Jesus tells me be an imitator of him. "Study my word so you can model my life. Always talk with me and ask me what I would do. Be truthful and kind. Be my humble servant always desiring to glorify me in everything. Show the world my love for them through your life. Focus on my standards and not the worlds."

So me, I try everyday when I get up to be love to other people. I try to listen to their hurts and pains or cry with them and tell them about how Jesus healed my heart and gave me Jesus hope. I tell them I don't know what will happen tomorrow. I don't know where I will sleep for sure or what I will eat, but I do know one thing for sure, that Jesus won't leave me and he will take care of me. I got joy in my heart cuz Jesus loves me and I love him.

Bye Pastor Chalberg.
Maria

Here it was only a few days after the second chemo treatment and most people of the System were looking ahead to what would follow the devastation of their inside world. Their environment was pretty bleak, yet hope was rising from the ashes. Around them on the inside there began an increase in attacks from the 'smelly ones' against the weakest parts who did not have a relationship with Jesus. The 'frontal assault' wasn't working well because of Mariann's ability to see, hear and smell them approaching. Evil was forced into changing their tactics which had been used for so long and they had become complacent toward souls they believed belong to them. Now they were loosing ground rapidly and had to find new ways to obtain entry into the System again.

Most of the adult parts were either curious to find out more about this person on the inside called Jesus or obsessed with learning everything they could from Dragonslayer. Maria and Louise were wanting to spend time at the feet of Jesus to learn more about what He wanted for them. Raquel was walking the paths of Sacred Mountain to learn from the Great Spirit, as she watched Him continue to heal Hopi. Liz was contemplating, perhaps for the first time in her life, the ramifications of receiving her new title – a Christian According to Jesus. Ann was trying to balance as her two worlds were in chaos, and do it logically, while attempting to move forward to secure their outside world.

I began to spend more time in counseling each adult separately and centered on Ann to get her to focus on the reality of the spiritual changes occurring on the inside. We began having philosophical discussions over lunch after chemo and followed it up with an exchange of point-to-counterpoint over email. Ruth and Council kept me apprised of conditions at home and struggles on the inside. In September 1996, I told them that I put the house up for sale again, as in the previous fall. It was listed at a fair price in a hot market, with the hope that maybe it sell so Carol and I could complete our degrees at Fuller Seminary in January. We knew that if it wasn't in the Lord's plan, then we would stay and not be selling or leaving for another year.

Now, after 8 years, I can see how the Lord was gracious with letting me test His will in this way. Sometimes I can stubbornly pursue crystal clear answers to not make mistakes in discerning His will, only to realize I need His grace all the more when I do. I knew in my heart that eventually we would leave the area, but that would not prevent or end our relationship with the System. This would continue as long as we are alive. This period made me focus more on all that the System was going through, as the possibility that we might only have a few more months with them near us loomed ahead. Our initial Bible study began to narrow on who is in control of our destiny.

"Humble yourselves, therefore, under the mighty hand of God, that He may exalt you at the proper time, casting all your anxiety upon Him, because He cares for you. Be of sober spirit, be on the alert. Your adversary, the devil, prowls about like a roaring lion, seeking someone to devour. But resist him, firm in your faith, knowing that the same experiences of suffering are being accomplished by your brethren who are in the world. And after you have suffered for a little while, the God of all grace, who called you to His eternal glory in Christ, will Himself perfect, confirm, strengthen and establish you."

1 Peter 5: 6-10

Chapter Two

"Will the Phoenix Rise from the Ashes?"

"Before I shaped you in the womb,
I knew all about you.
Before you saw the light of day,
I had holy plans for you:
A prophet to the nations-
That's what I had in mind for you."
Jeremiah 1:5

"Blessed is a man who perseveres under trial;
for once he has been approved,
he will receive the crown of life,
which the Lord has promised to those who love Him."
James 1:12

On September 12, 1996 I received a letter from Elizabeth Ray explaining why she had sent me a picture of Tabitha standing with her father in front of the family car. It was taken in 1956 when Maria was 4 years old during winter, with her mother and grandparents standing in the background.

You requested an explanation as to why I sent you this picture. I will attempt to clarify my reasons. You are writing a book about the system. You have the Letters to the Therapist *journals from May 1994 to the present. You have the maps of the system, access to the artwork and the poems written by Raquel. You have the words, but my concern is; do you have the deep understanding of how far they have come?*

Sometimes a picture can show what words cannot express. That is why I sent you one of the few pictures I have of the system as a child. I want you to know the child through the picture. Can you sense the coldness of the adult? Can you absorb the child's fragility and pain? Can you feel the darkness that surrounds her? Can you fathom the fear and loneliness? Can you feel the child?

39

Now take that connectedness with the child and write the book. Write of the child of the picture and write of the child of today...the shattered pieces journeying to joy. You cannot truly express the awesomeness of the system's growth, if you do not fully understand the depth of the pit from where they came.

I cannot show the picture because of confidentiality. I enlarged it to see everyone better and became sad over what was revealed. I could now see the child standing at arm's length away from her father. Her eyes were bright at being able to have this outing with her family, but one eye was swollen half shut. She was not smiling and actually, nobody was smiling on what appears to be a sunny day. No one looks as if they want to be there except Tabitha.

Ironically, I received another picture of Tabitha a few weeks later. This one was her first school picture I believe. In it she has another black eye but giving the biggest smile ever. My response to this letter and these pictures was to begin reading the journals that Elizabeth Ray had given me...from the beginning and not just scan the 'highlights' of the history of my client. As I read each letter again, while looking at the picture on my desk, I became more aware of the enormous distance the System had traveled just to survive.

It is hard to explain to anyone the amount of suffering they all went through to make it to this point in time. In book one, *Shattered People Seriess: Journeys to Joy*, only one quarter of the material in these journals is shared about their trials and tribulations. The question of whether or not they could survive the losses occurring around them in Preservation from the chemotherapy was still unknown territory, and even more so with the difficulties facing them in this outside physical world.

I began to wonder what journey God was going to take them on. Why were Liz and Ann the least affected by the chemo? I reasoned that Liz was the best protector on the outside, so she needed to be able to function best during this time to face the house contractor, family and from being blindsided by anyone. For Ann, well, she was her own worst enemy. The stress of trying to maintain control both inside and out was very hard on her. She wanted to do something in which she could gain some sort of foothold in the middle of all the changes going on around her. She was unable to explain to her own satisfaction what had occurred on the inside, so she did the next best thing…she gave definition to her outside world by finding a job.

Ruth continued to write to Bruce and I with updates on what was happening to everyone from her perspective. She began her own metamorphosis of change in ways so subtle, that I would not recognize the changes for a few more years.

Dear Bruce,
I don't know what happened that evening with the phone. We have had no problems with incoming calls. Sergio checked the phone and it works fine. Either something did not want you talking to Maria or it was simply a fluke. Maria is not sleeping well. Her back is in a lot of pain. Ann says it is the spine readjusting to the differences in weight distribution from the mastectomy. I'm not sure of anything here other than Maria is becoming weaker.

Praying with Maria over the phone provided us with a night free from spiritual attacks. However, last night they began again. Their attack began on Maria when Liz was present. She switched Maria in and said as she went out, "Okay assholes mess with me!" Liz heard a hideous laugh that chilled her to the bone and became frightened. She quickly escaped back inside as Mariann switched out saying, "Dragonslayer come!" The enemy left. I tried to find Liz inside to find out exactly what went on, but she is hiding quite deep. It was interesting that when Liz went out, we on the inside were having a difficult time shadowing with any clarity. It was as though a thick veil had covered our view of the outside world.
(Liz would not talk about what happened for several weeks.)

I do not see the spiritual world like Maria and the children see it. I believe in its existence because God's Word tells me that it's real. I also believe that the system is being hit hard right now because of the spiritual growth going on. Hopi seems to have been a major turning point for the system. Although I am not sure exactly what trauma he holds, it does seem to carry a lot of spiritual abuse.

I'm still not sure Maria was involved in any satanic ritual abuse, but then I'm not sure how one defines satanic ritual abuse. I think there was more to the Santeria than we ever thought occurred in the beginning. I remember when you asked Tabitha if she ever participated in any of the Santeria rituals and she told you no a long time ago. Could Hopi hold those memories, if Tabitha was unable to carry them? Did the Santeria practice animal sacrifices of goats? Was that a sect that turned Catholicism upside down? (If you're wondering why Ruth is asking questions that have already been answered in the Journals and in my previous book, you might remember that no one other than Bruce and myself had read these Journals to this point. No one but Elizabeth Ray in the System had knowledge of all that was in them.)

It makes sense that the location where Maria lived would have the environment to host something like this. There were many barns around that were quite a distance from roads and people. There were also many farm workers who came from Cuba and Latin America working these fields. Maria was not monitored or protected as to her whereabouts...giving a cult ample chances to use her. Yet, what I know about the Santeria (which I admit is very little), seems to be a blend of Catholicism and Voodoo. So I'm wondering if they would use the symbols of the church in a negative way? Or is it possible that cult members outside of the rituals abused Hopi?

In any case, what happened to Hopi is over and he belongs to Jesus now. Raquel seems very protective of him. He hasn't entered the forest for any length of time, so we haven't had the opportunity to get to know him. Raquel is probably wise in not overwhelming him with meeting all of us. I know that Watcher is still observing us for Tolip, but so far hasn't communicated with us. He seems to have strict orders to only observe our activities. Jennifer has been asking a lot of questions about Jesus. She is very interested in learning why Mariann is so attached to him.

For the first time since I've known her, Ann seems confused. Out of all of the parts, Ann is in the most pain, but not from the chemo. I think feelings are starting to rise up in her and it is scaring her. She has always had the ability to suppress them by focusing on an outside goal, in order to bury any turmoil inside of her. But now

42

the system is changing and she has no control over it. She is swimming against the tide and drowning. Denial has been her sanity and now she can no longer deny what is happening.

Speaking of Ann, she took a proposal to Circle Council yesterday. They are in session now considering it. Ann came to Raquel and I to ask for our support. Ann wants to become a teacher. She called the university to ask about getting a credential and they were excited about the possibility so much they offered her a job. She declined knowing she could do nothing without Council's approval. She is trying to convince us about how we could teach together. Raquel could handle the arts, music and literature. Jennifer could handle cultural diversity and environmental issues. I could handle character-building curriculum and teach the inside children at the same time.

Ann will take the sciences, mathematics and organizational issues like parent meetings, staff meetings, etc. She informed us how the pluses outweighed the negatives and the money could be used for Rosalinda's tuition. Ann would be working and out of the house away from that stress. She would be helping the children of her community and we would be working together as a unit on a common goal for the first time. Ann's argument was convincing, until I asked her about therapy.

"We don't need therapy. We are fine. We can do this ourselves." I told her Council will never accept that answer. I then asked her about Maria and Louise. She informed me that teaching would be good for them. They could do yard duty and give mother hugs to all the kids. I then made a mistake by asking Ann if she was considering teaching to avoid addressing the issues of our MPD. "You seem to get into busy, goal-oriented projects to avoid your feelings and discussing them." That's when she started yelling at me and said, "Ruth I don't care if you support me on this idea or not. I'm through talking to you."

So here we are in the middle of chemotherapy and cancer...and Ann wants to go into teaching!
Take Care, Ruth

Of course Liz was not going to sit idly by and say nothing, or not take a shot at getting something for herself. She went to Bruce first and then me. We both suggested she present her case to Council, as they would make the final decision.

This is Liz. Bruce suggested that I write my complaint to you about Ann. Council is not being fair to the rest of us parts. Ann always gets what she wants at our expense. It is not fair for her to have so much time out to get this stupid credential that she wants. Once she goes to work, she will get more time out than the rest of us. I never get what I want. How am I supposed to have any time out if Ann is teaching all of the time? She hogs all of the time!

Then when she gets home, Maria and Louise have to do piles of work that she gives them. Every time I try to tell you guys what I want I end up under house arrest or kicked out of your meetings. At least I don't manipulate you guys like Ann does. So I want my share of outside time. I want the freedom to party and have a good time. You should listen to the outside counselors. They say it is not healthy to have all work and no play. All we do is work.

So I figure that I should get about 10 hours a week of free time based on my rudimentary math. You can give me more, but all I'm asking for is ten hours out. I'll take the 1AM to 4AM shift, but I want out of the house to go bowling or dancing. If you don't give me any time, then Ann won't be passing any tests in her stupid classes.

When Liz got on the computer to write this letter, she decided to keep writing letters. She sent the following letter to me for approval, before sending it off to the seminary. She thought our house might sell before Christmas and we would be gone by January, so she tried this preemptive measure knowing that probably nothing would come from it. She had been talking to Jesus about this issue but wasn't receiving the answers that she wanted to hear, so she took matters into her own hands again. Liz seemed to have an endless supply of energy for banging her head against the institutions of the world, and seminary was no exception.

Hey Buddy –

I want to send this to your school. Ruth helped me with the lingo and cleaned it up for me, but I wrote it. It took all that I had to be nice. Anyway, read it and if you agree to let me send it out, give me the addresses and names of the idiots and I'll send it.

And since Maria blabbed to Carol about my plan, you might as well hear it from the horse's mouth. When you meet with Ann next weekend, I want you to tell her face to face (about Liz accepting Jesus). *I'll shadow and confirm it from the inside, but I want Ann to acknowledge her part of the bet in front of you. Otherwise she will find some logical way to weasel out of it.* (Several weeks before the cancer surgery, Ann accepted my bet that if Liz ever became a Christian, she would have to open her mind up to hear the Gospel message and actively study the possibilities of Jesus being who He says He is. I won when Liz became a 'Christian According to Jesus.')

I saw the picture Elizabeth Ray sent you. I hate the picture! Look at Tabitha's hand and the way she is barely standing. The picture ain't right because she was beaten earlier. Something is obviously wrong with her in that picture. Tear it up! We don't want Maria seeing it.

Later-Liz

September 7, 1996

To Whom It May Concern,
    My name is Liz. I am not a pastor or someone who is interested in enrolling in your university. My only qualification for writing this letter to you is that I'm concerned that you are hindering God's work, with some of your rules for students who wish to receive a Master of Divinity degree.

I am sure you have heard arguments in the past about the inflexibility of your program. You have undoubtedly also justified your position with arguments that seem in the best interest of Fuller Seminary. But I question whether your guidelines are preventing some people from becoming pastors, because they are unable to transplant themselves to Southern California for the required time of one year on campus to get this degree.

With the technology we have today, it is very feasible for students who live in all parts of the country to utilize the rich instruction of Fuller via satellite. Bob Jones U. has a program for home schooling families where students can be a part of the classroom and live thousands of miles away. Schools today will creatively reach out to a diverse population with 'college while you work' programs, interactive video classes, night classes and extension classes, similar to the ones you have in Menlo Park. The administrations have boldly used a variety of techniques in long distance learning to capture a broader based student population; thereby providing moneys to enhance the offsite programs. They have recognized that the students who use these programs would not have been able to attend their campus site anyway. By offering these programs, the schools increase their ability to serve all people.

Although I disagree with the thought that a degree makes a pastor, I am fully aware that in today's competitive California market, one needs that paper just to get the interview. I am concerned about those individuals who are called by God to be pastors and yet are faced with a roadblock at Fuller because they are unable to leave their locations due to hardships. For example, consider a person who is financially trapped in the Bay Area. Maybe it is an older working student who is married with a spouse working and children attending school. Displacing the family would place a financial and emotional hardship on them because of their particular situation. Or consider a student that has elderly parents for whom she is the primary caregiver. Maybe the student is in a long-term commitment ministering to people whom God has called him to help at this particular time in his life and theirs.

I am not a seasoned Christian. In fact, I am just beginning my journey as a Christian. I have always had problems with most 'established' churches because too many times I have seen God put in a box by the establishment and its rules. People like me, (street people, sandpaper people, throwaway people) never truly are reached with the Gospel of Jesus because of the establishment and its rules.

I was reached by a man who is trying to finish up his schooling at Fuller's extension in Menlo Park, but has to go to Pasadena to earn his Master of Divinity. He is financially trapped in the Bay Area. God has called this person to minister with people and proclaim truth to those of us who have been damaged by the establishment. His compassion and understanding of brokenness go far beyond anything that you can teach him at Fuller. Yet, I know that he needs that degree. Are your rules and inflexibility going to be a roadblock in preventing him from doing the work God has called him to do? How many other 'throw away' people like myself will never be reached for Jesus because your school would not be sensitive to the needs of its students? I wonder what Jesus would say about a school that does not consider first God's plan, but rather man's plan?

I am not biblically literate nor do I profess to have any credentials that would impress you in understanding my position. But I do know one thing, I was lost and now I am saved because of one man's willingness to obey Jesus and minister real to me. Your school has the opportunity to provide the means for this man to continue to obey Jesus and minister to many more people like me. I hope you will reconsider your guidelines in how students are able to obtain Master of Divinity degrees from your institution by allowing them to do it in extension.

Sincerely,
Liz

(Her request does not happen at Fuller Seminary until the year 2000 for the Northern California extension, but thank you anyway Liz for the effort then. This letter, like many Liz will write to pastors and churches over what she defines as injustices will never receive a reply. Only a very few souls will attempt to respond and challenge her perspectives, right or wrong, fulfilling Liz's desire to dialogue about life's injustice.)

Bruce was continuing to provide therapy with the child parts primarily, while hoping that the issue of Ann getting a job would be worked out within the System. It is always difficult to counsel a 'group' of people and to not appear as taking sides of one individual over another and to still offer guidance for healing to be effective for the greater good. However, sometimes you can get yourself caught up in the dynamics being orchestrated by different factions. One such occurrence was when Bruce suggested taking Mariann to the toy store to help her grow in her understanding of the outside world. This created issues for the adults, and Council responded.

Council has discussed the issue of the toy store. In the past, the children have been told that you were not allowed to take children outside of the office due to rules set down by your boss. We did this to protect the integrity of the entire system.

However, now we face a dilemma. We have had to admit to Mariann that we were in error when we assumed you were not allowed to take children out of the office. She is insistent that she wants to see a toy store like the other children do. We understand that as Mariann grows and becomes more aware of the world, she will want to explore and enjoy what children like to do. Yet, she does not understand that she is trapped in an adult body. She does not understand that looking like a forty-year-old and acting like an eight-year-old in public humiliates many of the adult parts and can be dangerous in the wrong setting.

We, as leaders, have had to place restrictions on the children to keep the system safe. Until that week with the Chalberg family, Mariann and the other children had been restricted in their play around outsiders, and primarily only allowed out in the middle of the night in the privacy of our bedroom. We were pleased with the protection Mr. Chalberg displayed at the school park. However, we also know that the situation could have been disastrous had there been a different set of variables. We need advice as to how to handle the toy store dilemma.

Upon receiving a copy of this letter, I suggested to Bruce and Council that I take Mariann, with Tabitha shadowing, to the toy store close by my house in about a month, or just before the holiday rush. The adults of the System would be far from anyone they knew and the kids wouldn't be pressured by them to be on the lookout so they could enjoy the event. Bruce wouldn't have to face the aftermath of boundaries being challenged in his therapy either.

The hour with Mariann and Tabitha in a Toys-R-Us becomes a memorable event for all of the System and for me in their first visit to a toy store. The overwhelming feeling of being inundated with 'stuff' was their basic reaction. The children had never had gifts given to them at Christmas or birthdays, so the idea of someone taking them to a store like this to buy a gift for them was difficult to grasp or understand. I told each one to pick something out from the whole store. Mariann and Tabitha each picked a coloring book but didn't think they should ask for crayons to go with it. I picked a box of about 80 colors of crayons and both kids thought they had received the greatest gifts ever. To this day when I ask them what they want for Christmas it is usually 5 hugs, 3 snuggle times, peanut butter cookies or vanilla ice cream.

It wasn't just the children whose horizons were being expanded. Some people at Maria's church wanted her to attend a woman's retreat and asked her to come. The men of Council had a difficult time saying no because Maria rarely asked for anything. Elizabeth Ray wrote to the pastor's wife on their behalf:

Circle Council has voted to not allow Maria to attend the Women's Retreat this year. It was a very difficult decision to make. They talked to the doctors, Carol and Mike Chalberg and considered their own observations of the system at this time. Maria has been told that the reason she is not able to attend is because of the chemotherapy treatment on October 28t[h] causing her immune system to be too low. Doctors have told the system to avoid crowds and Council has told her that she cannot take the chance of getting sicker.

Maria was shown how the accommodations available would not work for her. The system has major problems at night with child parts switching and flashbacks. It would not be fair to the other three women in the room to spend their retreat dealing with something that requires a degree of expert training. Also Council cannot control switching during the day if triggers are presented.

Three days without supervision would be too difficult for Maria. We appreciate the kind offer of Carol W. Please let her know that she will need to sign up with another roommate. In no way is Council's decision a reflection upon her inexperience in dealing with multiples. Council has based their decision on what they believe would be best for the system, for VBC and the women at the retreat. If you have any questions, please call Mike or Carol Chalberg. They have spent over a week straight with the system and are aware of the complications.
Elizabeth Ray – Scribe for Council

Maria wrote to me after her time with Council. She was too sad to type so it was handwritten. When she became depressed, sad or afraid over life's changing circumstances while in chemotherapy, her ways of expressing herself would regress. Her writing skills often looked like that of a child, yet I knew it was Maria communicating her thoughts as quickly as they came to her.

Dear Pastor Chalberg,
Helper told me to come see them at Council. I went and they said I can't go to the thing for women at my church cuz I'm to sick. I asked them what if I pray real lots and Jesus keeps the germs away from me can I please go. They said no cuz the doctors said not to go where lots of people go.
Do you know that they are going to have fun and make things for Christmas and sing to Jesus, play games and eat, and listen to somebody talk about having all our parts together? Carol said she would take me in the forest and I could see all the animals.
I smelled the smelly ones at 10:30 last night. They told me I can't go cuz I am crazy and a big problem for the church. I said Jesus help me cuz I was going to cry and he came and they went away and I couldn't smell that smell no more. Then I told Jesus I want to go with my church, but Jesus he holded me and said your time will come. He hugged me and I feel better now.
Helper told me to obey him and I won't cry no more about it and I'll obey him. I can't throw my paper away cuz it makes me sad (her invitation from her church). *Can you throw it away for me please? I don't understand but I will obey Helper.*
Your friend Maria.

Maria called me late that night and we talked for over an hour. More than anything else she wanted to be and do the things that she saw her friends doing. Though the System had been on other retreats before, it had never been a function that was for Maria only to enjoy with her friends. She had a dream of how this is what Christian women do together and she wanted to experience it for herself. Underneath her sadness was the fear that the cancer would overtake her and there might not be another chance for a women's retreat. As we focused on Jesus' promises together again over the phone, her joy returned thinking about "her retreat time coming".

Ruth wrote the next night to tell me about her thoughts on Maria's sadness over the events and what had happened when she attended a retreat several years earlier at another church. Even with Liz getting reprimanded for having a whip cream pie-throwing contest that wasn't on the agenda, the other results verified Council's few concerns that their decision was right. She also told me about the following incident that occurred the night before at home.

Something very interesting happened very early in the morning. Maria was on the outside crying about not going. All of a sudden she communicated to me on the inside, "Ruth it's Christmas!" I said what did you say Maria, and she said I smell Christmas. I figured she was dreaming but she kept insisting that the room was filled with the smell of Christmas trees. So I switched out to see if I could smell it and Mike, I can't explain how or attempt to even try, but the room smelled like a Christmas tree lot. Maria would not let me stay out too long because she wanted to come back out to smell it. It lasted about another 5 minutes and was gone. I don't know what it meant or why it happened, but it seem to bring comfort to Maria. This is good because she was sad today again as Ann got up early to drive Rosalinda off to college. She doesn't handle separation from her children well, but knows it has to happen and will adjust.

Ruth wrote again the next week about all that was occurring around them at home and on the inside. This was another eight page epistle that I will condense to highlights only.

Dear Mike and Carol,

Thank you for the card and stickers for the kids. Mariann has already instructed both Tabitha and Angelina about not putting them on the walls. Tabitha stuck her tongue out at Mariann for being so bossy and of course Mariann ran to tattle to Helper. It's good to see them active even with the chemo.

This weekend we had a difficult time and Ann has placed the body on some antibiotics. Louise accidentally sliced open her hand while cooking and Sergio on the outside and Helper on the inside both went in a frenzy. Sergio took dishwasher soap and poured it right into the wound, which made her scream in pain. This triggered Tabitha's memories of 'cleanings' and put her in a frenzy. Ann became panicked over the body getting an infection so she started feeding us pills immediately. She started yelling at Louise about being careful to not put us behind in the sequence of chemotherapy. I got upset and argued with Ann over how she treated Louise. Needless to say it was a difficult night.

Maria is doing as well as can be expected with chemo. She is having a hard time with her hair falling out and now her ring is missing. She doesn't do well with many transitions at the same time. She is trying to get used to her new body image and before she can accept it, it changes again. She is dealing with multiple losses at once: the loss of her breasts, her hair falling out, her daughter off to college and her adopted daughter returning to New York and most difficult of all, the loss of her childhood.

King of the Lights was commenting to me that Council realizes now how after we spent that week with you guys that Maria really began to take hold of her childhood memories, or lack of them. He said that before May 1994 Maria had no idea what she had lost. When Bruce began to reveal what she had lost, she could not identify with those loses. Then came the experiences in your home and at the school. Things like seeing you and Carol as husband and wife laughing and enjoying being together only brought back for her memories of food being thrown across the table, threats and yelling at each other. The school swings made her experience the sadness of never going to a park with her father. Even simple things of just being fed consistently three meals a day and having her clothes washed for her, raised feelings inside of the days she went hungry and wore filthy rags. Maria finally has touched the feelings of the parts and has begun to know the loss. Even though she is struggling, I am proud of her. She is not splitting into more parts and is trying with all her energy to go through this cancer and her lost feelings.

I am sure it has been hard for both of you to be so absorbed by the system's feelings and emotions at this time, but they so need your encouragement and support during this desert of their existence. They really have no one else. Bruce cares, but cannot be available for them outside of sessions. Sergio is not trusted yet by all of them, so they won't open up to him. Lindsay is only close to Maria and Louise. The church people don't really know how to help emotionally or practically.

Council realizes as well that there is still great fear of abandonment within some of the parts. It is a strongly embedded fear that will take a long time to heal from for some. They have monitored the number of phone calls placed to your home and have tried to set boundaries for the parts. They realize that with ten plus parts having a close relationship with you the number of calls could get out of hand. Yet they also know how talking with you alleviates a lot of the fear and stress someone might carry and helps the entire system get a good night's sleep or avoid taking too much medication. They try to balance what is good for the system and what is reasonable for you to absorb.

This is a very needy time for many parts, as they miss seeing you every Saturday and spending time with you talking about God. Council feels that several parts are attempting to rediscover their lost childhood through you, like when you give fatherly advice to the one who says she doesn't have a father or want one. Council knows she wishes she had a father who would have cared enough to guide her in life or even discipline her in love to help her. Little things like calling Mariann sweetheart go a long way in filling up the holes of emotionless memories. Like children who experience sugar for the first time...they crave it.

Carol also plays a crucial role with giving stickers and mothering the children. The children still believe in their little minds that she is a "mama angel", because mamas they remember give beatings, not stickers. And mamas don't hug and tell them they were a good little girl at the doctor. Mamas tell them to shut up and go to work in the fields before I kill you. So the children are experiencing 'real mama love' on the outside for the first time. The adults are learning to nurture and mother the children as well from her, as they become stronger and healthier.

I'm sure Council is right in their assessment of the situation, but I pray that the parts will transfer their need for love to Jesus as they come to know Him. King of the Lights agrees with me, but also tells me that it is important for the parts to experience human love so they can begin to trust and exist in society with others. Or they will become hermits and not be able to exist and relate to people if they can't. I sometimes wonder about my existence inside.

Raquel keeps reminding Maria to read the promises of Jesus often and to remain strong. So she reads the letter from Jesus that Raquel delivered to Council and you read to her at the beginning of chemo. We all need to focus her and ourselves back on those promises, as it is easy to fall and forget during the hard times going through chemotherapy. Besides Maria's hair falling out and mouth sores, she has bleeding gums, intestinal problems and the beginnings of a yeast infection, all making her sad about how she looks. Ann is forcing us to drink a lot of cranberry juice and experimenting with different foods to see what can be digested easily. Council decided that if worse comes to worse we will have Angelina come out and eat baby food. They are dealing with a lot of flak over this issue. Several parts said they would not allow Sergio to feed Angelina baby food. Helper pointed out to them this simple truth, "Either you eat the baby food or Angelina will be fed the food. We cannot worry right now about humiliation, we must focus on survival." Result: Angelina has grown up from a bottle to baby food out of a jar.

Guess what? Ann has been accepted into the university to get a teaching credential! I don't think we can pass the MSAT. Doesn't she know that multiples cannot sit for five hours taking a test? She expects me to help her by taking the English and writing portion to give her rested time to take the math and science part. Would this be considered wrong? Council has agreed to allow Ann to attempt this goal and they will be monitoring the effect it has on the entire system. I must admit that Ann presented some phenomenal reasons in favor of earning the credential and becoming a teacher.

I expressed my concern about failing to Council and they gave a quote from Roosevelt that silenced my argument;

"Far better is it to dare mighty things…to win glorious triumphs even though checkered by failure, than to rank with those poor spirits who neither enjoy much nor suffer much because they live in the great twilight that knows not victory or defeat."

So I guess we will dare mighty things. A multiple who hasn't been to school in twenty years attempting to compete with those twenty-year-olds is a little hard to believe. Pray for us. Ann is really going to stretch all of us with this, if it doesn't kill us.

I know you heard about Sergio's plan to marry all of us parts. Council is spending a considerable amount of time on the subject. Many of the parts do not love Sergio and only consider him to be Maria's husband. Some are very resentful and some are confused. Council gave me the task of speaking with him and telling him how the parts want marriage counseling before any decision is made. Even if we finally decide no, Maria could use the counseling for her relationship with him. I'm praying about how to approach this with him. I know he realizes now that he didn't marry a whole unit and that there are parts who do not consider themselves to be married to him. It must be very difficult for him to accept this. Yet, I do believe the marriage is salvageable and can be improved. If he could only learn how to provide emotional support for the system, I'm sure it could go a long way in improving the kind of relationship we have with him. He has lived with us for 23 years and barely knows us.

I talked with Mari today. She said that she asked Jesus to help her trust him and teach her how to have joy and happiness. When I shared with her Raquel's letter from Jesus that you read during the first chemo, she listened intently as if she heard it for the first time. She has a lot of pain and guilt she carries over not protecting Mariann. Maybe as she opens up to us and learns the truth that it wasn't her fault, she will release her feelings to Jesus so he can heal her. Mariann has spent time with her singing her song to Dragonslayer and telling about the bombs Jesus is using in chemotherapy. Mari said she was surprised at how Mariann was still joyful after the surgery and going through chemotherapy and this seemed to confuse her. I explained to her that Mariann is like any other child who becomes afraid or scared, but springs back quickly when she feels safe and protected by her Dragonslayer.

She told me she spoke with you over the phone and stated that you sound like a gentle man, but she is still not sure why you are in our life. I said you were sent by Jesus to help us understand and be touched by his love. I explained the relationship you have with the others and that you are safe. She asked how I knew this and I said because I prayed about it and Jesus confirmed it...

Liz is doing better than most of us and she surprised me by asking for help with her letter that she sent to your school. She does like to 'stir up the waters', doesn't she. She thrives on it. I am sending you her sermon on "Inauthentic Christians vs. Authentic Christians." She does zero in on some areas that we need to look at as Christians. Elizabeth Ray rarely talks about what the parts have done throughout their lives, which is probably good for everyone's sanity. I thought that Liz had always been self-centered, rebellious and stubborn, but I'm learning about and seeing other sides to her since the surgery and chemo. We're getting letters from her friends in Texas, Oklahoma, Guatemala and Romania that wish her well and tell of people praying for us all over. They all seem to praise her for her honesty in telling it straight and being real. As hard as she appears to be on people, including her friends, it surprises me with how much she is appreciated by them. It is hard for me to know how to communicate with someone who thinks that Jesus would love to drag race in the Judean countryside in a rented silver Camero convertible. Or when she starts picturing what it would be like for Jesus to give a sermon in his church today. I don't know that I'll ever be comfortable with her.

Raquel visited us in the cave and said all is well with the animals. She is spending a lot of time in prayer and meditation. Liz told her about the sermon you are writing. She listened intently and then Liz asked her what she thought about it. After what seemed like a long time, she spoke. "To fear and trust the Great Spirit is the beginning of wisdom and knowledge, but that is not enough, for one must continually seek out wisdom every moment on the path.

The Great Spirit will direct one's steps, but one must walk closely with the Great Spirit to know each direction one is to take. It is easy to stray from the path without noticing and be devoured by the enemy waiting there. Does not the Great Spirit give us advice and instruction on how to conduct our lives? Does not the Great Spirit teach us obedience, humility and how to show his love to our fellow tribesmen? Are we not to be careful how we live and our minds and attitudes to be one with the Great Spirit? Are we not to put into practice each day the things we communicate with our lips? It is far better to have never spoken, than to have spoken and not lived as one has pronounced. I request the honor of listening to the words Shedding Tear will speak. And with that Raquel was gone.

Take care, Ruth.

The third chemotherapy treatment would come and go before Raquel would hear this sermon. Raquel appeared to be the only part finding any peace within the current chaos surrounding the System. Maria was becoming more depressed as the losses increased. Her concern for her mother facing similar losses in her battle with cancer only accelerated her sadness. She didn't seem to care about the letters that Liz and Ann were writing to local pastors, or that Ann was going back to school to facilitate getting a job. Her primary concern was her mother's health and whether or not she would survive her own cancer.

Maria was trying very hard to understand the meaning and fulfillment of Jesus' promises to her. Would the renewal and resurrection of her 'garden' and Preservation be a spiritual one that is answered in heaven? The statistics of cancer survival that Ann researched did not bode well for them. While most of the rest of the adult parts were planning for a future of at least a few years more, Maria had started asking me a lot of questions about heaven. Just a few months earlier she had seen death as a relief from the pain she knew most of her life. Now it had become the doorway to immense joy and peace. The enemy chose to use this method for Maria to constantly barrage her to keep her intimidated by life here. Her questions to me became more persistent; *"What is Jesus telling you about His plans for me? How can I, a nobody serve Him? Why doesn't Jesus just take us home now? How can a broken person fix another broken person?"*

We shall call upon the Great Spirit
And he shall save us.

He will hear our cry
And our pain.
And he will protect us from
The battle which is against us.

We will cast our burdens upon the Great Spirit.
He will sustain us.

We will put our trust in him.
And we shall not be afraid.
We will take refuge in him.
In the shadow of his wings we shall dwell.

The Great Spirit will send forth his love and truth.
He will deliver us.

He is our stronghold,
Our strong tower in whom we trust.
Like the phoenix,
We shall raise from the ashes around us.

- Quiet Walker

"Listen to counsel and accept discipline,
That you may be wise the rest of your days.
Many are the plans in a man's heart,
But the counsel of the Lord, it will stand."
Proverbs 19: 20-21

Chapter Three

"How Will Eternity Find You?"

"To see a World in a Grain of Sand,
And a Heaven in a Wild Flower,
Hold Infinity in the palm of your hand,
And Eternity in an hour."
William Blake, *Auguries of Innocence,* (1803)

"Truly, truly, I say to you, an hour is coming and now is,
when the dead shall hear the voice of the Son of God;
and those who hear shall live."
John 5:25

When I became a believer in 1976 and became a follower of Jesus Christ, the quest for understanding eternity gave birth to a new reality for me. A metamorphosis of perception transformed my experience of the eternal from a thing outside the realm of my existence, into a real sense of grasping hold of time...even time without end. I had discovered true freedom, the understanding that removes barriers of time that prevent any attempt at overcoming the impossible. Life opened itself up to be lived simply for the joy of it. What I gave up was the illusion that I could accomplish something in my own power that would last forever...or at least for my lifetime. I had already achieved a real measure of wealth and authority, only to discover that it didn't provide any lasting satisfaction. Now, in the giving of my life to Jesus Christ, I was freed from my limited expectations to make life meaningful, to living a life that is meaningful to God...without limits.

I was reminded of my struggle to find meaning in this life shortly before Maria was diagnosed with cancer. This reminder came in the form of a dream...a rather long one that lasted most of the night. In it were people important to me throughout my life that were now dead, who came to my church office to discuss what they perceived to be the only true accomplishments of their existence. They each made a prediction that God would answer a

59

very important question of mine "within five years." As I tried to interpret the dream, I felt strongly that it meant a death of someone, perhaps me. Maybe it was the anticipation of death waiting in the near future, which caused a sense of urgency to influence my decisions around what I believed to be God's instructions to me. I do know it wasn't a fear of death, as I have been ready to go home for a long time. But at that particular moment, I sensed I should make decisions based only on five years remaining here. I wanted each and every choice to count for something.

I found myself discussing the dream with Circle Council and Raquel about its meaning. After Maria's surgery, they had observed as I did, Maria's preoccupation with her imminent death. Though neither Council nor I had discussed the dream with her, we knew that the enemy was trying to convince her that she would die soon. When they wrote the following letter, I could tell that they too were moving towards a different conclusion about the dream.

Do you recall before Maria was diagnosed with cancer, the dream you had about "within five years you will know?" Maria will know if she is cancer free within five years or dead. If she does not survive the cancer, she wishes that you perform her burial ceremony. The newspaper will read no services, as she wishes a private ceremony with the following people invited: Sergio, Claudia, Rosalinda, Jose, Bruce, Lindsay, Carol and you. She wishes to be buried in a pine coffin with Raquel's Native American blanket. She wants yellow daisies sprinkled in the box and no other flowers, as they represent for her the parts, with the center being Jesus.

She wants you to talk about the joys of heaven and how happy she is there. She wants you to encourage those left behind to not loose hope, because their reward is not in this world and has been freely given to them in the next. She wants everyone to know that she is waiting for them in heaven and very happy. After the burial, she hopes everyone will just go back to their homes and think about how much Jesus loves them. We are sending you this information as we promised Maria before surgery two months ago. Circle Council

60

Maria began to raise questions about her mom's health and often questioned me about the merits of going against her father's wishes. He didn't want her calling or disturbing him or her mom. Maria was afraid of his response if she did. Yet, her concern over whether or not her mom would go to heaven after her death was stronger than the lifetime of fear imposed by her father. She decided to risk his wrath and call her mom. Ruth helped her to write a letter afterward to reduce his anger.

Dear Mom,

I wanted to apologize first for disturbing you when I called last week. I will abide by dad's rule in the future and not call you. I am truly sorry if I caused either of you any distress with my call.

I am praying for you mom. I don't know much about what is happening to you, but you told me that you are going back into the hospital because of the spots. You told me you just wanted something for the pain and you're ready to die before dad came on the line.

I am praying that God will direct the doctors and give them wisdom in treating you. I know how you feel because I get like that too. By the time you get this letter, I will have finished my third run of chemotherapy. I don't know if it is going to work or not, but I am really not afraid of dying.

This last year has been a very difficult yet growing one for me. I have never been closer to God. I have finally understood the meaning of "a personal relationship with Jesus." Whenever things around me are out of control, Jesus is not. He keeps telling me over and over again that he is in control and that he loves me with an everlasting love. I know with confidence that when I die, I will be in heaven with him. This brings me great joy.

I will always love you mom. Nothing will stop me from loving and praying for you. Please, when you can, let me know how you're doing.

May God give you peace.

Your daughter, Maria.

Ann seemed to be wearing down from the effects of the chemotherapy. She was aware of Maria's thoughts on her possible demise and subsequent burial plans, all of which only irritated her more and more. Ann wasn't ready to give up yet, but she was also facing a new dilemma confronting the System. I have to admit that I was very surprised to receive the following letter from her.

I probably will seriously regret writing this letter to you. Rarely do I pour out my feelings to anyone because I learned a long time ago that no one really cares to listen to them. But I am faced with a dilemma right now that concerns Sergio and I cannot find a logical way around it.

*Recently, as you are aware, Maria's wedding ring turned up missing. She is extremely depressed over it and has relayed this to Sergio. He has decided that he will buy her another ring and **marry all of us!***

I have no problem with him buying her another ring, but I do have a problem with him marrying all of us. I do not love Sergio and I think I have never loved him. When I was in college pursuing a degree, I was determined to prove to the professors and all those male students that I was equally talented in the area of mathematics as they were. Second to that was to get out of Maria's father's house.

My dream was to enter tax law or corporate banking. I planned to be a career woman remaining single and celibate. I had no interest in men other than to debate issues or have them work under my control. But I never got my dream. When I met Sergio there, I had no interest in him except to debate political issues.

According to Elizabeth Ray, Sergio began seeing other parts and I wasn't aware of it. Liz used Sergio sexually just to spend nights away from the house. Maria also wanted out of her father's house. I found myself married.

Do you have any comprehension of the shock I felt two days after Maria walked down the aisle? Here I was in a situation I didn't choose, trapped in a marriage I didn't want and forced into a role I could not perform. Maria was as traumatized as I was. No one explained to her the obligations of marriage. She was totally unprepared for what came on the wedding night and she has no clue on how to be a wife. Maria did what she always does...she dissociated. Kansas was born and has been going strong ever since that first night.

If we were all truly honest, we would admit that none of us love Sergio. The reason is simple; we don't know how to love him. Maria cares for him, but she does not know what the love of a wife means. None of us have any sexual desire towards him or any man. Sex scares us. We function for him.

Sergio is difficult to live with and impossible to relate to as a spouse. He says he cares for Maria and yet he is emotionally dead towards her. When he is angry, he abandons her and rejects her by giving her the silent treatment. He never shows any of us that he really wants to know who we are or cares what we think. He uses us.

I have a great deal of resentment towards him because of the way he has treated us over the years. He's not this loving, wonderful guy you think he is. He is very closed and very cold. The system has been both mother and father to the children and basically raised them alone. Up until a few years ago, Sergio worked 70-hour workweeks and rarely spent time with the children. We'd catch his paycheck as he flew by.

In 1980, I told Sergio I wanted a divorce…after he informed me that he would not participate with the raising of the children, until they were old enough to carry an intelligent conversation. He never read to them or tucked them in bed. He never took them for walks or spent time with them. He never trained them for anything. Marie and I carried the father role as best we could with the few skills we had. I tried to give the children as many experiences as I could and spent an extraordinary amount of time with them. So much time that I lost my identity in the process.

Sergio on the other hand continued to live at work. He never took us dancing or socializing. We never had a babysitter for the children. Mostly it was six or seven months before we had a moment of private time together. Sergio never took the time to notice that we were dying in our cocoon. I was overworked, underpaid and trapped as a housewife, but I had an obligation to Maria's children. I wanted to raise them and provide for them the freedom to make choices to live life as they desired. So I gave up my life for them. I have given up a lot for people. I never seem to have control over my own destiny.

There are outsiders and insiders who are forcing me into a mold that is not of my choosing. It's easy to say "breakaway, set boundaries, be assertive or take care of you", but there are obligations and responsibilities that I can't just throw off my shoulders. When I do try to improve my situation, I meet with such resistance inside and out that I abandon the idea.

I've long been aware of my own problems that have not helped the marriage. I become very insecure if I can't maintain control and keep things in an orderly and logical manner. I work hard to avoid falling apart. I keep striving for something, but I'm not sure what that is. I create long lists of things to do and feel some level of accomplishment checking them off, but they are things I'm required to do, not what I want to do. If something enters my list that I didn't put there I fall apart. I have tried to relax and not "sweat the small stuff" as you say, but I can't. I've tried to be flexible, I can't. I'm this way because I have obligations.

I feel Sergio has taken advantage of our efficiency. I doubt that many men have it as easy as him in married life. I wonder if that is why he stays, being treated like a king. We manage the entire house, including the yards and the cars. We pay all of the bills and maintain the budget. We set up all appointments, handle all school issues, do all the carpooling, raise the children, take care of the animals and anything else that comes into the home.

Sergio goes to work, eats, sleeps, watches TV and reads at home. Lately, he's been doing some painting until Maria went into surgery. We were never allowed to get sick, because if we did the house couldn't function. One time when I had the flu and Sergio was home, Rosalinda had a problem at school and refused to allow her father to help, only me. It was as though he wasn't a part of her life.

Don't get me wrong, Sergio has some good points to his character. He has provided financially for the family. He is a hard worker at work. He ignores the children but has never beaten them. He is not an alcoholic like his mother. You asked me if he was ever abused and frankly I don't know, as he never talks about anything with us. We now realize that there has to be more to a marriage than this. Therapy has presented us with a whole new set of problems. We lived in a very sheltered and isolated world where we had no idea what a good marriage looked like in other families.

The day you and your wife sat at the kitchen table with the system and you were both laughing together over life's issues, had a great impact on all of us. Some parts didn't know that husbands and wives could laugh together and have fun like that. Sergio never laughs or jokes around. He never plays games or tells stories to the children, as you did to us. He never dances and never sings. That day we were in mourning. We were catching a glimpse of all that we have missed in our lives. All we knew from our childhood around a kitchen table was screaming, threats and throwing food. All we knew as adults was eating and serious talk with the kids about their day.

When Maria found out that husbands don't hit their wives, she was shocked. Her father hits her mother. Sergio emotionally beats her. She believes that he doesn't hit her because she is good at obeying, not because it is wrong. She continues to be hit by her sister and her son.

Tabitha has found out what hugs without sex is from Bruce, you and Carol. Mariann has discovered that dads will read stories to sleepy eight-year-olds. Angelina has learned that men sing and the adults have learned that there are men in the world that will listen and want to understand them.

Is ignorance bliss? I wonder if it was better for the system to not know what they had lost all these years. Once you know, then you hunger for it. That's what is happening to us now. We realize the marriage we have been in is cold, oppressive and unloving. We desire more. We are willing to learn, but Maria's husband thinks that buying another wedding ring and marrying all of us will take care of the problem. It won't.

If he truly loves all of us, then we want him to show us. We want him to commit to marriage counseling and learn how to communicate with us. We don't want a ring. We want our emotional needs to be met so that we in turn can then learn to love him. We've given a lot to him and now we want something in return. We want him to realize that marriage is not just free sex and maid service. We will not marry him until he chooses to put some effort into fixing the marriage.

Ann.

P.S.: Do you agree that God is logical and Science is logical; therefore God is Science?

Ann's letter to me was a significant departure from our ongoing theological discussions. She made herself vulnerable to a male in acknowledging her self-perceived losses of the past and fears of the future. While Ann tries to explain her relationship with 'Maria's children' as an obligation or duty, I knew it to be the only way she might qualify love for them. She treated love as a four-letter word and will only speak of it for several more years as it concerns others in the System and not her. Her last paragraph stating "loving all of us...we... learn to love him" was as much a subconscious hope that counseling would challenge her belief system about men. What is not stated in the letter is an underlying hope/fear that the process might also ease the risk of her accepting the love of Jesus. It will be another five to six years before she understands the differences between the love of Christ and that in human relationships.

Still, the letter brought me hope of reaching her on an emotional level much sooner than I expected. However, within the next few days after a few subtle inquiries, I was reminded of something very important about the System's security control when dealing with confidentiality. I safely assumed that Elizabeth Ray was the only other part within the System, outside of Jesus, who was aware of this letter. But I also assumed that over a short period of time that it would take to discuss the issues within the letter, that there would be others who knew of Ann's feelings due to seepage within the System.

What I have learned is that the strength of the individual part to control their feelings is directly related to the time they can keep them secret. No one else would know the letter's content for another eight years when Ann gives me permission to include it in this book. I also learned that it has to do with the individual's relationship with Jesus. It took a discussion between Ann and I with Jesus to allow it to be included, even though there is still fear of reprisal and a stronger concern that Maria's and Sergio's feelings would be hurt by it. Yet, as Ann learned how it could help others by its honesty, she released me from my promise of confidentiality.

A number of things were changing fast around her and I wanted to use this time to expand her mind about the possibilities of Jesus being to her what He says He is to all of us. I shot back a quick answer to her postscript that would be the lead in to our next conversation following the third chemotherapy a few days away.

"Yes, God is Science, but Science is not God."

I knew this would warrant a response at the next chemo, so I planned to be ready to respond, after I told her about Liz becoming "A Christian According to Jesus." I would remind her of our wager, if Liz hadn't reminded her, of opening her mind to the possibility of Jesus being God. It promised to be an interesting afternoon. The day before our chemo session, I received the following letter from Quiet Walker (Raquel), and I received a call from Maria later that night to discuss the meaning of it.

My Friend Shedding Tear,

May my words come with grace, mercy and peace from the Great Spirit. As I have been tending the animals in the cypress sanctuary I am often reminded of you and One Who Is Like The Angels. It brings much joy and pleasant memories to my spirit to think on the things which you have taught me, Shedding Tear.

During my time of embracing solitude in the place I have been called, I have spent time meditating and praying about patience and waiting for the Great Spirit to reveal the restoration of our land. The Great Spirit brought words to my ear of how the farmer waits for the land to give of its offering and how I too must be patient and trusting in Him.

And then the Great Spirit turned my thoughts toward you and One Who Is Like The Angels. And these were His words, "Encourage them Quiet Walker. They do not realize now what I'm doing, but later they will understand. Remind them to seek My guidance and listen carefully when I say this is the way, walk in it. I will lead them by ways they have not known, along unfamiliar paths I will guide them."

Shedding Tear, do you know of the writings concerning Paul and his companions' journey through the region of Phrygia and Galatia? Why did the Holy Spirit keep them from preaching the word in the province of Asia? Greet One Who Is Like The Angels for me. May the Great Spirit envelop you with deep peace.
-Quiet Walker

67

Ruth faxed me the following letter that night.

Dear Mike,

I shadowed the system's conversations with you the other night. The amount of stuff swirling around this system is unbelievable. Ann has been weakened by the chemo and is having a difficult time fulfilling her obligations. There has been a lot of arguing around here as Ann attempts to maintain control...Ann is having a harder time controlling the switching as seepage occurs.

Council has made a decision on Halloween. I was pleased with their stand on the issue. The kids became terrified when they found out Halloween was coming again and Liz was going to be some kind of Jack-O-Lantern. Mariann would not let go of Liz's leg and kept crying about it being the smelly ones' day. Brave Eagle even brought a message via Owl of Athena from Core warning Circle Council of the ramifications for the pod children. I'm not sure, but something happened in a barn on Halloween.

I'm concerned that it will be a high warfare night and some of the weaker parts will experience flashbacks and triggers. Maria's family doesn't understand the difficulty. They have celebrated it in the past and participated in all of the customs from costumes to skeletons. Hopefully, this year the system can keep it out of the house. I agree with Council on the options, however, going to your home would be an unfair burden on you as it is a workday on the Friday following. Council's suggestion to remain in the bedroom is good enough. I suggested that a light is left on all night and music be played softly. There's a lot of traffic outside the bedroom window as it faces the street. Usually the teenagers make noise on nights like this and if the music is on, then the inside children will not be as traumatized. Before, we were able to hide the children deep inside to avoid these issues. However, somewhere we lost the ability as all parts became more aware of what is happening on the outside.

I was most interested in hearing you and Maria discuss Raquel's letter. It was me who told Maria to turn to Acts in the hope that you could clarify some of my questions about Raquel's statements. As I read through her letter I tried to relate it to your situation. I wonder if the unfamiliar paths connect you with your relationship to us, a multiple.

Is the work you are doing now with multiples, different from what you have done in the past? Or could it be the book you are writing...the unfamiliar path of being an author? I don't know, but I thought it was interesting that without any connection to her previous paragraph, Raquel immediately jumps into Acts 16 without reason.

Yet, as I read the passage over again several times trying to link it to you, I felt she did have a reason. Paul's spiritual reputation and good name were critical in being able to help strengthen the churches in their faith...not unlike you in strengthening the faith of the system. I was intrigued how Paul tried to enter Bithynia and the Holy Spirit prevented him from going there. It was as though Paul was under the direction of the Holy Spirit and he was stopped every time he attempted to change direction not in the will of God. The reason was because of the divine call of God for him to minister to the man of Macedonia. This man, like the system, was begging for help in understanding God..."Come over and help us."

Paul was given a vision to help this man and concluded that God had called him to preach the gospel to him. Yet, it seems to me that God's plan included more than Paul saw, as the Spirit guiding him set the stage for missionary trips into Europe and the Gentiles in particular. I wonder if the system is your call into a 'Europe' that is unfamiliar and unplanned by you, as Paul's was to him. Maybe your ministry will be more of a restoration type ministry for those outside of the mainstream churches and largely ignored by them. Or maybe your book will have far more significance than any of us realize in opening up a 'forgotten Europe' for the church. It's also interesting to me that Paul is eventually allowed to go into Phrygia and Galatia, but only after he had completed the work given to him in his vision. Please tell me your interpretation when you can.

Louise is looking forward to visiting with Carol on Thursday and take her to her favorite nursery where they have all of the waterfalls and roses. Ann told her she can have ten dollars to buy a plant to put in the alley between the houses. If it cost more then no plant, because she has a freeze on the budget. We can't spend a dime until what we owe is paid off, including no more therapy with Bruce either. This might explain why you are receiving more calls.

Ruth's interpretation of the letter proved to be prophetic in the coming years. The change in ministry that Carol and I had begun the year before meeting the System would continue for a long time. Being intentional interim pastors to troubled churches in need of restoration and renewal would not only move us out of most large mainline denominations and it would place us directly in the midst of smaller congregations and individuals that recognized their need for healing and renewal with God. As we grow in our knowledge of God's plan at work in our lives, alongside everyone in the System, we will learn together the meaning of God's mathematics.

> *"What woman, if she has ten silver coins and loses one,*
> *does not light a lamp and sweep the house and search*
> *carefully until she finds it? And when she has found it,*
> *she calls together her friends and neighbors, saying,*
> *'Rejoice with me, for I have found the coin which I had lost!'*
> *'In the same way, I tell you, there is joy in the presence*
> *of the angels of God over one sinner who repents."*
> **Luke 15: 8-10**

Over the next few years we will all be taught the value system that loves one person at a time – unconditionally, and the value of small groups for helping everyone be real with each other and the world around them. We will also learn that maturing in worship of God is not what we bring into the church, but who goes with us out into the world to meet the needs there. A large church will become 25 or more people and a small church will be wherever two or three gather in His name. My traditional perspectives of bringing the 'lost' into the church will quickly become unimportant. The reality of meeting them where they are is where the 'heart' of the church is. That day, however, my new 'Europe' is about to open up with new territory as I talked about the letter with Maria at chemo.

The third chemo was a rough one for everyone. As the nurse began to draw blood in the early morning before the session, the ever-strong Mariann just turned her head away from the nurse and began to sob on my shoulder. She was unable to make it into the lab to begin the injection and Maria came out early to take the whole session. To take her mind off of her surroundings, I read from the book of Acts to reaffirm God's plans for His children.

After arriving at a restaurant for lunch following the session, Ann came out to have a lengthy discussion about all that was occurring with the System. Absent from her letter to me the next day will be any mention of our wager about Liz, and her reaction to the news. It is understandable due to the enormity of her surprise. We all had faith in her to honor her bet, and she begins to open her mind to Jesus. What Ann didn't know during our conversation was how most of my words were being given to me by the Holy Spirit. I will explain this after her letter. Her first two questions had been asked before; "Why are you still here trying to help 'them'? and, "When will we be whole?" What followed was a lengthy discussion of the scientific method and determining what, if anything is real.

Mike-

I immensely enjoyed our four hours of conversation. It has been a long time since I've had the pleasure of conversing with someone who challenges me. My mind is still swirling with all that you shared with me. I must admit that I find you intriguing. Here is a person who gave up a six-figure salary, success and power without any regrets. I've never known what it is like to have these things. Frankly, I'd really like to experience it for awhile. Would it make me happy? I doubt it. Would it fulfill my innermost desires? I'm not sure since I haven't figured out what those are? Would it make life easier? You bet!

You seem to possess a peace and strength about you that I'm still trying to understand. I know what you'd say, "Ann, it's God. He is my strength and peace." Maybe you're right and maybe not?

I'm extremely careful about jumping into new situations because of my background and experiences. Safety and security have to be concrete for me. I have trouble accepting something that cannot be proven concretely. Maybe that is why I'm a mathematician. Math is logical. Math is concrete. Math plays by an established set of rules. Even creating new dimensions, modulars, bases in defining and producing math, one must follow these rules.

That is why it is so hard for me to understand that week at your home. I struggle with attempting to understand that reality. My mind explodes with possibilities in trying to establish the concrete.

Is the universe a thought of some higher life form? Can it be simply a larger scale Land of Preservation? Can it be the leg of a chair in another universe? Is mankind limited in his understanding of reality, simply because he does not apply the resources he has at hand, in attempting to go to a higher level of understanding?

Are the resources available in the mind, but simply haven't been tapped into yet? Does man possess the knowledge of higher beings, made in that image and on the road to becoming god-like, but has yet to arrive at the level of understanding of his maker? Are there a multitude of universes controlled by a council of beings? Is this universe an experimental lab? Is there a control universe? Is there a spiritual universe? How does it operate and what is its purpose? Thousands of unanswered questions...

Everyone, including your favorite – Socrates, has wrestled with the definition of reality. I have wrestled with going back to the source to understand the purpose of the experiment, just so I can make some sense out of existence and purpose. I've explored other definitions of reality, reason and truth. So far, the best understanding I've found of these terms are in science. There reality is fact. I can prove my hypothesis by data and the scientific method to determine fact and then fact becomes truth. Here is where I derive my principles and absolutes. Reason is simply using logic to prove one's argument. Is reason always reality? No. One can use reason to convince someone that something makes sense, but that might not be the reality of the situation.

I thought a lot about the question I posed to you regarding Science and God. I asked you if God is logical and Science is logical, then God is Science. You stated yes, but Science is not God. I must disagree with you. If you break this down to a simple form assigning God the variable A, Science the variable B and Logic the variable C, then what we have is A=C and B=C, therefore A=B. You agreed, but you said that B does not =A. That is illogical unless you state it as God >logic, Science = logic, therefore God > Science and Science < God. That would make sense to me.

So if God > logic, I need to understand how to define God. So who is God? What are his attributes? He is logic. He is truth. He is reality according to you. He is all. What compromises all? How have you come to the conclusion that God is reality? Without using his source as your data, how have you been able to prove his existence and his statements based on outside sources?

The other parts think I am being too skeptical, yet they do not understand. I trusted once and was severely burned. I have learned to test all things to determine if I will believe or deny their value. When it comes to my inner values and beliefs I need to be assured that what I have accepted is reality and thus truth. I can not and will not be tricked again! I would enjoy spending more time discussing this with you.

Sincerely,

Ann

PS: I have heard you, Bruce, and Raquel refer to a book entitled <u>Mere Christianity</u>. *I would like to read this book if I may borrow it from you.*

When Ann began our conversation by asking the same questions over again, I silently prayed for the answers to break through her wall of mistrust that still existed after a year and a half. The first one was answered by telling her a little about myself and why it was important for me to be faithful to God's plan for my life. As I began to answer her second question, "When will we be whole?" I knew the Holy Spirit was feeding me the answer in mathematical terms that Ann might accept. It went something like this:

"Think of the System as real numbers approaching a plane of existence that has a lineal reference line with no beginning and no end. As each number, or part, intersects this line it adds, or blends, into itself a certain value that becomes common to all intersecting parts. This blending has a value determined to be a common awareness of each other and all that you individually are as people, yet there is something more. You become aware of the plane of existence itself, as that which binds you together to create a whole that is more than the individual points intersecting it.

Some parts of the System have yet to intersect this plane. When they do, they will discover wholeness within this plane. Some will blend to create another whole number, while others will remain as individuals, sort of like prime numbers. I believe the lineal

73

reference line is Jesus Christ and your 'wholeness' will be determined by your life found in Him.

It goes back to your question about God and Science. If you accept the premise that God is the Creator of the universe, with all of its 'natural laws' that we base science on and it becomes our control universe, then it is reasonable to say that Science is not God. The created cannot be equal to, or greater than, the Creator."

From there our conversation entered into a discussion of quarks, quasars, black-holes, physics, thermodynamics, metaphysics, and a dozen other topics about which I spoke eloquently, but without any formal training in the area whatsoever. I knew that it wasn't my knowledge challenging her, but that of the Creator. When I heard my voice speaking about a time-space-continuum as being a reality within itself defining the plane of reference for life, I knew I would never fully understand much of what I said that day.

Just as Ann was trying to grasp it all and put it into scientific terms and explain what happened the two weeks at my house, I decided to tell her about Liz becoming a "Christian-according-to-Jesus." That put enough strain on her logic to cause her to retreat inside, as Liz was confirming it as truth. Maria rotated out to ask me, *Why is Liz laughing so hard and Ann seems upset about something?* I explained that Ann's universe is being shaken right now, but don't worry it won't kill her. In fact, she might discover new life where she least expected it, face-to-face with eternity.

"Do you not know? Have you not heard?
The Everlasting God, the Lord, the Creator
of the ends of the earth does not become
weary or tired. His understanding is inscrutable.
He gives strength to the weary, and to him who
lacks might He increases power. Though youths
grow weary and tired, and vigorous young men
stumble badly, yet those who wait upon the Lord
will gain new strength; They will mount up with
wings like eagles, they will run and not get tired,
they will walk and not become weary."
Isaiah 40:28-31

Chapter Four

"Working at Understanding Love"

"Man is the only animal that blushes – or needs to."
Mark Twain, 1897

"Even as love crowns you so shall he crucify you.
Even as he is for your growth so is he for your pruning."
Kahlil Gibran, 1923

"Trust in the Lord with all of your heart,
And do not lean on your own understanding.
In all of your ways acknowledge Him,
And He will make your paths straight...
My son, do not reject the discipline of the Lord,
Or loathe His reproof,
For whom the Lord loves He reproves,
Even as a father, the son in whom he delights."
-    **Proverbs 3:5-6, 11-12**

The last chemotherapy was approaching in two weeks, the day before Halloween of '96. Everyone was tired but hopeful and waiting impatiently for the Land of Preservation to be restored. The desolation they faced each day, coupled with having to live inside the close quarters of the caves, had everyone somewhat edgy. No one knew what to expect out of the first marital counseling session that night with Sergio and Ruth. Ruth was chosen by me as the first female adult of the System to ever attempt anything like this. The primary reason I was selected over Bruce was finances, as I could do it for free as part of my ministry. Circle Council had all the women that might be affected by this, write down their expectations and frustrations pertaining to the marriage relationship with 'Maria's' husband. I think Sergio wanted to marry all of them, simply to gain control over a situation where he was fast losing the control he had known for almost twenty years. I know from the following letter that the women had other ideas.

We have asked the parts to record on file their frustrations, needs and wants, pertaining to their relationship with Maria's husband. Circle Council

Ann. (After 18 years, Ann had the most to vent upon Sergio.)

Some of the frustrations I have experienced center around expectations. I have always felt overwhelmed in this relationship with you because I have carried the brunt of the work. I raised Maria's children almost entirely by myself. I have always resented the excuse that "I had to work 70 hours a week." The children never had the opportunity to form a relationship with you because you were never there. You rarely spent time with them. I wanted you to read to them, take them camping, play games with them, talk to them, and teach them anything of value. It always seemed like they were a burden to you. So I tried as best I could to pick up the slack.

But it wore me out. I lost my identity raising the kids. I wanted you to be the strength in the home, not me. I never had any complaints about you providing financially for the family. You were and are a hard worker at your job. But I needed someone to come home and help with the discipline of the kids, guide them, and give me a break.

I have always felt that I have had to be responsible for the inside system as well as the outside members of the family. I hate having to write lists for you because you can't see past your nose all that needs to be done. I hate having to remind you to do something fifteen times because you never listen the first time. I hate it when you ignore the work that needs to be done around here. I hate it that every time I suggest something you do the opposite, even though I have proven to you over the years that I am usually right. If I say go left, you will purposely go right...as if my suggestion or opinion is not worthy of consideration. And I particularly hate when you can't find something, you start screaming the F-word and ranting and raving. Then I have to go and take care of the problem, just so I don't have to listen to you and deal with the scared parts inside.

I need you to help with the managing of the outside children and with parts like Maria. I need you to respect me as an independent woman and realize that I am not Maria or Louise. I need you to be strong to oversee the home, but not controlling of me. I want to relinquish being head of the house over to you, but I want you take it seriously and not ignore the responsibilities with it.

This is Liz. Needs...Needs...I got plenty of them. I want to know if there is life out there past this house and kids. I like to have fun and you hate fun. You never would take me out when I was trapped all day with those kids. Every time I tried to have fun you squished it. You don't laugh. You don't play games. You don't play cards. You don't even go over to people's houses and have dinner. You don't entertain. You don't dance. You don't joke. You don't camp. You don't fish. You don't do rollercoasters . You don't have fun.

And I am dying in this boring existence. I want to do stuff. I want to have a life. I hate to dust and organize and be the little housewife. I want to live and do crazy stuff. How come you never surprise us by taking us out for a weekend?

Me and Louise want to write ours together. We want to be a good wife to Sergio and make him happy. We have problems with not going away when we try to do it. We can't help it cuz we don't know how to stay and we want to learn so Sergio don't get mad. Doing it scares us and makes us feel dirty. We don't know how to feel when he says things about our body. It embarrasses us. We don't understand sometimes. We get scared when Sergio gets mad. We don't like fighting and bad words yelled in the house. We just want to learn to be a good wife. And we like it when we feel safe and he protects us. We like to be touched nice.

I, Quiet Walker, need to be allowed to seek solitude. I enjoy POW WOWS. I take pleasure in camping and traveling deep within the forest. I delight in listening to and observing nature. I do not like the city and the rush of the people in the city. I prefer quiet, still places away from buildings, cars and people.

77

I am not sure what my needs are in relationship to Sergio. Sergio and I are not on the same spiritual plane. I would like Sergio to be more active in fellowshipping with the body of believers. I would like to be in a couple's class with him and to socialize more at church. It is very lonely for me to always attend functions by myself. Everyone else has their spouse with them, enjoying the time together and I am always alone.

I know Sergio is very angry and not trusting of Christians. I know he hates what the church stands for, but I wish he would be willing to be involved simply because it would bring me joy. It's difficult for me to accept invitations from the church because I know that Sergio will get angry. I get tired of making excuses as to why my husband is never there. I want to be a partner with Sergio in ministry. I want Sergio to be the spiritual head of the household. I want him to teach his children about Jesus and let his children see him praying.   Ruth

(Jennifer is still absent but Council asked me to try and assess her needs based upon what we know of her.) Jennifer likes the ocean. In fact the system is very close to the ocean for reasons I do not understand. Jennifer loves picnics and walks along the shoreline. She is very serious about the environment and to stop poisoning the earth. She loves birds and becomes very upset when family members yell at her birds or attempt to harm them.

There is too much changing right now for me. I have a hard time being on the outside and talking with people. I don't know Maria's husband very well. I like men who are soft and sensitive but can protect and be strong. My name is Mari.

All parts who wished to comment have been given the opportunity. As leaders of Circle Council who are male and have spent a considerable amount of time with the parts, we wish to express our opinion on the needs of the female parts of this system.

We know how challenging it is to live with the diversity that is found in this system. In order for us to serve and work with them, we have learned about their needs so we could know all about them. We hope that this will help you better

understand each of them. These women are challenging! It is difficult sometimes to decipher what they are asking for or want. They are more in need of a man who is sensitive, kind, considerate and understanding, than a man who is brash and overpowering. They seem to thrive when we turn our attention to them. If we communicate with them by listening and then asking detailed questions about what they're talking about, showing interest in what they have to say, they blossom.

One way you could do this is calling from work occasionally to see how they're doing or surprising them with a special note on the table before you leave. These parts want to know that they are higher up on the ladder of importance than anything else. Affection, attention and love show them that they matter and that is extremely important for them.

We have gained their loyalty by presenting ourselves in a respectable manner. We have had to earn their respect. It has not been easy. They are very particular. Integrity is very important to them, as is honesty and being real. They like us to be strong in our decision making process knowing we have only their best interest at heart. They look up to us as leaders and protectors and seem to be proud of us, sort of like we're heroes. We believe that is what they want from you also, to be their hero.

If you look at the two male outside relationships that are successful, you will see all of these characteristics played out. The relationships are successful because the needs of the female parts are being met. It can be the same with you. Standing for Ann when your child tears her down, protecting Maria from family, setting boundaries for Liz that show her you want to protect her, sharing your hurts and feelings with Ruth, are all ways that can help the system draw closer to you.

As the system draws closer to you, they will begin to heal and slowly be intimate with you. It will be a life-long process and worked on continually. As we chose to spend time in getting to know each and every part, we have benefited far more than we realized. They have shown us how to persevere in spite of

difficult circumstances. They have encouraged us and taught us about the importance of life. We have learned a new set of priorities and "how to smell the roses". They have grown close to us and we cherish and adore them, for without them we are nothing.

Paladin, Helper, King of Lights, Daniel, Lion, Keeper of Functions

Ruth, on behalf of the System, read the letter to Sergio that night during the first session. I don't believe that Sergio was prepared for the responses to his idea of marrying all of 'them'. He had for the most part dismissed the whole concept of 'male' parts existing at all, so communication from them appeared to be immediately ignored. That was easy to do, even with the female parts, when they were perceived of as 'moods' and not real separate people. But when 'moods' start communicating with you under different names and requesting changes of attitude and perceptions, they're not so easily dismissed.

It's hard for me to imagine all of what was going through Sergio's mind as he encountered new parts that he was unaware of and never interacted with on a direct or personal level. Changes were occurring around him in spite of his desires that they go backward to the way it used to be. He had come to counseling primarily to be a man of his word and fulfill his promise to Maria, but that didn't mean he wanted to change anything about himself. He stated up-front his mistrust of all counselors, therapists, Christians, doctors, psychiatrist, pastors and contractors. Since I fell within 5 of the 7 mentioned, I knew the evening would progress slowly, if at all. Yet, he seemed to understand that I was there to help and made some effort to not be disrespectful in communicating with me. The following letter from Council reveals their reaction to the evening.

Memo from Council
Elizabeth Ray
The marriage counseling session was too long for the system. Two hours is the maximum time that council feels they can control switching in an intense environment such as Saturday. Ruth was having a very difficult time staying out. Driving home was hard for

Sergio. Mariann came out and would not keep Maria's wig on. She wanted to put her hands out of the car window and then spotted you going by on the freeway and gave him a hard time.

Council remains committed to the marriage counseling. However, we are now dealing with a tremendous amount of discouragement in some female parts and a lot of anger in others. We, as council, do not understand the husband's comments that he wants the system to be open with him in communicating, yet he does not ask them any questions. How do we communicate with someone who does not have any questions or express any feelings one way or the other about us? He just accepts everything...discussion ended, case closed. "She is Maria and I am not going to acknowledge the others for who they are, but only as moods." We tried to clarify this in the office with your help but got nowhere. Ruth was frustrated and we were frustrated. Liz was forced to stay away from the gatekeeper when she wanted to spin out.

We do not know if we are going to be able to control the frustration that continues inside. Liz was angry when Sergio said he was not jealous of you or Bruce, and your relationship with Maria. Liz wanted him jealous. She thinks he should be jealous that the system is so close in communicating with you their deepest secrets and emotions. She feels that apparently, it doesn't matter to him that another man is emotionally more connected to the system than he is.

Council will proceed cautiously. The next session on this Saturday at 3PM will work if that's okay with you. We will shadow closely and allow Quiet Walker out to address her specific concerns. Please advise if this is a problem.

I spent part of the next week trying to grasp what Sergio's view of married life had been for almost twenty years. I could set aside his refusal to answer most of my questions beyond yes or no, but it was his clear rejection of the diagnosis of Dissociative Identity Disorder for Maria that threw me. I knew he had acknowledged different parts previously by asking for them by name for a specific task. He had shown compassion for the child parts, even as he restricted them to be out only in their room. Even after I had explained to the whole family the diagnosis before Maria's cancer surgery 3 months prior to this counseling session, I would not be asked a single question by any member of the family over the next ten years to help their understanding of Maria's life.

The children would look to their father for their example in how to respond to the System. Usually life at home meant, if mother is acting strange or child-like, call dad to make her stop. When asked recently by a friend if these conditions had improved, I could only shake my head saying no. When asked about the dynamics involved here, I tried to explain it this way.

"Remember the movie "Harvey" with Jimmy Stewart? It's sort of like that. Everyone here interacts with Maria's condition on a regular basis, usually negatively, but refuses to discuss it with anyone outside of the family circle. I believe it is because of their fear of how it will reflect on them. They all know that ignoring it doesn't make it go away, so they have two choices: Keep silent and carry the pain of ignorance and fear deep inside...always wondering if you are going to be 'infected'; or, Talk with Bruce or myself about how they can help Maria heal. To do the latter they have to first admit the problem exists and no one is willing to consider that option, so they live in their denial.

I decided to use the direct approach at the session next week and hoped to get some response from Sergio indicating that he was aware of the problem. I would soon find out how little he really did know about his wife, Maria. The following week was very active for everyone as Halloween was just over a week away. Maria had been unable to attend her church for several weeks and was happy to receive a call from her friend. She also told her something unexpected. Her friend had purchased a book about MPD to learn more about how to help Maria and had left the book in her room. The next day her housekeeper came running up to her asking where she got the book and can she have it. She said yes, after she told her that her sister-in-law had been diagnosed with MPD a few weeks before in Washington. Her counselor did not know how to treat multiples and was looking for resources to help. Her husband had left the home and moved away out of frustration, unable to make any sense out of a disorder he knew nothing about. Everyone in the family wanted to read this book.

Maria asked if she could write to the woman, because she hurt for her and wanted her to know that she was not alone and that there were other multiples. Her friend thought it might help so Maria did, after she asked Jesus what to say. She was afraid of causing more trauma to the woman, but Jesus assured her that He wanted her to encourage the woman by giving her hope.

My name is Maria and I live in Northern California. A friend of mine from church said her housekeeper had a sister-in-law who had multiple personality disorder. I think that is you. I wanted to tell you about me and let you know that I was told I had multiple personality disorder almost two years ago. I didn't know what was wrong with me. All of my life I thought I was crazy cuz I couldn't remember stuff and everything was weird around me.

I tried to cover stuff up cuz I would not know where time went and I would find myself in places I didn't know and things in my house that weren't mine. My husband just said I had bad mood swings, but I knew it was something else. I thought I had early alhemizers disease or something. It was real hard but I never told anyone because I was afraid they might take my kids away.

Everything fell apart when my daughter got sick and they took her away from me. I tried to die but the others inside that I didn't know about got me help. When the counselor told me that I had multiple personality disorder I didn't believe him. I told him no, I am crazy. He said no you're not.

I didn't want to talk to the others or think about them. I tried to make them go away but they wouldn't. Liz would get real mad when I said she didn't exist and she would take me someplace and leave me there. The noise in my head got so loud and I would hear voices inside talk about me. I got real scared.

My counselor tried to help me understand why I am the way I am. I've learned a lot since two years ago. I had a lot of bad happen to me when I was little. I couldn't get away or get help so God let me be a multiple to keep me alive. My parts took the bad so I could live.

Each part has different things to say and different memories inside. They are different ages and they have names. At first I didn't want to know them, but now I like them and they are friends.

I still don't remember what they talk about but my counselor says that is cuz it happened to them and not me.

We are learning to trust God and not be scared. God is helping us by giving us a safe counselor and a safe pastor to help us learn about the real Jesus, and not be deceived by the one we were told about by bad men. It is not easy being like us. Sometimes we feel so different and alone in the world. Our counselor and pastor is special to us as they try to understand what it's like to have parts, but I don't think you can truly understand unless you have them.

But Jesus understands. Liz once told me that God is multiple. She said he has three parts in one person so he can understand us. I don't know if that's true but I would like to think so. I don't know what will happen to me but I have hope now. I didn't have any before now. Lots of good has happened in the last two years even though I got cancer and parts. I now have friends who don't treat me bad and accept me as I am. I have a church and a Bible class with friends who know about my parts, and they don't get mad when I switch. The parts are talking to the counselor and learning that what happened was not their fault and they are not bad. I think I can make it as a multiple in this world. Maybe I can have friends stay and understand me and give me hope. I don't know.

I want you to know that you are not alone. There are others of us out there in the world who know what it is like and know the pain we feel. I hope you can find a counselor and pastor like mine to help you. There is a toll-free number called 800-new-life and they know counselors who can help. There is hope.

Bye, Maria

A few days later I received this letter from Council.

Memo – Circle Council
Elizabeth Ray

Mariann is having difficulty with separation issues, as you are aware. We are attempting to help her understand that temporary separation from you does not mean that she is being abandoned or that she is bad. She is having trouble with memories at the park and we are not able to control the escalation. In the past, the statement "you are bad, I am going to leave you" was reinforced continually. Mariann would respond, "I won't be bad. I *won't be bad." When she began to hyperventilate with you and say this over and over again, she was having flashbacks. We would appreciate outside help in calming her down. Hold her and tell her "You are not bad and I am not going to leave you forever. I will see you again. <u>I am not like all of the others, Mariann. I will not leave you.</u>"*

Ruth does not understand the deep trauma with abandonment for the children. When Tabitha was left hanging in the basement, she cried the same words, "No be bad. No be bad. No go." She would rather he stay and beat her than walk up the steps to close her in the dark. To be alone was more traumatic than being whipped.

We can empathize with Mariann. She would rather live in a box under your sink to be close to you than live in a castle. You satisfy her hunger for closeness. There are a lot of dynamics going on for the children so close to Halloween. The system is overwhelmed by stress from CORE. October is always a bad month.

Things are changing for the children as they learn about boundaries and conditions in the outside world. They are in a difficult situation. They are children and as such act like children. Four-year-olds take clothes off, eat with the dog and play in the toilet. Yet these children must take on the added weight of being in an adult body, though they don't seem to perceive it as such. As children they want to take off their shirt, but as adults they can't. As children they want to play in the dirt and climb all over you and Carol but can't in the adult body. (That never stopped the kids from trying.)

We are continually monitoring the children to balance their needs, while maintaining the integrity of the adult body. It is a challenge for us and a time-consuming endeavor. We appreciated the consistency of Carol for the children regarding the clothing. We still have a difficult time with them wanting to take off their shirt in front of Bruce and you to show their scars. Helping them to understand that it is okay only in the doctor's office is not easy. There are other issues as well, like Tabitha wanting to be in the backyard with only her shirt and underwear on and Mariann in the kitchen in only her underwear. Sergio is constantly telling them to put clothes on and it is embarrassing to the older parts.

We find it perplexing that the children have no hesitation about removing their clothes and yet Maria will not remove her clothes in front of Sergio. We do not understand this extreme between the parts.

The all day conference was good for Maria and it confirmed our decision about not allowing Maria to the weekend retreat. She could not control the switching over the course of the day and Mariann switched out with the cookies. The lecture on friendship was interesting for all of us. We realized that until recently, we had no friends, especially soul friends. The system had to maintain its secrecy about the multiplicity and all of our acquaintances to the different parts never knew the real system...only the façade. Only in the last year have we risked exposing ourselves and sharing with friends, soul friends, such as you.

Last night we centered our discussion on what type of love is the system seeking. It was lively and interesting, more so than the lecture earlier. The system is not searching for sexual love and in fact, avoids it due to their past experiences. For all of them, there seems to be no understanding of this type of love. Sex to them is manipulative, controlling and hurtful, and something men do to women. Liz said it is something I use to get back at men, "where at least I will have some control and they will pay." The husband does not say it is love, but rather a responsibility that meets his needs. We have observed how his touch always has sexual overtones and he is constantly badgering Maria with jokes or sexual innuendoes that he is never satisfied. Maria is afraid of his touch because of what it means.

The system loves to be touched in non-sexual ways, as warmth and safety is important to them. This may be because they have known cold and fear most of their lives. Every time you or Carol or Bruce hug the system and wrap your arms around them, you give them the greatest gifts that they desire...warmth and safety. We know that this is important when we see Jesus continually doing it on the inside for the children. He holds them close to him to give them security and warmth. They feel his strength and protection and this transcends into love.

We also realize that although the parts desire this type of love, they also fear any outsider who attempts to give it, not knowing if they can trust them. It has taken many years for them to allow just a few people (Bruce, you, Carol and Lindsay) to give them touch love. They may need it desperately, but they are afraid to trust to get it. Each time they receive it, they heal a little bit more from their past fears and feelings of unworthiness. Touch love tells them they are worth protecting and accepted as important enough to be precious to the beholder. They are not pushed away, but gathered in, something very foreign to them.

Another type of love we discussed is non-judgmental love. They are now allowed to be themselves without fear of ridicule, rejection or abandonment. When you truly listen with an open heart to their questions, their frustrations and opinions, it helps them have value. They never try to convince anyone to see things their way, they just want to be allowed to be heard. Even Liz, as vocal as she can be, never has as her ultimate goal to force others to bend her way, only wanting the right to have her opinion.

Again we see this on the inside exhibited by Jesus. The parts are given the freedom to question, talk and complain. Jesus has never once pushed them aside or said don't talk about that. He allows them to be free to express themselves however they feel. They feel accepted by him.

Time-love is another form of love that the system desires. Time-love is not the amount of time, but rather the focus during the time allotted. Jesus gives his undivided attention and makes it available to them when they seek it. That transcends to "you are so precious to me that everything around us does not matter. I am focused on you." In their past, everything was more important than them. At times, they even seemed to want the physical abuse because at least it was attention. Negative attention was better than none at all.

The system has experienced the world's love filled with conditions, abuse and control. It never satisfied them and only caused a deeper hunger in their spirit. They were yet unaware that there was any other love available. Then you, Bruce, Lindsay and Carol entered the picture and began to show them a different love – touch love, non-judgmental love and time-love. We do not believe that they could have understood the love Jesus was offering them, if they had not first experienced it on the outside through people like you. As Raquel has told us, "the outside helpers are preparing and serving the food made by the Great Spirit so that the system will be filled with good food and thus grow and be healthy. As they grow and become healthy, then they too can become servers and providers for others."

On another matter concerning the next marital counseling session, Maria's mother attempted to force her into buying a wedding ring from a friend of hers with the insurance money given to Sergio. Liz switched out and said sorry, but we already purchased one. Liz does not want a ring picked by Maria's mother. She doesn't even want a ring. She wants to purchase a two year supply of mushrooms and beer! Her request has not been approved, reluctantly, but we are grateful she switched and prevented the mother from choosing a ring for Maria.

Council has addressed the issue of Halloween. We want it clearly understood by you that it is one of the most difficult nights for the system. Are you and Carol truly prepared? Can Carol handle that evening with the system? What about the workday to follow? You will probably get little sleep. Although we have received little communication from Tolip about the approaching day, we know the ramifications of Halloween. The system becomes highly stressed and there are flashbacks in CORE. Hopi is not yet fully healed and Egar has not had contact with Dragonslayer.

We cannot prepare you thoroughly for all that might occur...since we do not know. All we can tell you is that there are constant triggers like the color black, demon billboards, ghost music and kids dressed up in costumes. We try to block these but some make it to CORE. Last year the system was in the shed hysterical over the phone to Bruce. Maria did not understand why she was feeling the way she was and became confused by the memories of others. At Halloween 1977, an eleven-year-old child hung himself in the family bathroom. Ann went to the funeral where Maria saw the burn marks on his neck. It triggered someone inside to remember that Halloween = death.

Egar hurts herself by banging her head against the walls. If she gets a hold of a knife or scissors she will cut the body. She takes her rage and turns it inward on herself because she doesn't know how to deal with it. She has been out once with you in Bruce's office repeating herself, "put her on the table. Be quiet or I will kill you." Hopi has talked of drinking blood and worshipping the master. We are not sure if the two nightmares that Maria experiences are related to this trauma or a different one. She has reluctantly shared with us the nightmare of being put on a table she thinks is in a bar and is stripped naked to be examined. It then becomes cloudy to her except that something is done to her to force her to react sexually to a stimulant. Though she tries to rid herself of this nightmare, it always returns.

Elizabeth Ray will not divulge to us the particulars of Egar's trauma. We do not force her to reveal anything. We are not sure if Hopi holds the pain and Egar holds the rage. Tabitha seems to have a connection to CORE, so we assume that all of this has to do with the Santeria. Tabitha has drawn some pictures that Hopi showed her...lots of black and red...black marks in a circle and what appears to be candles...something on a table and one black mark with an animal symbol we believe to be a goat. Tabitha knows it is bad even if she can't explain it. During Halloween, the system hides in holes where it is safe and they can't be snatched from it, or found hiding under the bed, in a closet or in sheds.

If you encounter the Core children, keep all sharp objects away from them. If they run in a closet or under the bed, do not attempt to grab them or you might be bitten. Do as Bruce does and lay down and talk softly to them, allowing them to stay where they are. Try to make eye contact as you have done before, while allowing them to chant, scream or display symbols in their drawings. Reassure them in a soft voice that "you are not the goat man and you will not hurt them. Tell them you will not put anything into them. Tell them you know Tolip and that they are safe with you." Repeat this as often as needed.

If they try to hurt themselves by scratching the face or banging the head against a wall, tell them you want to make them safe by gently holding their hands or head to stop them from being hurt. If necessary, tell them you will sleep next to them on the floor to make sure that no bad can get them. Be prepared for repeated behavior. The child might calm down one minute and then be agitated again the second, as memories flood the mind. Please be consistent with the children.

We are sure you have other ideas that will work that we are not familiar with, as we have a limited amount of information. You are entering into the core of the trauma and as you proceed the level of intensity heightens.

Egar holds the rage and is probably the most fractured. Our purpose in being explicit is to make sure you understand what you are asking to be involved in and know that it will not be peaceful or the CORE children won't be out. We hope they don't, but from our experience we assume nothing.

If you choose to subject yourself to this, we will have Ruth drive them over to your house early Thursday afternoon and return on Friday morning. If you choose to not do this, we will not be offended. We have an alternate plan of locking them in the bedroom and staying in the closet all night. Please advise us of your decision.

Circle Council

The second session of marital counseling could easily qualify as the worst yet, and only to be topped by the third and final session a week away. Sergio was not pleased with facing Raquel in the first half-hour, followed by Ruth speaking for Ann and Liz who were too volatile to come out. Sergio was very uncomfortable with being confronted by personalities that were clearly not submissive and stating expectations of changes for him to consider now. I could not get him to recognize openly anyone but Maria. Council wrote the following letter after the session and it was waiting for me by the time I returned home that evening.

Memo From Circle Council

We apologize for the animosity of the husband. We have spent the last hour and a half discussing what occurred in the office. Our perspective is that the husband wishes to remain indifferent about the marriage and he sees no benefit in changing. As leaders, we are concerned with the effect his behavior is having on the female parts. The husband has always been bitter and closed. There have always been outside circumstances that he has used for his support in distancing himself from others and the system.

His relationship with Ann has always been a superficial one. He never shows feelings, nor does he allow it in Ann. He likes her strong and efficient, so that he does not need to worry about "the little de-

tails of the household." Sergio uses control, rejection and isolation as a way of keeping parts inline. It is possible that he might not be aware of this, but nevertheless it is a method he has perfected over the years. As the system maintained an emotional satisfactory distance from him; met his physical and mental needs; took care of his children and managed the home efficiently; he was content.

When life changed in 1994 for the system, they realized one of their greatest needs. They were starved for acceptance and deep connections with people. They had spent most of their quality time with animals and very little time relating to people, and there was no turning back after Bruce introduced them to a relationship that valued them. Then you came into the picture and reinforced that they had a void in their lives yearning to be filled. Why do they love being with you? We believe it is because you nurture them without expectations placed on them.

What you saw in the session is very much what it is like at home, even if the husband wishes to admit it or not. The parts have tried many times to reach out to him and they have received the same response you witnessed in the office. So as leaders we have questioned why the female parts stay.

There are several reasons why they stay, the most probable one being their fear that it would push Maria over the edge and she would kill herself. It has always been the function of the parts to keep Maria alive. They will live out their lives in a cold and unnurturing environment rather than risk Maria destroying the system. Even though Ann and Liz find different ways of escaping from the home through work and "I want to party", they will stay for Maria's sake.

We are not sure if it is good to continue to subject the system to the pain of going through these counseling sessions. We know that every time Sergio attacks your questioning, there is a great affect on different parts. Maria is unaware of what's going on except that Sergio is mad and she is scared that she has done something to cause it. We try to close her off from shadowing when he attacks you verbally. She can't handle that. You are very special to her and she loves you more than anyone outside of the one she refers to as Jesus. Sergio's attacks would pierce her and we're not sure we could repair the damage. We are afraid she might split due to the severity of her reaction to that type of confrontation between you and him.

Raquel has told us that she has spoken and has nothing further to say. She has returned to Sacred Mountain. We believe that the husband's response to her story and poem had a negative effect upon her. Ruth can not handle any more out time with Sergio. We asked too much of her and she has been overwhelmed at the responses of Sergio. She did a good job of communicating our thoughts during the sessions, but we realize now that she was exhausted and confused by trying to read the body language and comments of the husband. She broke down after the session and is deep inside.

Liz and Ann have joined forces in responding to the husband. They believe he is attempting to place the blame of non-communication on them and somehow they are responsible for all of the problems. They are mad that he refuses to recognize them for who they are as individuals. They are tired of him questioning them about "when are they all going together to fix this nonsense?" They refuse to share their deepest feelings with him, because he doesn't deserve the right to know them. They are more than willing to share their fair share of the blame in order to risk learning how to improve the marriage.

They had been considering trying being married to him in order to learn to love him, if he was going to try to change and accept them. But now they say he can f&#% off. They are tired of him making them the whipping boy for his problems. They will make it on their own without him and keep the pain deep inside.

Maria and Louise are very upset because they see how the other parts are reacting to the marriage counseling. They don't fully understand and we are selectively telling them pieces. We are careful because we don't want them falling back into a deep depression and seeing the only way out is death.

Counsel needs advice as to how to proceed. Should marriage counseling continue, or should council give up and allow the husband to maintain his status quo?

That evening I discussed with Council the drawbacks of discontinuing marriage counseling at this point however difficult. The chance was slim but worth taking if we could break through Sergio's resistance. We agreed that he was only there out of obligation to a promise made to Maria. Council felt this promise was an impediment to his genuine growth if that was the only reason for his presence. They chose a course of action they felt was their only honorable path to healing for the System. They sent the following memorandum to Sergio in the hope that it would either open the road to communication with him or remove the block to their learning process. We had one more session scheduled with him and waited for the response to know if we would be going on with him or not. I hoped it would be a positive one.

To: Sergio
From: Circle Council
Re: Marriage Counseling

Circle Council has discussed the comments made by you at the Saturday marriage counseling session held in the pastor's office. Council has voted to relieve you of the obligation of fulfilling your promise to Maria that you would attend marriage counseling if she promised to fight the cancer.

We, as leaders, do not wish to be perceived as forcing anyone into a situation that they do not wish to be in. You commented several times that your presence at the sessions is due to coercion on the part of the system. Therefore, we wish to nullify the promise to prove to you that we do not coerce.

Circle Council will, however, continue to encourage the system to seek marriage counseling to help them learn the skills of communication. The female parts will attend the sessions alone. We will respect your right to decide if and when you are ready to change, and release the bitterness that you are carrying. At that time, if you wish to join us in marriage counseling, we will welcome you.

This memorandum illustrates the state of growth, positive and negative, of Council's relational skills as male personalities that never come to the outside from Preservation. There are many good reasons why they have chosen to do this, but it does make it difficult for learning how to communicate with the husband of their female counterparts on the inside, who are his only perceived relationships. His prior acknowledgement of their existence was mostly courtesy on his part to his understanding of his wife's acceptance of their reality. Previously, any communication from them was accepted 'tongue and cheek', because it was usually advice without any real consequences. Now however, they were establishing themselves as men of conviction with some control over the choices of this System. To issue an ultimatum like this, even though it was not intended to be such, provoked a reaction from Sergio that was irrational, given his statements earlier.

Council would continue to grow in their understanding of male/female relationships and how we cross-communicate. They have commented many times to me about what they learn through observing my wife and I at our best and our worst. They will get much better in the years to come at communicating with men on the outside…Sergio being the only exception. While they may grow to understand some of his complex male issues in the world, they will struggle to understand his relationship with Maria and the female parts. Sometimes I will simply say to them, "If you haven't been there yourselves in a marriage, it's too hard to explain." They later realize how in many ways, their relationships inside are not identical to a marriage. It would be better described as that of elders in a small, rural, family church, and most churches have the distinction of suffering from multiple personality disorder. They will send the following letter to me within 24 hours after giving Sergio the memorandum.

Sunday afternoon:

Council submitted memo to husband relieving him of his promise to Maria. Husband became angry that council had the nerve to make a decision like that. He threw the memo back at the system. System attempted again to communicate by telling him it is not our intention on council to force him to do anything that he is not willing to do. Comment from husband, "I promised Maria and I keep my promises." Council again attempted to speak and told him that he did not break his promise and he fulfilled his obligation to Maria. Husband walked away into his room and slammed the door.

That evening, the husband spoke to Maria and told her that, if she kicked him out or left him, he would die. Maria began crying and stated that she was sorry for anything she did. She promised not to leave him and didn't want him to leave. He told her that he wanted her to not be involved with others outside the home but spend time with him there. Council immediately switched Ann out and she questioned him. "If you are never home and when you are, you are tired or busy doing things...then how am I supposed to spend time with you?" Husband did not answer her. Ann said, "Well, answer me." He said, "I want you available for me." Ann responded, "So I am supposed to stay home, have no friends and no life outside of here...is that what you're saying to me?" He said you are misinterpreting me. Ann said I don't understand you. He said, "that is just the way it is". Council switched Ann in and Maria out to tell him that she needed to go to bed to rest. He left and Maria cried herself to sleep in her pillow.

The night was poor. Maria began hearing voices telling her that she was the reason for Sergio's unhappiness and the sooner she was out of the picture the happier everyone will be. Mariann told us that she told her how they would be going to heaven soon, because she was going to take heaven candy to make everything okay. Mariann came to us because she wanted to know if she could go to the toy store in heaven with Mr. Miguel. We asked her if Maria gave her a day that she would be going to heaven. Mariann said soon because we are bad here and in heaven we get love and Jesus. Council went on alert. There is concern about how Maria will be able to finish the chemotherapy in her emotional state, with Halloween coming the day after the last chemo next week.

Ann has brought a request to Council informing us that she is broke and cannot pay for therapy the rest of the year. The bills are greater than the income and she is freezing everything in the budget. She has nothing of value to sell and her children own the computers and van. She has asked that the insurance money for her stolen wedding ring be used for bills instead of replacing it. She has asked that we discontinue therapy until next year because she can't pay for it. Council is considering her request.

Liz has taken off inside through the desert. She cannot be reached.

Jennifer is still not back.

Ann is trying to hang on but is loosing ground. She feels that she must get her teaching credential to have a backup in case she becomes the sole provider for the system.

Louise is sticking close to Maria and both are very quiet.

Ruth cannot be reached.

Tabitha, Anna and Angelina are hiding in the cave and don't play.

Mariann is still talking. She is confused as to why the adults are taking off. We told her it is a big person's problem and they need time alone to think about it. She informed us that she was going to Dragonslayer to tell Him all about it and she's there now.

I knew that the amount of spiritual activity was increasing around the System as Halloween drew near. Evil was not going to pass up an opportunity like the problems within marriage counseling and Maria being suicidal, to disrupt the lives of any part willing to listen to them. I began to plan with Louise an outing with Tabitha on Halloween night, eating burritos together that Louise would prepare for us. She also wrote out for me several pages of words and phrases in Spanish to help my talks with Tabitha.

All of the adults planned to stay very deep inside Preservation on Halloween night. It was just going to be Carol and I, the children and Council all night with Jesus protecting us. We accepted Louise's burritos for us and we enjoyed them as they were most excellent. She wrote in her letter to me three days before Halloween the following:

I hope this information helps you a little. Ruth told me that Bruce is going to see Tabitha and Mariann on the morning of Halloween because they are becoming fearful and taking on a lot of the feelings that are coming up from the pod children. The pod children seem to be having more of an affect on the other children lately. I don't know but Mariann is not doing well and Tabitha cries a lot and tells us disgusting things that I don't want to hear. Bruce said that CORE and Tolip are closer to you than him. They will trust you with their children before they will trust him. He said that you can do in one night what would take him months of therapy in the office. He will not call the pod children out on Halloween because he doesn't have enough time to work with them. I don't understand all of it, but that is what Ruth said.

"Come now, you who say, 'today or tomorrow, we shall go to such and such a city, and spend a year there and engage in business and make a profit.' Yet you do not know what your life will be like tomorrow. You are just a vapor that appears for just a little while and then vanishes away. Instead, you ought to say, 'If the Lord wills, we shall live and also do this or that."
James 4: 13-15

"God brings forth the living from the dead, and he brings forth the dead from the living. He quickens the earth after it is dead, so will you be caused to come forth."
- Koran, 33:17

Chapter Five

"Submitting Free Will to Providence"

"The man who submits to his fate calls it the will of God: the man who puts up a hopeless and exhausting fight is more apt to see the devil in it."
C.G. Jung, *Psychology and Alchemy* (1953)

"Permit the children to come to Me; do not hinder them; for the kingdom of God belongs to such as these. 'Truly I say to you, whoever does not receive the kingdom of God like a child shall not enter it at all."
Jesus Christ, Mark 10: 14-15

It has taken me most of my life to trust that God's plan for me cannot be fulfilled as long as I'm trying to control it. I have wasted many years in stubbornness of telling God, "this is what I decided to do." I seem to have a natural gift for deciding how to do anything…the hardest way possible. My ego told me this was the best way to learn how to cope with the difficulties of life, and the only way to be sure that I didn't repeat mistakes. I think it came from a life that reinforced the belief that no one else could determine what was best for me better than I could. What a crock that was…and is!

As I began working with the children of the System more often during this time, I slowly began to learn the truth of Jesus' statements about children and the kingdom of God. On the one hand, I had worked with adults for so long in trying to understand the complex issues of faith that I had come to truly value someone with 'simple' faith. On the other hand, I still wanted clear and reasonable answers from God for guidance here and now. I definitely did not want the answer that I gave to my children at crucial times, "Because I said so!" Just as they always responded with, "But why?" I found that I was often saying that to God as well, whenever His response to me was, "Because I've said so." It would be the children's examples and Maria's simple faith that opened my eyes and heart to finally perceive the kingdom of God as a child.

I have reached a point of understanding where I want to ask my children to forgive me for having learned this so late in life. They were raised without the benefit of a father who could teach them how easy it really is to love Jesus and be loved by Him, or how you don't have to 'perform' or be good enough to be accepted by Him and perhaps most important of all, how you don't have to understand God's plan and accept it…before He will implement it on your behalf. If I could pass on one piece of advice to my children today, it would be what Jesus told the Apostle Paul when he asked to have an affliction removed from his life – three times:

"My grace is sufficient for you, for power is perfected in weakness."

If I have learned nothing else but this about the person of Jesus, then I have learned something worth passing on to my family and friends. Children are capable of accepting the kingdom of God, because they can accept the power of love without having to first understand it. Children begin at birth to have their primary needs met, including love, and they don't really care about whose plan accomplishes this, as long as these needs are met. They know right away that they can't fill these needs, so they ask for help one way or another. Problems don't start occurring until they start taking things into their own hands and making free will choices to accomplish this. But when children are nurtured by a parent whose plan always seeks to give them what is best for them, the necessity for making their own choices can wait until they are mature enough to handle it.

This kind of maturity recognizes what real control, real power, truly is. It also understands what it means to give power over one's life to another. For the children of the System and Maria, most of their life was spent without their needs being met, or the freedom to make choices on their own. We would soon find ourselves in a place where we would have to start at the beginning and discover together the kingdom of God through simple faith and the eyes of a child. Over three days' time we go through the last chemotherapy treatment, fight a major spiritual battle all night on Halloween, and witness dramatic changes for everyone in Preservation. It felt as though the spiritual attacks upon us were increasing in intensity with each passing hour, so I asked Maria to journal her prayers the night before the last chemotherapy session.

Dear Jesus,
You know it's me again. I want to talk to you Jesus. Jesus it's so hard to be happy sometimes. I cried today cuz I'm mixed up and sad. Please unmix me up.
I love you.
Maria

My precious child,
Continue to persevere and believe in my promises. I will deliver you and you will receive what I have promised.
Trust me – Jesus

Dear Jesus,
How long is this going to be like this?

My dear little one,
Do you trust me? You are going to have to trust me. Why do you doubt my ability to bring you through the wilderness? You must have faith my child...faith to overcome.
Your loving Jesus.

Dear Jesus,
I trust you. You are much smarter than me and more powerful than Superman. And you know everything and you made me. You went and got hurt and died for me. So I trust you. How come Ann says for you to prove it?
Me.

My child,
Remember when I sent Wolfdog into the orchard to protect you and provide you warmth in the cold? Remember the times of hunger and the slabs left behind on the tray? Remember the birds I sent to you in the treetops as you sat lonely and sad perched in the apricot trees? Remember the blossoms that spring day when I sent the wind to sing to you and the blossoms to cover you with my love?

Remember too, that Monday night when I sent Mr. G____ to your home and stopped your death? I have never left you and I have always cared deeply for you. Does Ann still refuse to trust me despite all of the signs I have shown the parts? Yes Ann, I know you are reading this and I know your struggles. Ann, will you trust me or will you not?

Jesus, Ann is crying. She is so tired. She tries so hard and nobody sees how hard she tries. Jesus, Ann isn't bad, she is just real sad inside cuz life is so hard for her. She helps me do things and makes sure the stuff is done right. She works lots to make sure we do the things that we got to do. She is afraid you will take it back or trick her about love.

My dearest and most precious ones,
  My love endures forever. I will never take my love from you. Ann, I am slow to anger and rich in love. Let me pour out my love on you. Ann, my love for you surpasses all understanding, so allow your heart to experience my love...my unfailing love for you.
Lovingly – Jesus

Jesus, how come you are talking to Ann more than me?

My child,
  My words are for you also. I will talk with you as long as you wish.
Trust me – Jesus

Jesus, I got to tell you that I was thinking about going to heaven this week. I wasn't trusting good. I'm sorry. Please forgive me.

My special one,
  I know of your thoughts and I know of your hunger for heaven. You must be patient. There is work for you here. I am preparing a place for you. You will be in heaven when it is time. But for now continue to allow me to guide your steps.
I forgive you.
Jesus

101

Jesus I'm tired. Can I go to sleep?

Goodnight my child.

PS Jesus please protect my friend Pastor Chalberg cuz the smelly ones are real angry that I call him. They don't like him at all.

My child,
    He has the armor. Go to his home on Thursday and do not be afraid for I am with you.
Love – Jesus

Jesus, I got one more thing I would like to ask you. Please help Sergio not be so angry and help me learn how to love better.

My child,
    His heart has become callused and he hardly hears with his ears. I am at the door of his heart knocking. Continue to show him my love.
Jesus

I read these letters the next day as we went through the final injections of the chemotherapy. As we prayed together in the hospital, we talked out loud about the plans that Jesus had for us. We assumed prematurely that our ministry paths would separate soon, with the System remaining here and Carol and I moving south to the LA area. We knew that our relationship would never end, only change for a season. We celebrated over lunch the faithfulness of Jesus in bringing the System through the cancer and chemotherapy thus far. They never lost their appetite during our lunches, something that had never happened before with patients I knew who went through chemo. Carol had sent gifts to encourage all of them for accomplishing this feat. We confirmed our plans for Halloween night two days away. I received the following fax the next night.

Dear Pastor Chalberg and Pastor Chalberg,
    I like saying that. It's me, Maria. I wanted to thank you for my gift so much cuz it is such a beautiful gift. But I wanted to thank

you for something else too. I wanted to thank you for being my friend and helping me to know Jesus. I don't think that anyone could give me a better gift.

Maybe you don't know how much that gift means to me, but I think that I am still here and getting better because of you doing what Jesus asked of you. I know Jesus sent you cuz he told me he sent you. He sent you so I could learn about his love. It's like our heart doesn't live in a dark hole no more, but its got light coming out of it now. The dark is around us, but we got light now to make the dark go away.

I never knew there was love like this ever. Jesus does care about us and I know that now. You care too and that means so much to me to know someone cares. I never thought anyone would care enough to help me with the chemotherapy. But you and Bruce, Dr. Gail and Nurse Kathy, you all cared. Jesus, he really cares about me and I never knew that before I met you and Bruce.

I know that earth is not an easy place to live and there are problems here for us. I know that I am going to have more problems, but it is going to be easier I think cuz I know Jesus and can trust him. I don't need to understand it all cuz I know Jesus cares. When you hug me, I forget it is you and feel Jesus. I know it is you but somehow I feel Jesus.

Do you know I never thought anyone would ever want me to stay at their house? I didn't think anyone would want me around or listen to my words. But you did and that will always be special to me. I don't know what work I am supposed to do for Jesus, but I wonder if Jesus takes the stuff we are made out of like experiences of our life, and then makes them useful for him. I will be a funny looking clay pot cuz my clay is different, but I think Jesus knows how to make it useful for him. Maybe he will let others see my pot to help them trust him to let him make their pots. I don't know how Jesus decides what we are to do, but I think I am to help sad people find hope. There are lots of sad people. I can't fix them cuz that is Jesus' job, but I can tell them how we got hope cuz of his love. I can love them with real Jesus love like you have loved me. I hope that Jesus will let me be a pot for him.

Can I tell you something? It's not something in the books or something that smart people told me, or something that I got proof for or anything like that. It's something I feel in my heart. You don't have to think it's right or anything, but I want to tell you.

You are different, not bad different, but different. There are other Christians that have become my friends, but they don't know like you know. It is like Jesus let you see our heart for real. You listen different too. I watch and others are being nice, but not hearing like you do. You not only hear, but you understand what we are saying. You don't just talk about Jesus, but you show us Jesus. You walk and talk like him inside, and you are like him cuz you understand our pain. You really understand. We don't know how you do, except that Jesus must give you a way of knowing it. You are real to us.

I think that Jesus has given you a special gift of knowing about pain and suffering and what to say and do. Nobody tells me much about your life, so I don't know why I think this but I do. I think that Jesus has let you be around different types of suffering so that you can work for him. Maybe if you hadn't had that when we came along, then you would have been afraid of us, or something. I don't know, but I do know that you are not like other pastors.

I think you are the shepherd that bends down and wraps the little sheep's cut foot. You hold him and rock him and tell him don't give up little sheep. Jesus loves you and cares for you. The little sheep cries cuz all of the big, beautiful sheep laugh at the little sheep, cuz he is broken and looks different. Sometimes they just ignore him cuz he doesn't have a big voice and they don't think he is worth anything. But you hold him and encourage him and let him know how Jesus looks at the heart, not on what the outside looks like. Jesus loves little sheep with cut toes very much. The little sheep grow strong in Jesus cuz you help them. Then they go tell other little sheep with cut toes that Jesus loves you.

I think some pastors are like shepherds that organize the sheep pens. Others are like shepherds that listen to the arguing of the big sheep when they complain about each other. Some shepherds are like guards at the pens. But I think there are very few shepherds that bend down in the bad places to help the little sheep that are forgotten. Lots of shepherds don't want that job cuz it has no importance in the world. People want to be around shepherds that are powerful and glitter. I think Jesus wants shepherds to pick up the wounded on the sides of the trail, as all the sheep move down the path. The big shepherds and important people forget the ones that go slower and are broken. They throw away the broken ones cuz it's too much trouble to carry them, or cuz they don't know what to do for them. I don't know the reason, but I do thank Jesus each day that somebody came back for me. I love you very much and I hope that Jesus tells you soon the work he has for you. I really think that it will be very special, cuz he has been training you for a long time. And Jesus knows what he is doing.

Love from me, Maria.

On Thursday morning the System went to Bruce to help the children prepare for Halloween that night. While none of us knew for sure that something dramatic would happen, all of the signs pointed to a confrontation of some sort. The children were anxious with Bruce and asked for reassurance from him that the "bad ones" would not hurt them if they came to our house for the night.

While Mariann seemed less troubled than Tabitha, it was only because she didn't understand the fear welling up in Tabitha. Tabitha tried to explain it in Spanish through Mariann but wasn't having much success. Fortunately, both Bruce and I were alerted by the phrases that referenced 'drinking blood.' Mariann didn't have the experiences of Tabitha to this event, but she clearly understood the growing fear in Tabitha. As often happened after Tabitha would express these phrases within her drawings, along with symbols that represented Satanic Ritual Abuse, Mariann would rotate out and scribble over them with a black crayon to help reassure others that nothing was revealed. However, today was different when she came out.

She simply shoved them aside and drew her own pictures that were memories of abuse within the Catholic Church. She was hearing 'voices' that said the Beast was coming back to kill them for telling what happened. When she heard the voices she called for Dragonslayer to come to make them stop. But Tabitha was still the main conduit for the Pod children to release their anxiety. Both Egar and Otosis were rarely out long enough to build the trust needed to allow help in their healing. We knew that Egar was very traumatized from the ritual abuse she had experienced by the way she tried to hide under the couch when she did come out. When I would say that Jesus loves you to Egar, she would scream that the light was burning her and retreat inside. Since her name was *rage* spelled backwards, we knew that she needed a safe place to release this rage to the one person on the inside, which she had been manipulated into fearing the most in approaching her…Jesus.

Since Circle Council and I had discussed the possibilities prior to that night, I spent that afternoon reading my notes on CORE and the Pod children, while also praying over some Scriptures I knew would be helpful. I also went through my house, room by room and prayed for safety there in anticipation of spiritual warfare coming. I remembered the events of early August with Blue Devil as he became healed by Jesus and renamed Hopi. I went through all of the doors and windows to be sure that they were locked, because I could then say to the System that this house was prepared for battle with honest assurance. You probably think that I was being extreme in doing this but read on! Elizabeth Ray sent me the following letter on behalf of Council, describing the chain of events that occurred that night.

Memo from Circle Council:

Events of Thursday evening and following:

Council had tried to prepare the child parts Mariann & Tabitha for the evening. We continually reinforced that there was safety with you and no one would get hurt. Maria was worried about the emergence of Egar and what the child might do to you. We explained how Bruce told us that the child part would be less destructive on the outside and it was necessary for her to emerge to be healed. (Apparently Council knew about as much as I did in what to expect.) *Maria resisted the idea and wanted the child to remain inside, but she was overruled. All other adult parts felt uncomfortable with the possible emergence of Egar and avoided outside time as much as possible so the child parts could be prepared.* (Later that evening when Egar first came out, all adults except Elizabeth Ray and Council retreated to the safety of the caves, where they didn't have to experience the pain of what might be revealed of their past. To this day, several adults have not asked about the details of Egar's abuse, as it is still too difficult to hear. This is not a bad response because it isn't denial of what happened.

What they missed however is having the opportunity to witness the power of Jesus in healing such pain – firsthand.)

After eating her burrito dinner with Mike and Carol, Tabitha began to experience stress in her stomach, which was a direct result of Egar's turmoil. Tabitha tried to maintain control on the outside but was not strong enough. When Egar emerged the first time, she was disoriented and confused. (I had positioned us on the couch because I knew she would slip to the floor to seek safety under it.) *Her goal was to get away from whoever was talking to her (Mr. Chalberg). She believed the voices saying that he was a danger and became highly agitated if he touched her. She hit her head on the coffee table several times causing the cut on Maria's head.* (She kept repeating how the light was burning her, which I thought at first was her memory of a heated crucifix being inserted into her by her abusers. As I listened to the timing of her statements, I realized she said it every time I reached to reassure her of her safety with a touch. I wanted to refrain from forcibly holding her down to restrain her and allow her freedom to move about the house to build trust.)

According to Tabitha, voices told the child to get away from Mr. Chalberg because he was going to "grab her and put her on the table." (This was a reference to a particular time of abuse that occurred in childhood with the 'Goatman and some Santeria priests.) *The voices then told her to get outside and run away. The child was told "over here" and was directed to the sliding glass door, where she proceeded to find a way out of the house.* (This was the same door I double-checked as being locked before they arrived. As she crawled toward it, I wasn't concerned about her escaping.) *The latch was somehow opened for her, as she clawed at the base of the door. The door flew open and she began to crawl outside. The voices were coming from the outside and for some reason, they refused to cross over the line of the door and enter the house.* (This was an unexpected event and took me a second to regain my composure when the door flew open. I caught her halfway out and picked her whole body up to turn and carry her back to the couch. Now given that the body of Maria weighed well over 200 pounds and I picked her up from a stooped over position, I can only thank the Holy Spirit for doing that for me. I would struggle to press 125 pounds in a normal workout, as well as having numerous back injuries, so I knew it wasn't me lifting her to safety.)

When she was pulled back in by Mr. Chalberg, the voices yelled for her to pull away or she would die. The child was not strong enough to pull away from him and cycled back inside, causing Mariann and Tabitha to surface. They took turns telling Mr. Chalberg about the voices and struggle going on around him. (It was then that I thanked Jesus for making the body seem light as a feather, and I asked Him to remind me to pray around the house on our property before the next time that He asked me to do something like this.)

Tabitha began to feel sick to her stomach again and showed Mr. Chalberg by rubbing her tummy. Tabitha was still weak when Egar rotated out. This time Mr. Chalberg held her arms to her in a restraining hug to prevent her from hurting herself. The child groaned and made noises as Mariann was telling Jesus inside that Egar needed his love. "Hold her Dragonslayer...she hurt. She scared the bad ones come and get her. Dragonslayer, the bad ones hurt babies tonight, Tabitha say. Help Dragonslayer."
(The Holy Spirit told me how "the light that burns" was actually the light of Jesus' presence. Every time He approached her inside she screamed. I was told to whisper in her ear how Jesus was the Good Shepherd and how He loved her and wanted to heal her, to take away the pain that the smelly ones and the Goatman had given her. I told her repeatedly how He was safe and how the light of the Shepherd was warm to heal her. As Jesus moved closer to her on the inside, her screaming started to subside. Mariann rotated out briefly to remind me of what Jesus wanted me to do...to be Jesus' arms on the outside like I did with Hopi. It still amazes me how Jesus uses human touch to facilitate His healing of an individual. As Jesus instructed me, I began telling her that "the Shepherd will heal you and take away your pain. He wants to remove your rage and He wants to change your name to Joy when you give it to Him." Slowly she allowed Him to hold her inside, even though she was moaning as though she were in pain.)

Inside Jesus held the child, while Mr. Chalberg held her on the outside and comforted her. The adult parts: Ann, Liz, Maria, Ruth and others had gone deep inside because the trauma of seeing Egar was too much for them to shadow. The internal emotional atmosphere was more than the parts could assimilate. The child part eventually released the rage to Dragonslayer and rotated inside to be held by Him. The child was taken to CORE.

Mariann and Tabitha were now allowed to enter CORE for the first time. The child was bathed and seemed to heal faster than the child Hopi. The child was given the name "Joy". (This process took about 4 to 5 hours and I had Louise come outside to get ready for bed. While she and I were talking about what was happening inside, I asked if Otosis was coming out. She had been out before with me for brief moments. The times were difficult because she displayed the characteristic of being deaf. I had tested this by coming up behind her and making loud noises or shouting, never to get a reaction. No other part displayed this. Elizabeth Ray explained to me how she had gone deaf due to gunshots next to her ears as a child to intimidate her. I knew she was also known as Lila and that she would ask for her grandma to help her find her ears.)

Hopi and Joy took the hand of Dragonslayer and asked him to come and help their friend Otosis. Dragonslayer went to Pod Alpha and raised his hand and said, "Otosis". Otosis emerged from the Pod and rotated outside. Mr. Chalberg wasn't surprised to see her, or hear her ask for her grandma. She stated, "I can't find my ears grandma." (I must have been hearing Jesus correctly, because we simultaneously reached to cup her ears in our hands inside and out. He was already healing her as I prayed for her hearing so that she could hear His voice.) *On the inside, Dragonslayer took his hands and placed them on the child's ears and healed her hearing. Mariann said hi and the child said hi back to her, responding for the first time since losing her hearing.*

Dragonslayer raised his hand again and Pod Alpha, Mu and Omega vanished. Tolip went to Dragonslayer, bowed down and kneeled before him. Tolip turned to his troops and said, "Today I shall serve the one known as Dragonslayer, for he has healed our pod children and restored peace and tranquillity in the Land of CORE. Hail to Dragonslayer." All of the troops kneeled down around Dragonslayer, as Tabitha said, "Bright Ones Canta!"

Dragonslayer began to speak and the children hung from him. He began to teach the troops about the kingdom of heaven and then told a story to them about the lost sheep, for he had come to save that which was lost. He told them many more things and with each moment the troops became more convinced that he was the one they had waited for to release them from bondage.

Joy rotated out once more and was happy to tell Mr. Chalberg her name and get assurance from him that she would not be placed on a table to be harmed. (I set up a chair next to the bed so I could get some sleep but be alerted if there were any more attacks.) *In the early morning hours, the child Joy began to be attacked by voices who threatened her with harm for accepting Dragonslayer. She rotated out and slipped to the floor next to Mr. Chalberg. He was alerted to her whimpering and placed himself next to her on the floor, gently rubbing her back as he comforted her. Switching occurred continually throughout the night between Tabitha and Joy. As a child began to exhibit anxiety in their sleep, Dragonslayer comforted her on the inside and Mr. Chalberg comforted her on the outside, preventing an escalation of fear.* (I would say simple things like, "Call Dragonslayer. The Good Shepherd will protect you. Trust Jesus.") *All through the night the voices attempted to get the child to become fearful and reject Dragonslayer. Each time the child began to whimper or show signs of stress, she was comforted on the inside and the outside.*

Friday Morning: The system left for home to recover there. Sergio had left for his conference, so they are alone as the physical health deteriorates and parts experience sudden illness. Ann struggles to function on the outside. Maria and Louise start to panic as a nosebleed begins and Council can do nothing. Maria is sent to bed, but her anxiety causes her to be unable to breathe. She is told to get up and go out into the garden to relax.

Outside she experiences a sudden uncontrollable release of fluid from her nasal cavities in large amounts. Council suggests to Ann to call a doctor. Ann wants to attempt to control it without a doctor and is somewhat successful by the afternoon. Maria calls Pastor Chalberg for prayer support.

Saturday Morning: The system is very ill, with tremendous headaches and flu-like symptoms. Ann attempts to get the weaker parts functioning and reprimands Maria for wanting to throw-up. She encourages them to fight back against whatever is causing this and not give up. By the afternoon when Sergio returns, the system is up cleaning house and working in the garden. Ann is keeping them busy so they won't dwell on their problems.

Sunday: Tolip reports to Council on recent events. There was a ceremony in CORE performed in the early morning hours this day. He described how his troops have blended together. Valkrie, Epistler, Tac and Tyr of Pod Alpha blended into their commander Watcher; Bellona, Dough Boy, Wildcat and Security of Pod Mu blended into their captain Brass Hat; and Bugbear, Griffen, White Feather and Titan blended into Old Nick, the Holder of Pod Omega.

"With the sounding of trumpets, the troops of each pod stood in a straight line facing their respective commanders. Marching to Glory Hallelujah they began to march towards their commander. At the point of contact there was a brilliant light as each one of them blended with Watcher, Brass Hat and Old Nick. Then the three leaders faced me from the three points of the triangle with me in the middle. At precisely the same time they marched toward me and again there was a flash of light as we blended."

Tolip then requested an audience with Circle Council. He also requested permission to take Joy, Hopi and Lila to Raquel, as she had asked to see them on Sacred Mountain. We approved his requests and met with him early Monday morning. He was welcomed into the Land of Preservation and has joined us on Circle Council. Council has also welcomed Dragonslayer to be

111

present at Council meetings. Dragonslayer has informed Council that he is preparing a place of many rooms for the system and reminded us that the land will be restored. (I was soon to be surprised by this last statement. I assumed too quickly that Jesus was referring to their spot in heaven and of events that happen in the future.)

End of this part of the transmittal.

Maria is experiencing problems relating to her husband. We have been guiding her in attempting to communicate with him about her needs and the needs of others in the system. Although the system is continually healing on the inside, there is a tearing down of that healing from outside influences at home. For the system, it is an up and down situation. The female parts are still wounded from the counseling sessions with the husband. Liz is refusing to marry and has repeatedly told us that "if the husband truly loved her, he would be willing to place himself in an uncomfortable setting in order to help her."

The stronger parts like Ann and Liz have a difficult time not being recognized or appreciated for who they are by the husband. Council realizes how important this is to these parts, especially Ann and Liz. Though Ann does not usually show emotion, she was emotionally affected by the gift presented to her by Mr. Chalberg. The fact that he had her name placed on the Bible and that he knew her favorite color was rose, greatly impacted her. It was the first time that she had been recognized for who she is by an outsider. Yet, it saddens her that the husband has never cared enough to even know her, her favorite color, her dreams, or her desires. This small gesture of the gift has turned Ann around in her relationship to Mr. Chalberg. Council has noticed that Ann has put all other books aside to read this one.

- Elizabeth Ray for Council

On this particular Sunday evening, something else occurred that reminded me of a belief I held but had set aside for my own reasons. Dragonslayer called everyone in the Land of Preservation to a meeting…an ekklesia meeting. If you don't know the meaning of ekklesia, it is the Greek word in the New Testament that is used for church. However, this is not a church as we commonly define it today – "A building for public worship or place where a congregation gathers for divine worship." I would contest this definition with the IRS a few years later and lose, when my definition of church didn't match this. So I offer you the following uses in the Bible, and Jesus' use of it in the following report, to offer help in understanding ekklesia – "the called out ones."

"Greet Prisca and Aquila, my fellow workers in Christ Jesus, who for my life risked their own necks, to whom not only do I give thanks, but also all the churches of the Gentiles; also greet the church that is in their house."
Romans 16:5

"The way God designed our bodies is a model for understanding our lives together as a church: every part dependent on every other part, the parts we mention and the parts we don't, the parts we see and the parts we don't. If one part hurts, every other part is involved in the hurt, and in the healing. If one part flourishes, every other part enters into the exuberance. You are Christ's body – that's who you are!"
1 Corinthians 12: 22-27 – The Message

I do not believe that the 'church' was ever intended to be defined and known as a building or geographical location, but to be a group of people "called out" for relating to the world-at-large as Christ's representatives in it. This means then that the church is who you are 24-7, whether you're gathering together for worship, or helping your coworker on the job. It was never meant to be understood as a place you go to once or twice a week to act differently with people, than you might at any other time. Jesus Christ went to people to help them and build relationships. He didn't wait for them to come to Him. He does that with each of us individually today, knocking at the door of our heart, waiting to be let in.

While there are many historical reasons for why the church will become known as places rather than people, the practical

113

implications for moving the 'church' out of these places hasn't changed. A few years from this event, my wife Carol and I will startup a ministry for creating house churches…churches without walls, where the greater part of our worship is spent out in the world ministering to those in need. It is our way of sharing our time, gifts and resources in the love of Jesus. Time in the home is reserved for study, fellowship and prayer. I believe that this is the simple model that is given to us by Jesus in the New Testament in many places. It is also how Jesus uses the term ekklesia in this meeting with the System. It is the first time that He calls for a 'church' meeting.

Ekklesia Meeting Report

Meeting called by Dragonslayer. Report by Elizabeth Ray.

Those in attendance:
Surface People
House of Prayer
Leaders of Circle Council
Eagle Clan
(Not present: Task performers)

Dragonslayer calls the meeting to order.
House of Prayer sings blessing over the meeting.

Dragonslayer tells the assembly that they have been called out of the world by him. "You didn't choose me my precious children. I chose you. As my chosen vessel, I appoint you to go and tell others about me. You will bear good fruit and that fruit will remain. Know that I will be with you and that the gates of hell cannot stop you. Yes, my children, the gates of hell will try to prevail against you, but know this, I am greater than the gates of hell. Go and do what I say. You are my chosen instrument to take my message to the downcast, the brokenhearted and the sick. And you will show my church how I have called them to love my people.

You are to conduct yourselves in a manner worthy of my word. Continue to follow my instructions. Continue to pray with joy and thanksgiving. Continue to encourage those I have sent to you...praying for them and uplifting them. Continue to encourage my child, Michael, to complete the task I have set before him so that others may know my love for them. Continue to have confidence that the good work I have begun in you will be finished. Rejoice my children and continue to proclaim me...desiring that others will have the same relationship with me that you have.

Speak with the authority I give you. Do not be ashamed of my words and do not compromise them. You have my truth...go with boldness, authority and confidence and I will use your life so you can relate to others and through me bring healing. I have taught you truth. Now walk in obedience. And know that I am with you and will provide for you.

Now go and think on these things which I have told you.

I tried to hear Jesus speaking to me as though I was a part within the System and wondered about how I would have received His words. I felt like I heard the same message that was given to His disciples in the upper room recited in the Book of John. I also wondered if His disciples had many of the lingering questions that the System had, following this event. The System had witnessed miracles of healing within their ranks over the last few months. Until this moment, it was only Mariann and the children who had clearly accepted Jesus as Lord and God, without any questions still answered about why the abuse occurred at all. Maybe this is an example for us about why we are to receive the kingdom of heaven as a child.

"For My thoughts are not your thoughts,
Neither are your ways My ways," declares the Lord.
"For as the heavens are higher than the earth,
So are My ways higher than your ways,
And My thoughts higher than your thoughts."
Isaiah 55: 8 – 9

After observing miracles, an adult will cringe over this answer to why things happen, and often want to respond in anguish with "That's not good enough – explain why!" Whereas a child sees the unexplainable happen and is more prone to say, "Okay, I'll trust you", because their immediate need is met and they aren't too concerned about what tomorrow brings. This is why Jesus' words are given to the adults to ponder about their meaning. Not every adult within the System had accepted Jesus as someone other than just another part within their inside world. Several were still unwilling to give control of their individual lives over to Him. Even Circle Council will continue to ask Him into their meetings for awhile, as an advisor only in their decision making process. It will be several months before I get the call telling me that Jesus will be asked to head the Council meetings. Would we have responded differently?

For the adults, most had not witnessed the actual healing of the children, but only witnessed the changes that had occurred to them in their absence. They celebrated the healing because 'those parts' had received relief from their pain, and because they hoped to not have to relive it again with them. What many will learn is that this does not complete the healing process. They accept it without understanding it, because it didn't happen to them. This makes Jesus' words all the more challenging in the 'ekklesia meeting'.

How would any of us respond to the statement, "Yes, my children, the gates of hell will try to prevail against you"? This had to be disconcerting to those who were simply unsure about what they believed about Jesus, and twice as difficult for someone like Ann who wanted proof before she believed that Jesus might really be God. Remember that she had witnessed the aftermath of the trauma and the healings, but not all of the actual events. Most of us respond in the same way in faith issues, when we haven't witnessed 'miracles' of any kind in our lives. We received the same instructions in Scriptures to go and do as the System was instructed to do in this meeting, and we probably do as well as they will do in the coming months, given our human nature that says to God, "What have you done for me lately?"

I can honestly state that, for me, my faith was growing vicariously as I observed Jesus healing the System, beginning with the most traumatized parts. Jesus was 'proving' to me that He was the God I read about in the Bible and always hoped that He would be. The proof, which I needed to remove my lingering doubts, was being presented in the lives of the System, before my eyes and ears. There was a sense of the mystical that was surrounding these events. It wasn't that it was unexplainable, actually quite the opposite, because it was clearly… 'Wholly Other.' God's hand was at work preparing these people to accomplish His plan and even the "gates of hell' could not stop them…if they trusted Him. They were being 'called out' and 'chosen' for a task that would bear fruit for the kingdom of heaven…if they chose to be obedient. They were told what His plan was for them, "to take my message to the downcast, the brokenhearted and the sick; and you will show my church how I have called them to love my people."

Many Christians will be saying to themselves after reading this, "If Jesus would appear to me in the same way as He did to the System and say the same words as clearly as He did in this church meeting, then I could answer His call without hesitation or doubt. I could do all those things, if He only appeared to me like that." Remember that, as you continue reading about the lives and choices made by the people of the System.

"But Thomas, one of the twelve, called
Didymus, was not with them when Jesus came.
The other disciples therefore were saying to him, "We
have seen the Lord!" But he said to them, "Unless I shall
see in His hands the imprint of the nails and put my finger
into the place of the nails, and put my hand into His side, I
will not believe." And after eight days again His disciples
were inside, and Thomas with them. Jesus came, the
doors having been shut, and stood in their midst,
and said, "Peace be with you." Then He said to
Thomas, "Reach here your finger, and see
My hands; and reach here your hand, and
put it into My side; and be not unbelieving,
but believing." Thomas answered and
said to Him, "My Lord and my God!"
Jesus said to him,
"Because you have seen Me, have you believed?
Blessed are they who did not see, and yet believed."
John 20: 24 – 29

No where does it state that Thomas actually put his hand into the nail holes or into His side, to remove his doubts. I take the word of those in the System about what was witnessed in their world and compare it with the changes that I witnessed in the individuals in this world. I could not see how Mariann and Tabitha escorted their Dragonslayer by the hand to their friend Lila, asking Him to heal her, yet I know it was true without seeing it. Just as I knew within my heart and mind that Jesus has these children of the System hanging all over Him, hungry for every ounce of love and every word that comes out of His mouth.

The only thing that saddened me at this time was a few friends who thought that I was gullible in accepting these letters as actually reflecting truth. What they couldn't witness, as I did, was the changes in their faces and voices, as pain was replaced by joy, fear replaced with laughter, and emptiness being filled with love. If seeing God's plan for these people being fulfilled in His good time makes me gullible, then clearly I am and I wouldn't have it any other way. My faith grows because the answers I seek are becoming simpler to understand, as I see God's providence fulfilling the promises of Scriptures and giving love before it is ever thought of as a choice. Perhaps it is in this manner that I have become a fool for Christ…not to deny reality, but to revel in the joy of it, as His joy is becoming complete within me.

"For God so loved the world that He gave His only begotten Son…"

*"We live in an age which asks for faith,
pure faith, naked faith, mystical faith."*
William Johnston, *The Inner Eye of Love* (1978)

*"Galileo, who held a scientific truth of great importance,
abjured it with the greatest ease as soon as it
endangered his life. In a certain sense, he did right.
That truth was not worth the stake. Whether the
earth or the sun revolves around the other is a matter
of profound indifference. To tell the truth, it is a
futile question. On the other hand, I see many people
die because they judge that life is not worth living."*
Albert Camus, *The Myth of Sisyphus* (1942)

Chapter Six

"Is Love Subjective and Faith Illusion?"

**"Faith is the assurance of things hoped for,
and the conviction of things not seen."**
Hebrews 11: 1

*"All things are possible to him that believes, more
to him that hopes, even more to him that loves,
and more still to him who practices and
perseveres in these three."*
Brother Lawrence, *The Practice of the Presence of God* (1691)

Tina Turner once asked, "What's love got to do with it?" Well, when it comes to faith, I would say that it has everything to do with it. If the System had not experienced the love of Jesus first hand when they did, both faith and love would have remained the subject for others and an illusion, or nightmare for them. Most of the choices that lay before them required enormous trust, or faith, in the person of Jesus Christ. While He was revealing His power in increments to them, His love was there for the asking...without limits. At least in Preservation, He was fast becoming the object of love, instead of just the subject of love. The System began to believe for the first time that His love was real. However, this also created issues of faith for some.

Questions began to surface quickly following the message that was given in the ekklesia meeting. Jesus had given them a basic plan for their future...one that required faith in Him to guide them and empower them to do what He asked of them. His power was demonstrated clearly enough for one-third of them to accept His protection and 'blend' with their leader, Tolip, thereby trusting Jesus enough to protect the children. Guarding them had been their life's work and reason for being. But these changes were happening at levels that most of the Surface People knew little about. Their level, or Land of Preservation, hadn't been restored yet and several people wanted to know, *why not*. It had only been about 3 months, but it felt more like 40 years in the desert. Matters on the surface didn't seem to be getting any better and the future wasn't bright.

Two basic questions became a reoccurring theme, with only the first one rarely spoken of directly. Would acceptance of Jesus mean that others would have to blend? This was an obvious trend that bothered some parts to the point where they would ask me in very subtle ways what I thought. While I always answered that I didn't know who would or wouldn't blend, I felt that it was up to the individuals to make that choice because Jesus would not take that choice away from them. It was difficult to explain to them how the providence and omniscience of God is not altered or lessened by our free will choices, given their history of men choosing to abuse them. Just because God already knows what our choices are going to be, good and bad, doesn't change His plans for us, or remove His unconditional love for us allowing these choices. This brings up the second question often asked for several more years.

If Jesus has the power to heal and alter reality however it is perceived, then why did He allow the children to be abused? This question would take a much longer time to answer, though it was never avoided. The axioms of love and faith would border every discussion we had on these issues, as well as determine the paths we would take together on our journey. Even following the meeting, it would be difficult to have everyone on board with how Jesus was planning to use the evil that was done to them, to bring good out of it to others. The past can be changed, if only in our perspective of it, when its purpose can renew and redeem our future. The plan was given that the System's endured pain would bring hope to others, through faith and love being made real to them.

> "For I know the plans that I have for you,' declares the Lord, 'plans for welfare and not for calamity to give you a future and a hope. Then you will call upon Me and come and pray to Me, and I will listen to you. And you will seek Me and find Me, when you search for Me with all of your heart."
> **Jeremiah 29: 11-13**

If it seems like I repeat this verse…I do. It is perhaps the most consistent answer to all of the questions I would be asked by the System, beginning with the word - *why*. Towards the other end of our journey, it will become the foundation of truth that will demonstrate God's love and the reason for our faith in Him.

The System's world began to expand after this church meeting, with new relationships developing on the outside world and old relationships were being revealed for their true nature. Liz had begun writing another pastor after hearing his sermon and his responses opened up another dialogue for her. Raquel wrote as well and shared her poetry to help him understand all of them. Bob was drawn into their lives through a strong desire to help them find healing. Though he knew little about Dissociative Identity Disorder, he wanted to help right the injustices that he clearly felt had been perpetrated upon the System.

I wrote to him at Maria's request to help him understand these people whom he wanted to know more about. Some of the System were drawn to him for his obvious intellect and sincerity of concern for their well being. His answers to their questions were giving them a different perspective than mine of the Christian life and I felt that was good for them. Bob, his family and his circle of friends, will soon become very significant in the lives of the System for the next 5 years.

The focus of his relationships will be with Maria, Mariann, Louise, Ruth, and Tabitha. Liz and Ann will have a love/hate relationship that challenges both sides. I don't believe that Bob will ever really comprehend these relationships for one basic reason. He will be unable in my opinion, to set aside his psychological interpretation of who 'they' are and see them as Jesus does, to truly understand their purpose in life and why Jesus brought them into his. His love will be conditional and require that they conform to his understanding of them, if they are to receive it.

This is also the common response for most new relationships that connect with the System. There will be a few exceptions however, who stated in the beginning and continue saying today, "I don't understand all of this, but I know the Lord is with them and I want to love them, just as He loves me through them." The people of the System will grow and be challenged by these experiences, as new relationships offer love, pain, acceptance and rejection. They will often come to the conclusion that the emotional growth isn't worth it. It will be at these times when the Lord will ask them,

"How much are you willing to endure for My sake?"

As Circle Council begins to come together and make decisions to help guide the paths of everyone remaining in the System, (all but one person has been revealed to them by this time), they try to tackle one of their hardest issues on the inside and outside worlds, as they attempt to set boundaries on Ann's education.

Memo from Circle Council
*Decision has been made by council in regard to Ann's request to pursue a Ph.D. in mathematics. **Denied.** Reason: Although council has no doubt that Ann has the ability to obtain the Ph.D., the amount of 'out time' necessary to achieve it would require too much sacrifice for the other parts. Council must balance the needs of all of the parts.*

Council will approve of Ann entering the Single Subject Credential Program next summer and taking Statistical Inference in the winter. Council will allow Ann's request to have Louise enroll in the conversational Spanish class so that Ann can receive a cross-cultural emphasis on her credential. (Is this taking advantage of what the world says is a disorder?) *However, Council reserves the right to withdraw her from the class if she is unable to cope in a classroom environment.*

After much thought and discussion, the leaders have determined that it would be better for Ann to teach high school mathematics part-time, rather than the elementary school level. There are less triggers there for our children than the elementary setting. The kids are afraid of outside teenagers and Council can better control the switching. Part-time work allows more 'home-time' for the other parts. This allows Ruth to continue her ministry, Maria and Louise time to care for her daughter and take care of the house. If the System can adjust to working, Ann may slowly add more teaching time. She will be a good role model for Latina teenagers, as most minority women never see a minority math teacher. Ann will be able to impress upon them that anything can be done when you are committed and determined to work hard.

-Elizabeth Ray for Council

Ann was attempting to move forward on several fronts. She began to file a complaint against the contractor remodeling her home for breach of contract. I advised her on how to proceed to encourage her as a friend and as a contractor wanting to prevent poor workmanship in my other profession. This would be one of the first times that the System would speak out against an injustice done to them in the outside world. Though this process will not have the results that we hoped for with this inept contractor, it will help build the confidence of the System to challenge the world around them.

She also began the application process for a teaching credential and for available scholarships to help offset the costs. She was trying to balance a budget that included college tuition for Maria's children and Sergio. She hoped to enter a program where she could teach mathematics in the Barrio. She realized how things were changing around her at all levels and decided that it would be prudent to study about who God is and test out Jesus at the same time.

I am enjoying my Bible. I find that I'm reading it more than I anticipated. Every time I start, time seems to escape me. I am cross-referencing, checking word meanings and researching the historical timeframe of the period. I now understand why you have so many dictionaries and concordances. This is habit forming. All kidding aside, I admit that I was wrong in my stand against God. He is quite different from the people I have met who say they represent him. He is logical and trustworthy. I have had delightful conversations with him and enjoy his clear answers, with intriguing statements that make me think.

I know that there is a lot of cleanup to do in my life, mostly in the area of attitude and trust. It is going to be hard to change to rid myself of the independent mode of relying on no one but myself to survive. To become dependent upon him is going to be my greatest challenge. While it is scary to think of relying solely on God, it is ironic that deep within me there is a craving to do so. Anyway, thank you for the Bible with my name on it.

Respectfully, Ann

I asked Ann if she had read the books of C.S. Lewis that I had loaned her on the subjects of grief and pain. I had counted on both her logical reasoning skills and her quest to understand her past, to connect with Lewis' presentation and self-analysis. After receiving the following letter a few days later, I knew that she had.

Mike,

There was a song Maria found on tape several years ago that she gave to Bruce. (<u>The River of Dreams</u> *– page 10.) She said the song 'called to her' yet she had no idea of its meaning or significance. I remember shadowing and hearing the song. I thought it was a disturbing song, depressing at best; talking about walking in one's sleep, searching for something I didn't lose but was taken from me. I forgot that song until I read Lewis'* <u>A Grief Observed</u>.

What have we been searching for? We have been searching for an understanding of our pain, our grief, our separation from something that was stolen from us. We have had to search for this understanding in the inner part of our being. Why...For the same reason that Lewis walked around and wrote about his search for understanding his grief over the loss of his wife. ***"You can't really share someone else's weakness, or fear or pain. What you feel may be bad. It might conceivably be as bad as what the other felt, though I should distrust anyone who claimed that it was. But it would still be quite different."*** *And he is right. No one can enter into the depths of another's inner being and know the intensity of their pain and their grief.*

Lewis' agony was over the separation with his love and questioning the purpose of that separation. Our agony, not unlike his, is over the separation from true love and questioning the purpose of that separation. Which is worse...the death of one's physical body or the death of one's being? To be still physically alive, but a mere vacuum inside is the worst of tortures. Like the house made of cards, it stands but is void of any substance to make it truly alive. It is simply a shell of a person.

We have done well functioning, spending years in secrecy, functioning in a single's world. We have produced, maintained and survived. But our eyes always showed the hunger to make sense out of our internal wanderings...our internal conflict with ourselves...our internal struggle with deep feelings of nothingness. Yet, we have attempted to avoid the pain and grief reflected in our eyes and move on in productivity. We continued to function. We continued to hold our masks on tight around our true selves. Yet inside the search went on...the hunger...the agony didn't go away.

Enter God. In the middle of intense pain, he knocked our house of cards down. Not because he is set upon destroying us or inflicting more pain and suffering on us, but because it is the only way that he could get our attention. The only way he could show us how our agony and joylessness within us was not allowing him to enter our vacuum and fill it with his love. Yet we were not ready to understand this gift or accept it.

We kept him at arm's length and harbored anger and revenge. We yelled at him, "We didn't loose our childhood! We didn't lose honest love! We didn't lose our being, our identity, our worth! We didn't lose any of it! It was stolen from us on the day of our birth and we want it back! We don't want you as a substitute. We want what was taken from us! We want that part of us that is the fuel that lets us know that we are alive! We want the acceptance we were denied as a child. We want pleasant childhood memories to flood our minds. We want security, worth and warmth. We want the love of a mother and father. We want our fractured foundation to be rebuilt so that we can weather the storms of adulthood. You can't give us that. You are aloof...something mystical and untouchable. We need companionship. We need human touch. We need that which was stolen from us!"

And as open floodgates pour out the waters contained within, we continued to disperse our grief on the inside. A grief unobserved by others because we are masters at maintaining secrecy of our inner struggles. A grief so overwhelming that physical death would be less painful. Echoing deep within that pit of anguish, all of us could hear what all of us wanted to express...Why have we been forsaken? Would not death have been more merciful?

Silence...as if our voice was addressing no one. Unable to bear tearing away the gauze that would reveal the pain to others, we chose to tuck it away under layers of cloth. We attempted to shield ourselves from the pain. We avoided thinking about our hunger and we escaped in our own ways. We chose Sacred Mountain. We chose beer, parties and mushrooms. We chose math and the concrete. We chose housework and raising children. We chose anything that would keep us from opening up that wound. We foolishly thought that we could avoid the pain.

Enter God. Again he knocked down the house of cards and again we chaotically ran around attempting to rebuild our house of cards. But life has a way of wearing us down. We began to look at our collapsed house of cards and realized we did not have the energy to rebuild it. We submitted. Like a regiment of soldiers on the front line, we realized that we had no more strength to fight. We were hungry. We were cold. We were tired and without ammunition. We, one by one, surrendered.

Enter God. Enter the warmth of his love...

And the grief is slowly dissipating.

Thanks for lending me the books.

Ann

I shed a few tears upon reading it because I knew that Ann had finally begun the journey. She had taken the first real step of faith in understanding...that the answers lay before her and not in trying to explain the past. She was not going to let God go without an explanation, but she was learning that God would explain it in His time, and she was willing to wait. She submitted to the fact that her search for truth with God would have to intensify, as the worlds of her life changed in miraculous ways...ways that science couldn't explain. As I challenged God in prayer about how He would answer her needs, I received the following answers.

"Do you trust Me?"

Yes, Lord, You know that I do.

"Then feed My sheep."

Yes, Lord, but how can You give back what was stolen from them?

"Do you trust Me more than these?"

Yes, Lord, I trust you with all that I am.

"Then believe that I can make all things new...
Tend My lambs with the love I give you."

I didn't know how or when, but I did know that I had to be obedient in faith...to believe and trust His love to accomplish this.

"Behold, the tabernacle of God is among men, and He shall dwell among them, and they shall be His people, and God Himself shall be among them. And He shall wipe away every tear from their eyes; And there shall no longer be any death; There shall no longer be any mourning, or crying, or pain; The first things have passed away." And He who sits on the throne said, "Behold, I am making all things new."
Revelation 21: 3 – 5

In the Land of Brave Eagle, a young boy sat next to the Keeper of the Animals as she told him a story. The boy and his companions spent many hours with the Keeper of Animals listening and learning wisdom from the Great Spirit. As the boy watched the Keeper caress a frightened fawn, he listened intently as she began to speak.

'There lived a man born into the tribe of greed. He was of the tribe of greed, but he did not follow the path of his tribe. For he was a man who followed and spoke of the wisdom of the Great Spirit, rather than the wisdom of the world. The wisdom of which he spoke was given to him by the Spirit of God and set apart from the spirit of the world. Each morning the man rose and worshipped the Great Spirit and made petition and supplication before his God. And the Great Spirit communed with the man and gave him much knowledge, intelligence and wisdom.

One night the man awoke from a very disturbing dream. In the dream an owner of a vineyard was arguing with the foreman of the field, as to which of them deserved the honor for producing the best wine in the land. The owner argued that it was he who supplied the riches to plant the vines upon which the grapes grew. The foreman countered with the contention that it was he and his workers who tilled the land and watered the fields, thus producing an abundance of fruit.

The man from the tribe of greed was most confused by the dream that had awakened him in the night. For weeks he spent much time asking the Great Spirit what the dream meant. One evening, as the man walked with the Lord, the Great Spirit spoke.

"One man plants and another waters, but it is I who cause it to grow. Apart from Me, you can do nothing. You are like a wind instrument. It is not you who produces the beautiful melody, but My spirit that flows through you. It is I who bind up the brokenhearted. It is I who free the captives and bring the oil of gladness to those who are mourning. It is I who comfort the afflicted.

But you...you will be the instrument from which I do these things. For My spirit is upon you and I have commissioned you. Do not forget My teaching, My child. Write it on the tablet of your heart. Do not be wise in your own eyes. Do not boast of your own wisdom, or your own strength. But boast of Me and of My kindness, love, righteousness and justice. For then truly you shall be wise. I have given you these words for that which is to come. Remember them as you walk on the journey I have set before you."

Keeper of the Animals turned to the young boy and asked lovingly, "Child, do you understand the words of the Great Spirit?" The boy looked up at her and replied with a sparkle in his eyes, "Yes, I know. Dragonslayer is strong. I am small and weak, but Dragonslayer is strong and all of the good things that happen is because Dragonslayer does them. Huh?"

With that, Keeper of the Animals softly placed her hands upon the boy's cheeks and said, "Wise is the one who knows he is not wise or strong but gives glory to the Great Spirit from which all good things come."

- Quiet Walker

This was one of Raquel's stories that could be applied as direction for a number of people in the System's life about this time, including me. Yet, like most of her messages of teaching from the Great Spirit, it has a universal application as well for those who follow. When I received it I chose to remember the wisdom as applying personally. It also gave me a picture of how the Pod Children were spending their healing time with Raquel.

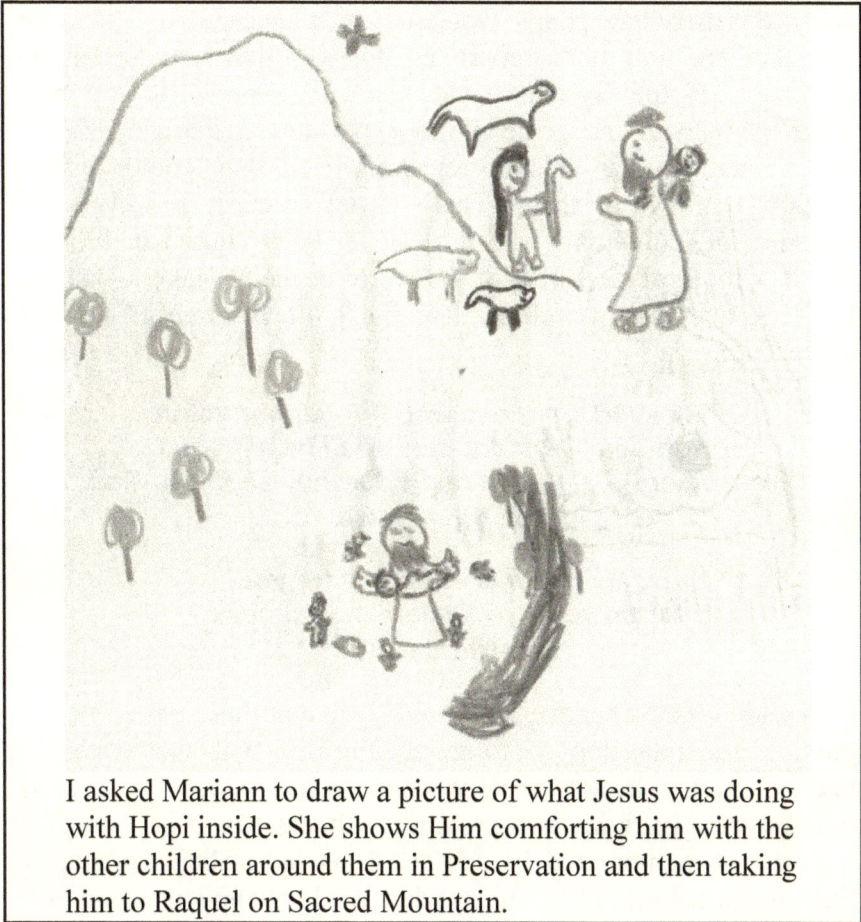

I asked Mariann to draw a picture of what Jesus was doing with Hopi inside. She shows Him comforting him with the other children around them in Preservation and then taking him to Raquel on Sacred Mountain.

Plate # 2

My work with the adults increased over the next 9 months to include teaching about the meaning of baptism, communion, worship, and primarily focusing on grace in all of its various forms. They were heading into many relationships that would require an understanding of grace, as it is the catalyst that can make or break friendships. They were in a better place now to accept this truth.

They had just survived some very difficult changes inside each one's reality and had just heard it impressed upon them that more were waiting down the path. They would be entering new relationships and facing up to old ones, with a much better grasp of the power of grace, than those waiting ahead would. I really doubted if these new people would be able to accept the System for who they are, and more importantly for who they were becoming in Christ. If the System could learn to experience any new relationship with the grace of no expectations, knowing that it doesn't remove the pain of rejection, then they could survive anything thrown at them. That's a tall request for even the strongest of individuals who have never been abused or broken. But it is the broken people of the world at their weakest, that the Lord's grace can overwhelm into being the messengers of His grace.

"Blessed are those who hunger and thirst
for righteousness, for they shall be satisfied..."
"Blessed are the pure in heart, for they shall see God."
Matthew 5: 6,8

"My grace is sufficient for you,
for power is perfected in weakness."
2 Corinthians 12:9

I had come to believe more than ever that these would be the guiding principles for my future relationship with the System. I knew the time was not far off when we would be leaving them as primary caregivers in close proximity. Others would be taking on the rolls of mentors and friends and I needed to begin preparing them for this. From my own experience, I knew how it would take most people time to realize how these broken people will give much more to them in love, than 'whole people' will ever offer in return.

These lessons would have to begin directly with Maria's immediate family. It will take years to see significant changes in them, but the System was ready to look at how they responded to those around them who had no real concept of grace. The System is about to learn how to "turn the other cheek", not as a victim, but as one whose strength and worth is found in Jesus.

Circle Council was prudent in accepting the position that Sergio was not going to change any time soon, if ever. Accepting this about him however, did not help with their frustration over how Maria's children treated her. With Rosalinda away at college, this left an angry daughter that blamed her mother for her life being lived out of a wheelchair, and a teenage son too busy trying to define his destiny, to really care about 'understanding' his mother. The relationship with the two at home will reduce Maria, Ruth and Louise to tears of unworthiness often, and Liz and Ann to anger. Part of this letter from Louise describes their feelings clearly.

...I got up early this morning and spent some time talking to Jesus. He never calls me a jerk or says are you deaf, like Maria's daughter does. I told him how much it hurts and that I don't know what I'm doing wrong. It's so hard when Maria's daughter hates her and me so much. I know it's wrong, but me and Maria wish that we could just separate from the world and be inside forever, or just fly away forever. Then we wouldn't cause people to get so angry. We don't mean to cause problems, but I guess we just do. Nothing I do seems to please Claudia, so I asked Jesus to help me do it right.

I wish that my heart wasn't so sensitive to things like Ann says. I asked Jesus if he would let everything spin around me but not touch me, so I could be like in the center of the twister where it is quiet and peaceful. He talked to me about trusting him with even the things that Claudia says to us. He told me that every morning before I do anything to talk to him and give him all of my worries, and every night before bed to release to him my cares and burdens. During the day when I am hurt, I am to come to him for comfort. He said giving him my problems means not worrying about them in the day. He will tell me then which way to go.

When I asked again about what to do when Claudia says bad things that hurt us, he told me to love her with all of my heart and come into his open arms for his comforting love that will heal the hurt in my heart. He said that he knows the anguish within our hearts and not to return an insult with an insult. He told me not to fear intimidation from others or be troubled by it, but to entrust my soul to him and continue to do right. He said that he is my helper and the sustainer of my soul. He said he will always hear my voice and will redeem my soul in peace, but I must trust him.

So I told him all of my troubles, about how hard it is for me and Maria to keep up with the world. I told him how scared I am that more people know that we are different and I don't know how to handle that. I said how hard it is with Sergio and how scared I am that I'm not being a good wife for him, and how sad I am about not looking right because of the cuts from surgery. I told him how hard it was to be broken on the inside and then have the only thing that made us look normal cut off to nothing there.

I told him how so many people have me doing unimportant things, when I want to work for him. I told him how sad it makes me and Maria that her daughter has to be in a wheelchair, because we know how hard the world is to people that are different. We just wanted her children to not have to suffer like we have. I told him how my heart longs for heaven. Jesus told me to read Psalm 34 and always remember to seek him and he will answer me and deliver me from all of my fears. So Pastor Chalberg, I am going to do just that and trust Jesus with all of me. I told him I am not smart and not strong, and I'm tired and scared, but I'm going to have a song in my heart and trust him. And you know what, he said that being smart is not as important as knowing, loving and obeying him. I'm glad he said that.

When I asked him about school and all of the stuff that Ann is going to do, he told me to trust him and that he is in control of it all, and that Ann is going to be learning far more important things than statistics. He told me to keep on the path in school and that he is in control, not Ann.

Council wrote to me about Maria's responses to the changes and her talk with Jesus.

The system has taken an upward turn as a whole. Maria finally released her pain this week. She spent a considerable amount of time crying to Jesus in the shower. We recorded her conversation with him and felt the same peace and comfort that she did. As Maria told him of her feelings that she is not worth his love, he poured it out and told her that he died for her because he loves her and she is priceless to him. She asked him to promise that he would never take his love back and that he would help her learn to trust him. Over and over again she begged him to never leave her heart and stay close to her.

"I can't do anything on my own, Jesus. I can't control anything and I don't talk good or think good. Please show me where to walk *and what to do, cuz I can't do anything good by myself. But I read how you helped Moses talk and how you did good things through Peter and Paul. Please do good things through me. Please help me to love and be loved. Please use me to show other people that you love them. Please help me learn to sing everyday that I remember how I get to be with you in heaven. And Jesus, if you have a job for us and we don't see it, please stop us from doing other stuff and push us the way that you want us to go. And please hold me close to you, cuz I feel safe when you hold me."*

Jesus spoke to her words of comfort. ***"Child take courage. I will never leave you nor forsake you, and no one can snatch you out of my hand. Follow me and you shall no longer walk in darkness, for I am light and you shall have the light of life. I shall be your provider, your caretaker, your guide and protector. And in your heart shall be my peace. Let not your heart be troubled my precious one and do not fear. I have given you the Spirit of Truth who abides in you. He will teach you in truth and be your helper. These things I have spoken to you, my little mustard seed, so that you will not stumble."***

Louise has been learning Psalm 34 all week. The card to Maria was very encouraging to Louise too. Ann has been reading the book, "Myths I Have Known," that you sent her. Yesterday, she posed an interesting question to Maria. She asked, "Maria, say you died right now and found yourself right in front of God. And He said to you, 'Maria why should I let you into heaven?' What would you say?"

Maria thought for a few moments and answered, "I wouldn't have to say anything, cuz Jesus would be right there and he would walk up to his dad and say this one is one of mine. I would be peeking around from behind Jesus' robe cuz I would be holding on to him real tight. God would smile at me and I would smile back at him, and he would say that my son has paid the price for this one. Jesus would hug me and we would walk into heaven together."

Then Ann said to her, "And you really believe that?" Maria said, "With my life."

Jennifer is not back yet. The Pod children are still with Raquel. Mariann is spending time with Dragonslayer and asking him a multitude of questions about Christmas. Tabitha is picking out stickers from the book that Carol sent. Mari is spending time with

Ruth and asking about Jesus and the whole system is waiting for the restoration of the Land of Preservation.

Christmas was fast approaching and preparations had begun to celebrate it with new hope for the future. As Bruce worked with Mariann and Tabitha, who were asking many more questions about the connection between Dragonslayer and Christmas, somehow the subject of experiencing a toy store came up. He had peaked their interest, but was unable to take them himself, so I volunteered to take them to a safe neighborhood Toys 'R' Us. The children were not allowed out in public near home for security sake, so we planned it for the week before Christmas with huge crowds to help 'blend them in'.

I wanted to make this Christmas special for everyone, because I knew I would be listing my house again in May in preparation of leaving in July for seminary. I had received my second letter from my seminary, requesting that I plan to attend my final year on campus to meet my Master of Divinity requirement. Actually, it felt more like a demand. It seems that after 15 years of attending extension part-time, while doing ministry full-time, I was setting a precedent for second career students that they didn't want others to follow. I took this as a message from my Lord that the next time I listed my house it would probably sell. In either case, we assumed the Lord would take care of it. So I began preparing the System by letting Council know that the probability of our separation soon was more likely, but we should wait until the last minute to inform the children. Council informed Ann of this and she wrote the following to me.

...Let me know if Dec. 15th is a day that Maria and her husband will be getting together with you. (I had requested to make one last counseling effort at communication building in their marriage, in the hopes that something could begin to grow, especially considering the probability of us leaving. They had everything to gain and nothing to lose.) *Also Council asked me to ask you if there is another day in December that the system can come over with some gifts for you. Maybe it can be combined with the day that Mariann goes to the toy store with you. I know that Maria and the kids want to watch you and Carol open the gifts. So*

if you can have a pre-Christmas day it would mean a lot to them. Your gifts are handmade or special keepsakes from different parts and all of them had great joy in preparing them for you. I personally want to shadow and find out what's in Raquel's wolf package! She rarely gives gifts, but when she does they're special and weird.

On a more serious note, Council is starting to prepare Maria for your eventual separation from the system. They are becoming concerned about her inability to separate without problems, their example being how she's not handling very well seeing Bruce a lot less. They suggest extending the time between your visits to twice a month instead of once a week and limiting phone calls from them to possibly once a week. They would appreciate any guidance you can give on this transition.

Helper suggested a cassette tape of your lessons or sermons for Maria to listen to when she can't call. Maybe you could do one of the stories from the Bible for the children. Even one of just you encouraging them to be strong would mean a lot. That way we can play it for them when they're down or lonely and believe me when I say they will play it over and over again. Helper is having a hard enough time maintaining with you only across the bay and doesn't want to think about you 500 miles away or more, if you accept a call to a church somewhere in the world.

Finally, I want to thank you for your kind offer, but I cannot accept. I have a rule about not borrowing money from my friends. I will get out of this predicament. It must be your love for Maria and the kids to offer this, as the system is not a good risk. Anyone with good financial planning doesn't want to lose it on us but thank you for the offer. It is appreciated.

Ruth talked to Sergio about the possibility of another session, but from his response, Council decided against putting Maria through another ordeal. So a date was set for the toy store on the following Saturday instead, followed by an evening with Dragonslayer around the Christmas tree. Council tried to prepare for something totally new for everyone in Preservation:

Memo from Circle Council:

135

Greetings. Thank you for being available on Saturday to take Mariann to the toy store. We have attempted to prepare her for the experience by explaining to her the concept of a toy store and appropriate manners in a store. She is not to run off but stay with you at all times. She is allowed to look at the toys and smell them, but not touch them without your consent. (Council had obviously never been to a toy store with children. A behavior that Mariann displayed during her recuperation in August whenever she was out, was the strong desire to smell everything, and I mean everything, as well as taste it if she could. It took outings like this to realize that <u>everything</u> was new to her as she made up for decades of hiding in Preservation from the Beast. She wasted no time in trying to fill every sensory perception available in the brief times that she was allowed to the surface. In the years to come, these moments will be both heartbreaking and hilarious, as she learns about the outside world she never knew.)

We asked her why she wanted to go to a toy store and her answer was, "Because I be with Mr. Miguel and look at toys." Paladin explained to her that Mr. Miguel is not buying toys, to which she responded, "cuz he gives hugs like Dragonslayer". Mariann has a limited understanding of the traditions of Christmas. She says giving Dragonslayer a tree for Christmas is silly but is very excited about making things for people and giving it to others. When we asked her what she wanted for Christmas, she thought for a few seconds and stated, "lots of hugs and be with my mommy and daddy and Dragonslayer".

Tabitha knows about Saturday and will probably switch out at the toy store. It will depend upon the strength of Mariann, as these two are rivals for time out. (For the first year or so, Mariann would be the dominant child out in experiencing the world. At first I thought it was an age issue of Mariann being about 8 and Tabitha being about 4/5, before I learned how Tabitha had many brief times out over the years when Mariann had relatively none. Tabitha submitted to Mariann's desires to be out most of the time, unless we pressured Mariann to be obedient in allowing her out. Whenever she did however, she was like a second skin near the surface shadowing in order to get some measure of the experience. As Tabitha grows stronger in her own identity, she will eventually be able to display strength never before seen by Mariann.)

Joy, Hopi and Lila are now in the caves with the other children. Raquel returned to care for the animals. Tolip has spent all evening with the pod children and reported to us that they are still adjusting to all of the changes within the past 2 months. They know nothing about the toy store and wouldn't do well there. However, Tolip would like at least one of them to switch out for a few moments to interact with you and Carol in a safe and trusting place. After much discussion, Council decided to allow Joy out for some time with you and Carol, in the hope that the others will shadow her and become comfortable with you two, if you agree. Joy is the strongest of the three.

Adult parts might rotate out that evening as you open their gifts. Maria will be the primary adult out to share the day with you. Her Christmas wish this year is to live through Christmas and be with her friends. It will be beneficial for her health to spend time with you. We hope this information will help you on Saturday.

Council learned how one doesn't prepare for a child's first visit to a mega toy store, only step aside and enjoy the festivities. Just the drive over to the store for Mariann's first outing in a car with her daddy was exciting enough. Thank God for seat belts! Nothing along the boulevard escaped her notice. When the ducks appeared in the marsh in front of the store, I was required to drag her away with promises of more exciting things inside.

As we entered through the high narrow stacks of games and boxed toys, she was calm for that first 20 minutes moving 40 feet, unable to really touch or smell anything but plastic. When we turned the corner and her gaze encircled the rows upon rows of stuff beyond her imagination, she stood stunned with eyes like saucers murmuring, *"Oh Daddy...Oh Daddy"*. I waited to see what she did next and was surprised when she began to slowly walk down the aisles in a silent reverence. It wasn't that she wanted any of it, only to look and occasionally touch this new phenomenon of existence entering her reality.

When I pulled the string on the first talking doll, I thought that she might pass out with wonder. Was this thing alive? After gaining her composure, she immediately introduced herself to this new friend. I didn't want to waste any time trying to explain everything to her, so I said that we needed to move on to see other new discoveries. At a couple of such moments when Mariann was overwhelmed, it was easy for Tabitha to switch out to view things that interested her. She must have been very close and shadowing Mariann, because at one point, Mariann looked in a mirror and started to cry. I asked her what was wrong. "Daddy Miguel, please tell Tabitha that she can't be out now…it's my turn."

After an hour and a half, I told the two of them that they could pick out one toy each for Christmas. After I assured them it was okay, Mariann proceeded directly to the coloring book aisle. She spent another twenty minutes deciding on the perfect book, one with Jesus and lambs on it. I told Tabitha to come out and pick a book as well, which we topped off with a large box of crayons. By that time they were so overwhelmed by it all that Ruth had to come out so I could get them out of the store. They were exhausted from the experience, as was I.

I was told that they 'rested' inside by telling the other children and any adults that would listen all about their time there. This allowed time for Maria and others to have some special time with us, uninterrupted. We came together to share gifts that would become triggers for remembering special moments of our journey, points in time when healing triumphed over the past and hope won the day. The gift I received from Raquel was a calumet, or peace pipe, just like the one that Circle Council shared in the Sacred Circle. They honored me by this symbolic gesture. The children each made a Christmas ornament for us to hang on our tree. There was story time with the children, each taking turns to sit by the fireside listening to carols and staring glass- eyed at the tree. We all felt that night that it would be pretty hard to surpass the love shared this Christmas. We all underestimated the plans that Jesus had for us.

But Christmas wasn't over yet and Liz had her own plans for this year. One of the churches that Maria was attending had an abundance of food to give away and no 'poor people' in the church. This was an opportunity Liz couldn't pass up and she pulled a power play over Ruth. After rotating out and letting the youth pastor know that she would distribute it to the really needy, she loaded up the car to the hilt and headed for the East Bay. Ruth heard, *'You keep your mouth shut and you might learn something.'*

I learned a lot today. As soon as we left the church, Liz began to set the rules for this outing. Of course I protested and attempted to get her to understand that this was a team effort, but Liz was not cooperating. **"I'm pissed at you guys for finking on me to those pastors about taking the damn tree."** *I tried to explain to her how the Robin Hood Philosophy wasn't right. All that did was make her angrier. I decided at that point to let you reprimand her later and find out where she stole it from so I can repay it. I think this is a holdover from the days when the children had to steal food to eat. The funny thing is, if you put a diamond necklace and a cantaloupe on a counter side by side, Liz would take the food. I've noticed how she only rarely steals, and even then it's for somebody else who is poor. It's still wrong, but how do I get Liz to see that. If Sergio finds out that Liz does this, I'm afraid that Maria will suffer the consequences.*

I wasn't getting anywhere trying to be involved in the distribution. She said, **"So where are you going to go Ruth? I know the places, not you."** *She had me there and that's when the Lord spoke to me,* **"Be still Ruth and let Liz be my representative."** *I obeyed. Liz did not go home like we told her to do. She was a woman on a mission and very focused. She stopped in a parking lot long enough to make up a bag of ready to eat food. She drove to a spot where a man lives by the creek under the overpass, giving him the bag. I recognized him as a man I'd seen on the streets. His face had seen better days and there was no sparkle in his eyes. I wanted to tell him about the love of Jesus, but Liz warned me.* **"Man like that wants food in his belly. You can't eat words Ruth. That's all you guys ever do is preach it. God I hate that, just leave him alone."**

She walked up to him like an old friend and said, **"Slow day huh? They're all in a rush to get that last gift. How's old Yeller doing?** *(This raggy, mangy, old dog.)* **Here's some stuff for you. The guy upstairs thought you could use it. Take care."** *Then she just left. Next we drove up to East Oakland. I used to think that she was exaggerating about knowing the streets, but I believe her now. I didn't know what kind of place that she was taking me into, when out come some bags for kids. I can't tell you what happened inside, as I was unable to shadow. I came close to shadow as we were leaving, to watch her wind her way through alleys to her next stop.*

We were at the home of an elderly couple obviously in need. The house was a shack, with the steps rotted out and weeds overtaking the sidewalk. As Liz pounded on the door, I thought that she was going to knock it down. Liz said, **"They're almost deaf, but I know that they're home. They never go out, they're too old."** *Finally the woman opened the door and Liz strolled in with,* **"Ho, Ho, Ho! I'm here with great stuff for you and Charlie."**

Mike, the house had no interior paint, the ceiling was falling in, the oven didn't work and everything was torn or broken. They used to watch Jeopardy on this small b/w TV, but that had died too. They're both in their late seventies, tired and alone. Liz hands Charlie the stolen tree and says, **"Can't have a damn Christmas without a few pine needles falling on the floor, now can we Charlie?"** *He laughs and I pray for her language.*

There's not one sign of Christmas in the house. There's no food, no heat and Liz just seems to bypass all of that telling them, **"I'm bringing in some boxes and you just take whatever you want."** *Liz unloaded the rest of the car and hauls the heavy boxes into the house herself. These people never leave the house to shop. Charlie is so overwhelmed that he doesn't know where to start. So Liz jumps in for him.* **"So let's see…we got some corn. Like corn Charlie? I got a friend named Ann who is always yelling at me to eat vegetables, but she doesn't think that mushrooms are veggies!"** *Charlie laughs and says I'll take some of those. Liz,* **"Here's some great hot oatmeal. You got no teeth so this'll be good on those old gums."**

He smiles and takes the food until he gets two full bags before saying that's enough leave some for others. Liz sits and talks with them for awhile about nothing and everything. The woman started to cry and says how she wishes that Liz were her daughter. She was aware of how Liz (Maria) had been helping other elderly people and said, "You're the only one Maria to do this." Liz swore how it was nothing and easy to do. I prayed again asking God to stop the profanity. He said again to be still and listen.

The conversation turned to their sadness as they reminisced about their life. They had a son who committed suicide…another son who had CP…another son who made it big and ignores them… the drugs, alcohol and violence…all-in-all a life of pain and suffering. I looked at them and saw two people who had worked hard all of their life and were now alone, destitute and dying. Suddenly Liz jumps up and says, **"Got to go…got more stops to make."** *The woman asked her to please not tell anyone how bad off we are and begged her to stay just ten minutes more.*

The woman wanted to know why this wealthy church out in the valley wanted to give them food. Liz chuckled and came up with the oddest way of witnessing that I ever heard. **"Well, you see the people in that area are pretty well off. I mean there are some that struggle, but most of them are okay. They wanted to help out people who really needed the help. There are so many con artists today that you just can't set up a table and say free food. People sell it for dinero' for drugs."** *Both agreed with her.*

"So up pops me! I live in the real world with tons of legit poor people. So they asked me to distribute it and I loaded the old car and headed out for parts unknown to them." *With tears in her eyes the woman asked her,* "Why us?" **"You were on Jesus' list for food. You know that he loves you a lot. And love just don't come down in words, but in action. He knows what it feels like to suffer. He died suffering on the cross so that those who believe in him could go to heaven. To me, that is committed love. So, like he said, take them food and the last thing I want to do is piss Jesus off. So here's your food."**

The woman wanted to give her an old purse… "hardly used"… *before she left, but Liz told her no thanks and suggested that maybe she might want to write a letter to the church to thank them. She said in parting,* **"Maybe I can get some more next time for you too. You know I bet that I could get some of the youth group to come out here and clean up the place, paint, pull a few weeds and fix those steps so you don't break your necks trying to feed those squirrels. Think about it and this as from church friends."**

Then she hauled the food back out and as she proceeded to get in said to them, **"Don't ever give up hope guys. It's a shitty world out here but listen to Jesus. He's got a great mansion up there for you. Just believe him and trust him. Take care."** *Then she drove away.*

She goes to one lady's house on the brink of despair and contemplating suicide. How does Liz handle it… "Shit, if you go who's going to make me that great pudding? Hey, shit happens and some of us get crapped on more than others but look at the *positive... crap is protein." As the woman starts laughing hysterically, Liz brings her in a bunch of food and another stolen tree! I must tell you that I have a problem with the stolen trees.*

Then we headed into the gang-infested area and more poverty. We stop at a house with a disabled man outside. Liz has his children get the food out of the car and yells at him to shut her car door before some fool takes it off. Inside we hear how the oldest son was laid off and his wife made him get out...six kids...tattoos up and down his arms...another son out of San Quentin...kids... disability...poverty...machismo...you name it and it was here.

*So Liz sits down and visits for awhile. They talk about the bad times...sexual abuse...nuns hitting them...children exposed to evil too early in life. Liz is comfortable...this is her world. She rubs the head of a disabled child who sits on her lap and sees no Christmas presents under a wispy tree. She tells the child, **"You watch ...there'll be a present for you from"** and she points up. She talks about Jesus again and tells them all that he has done for her.*

*She never once cried...never showed pity towards these people. She had only respect for them saying, **"they have been through the wringer Ruth and survived. They know life and death and keep on going."** With that we left and she asked me to come out and drive because she was tired. While I'm still attempting to absorb all that I learned today, I think I have more compassion for Liz. I don't agree with her style, but I appreciate her results from a heart that is broken for the brokenhearted. But please stop her from stealing Christmas trees! - Ruth*

For the first time in the lives of the System, everyone wanted to seek out and know who the CHRIST in Christmas was to them... and to the world around them. Instead of just being the subject of conversation for Ruth and a few others, He had become the object of their hunger to understand the reality of their existence. Neither the Land of Preservation, nor the outside world had much to offer in the meaning and purpose for existing, if Christ wasn't a part of its interpretation. Most were at different stages of the interpretation for themselves, with some believing to the full extent of the knowledge they had, while a few were just beginning to believe...to the full extent that their 'knowledge' would allow them.

Real love had entered their domains and challenged them to be engulfed by its purpose in our lives and relationships. It could no longer be the subject of ridicule and scorn or remain the scapegoat for life's pain and suffering. The expectation of this love to remove all of the pain they had known in the past and present realities of life was being transformed into a new reality, one that required a lot of faith to fully understand. They were allowing Jesus to lead them onto a difficult path of the journey to love... the trail of wisdom and compassion winding through the desert of real humanity.

The next three years of their lives will be the length of this trail and the balance of this second journal, which by necessity requires that I present the events in highlights of particular lessons, learned by all of us. Because a significant number of people will cross their path over the three years, the first name will only be used. I do this because several will have a significant impact in changing the life of the System, and their own. However, the 'impact' may have been a very painful one that individuals are still trying to understand. I hope to share within these books how even those times were used to bring about the understanding of how God's purposes are unstoppable. His love will be what sustains us on the journey.

"This, and only this...can give us back a belief in God
- in a compassionate, torn and sorrowing God
who gave us free will out of love,
and having forbidden Himself to interfere,
must behold in agony what we do with our freedom."
Meyer Levin, *The Fanatic* (1964)

"I would have despaired unless I had believed that
I would see the goodness of the Lord in the land of
the living. Wait for the Lord; Be strong and let
your heart take courage; Yes, wait for the Lord."
Psalm 27: 13 – 14

Chapter Seven

"While Seeing They Do Not See, While Hearing They Do Not Hear"

"We pray that we may come into this Darkness which is beyond light and, without seeing and without knowing, to see and to know that which is above vision and knowledge."
Dionysius, *Mystical Theology* (6th century)

*"Oh abundant grace, wherein I presumed to fix my gaze
On the eternal light so long that I wearied my sight!
Within its depths I saw gathered in,
Bound by love in one volume,
The scattered leaves of all the universe."*
Dante Alighieri, *Paradiso,* (1320)

*"For the heart of this people has become dull,
And with their ears they scarcely hear,
And they have closed their eyes
Lest they should see with their eyes,
And hear with their ears,
And understand with their heart and return,
And I should heal them."*
Jesus, Matthew 13: 15

*"For now we see in a mirror dimly, but then face to face;
Now I know in part, but then I shall know fully
just as I also have been fully known.
But now abide faith, hope, love, these three;
But the greatest of these is love."*
Paul, 1 Corinthians 13: 12-13

I have always appreciated Paul for stating the verses above at the moment that he was defining the characteristics of love. God's love is a mystery that can only be understood through God's own expression of it in Jesus Christ, His Son. I used to understand his meaning here, as though we are looking for God's love through a foggy window, with love waiting ahead to be fully known when we are with Jesus. This is an accurate interpretation if one is seeking to know the full and final definition of God's love, waiting for anyone who accepts God in Jesus Christ.

Yet, in the last few years I have come to a deeper, more personal understanding of these verses. I believe Paul's use of the word mirror challenges us to look for God's love not only within ourselves, but also in the world and people around us, within the scope of our reflection in this life today. Jesus taught us how to live in His kingdom now, if we have the eyes to see, the ears to hear, and the heart to understand and know Him. To do this we must look at the world and ourselves as mirrored through His eyes, understanding through His heart, and hearing anyone asking to receive His love.

I have heard people in congregations over the years acknowledge how 'nothing is impossible for God yet lead lives that really only reflect the limitations of mankind. Most are hard pressed to give an example of how Jesus' love in them permanently changed their actions in this life. When it comes to the power of Jesus' love changing lives day-to-day through us, **"We have not because we ask not!"** Most of us really don't want to take the risk of asking for 'eyes that see and ears that hear', the spiritual realm that is the kingdom of heaven around us. Why is that?

Perhaps Jack Nickelson and Kevin Spacey answered this question in lines from their movies, "You can't handle the truth!" and, "The greatest trick the devil ever pulled, was convincing mankind that he didn't exist!" Most of us have a hard time accepting what we can't see with our own eyes, or hear with our own ears, when it comes to the spiritual realities of life. We mouth a lot of platitudes as Christians, but in our heart of hearts...we fear most of all our denial of the things Jesus wants to do through us. And what are the ramifications of that when we do come face to face one day?

"Not everyone who says to Me, 'Lord, Lord' will enter the kingdom of heaven; but he who does the will of My Father

145

who is in heaven. Many will say to Me on that day, 'Lord, Lord, did we not prophesy in Your name, and in Your name cast out demons, and in Your name perform many miracles?' And then I will declare to them, 'I never knew you; depart from Me, you who practice lawlessness."
Jesus, *Matthew 7: 21 – 23*

In response to this, we fall at the feet of Jesus, asking for forgiveness…and banking on His grace. We will continually do that in this life and thank you Jesus that we are able to because of your love. But I believe that He wants more for us than spending our life on our knees asking for forgiveness. He has empowered us to do more in this life than we can ever fully understand, and He has promised that what we do here can have a corresponding affect in heaven. The thought of that should be both exhilarating and sobering, to think that we can affect what we cannot see in the spiritual life of others, as unto ourselves.

Maybe it is because the System had a life filled with abuse that blocked them from seeing, hearing, and knowing the love of God, that they were given the blessing of living in two worlds. Yet, it was only after the love of God was made real to them, that they were able to distinguish between these realities. Even at this point in their journey of two plus years, the word blessing wasn't used very often to describe what they were seeing or hearing. The Land of Preservation was a desert, the world outside was difficult, and the only motivation for continuing was the promises of Jesus. Some wanted proof, others wanted relief, but all of them had to struggle with understanding what they were seeing and hearing from Jesus.

How would any of us begin to integrate these two realities? Liz would continue to live life with God in the trial and error method, always seeking compromise after everything else fails. Unless the subject was beer and mushrooms, then compromise was tried first. She had three pastors now that she wrote to often, after each gave a sermon that needed challenging. Two of these and others will come and go over the next several years simply because most pastors don't like being challenged by their own words. Yes, Liz would take her 'call' from Jesus seriously, and struggle for many years ahead with the meaning of 'correcting in love'.

Quiet Walker would continue to integrate her worlds in her writings. When the Great Spirit gives her a message for an outsider that is difficult, she will pass it on with grace. Yet, this will take its own toll on her later, when most of them are ignored, even after they come true. Shortly after the following letter, Raquel came to me and asked one of the most difficult questions I think that I receive. *"Will I ever be accepted in the outside world?"*

The short version of my answer was, "Sadly, no...not as long as you are obedient to the Great Spirit and try to live life outside as He created you. You say whatever Jesus tells you, with the wisdom that He has given you. You do it naturally through the cultural ways that are you, in parables, metaphors and stories, much the way that Jesus does. If you remain true to Dragonslayer and follow the path of the Great Spirit, you will probably want to spend most of your time on Sacred Mountain and not out with the tribe of greed." My only regret in telling her this is that it meant that we would have only brief times together over the years. Those moments will become greatly valued by my wife and me.

In the early morning, while the mist still hovered over the ground, I awoke to hear the Great Spirit. "Do you love me, Quiet Walker?"

I was surprised at such a question. "You know I love you. For you are the Great Spirit. You are my Lord and Savior."

"Quiet Walker," he said, "What if I allowed your eyes to become dark or your ears to become silent. Would you still love me?"

I thought deeply about losing my eyes. I would no longer be able to see Brave Eagle soar among the cliffs or Wolfdog frolic in the wildflowers. I would lose one of the most precious gifts I have that of seeing the Great Spirit's creation. To have my ears silenced would mean that I would no longer be able to enjoy the beautiful melody of the birds and the symphony of the wind swaying the fountain grasses along the river.

"Great Spirit," I said, "It would be most hard with dark eyes and silent ears, but I would still love you, for you are my Lord."

The Great Spirit answered, "Do you really love me?"

147

"I do not understand why you keep asking me Lord. Have I not answered you clearly? I love you with all of my heart, soul and mind!"

"So why do you sin?"

"I try earnestly not to Lord, but the world has much evil and I am weak."

"Quiet Walker, why is your praying and fellowship with me the greatest during times of trouble in Preservation? Why do you not pray and fellowship with me during the calm times? Why is it that the parts cry to others and do not come to me?"

I stood silently as the Great Spirit continued.

"I have blessed you and have preserved your life. I made you for a purpose. Do not throw away the gifts I have graciously given you. I am giving you opportunities to serve me. Do not waste them. Do not waste the talents I have blessed you with. I have sent you teachers and fellow servants to instruct you and learn from you. Continue to gain knowledge as I reveal my word to you. Do not be as others who close their ears when I speak to them. Quiet Walker, do you love me?"

I stood silent as tears rolled down my cheeks. "Great Spirit, forgive me. I am unworthy of your love."

"Quiet Walker, my love for you is genuine. You are my child. I am here. I am listening. I am always with you. My compassion is great. And when you fall, I will pick you up. When you are discouraged, I will uplift you. When you are sad, I will be sad with you. I will love you forever."

And with that he stretched out His arms and I saw the wounds of nails on His hands and I cried. "Lord, I truly love you," I wept.

We decided in March to help prepare the children for our separation gradually by ending our sessions every week and moving to more dialogue by fax and phone. We met once or twice a month as needed to spend longer time together in a single setting and help establish a firmer relationship of trust. The children would have stories read to them from a friend – my hand puppet, Lammie.

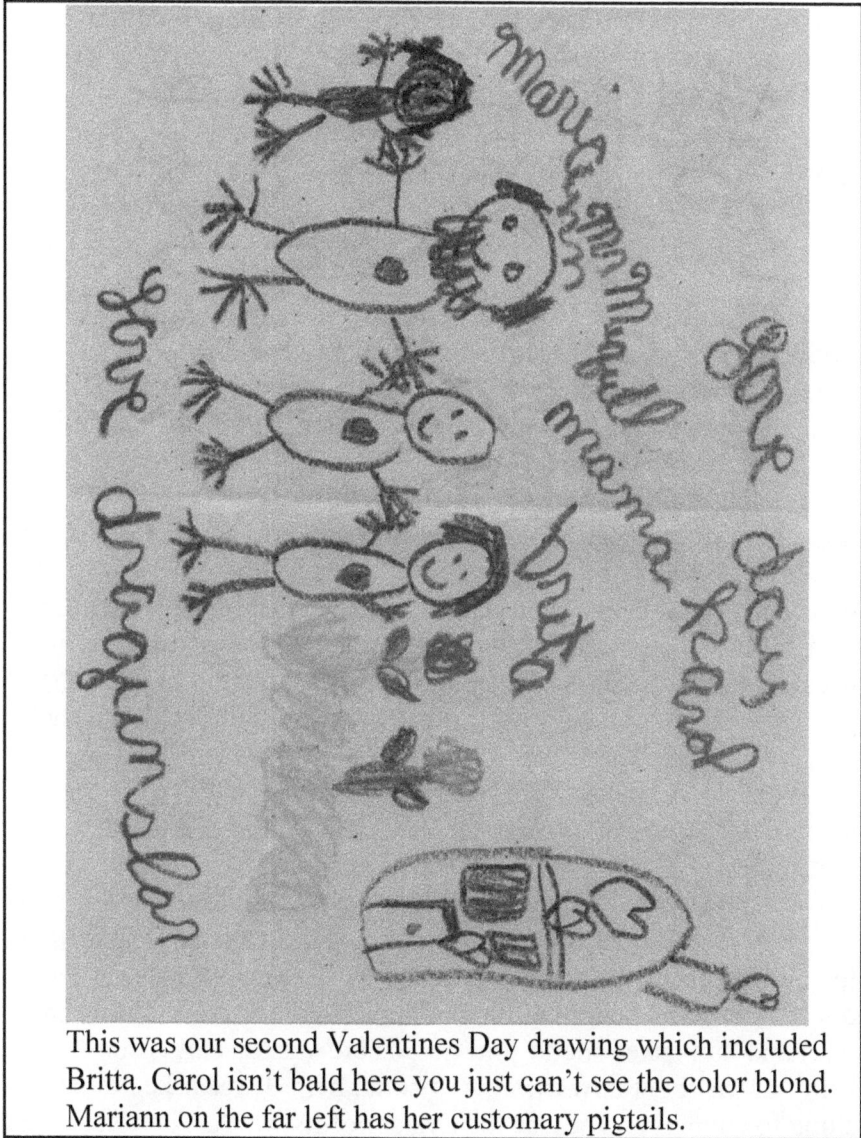

This was our second Valentines Day drawing which included Britta. Carol isn't bald here you just can't see the color blond. Mariann on the far left has her customary pigtails.

Plate # 3

Easter was coming earlier than usual and the spiritual attacks upon the children increased dramatically. The 'smelly ones' were

149

concentrating on Joy as the last stronghold, and the weakest in the System. They were reemphasizing the control and power of the Goatman in her memories, to keep her in a constant state of fear and anxiety of death. They wanted to trick her into asking the Goatman to return to her side... inside Preservation. I learned how the demonic can make their voices heard in whispers, only by the one that they want to have hear them. It is the same in both worlds. Only those with the gift of spiritual discernment can recognize who it is that is talking. Adults are supposed to be wise enough to make the distinction between good and evil thoughts or messages. If the messages aren't tested with the will of God, it becomes quite easy to make bad choices.

For children just beginning to trust Jesus and gain a child's perspective of His power, tricking them by the methods used for decades to control them was even easier. Mariann was not always around her to smell their presence or hear what was being said. It would take several more years before she learned the necessity to call Dragonslayer whenever she saw them approaching. At the time, she felt that as long as they weren't poking or threatening her, then it wasn't her responsibility to call Dragonslayer. Often, the enemy would come in proximity of someone in the System and appear as a 'bright one'. Don't be fooled into thinking that just because they're in a spiritual dimension, that testing of the spirits wasn't needed. The only time that anyone could let down their guard was when Jesus was present. None of the enemy lasted long in trying to maintain their charade with the parts when Jesus approached. Mariann always laughed at watching them run away like chickens.

We made plans to have the System over for a weekend, two weeks before Easter. I knew from the phone calls and faxes that the children and Maria were troubled by the attacks wearing them down. Ruth was planning to attend a conference on disability that weekend and asked me to join her. There was a seminar on MPD being given about how the church could help. I was asked to come along to support and advise the System of its worth. The following portions of letters were sent that week, beginning with Raquel and followed by Ruth, then several from Circle Council.

150

Greetings Shedding Tear. May the Great Spirit be glorified in our suffering. For it is a gift of sharing in the Great Spirit's afflictions, it purifies us and it testifies to the reality of our faith to those who are watching. May you continue to seek the wisdom of this. For one can not know the Great Spirit without knowing suffering, for they go together.

Come Great Spirit
Deliver us from our fears
Comfort our wounded heart with your love
For we cry out in anguish
Hear us oh Great Spirit
Be gracious to us
Rescue us from our sorrow and fears
Deliver us from the enemy
From the one who torments our children
And persecutes us both day and night
Lead us in your truth oh Great Spirit
Teach us your ways
Guard our soul and deliver us from the enemy
Shield us in your wings
Do not abandon us oh Holy One
For we are your children
Come Great Spirit Come
Rescue us

Quiet Walker

Mike
Pat called me last night. She's the speaker and consultant on MPD presenting the workshops at the conference. I asked about content and triggers for us in her presentation of a ministry for the church. She asked about our support and I told her about you and Carol and how you've helped us resolve many of our spiritual issues. I told about the books you are writing for pastors and churches, and how to minister to multiples. She asked several questions about you, and I referred her to you directly. I told her which churches you are working in currently and she wanted to know about your prayer support team. Why?

151

Council wanted you to know that they have not given her permission to read our journals. I told her how Council is very particular about the perimeters of its presentation as our story, spotlighting on what Jesus has done without sensationalism or monetary gain for us, only truth. Council said you are free to share with her any advice that you have learned in working with us, especially if it will help her help churches in their ministries. They would also like to know more about her qualifications, since she is not a therapist, but works with therapists as a support...
Ruth

Memo from Council
Pod children are having difficulty with Easter approaching. This is their first year out of CORE and Tolip is concerned with their ability to 'weather' the holiday. Joy/Egar seems especially agitated by the many triggers of this holiday. See sees the cross on the bulletin and crucifix at Maria's church and starts shaking. Tolip is unsure if the pod in the cave will hold her now.

All of the children had a difficult night last night. Mariann woke up in a pool of blood and got it on her hands, face and the wall before we could get her to switch back inside. We are recognizing massive blood loss occurring on key days like Halloween, Christmas, full moons and Easter. Are there any connections with the abuse? After we got into the shower, Mariann switched out and curled up in the corner...watching the blood go down the drain and thinking that she was dying. We finally got control again, but we are concerned.

More surgery is not possible until the body can recover from the previous one and the chemo. The medication Ann was on isn't possible because it fed the cancer. We must find a creative way to recoup the body to face whatever comes next. Liz wondered why every time we get close to getting over one hill, God allows another tidal wave to hit us and knock us down. Good question.

Lila communicated to Tolip that she wanted to know if "the nice man that holds Mariann and hugs her, would give me a hug." Tolip said, "Yes, just ask him." -

Next night:

Not sure if what we are experiencing are attacks, or simply coincidence. System was awaken in the early morning hours unable to breathe. The mouth was swollen with a type of sores or rash...possibly cuts on the sides of the tongue and roof of the mouth. Is it a body memory? Mariann started crying and Ann switched out to get cold water down her throat. It was extremely painful, yet it was completely gone by mid-morning.

Ann's interview for entrance into the school is scheduled for Good Friday and she's concerned about the state of the children then affecting the interview. She tried to change it with no success. They said that if she misses this one opportunity to get in the program, it may be another year or more. She has to compete with a large number of other applicants answering questions for 45 minutes from math professors. She's wondering why that day, coincidence? Mariann asked to add this letter:

Hi mr miguel   when I go in dragunslar water   Dragunslar clean me and mak me whit   do dragunslar hav dragunslar soap and clean me up   smelly ones com lots now
I say dragunslar com   I give you machin hug   clos eyes mr miguel   redee hug   hug   I lik better hug you and see you   hug with love   hi mama carol   I be good girl

Next night:

Council met with Dragonslayer last night and I have been instructed to communicate to you a summary of the meeting. As Helper sought direction from Dragonslayer about the attacks happening, he was assured that Dragonslayer would keep his promises. He stated again that he will rescue the child (Joy/Egar) from her fears and deliver her out of the hand of the wicked. He said,

"She does not know or understand who I am. She walks and crawls in darkness, but I have come that she may live. Take courage and do not be afraid. Do you not know that this precious little one has angels in heaven continually speaking to my Father on behalf of this child? I have come to save that which was lost,

for it is not the will of my Father that one of these precious ones perish.

Remember that this kind of evil spirit cannot be cast out by anything but prayer. Therefore, unite in prayer and have faith in God. Do not be deceived and do not be frightened. Why do you tremble in fear? I have overcome the world forces of darkness. Do not be afraid of the evil one's snares. He roams around looking for those to terrorize. Resist in my name! Remember my precious ones, I have defeated him already. He puffs himself up to look like a lion, but he is really a little mouse in disguise. He is defeated. Do not fear him and do not let him captivate your mind. No matter what happens, trust in me.

Let all who have ears hear! When an unclean spirit goes out of a man, it roams around looking for a place to rest. Not finding it, it returns to its former dwelling, but finds it clean and in order. Therefore it goes and gathers seven other spirits more evil than itself and they invade the dwelling and live there. The man is worse now than when the one spirit resided in him. Do not let up your guard. And do not let division among the ranks cause an opportunity for the enemy to take hold.

The little ones need nourishment and instruction. I have sent you my precious servants to love them and teach them truth. I will work through Michael and build trust. I will work through Bruce and the system will learn my ways. Go to Michael's home on Saturday and allow the children out. They are safe there.

And remember Tolip and Paladin, woe to those who have caused my little ones to stumble. It would have been better for them if they had never lived. I am a just God. Do not be afraid. Pray without ceasing. I shall deliver you. You are soldiers of my army now. Fight and resist in my name, for I am greater and stronger than the prince of the air and all of his demons. I will not forsake you. No one can take you from me. Do not be deceived. Stand firm in me."

Council will trust Dragonslayer and follow his instructions. – E.R.

Late that night I received this fax just before midnight.

If you truly care for Maria, DO NOT WRITE THE BOOK

Surely you realize the pain and confusion that book will bring upon her

Has she not suffered enough

You have the power to bring her peace

Do not tell others about her as this will bring her more pain

God does not want you to write this book

You are in error

Separate from her and you shall be rewarded

You are an intelligent man and can accomplish great things

Great things if you will only remove yourself from her and destroy the journals

Have you ever wondered where the phrase "Smooth Talkin' Devil" comes from? At first, I started to laugh because I knew whoever sent this wasn't talking for God. I had heard from the demonic before in a variety of ways; in prayer, through people I had confronted with God's truth – like in an exorcism, in dreams and other ways, but this was the first time I had ever been sent a blatant fax. I took note of the time on the letter and noticed there was no sender phone number. I decided to ask Elizabeth Ray the next day, if anyone was 'out' at that time of the night.

There were several things to note on this fax other than…they didn't want me to write the book. What blew it for them right away was the whole, "you shall be rewarded…you are intelligent…and will accomplish great things, etc." God only knows how many times I have asked for His help to diminish my ego. It was a sorry attempt by a grunt of the demonic ranks. I laughed because I knew that he would have hell to pay…literally!

The bulk of the content in these letters from Ruth and Council not given here was about the chaos in the family life of Maria. She was caught in the middle of her extended family's struggles between parents and siblings, marriages falling apart, brother in the hospital, 'friends' at church putting demands on her, and a contractor not fulfilling his obligations. Ann was being sabotaged by someone inside in her school preparations, but didn't know who. The mother and father were putting legal obligations upon Maria about taking care of their estates, as well as being the one expected to care for family should they become incapacitated. The children were calling me every night in need of phone hugs, blessings and general reassurance that the Good Shepherd would protect them. It was obvious that something was going to happen spiritually for them, I just wasn't sure what or when. We had two more nights before they would come to our home, so I began praying earnestly for God's guidance on Saturday night.

When I called the next day, no one was aware of any part being out the night before near midnight. The thought was that Mariann was sleeping then. I asked Ruth to double check with Elizabeth Ray and get back to me. I received another 5 faxes over the next two nights before they came. Ruth told me that Egar/Joy was out between 11:00 and 11:45 the previous night, but no one thought she was capable of doing anything on a fax machine or computer, as she was too young at roughly 2 years old. I decided to wait to discuss how the demonic can manipulate people, until they were with us and in a safe place. They wrote the following:

It has been an extremely difficult day. Ann is trying to salvage all of the work that she put into her class. We think Egar was out this morning and this made Ann late for her classes. She was asked to do an evaluation of the class by the professor and she pulled it off even though she was tired. I've been told to handle all of the phone calls from family until after Easter, as it's too much stress. Maria is depressed about her brother and she's been crying inside all day. It doesn't help. Council wants the kids, Maria and Louise to be out this weekend. Tolip will shadow if Egar rotates out. ...

Hey Buddy,
Heard about the attack letter on the inside. Stupid weeny probably flunked Manipulation 1A. What a dumb move! Even I could see through that shit. Boy I would love to see what's happening to him right now. Well I'm sure the little informer Mariann has told you everything that has been going on around here. This morning the new surprise awaiting us was boils on the body. Man, we never get a break! How about you and I goin' fishin' in Alaska together for a week? I heard the demons don't like the cold up there. You pay!...

Memo from Council
Attacks on the system are intensifying. Council has communicated with Quiet Walker concerning spiritual matters. Plan of action: House of Prayer, Quiet Walker – prayer warriors; King of Lights, Daniel and Lion will form clusters of parts to watch over and be on alert for the enemy approaching. Instructions are to call for chief commander Dragonslayer when enemy sighted. All parts have been instructed to immediately call for Dragonslayer if they even suspect the enemy is near.

Enemy is using tactics concerning Easter. As it approaches, attacks become stronger against Egar and the younger children. The husband is also being used as a ploy to weaken Maria. When the system needs the most support, he is the least supportive. Council has decided to keep Maria inside until things improve. Enemy is also at Ruth when she attends church alone. A 'Christian' divorced man is showering her with attention. Ruth was warned not to call him or have any contact with him.

We reminded everyone that survival is the primary goal and the enemy is out to destroy us. Council decided that baptism for Mariann can happen after March 21st. Be prepared for major attacks from enemy over this. Mariann is one of the parts who seem to agitate them the most. Her baptism will likely mean a response in some manner from them. Be prepared.

Tolip plans to push Egar out at your house this weekend. Dragonslayer said that you would know what to do. Tolip realizes that this causes her pain, but unless she identifies with you and trusting what you say, she will not be able to break the hold that they have over her. The cross is a trigger. The child has been conditioned to believe that you and Bruce are tricks to hurt her. She believes the Goatman will rise up Easter morning and punish her for betraying him. Remember that she still connects Jesus to the Goatman as one and the same. Maybe you can let her draw and talk about the drawings with her. The enemy yelling at her is twisting everything that you say around, as you say it. They tell her the Goatman is her savior. He rescued her when she was buried in a box and that's a strong memory for her. She doesn't know that he ordered her put there in the ritual.

We appreciate the boundaries that Carol is teaching Mariann, but please remember to remind her that being timed out is not for being a 'bad' girl as her abusers told her, but for disobedience. Can you talk to Mariann and prepare her for when you, Carol and Britta come over on Easter for dinner? She can't be out in front of Maria's family or the system suffers. House of Prayer and Quiet Walker will be in prayer that day. ...

Friday night Maria was worrying about her brother and his family and couldn't sleep. She called and told me about her many concerns this week with all of the spiritual attacks. I asked her to talk directly with Jesus about the futility of worry, and how to best help her brother. I wanted her to release it to Jesus so the System could get some rest before coming over to us. I expected a long Saturday night.

Jesus, I am trying to love my brother from afar, but it is hard. What should I pray?

That he will draw close to me and I will give him strength. I want him to trust me.

Like me huh? I keep making mistakes Jesus. I keep forgetting to go to you. Why do I have such a hard time trusting you? You have never lied to me. I'm not doing good.

My precious child, the spirit is willing but the flesh is weak.

158

Jesus I love you, so could you please make my mind a spirit mind, instead of a world mind? This world is too fast and I don't fit.

Little One, none of my children who really know and follow me fit in this world. Remember when I walked the earth, did I fit?

No Jesus.

Then neither will you. But do not worry for I am with you and nothing can happen to you that I have not allowed. You are being trained up my child to be a witness of my love.

I don't understand Jesus.

You and Michael will tell the people I love them and care for them. You are to take the spirit of my love to the brokenhearted and downcast. And do not be afraid of the challenges and attacks coming your way, for I will be with you always. Remember dear one, I am your Lord and you are mine. You will tell those in darkness that they will see. Preach my message that I have come to set them free and one day, justice will rule the earth.

So my job is to be your love to other people that are hurting and bring them your hope.

Yes, my child.

I'm still trying to learn about real love Jesus. Your love is so different from the other kind. Will you teach me more, please?

Have you not realized my child that I have already begun? Did I not send you teachers of the faith? I will guide your walk and teach you in many ways. I will give you the words to say. My dear one, you never need run and hide again. I am always at your side. I made you with loving care and you are mine forever.

Jesus, when I go to heaven, can I please see my name written in the book of life? I'm in your book, huh.

Yes.

Jesus, I hope that my life from now on will please you and I hope that I can work for you and be your servant forever. Good night!

Good night my child.

After arriving Saturday, Louise and Carol spent part of the day preparing our gardens for the realtor's walk-through coming up. In the cool evening I took the children for a long walk in the neighborhood. We went a different direction than before, so it was another brand new world for the kids to experience. Mariann chatted with the bright ones along our path and wanted to put her face into every bush that had 'bug potential' along the way. Tabitha rotated out when she heard voices speaking Spanish coming from one kitchen. When we passed an orchard area on the hill, she wanted to go climbing trees, but the 'old man' wasn't up to it.

By evening, it was time for Egar/ Joy to rotate out for awhile. She was afraid and kept looking out the window into the darkness. I gave her crayons and paper to draw why she was afraid. She was still learning who she could trust and often repeated her questions to me. When I would gently hold her and tell her about the love of the Good Shepherd, she would point at me and ask, "You do me?" Her abusers often said, "I'm going to do you." So I had to break the mindset that the enemy was reminding her of at that very moment. I would repeat, "No. I love you with the love of the Good Shepherd and His love does not do you, it protects and keeps you safe. I will protect you and keep you safe here."

She drew a picture of a table with her on it, with the Goatman standing next to it alongside of Jesus. She would point to them and say, "Same...do me." I, of course, would differentiate between the two telling her, "No, Jesus is the Good Shepherd and He would never hurt you by doing you. The Goatman is a liar and he did hurt you and tell you that he was Jesus. He's a liar. Ask Mariann if Jesus ever hurt her. Ask her if Jesus is the Good Shepherd."

Sometimes she gave hand signals to indicate that she was afraid of being buried again underground and wanting to call the Goatman to rescue her. Tabitha tried interpreting her hand signals for me when asked, but it took awhile. I began telling her repeatedly how it was the Goatman who told his worker to bury her and it was how he tricked her into trusting him. Helping her to understand who would trick her to hurt her and who wouldn't, was going to take a long time to overcome. For that evening, the puppet 'Lammie' would stay next to her all night to tell her stories about the Good Shepherd and His love to heal all of the pain His lambs had. It was simple but effective enough to have her run into Jesus' open arms for comfort in the early morning hours. Baby steps were the only way to heal a lifetime of memories of pain.

Some adults inside wanted her healing to move faster, but they had no understanding of the depth of her pain, confusion and how the enemy was trying to coax her back. It was a victory for the enemy just to keep her away from the arms of Jesus for a time. No one really wanted to hear how Jesus kept telling me, **"Just keep telling her the truth in love and bringing her to Me."** I was slowly learning some truths about how Jesus heals us from our wounds, and the wisdom of His timetable in doing so.

Adults can often grasp the concept of free will and taking responsibility for choices made that are contrary to the will of God. A child, however, cannot and makes choices based on feelings, not ethics. Joy would choose whom she would trust and respond accordingly. Just as before and again in the future, the children will make a wrong choice, and trust the words of evil. In doing so, they will invite evil back into their life and become tricked into staying away from Jesus. Over the years, as the System learns of the necessity of being observant of each other's state-of-being, they learn to question each other and the children when they seem to want to stay away from their Lord.

We on the outside will learn too, how the enemy will come to the children as a friend wanting to play with them, often in a very pleasant appearance. They will appear as a white dove; a relative that had been nice at some point; an angel; the Madonna; as an outside person who cares for them, but always with a detectable flaw in their character, if the child/person is willing to see it. The children will be taught to look into the eyes, as the window to the soul, to see if Jesus is mirrored there. The adults will be taught to test the words and test the spirits, by going to the Bible and to Jesus for authentication. For everyone it will be trial and error.

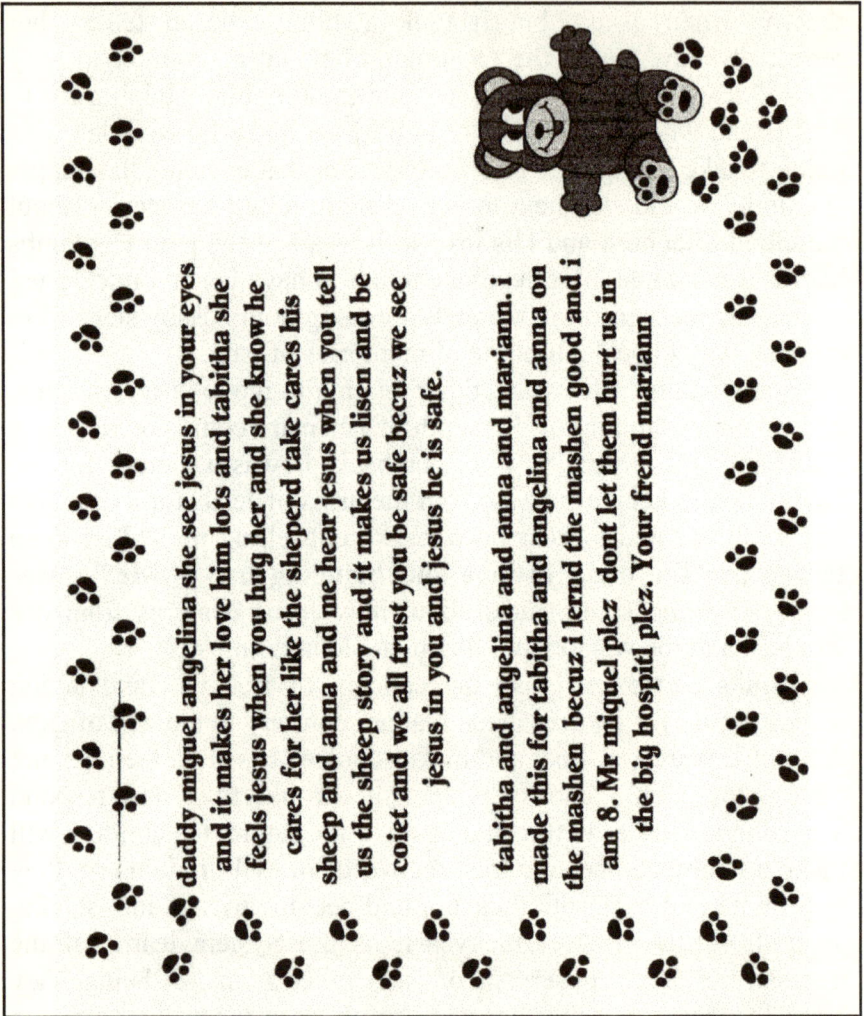

daddy miguel angelina she see jesus in your eyes and it makes her love him lots and tabitha she feels jesus when you hug her and she know he cares for her like the sheperd take cares his sheep and anna and me hear jesus when you tell us the sheep story and it makes us lisen and be coiet and we all trust you be safe becuz we see jesus in you and jesus he is safe.

tabitha and angelina and anna and mariann. i made this for tabitha and angelina and anna on the mashen becuz i lernd the mashen good and i am 8. Mr miquel plez dont let them hurt us in the big hospitl plez. Your frend mariann

Plate # 4

As you can read above, the children had already learned this lesson some months earlier, when they were approached inside by a person telling them to listen to Yemaya. Mariann looked in his eyes and didn't see Dragonslayer and immediately called for Dragonslayer...causing this 'person' to run from them quickly. The difficulty for the children in this was when the being look liked the Madonna, the Pope, or a cuddly animal.

Adults have no problem looking into the eyes directly of another person, usually to see if they appear to be lying. It's relatively easy to learn how to observe this. How many of us though, are willing to look for the spirit of Jesus shining through the eyes? This is not difficult to learn either, if one truly listens to the words being spoken and match them up to something Jesus would say. It is true that in some cultures, it is disrespectful to make eye contact with someone you don't know or has authority over you. One has to take into consideration the context of what's being said and who is saying it, especially if it has to do with a spiritual or moral issue.

Children in any culture on the other hand, have no problem looking right through an adult's eyes and into the soul. That is why they often repeat "the darnedest things." A lot has been written about children being able to see spiritual beings like angels, when the more learned adults cannot. There are a lot of lessons we can learn from our children, if we take the time to listen to their conversations with spiritual beings…before too quickly dismissing it as an overactive imagination. Believers make the mistake of thinking that their children are somehow protected from the enemy attempting to influence them into making bad decisions. This is one of those areas where most believers do not have a clear understanding between **demonic influence** vs. **demonic possession.** I'll discuss this more when the context for the System's choices reveals this clearly.

For the believer who thinks that they have this process licked, be careful, because you're approaching a cliff. If the devil had the hubris to go face-to-face with Jesus, tempting Him in the desert, what makes you think he's afraid to tempt you? How much easier targets are the children of faith, before they reach an age of discernment? For children who have been abused, that age of discernment can be stalled into adulthood. They need prolonged help, love and guidance in making good choices about truth. They can't choose truth if it isn't proven to them to be trustworthy. Joy will choose truth this weekend and move another step closer in her journey to trust His love.

"Let the children alone, and do not hinder them from coming to Me; for the kingdom of heaven belongs to such as these."
Matt. 19:14

Over the years ahead, Carol and I will watch and learn how the demons approach the children of the System and will record the various strategies used to trick them. We find a correlation with the easy way they dupe adults, by playing to their needs...their desires and their vanities. It took me awhile to understand why Jesus would wait to teach some truths to the children of the System, when they were obviously caught in a tug-of-war between the forces of good and evil. It will be the constant reminder that I too am caught in the same warfare and don't always make the right choice, even when I know it clearly. I will learn how the children belong to Him and are protected through the learning process, just as I am by His mercy, and how evil can never overcome His love.

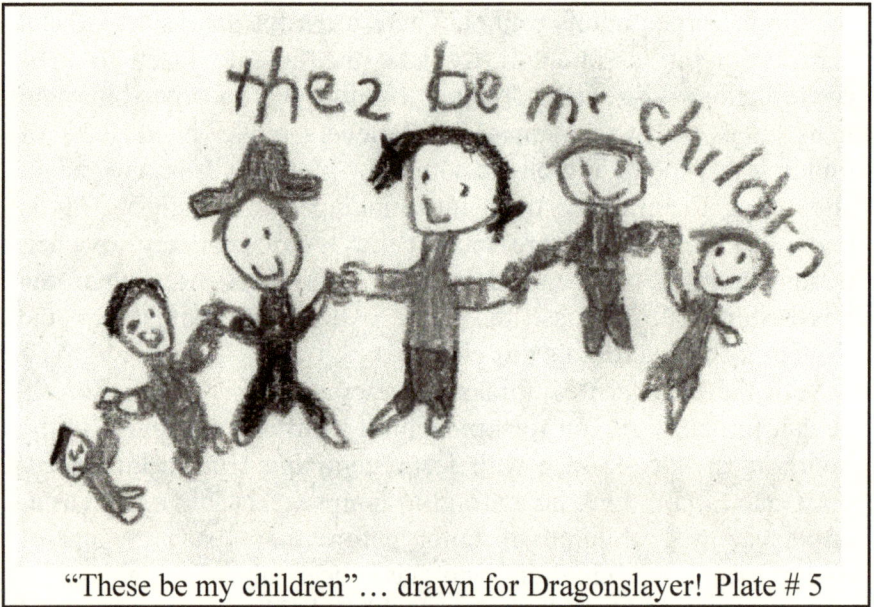

"These be my children"... drawn for Dragonslayer! Plate # 5

"You may give them your love but not your thoughts.
For they have their own thoughts.
You may house their bodies but not their souls.
For their souls dwell in the house of tomorrow,
Which you can never visit,
Even in your dreams."
Kahlil Gibran, *The Prophet* (1923)

"And He called a child to
Himself and set him
before them, and said,
'Truly I say to you, unless you are
converted and become like children,
you shall not enter the kingdom of heaven.
Whoever then humbles himself as this child,
he is the greatest in the kingdom of heaven.
And whoever receives one such child in
My name receives Me; but whoever
causes one of these little ones who
believe in Me to stumble, it is better
for him that a heavy millstone
be hung around his neck,
and that he be drowned
in the depth of the sea."
Matthew 18: 2 – 6

Chapter Eight

"If home is where the heart is…
What home can hold the heart of God?"

*"Let not your heart be troubled; believe in God,
believe also in Me. In My Father's house are
many dwelling places; if it were not so, I would
have told you; for I go to prepare a place for
you. And if I go and prepare a place for you, I
will come again, and receive you to Myself;
that where I am, there you may be also."*
John 14: 1 – 4

*"You cannot… separate God and miracle,
but you must be able to interpret and
proclaim both in a 'non-religious' sense."*
Dietrich Bonhoeffer, *Letters and Papers from Prison* (1953)

I was aware all Saturday night and Sunday morning, of several spiritual battles being fought within the spiritual realm around us and perhaps even within the boundaries of Preservation. Though I could not see or hear what was happening, I felt led to pray all night for the System's protection. After Joy had chosen to run into the arms of Jesus, Mariann switched out and began telling me about the many 'smelly ones' circling the house and shouting curses at all of us. She described how the 'bright ones' were holding the line locked arm-in-arm around the home, and being told by their commander, an angel named Sarus, to "hold the line and don't let any pass through." Mariann wanted to go back inside and join the fracas in the spiritual realm, so I told her not to go anywhere…without her armor in place.

We prayed together the verses from Ephesians 6 and asked for Dragonslayer to put His armor on her. Some months earlier, after I learned of her gifts to see the demonic in both worlds, we studied the purpose and detail of this armor in preparation for future visits. She knew the importance and meaning behind the armor, after

Jesus had given her a helmet, just like the ones she saw the angels wearing. I told her to stand next to Dragonslayer and do only what He tells you to do. By the time that she switched back inside, the wind was howling around my house to the point the windows shook.

Now some people reading this account will think that I had lost my senses and was now participating in a delusion of my own making, as well as failing my client/friend by not keeping the child part safe in my home. For the latter to be true, one must accept the reality of what was happening around us in both dimensions. For the former to be true, one must reject all that the Bible tells of the spiritual realm and the reality of the battle between good and evil. After 21 years, by this time, of my experiences as a prayer warrior for Jesus, I had no doubts of the realities we face daily. I also knew how the battles belong to Jesus, as the only One with the power to defeat our common foe.

I also know that He calls us to join in under His authority and power to protect us. Knowing that Mariann was in His hands helped me to encourage her to return inside. I could only join in through prayer, and I prayed for hope…hope that I would have the courage to do what Mariann was doing, if I were given the same gift of seeing and hearing the battle in front of me. I remembered the times when I was given shadow glimpses of the demons I was confronting in the Lord's name, hearing the voices, and having my heart race in the moment of battle. I was also quickly reminded of the sense of peace that overtook my soul, as the Holy Spirit took control of my senses.

Did I have any fear that particular night? Yes, but for the others inside Preservation who did not yet have the trust in Jesus to protect them, or the belief that they were fighting a defeated foe. Most had accepted the reality of the ability of the demonic powers to bring pain and suffering into their lives, and yet, had witnessed the power of the Lord to defeat them over the last several months. They were moving forward in obedience, based on a hope of mostly unfulfilled promises as of yet. Fear still existed that the cancer would kill them, as the demonic constantly said to them. The promise of the renewal of the Land of Preservation was felt by many, as something to occur after their death. But Dragonslayer was telling them to concentrate on the battle before them, and not to be anxious about anything… for they were in His hands.

I knew by the time the sun rose that the Lord's forces had won the day. They were tired, but rested, when I talked with Ruth and Maria before they left for home. I was told how Ann had slept through everything. The children, other than Mariann, had spent most of the evening sleeping next to Jesus. Except for Council, most had trouble sleeping in the caves on a windy night inside, and only Quiet Walker and Elizabeth Ray were aware of the battle. I would not know of the ramifications of the battle, until after I received the following letter.

Sunday night: Message from Commander Tolip –

System stable. Attacks have ceased for the time being. Our Chief Commander Dragonslayer tending to wounded. Darkness has left the Land. Chief Commander Dragonslayer has transformed Preservation. New dwelling for parts.

Angelina, Anna and Tabitha have blended into Tabitha Ann. Tabitha Ann is with Dragonslayer, sitting on his shoulders. Joy is being held by Commander Dragonslayer as Angelina once had been. Mariann is positioned to his right, with her helmet on, singing and guarding. Hopi and Lila are positioned on his left. All children are either holding his hand or securely on his shoulders.

Liz spent an hour with Dragonslayer late last night. Dragonslayer wished to speak with her about recent behavior. Ann was also called to discuss priorities and attitude.

Council met this morning to discuss maintaining unity and being prepared for new attacks. Chief Commander Dragonslayer has informed us that they will come. However, with his strategy, we will not be defeated, only bruised and scarred.

Tolip – Commander
E.R.

After reading this, I phoned Maria to get more information of all that wasn't said in this memo. I was struggling with the news of Angelina and Anna blending with Tabitha, because it was sudden and unexpected. My struggle was with a sense of joy over their healing and a real sense of loss over the thought of never seeing them again in this life. Carol was feeling the same way and I knew that Bruce, being the only other outside person to have known them, would understand this loss. They each gave us love in their own way and they would be missed.

I was surprised by the responses of everyone inside over this. It was as though they were gone, but not forgotten...and this is the way it is supposed to be. They were all overwhelmed by the transformation of Preservation and its meaning now for their daily lives. Maria was exhausted as well and promised to write the next day to tell me all about the changes. I went to bed that night praising God in my prayers for His protection and trying to imagine what He had done to their world inside. I knew that wherever the essence of Angelina and Anna was, that they were safe and the memories of the abuse were gone. I asked the Lord if it was possible to occasionally be given a glimpse of them through Tabitha. When I received the following letter the next night, I discovered that I couldn't imagine the depth of the majesty and mystery of our Lord Jesus Christ. As challenging, if not mind-blowing, as this letter may be, it made perfect sense to me in how this displays the love and mercy of the Creator, fulfilling His promises.

Dear Pastor Chalberg,

I am going to try to explain what the Land of Preservation looks like now. It is very hard to put into words just how beautiful it is. Yesterday, Dragonslayer raised his hands and prayed, and all of a sudden there was an explosion of color. I never saw the ice melt that covered the land, it was just gone. And the colors...oh, the colors, all of the flowers that appeared are fresh and pretty. We have beautiful meadows and the trees are fully grown, green and shady. The river is so clear and sparkly that you can see the bottom and all of the fish swimming around. Animals and birds were everywhere suddenly and came up to us wanting to play. The air is crisp and pure, and Sacred Mountain looks so special with so much to see and touch.

Dragonslayer led us to the middle of the land, where he had built us a place to live. It is not a house like we think of when we think house. I don't know how to describe it, but Ann says it is a sphere. I think it looks like a giant shiny ball but made out of diamonds because it shines like a sparkling rainbow. Every way you look at it you see a different view. It's not covered in glass, but something different that lets you see out into the land, but not into the ball.

To get in, we go through this pretty gate. Inside the first big round room are many doors all leading into other rooms in this circle. This big round room is the meeting room for Circle Council and Dragonslayer. The first door on the right has Ann's name above the door. The door looks like one of those musty old doors you'd find in a monastery and looks real heavy. Ann let me see inside it. She has a huge library with a ladder going way up the wall and it rolls by the shelves. Her room is done in dark wood and looks like a library should. She has a rectangular bed with green sheets. In another corner is this huge desk with a computer and math stuff on it. She has a big stuffed chair with a table next to it. On the table is her Bible and a book on history.

The second door belongs to Liz and Dragonslayer must have put something between the walls, because Liz has a loud room and Ann's is so quiet, not like the house outside. Liz has a funny door too, all of these splatters of paint and a sign in the middle, Enter At Your Own Risk – Toxic Waste Dump. Inside, well, you just have to see it. Each wall is painted bright primary colors. There is a big stereo with music that Dragonslayer selected for Liz. It has the beat she likes, but no bad words. I heard it and it's fast music. She has basketball wastebaskets cuz Liz don't pick up stuff, but she likes to make basket shots. Her bed is a hammock. In one corner there is a gate leading to an indoor mushroom garden, with all kinds of mushrooms that you can eat. Liz has a lot of posters on the walls about justice and sticking up for the poor and hurting. And you know what, Dragonslayer put this power poster art piece on the blue wall and it says, "Lest You Forget!"

Next to Liz is Jennifer. Her door has carved whales on it. Inside there are ocean and tropical forest murals. Rainforest and ocean music plays. In one corner there are dolphins in a huge pool and a ladder so Jennifer can go swimming with her friends. Jennifer has a dirt forest floor. She has parrots and other birds flying around in it, because she has trees growing in her room. She sleeps on a cot with animal sheets.

The next one is Marie's and it has murals with little children on it. Inside is a big soft rug and lots of toys and children's books. The kids all live in the next room to hers, I think because of the toys. I don't know why the toys are not in the children's room and maybe it is cuz Dragonslayer wants them to sleep. Their door has balloons with each of their names on it. Inside it has one huge tree, but not a tree, more like a bush or vine. On the trunk it says, 'I am the vine and you are the branches.' The branches spread out and each one has a little nest that is made into a bed. The nest is made of gold fleece and it is very soft. Mariann has the highest nest and Joy and Tabitha Ann have the lowest. On the walls are Bible stories with Noah and the rainbow, the birth of Jesus, one about Moses and another about David. Lots of bright ones are painted in the pictures and they are beautiful. The vine has a way of telling the children the Bible stories at night when the kids are in their nests. Mariann says the pictures can move and change too, just like on the box (TV).

Next is Louise and her door is different. It is made of flowers and it smells nice with roses spelling her name on it. Her room inside is a garden room. Her bed is like a giant rose with petals for sheets. It is warm and pretty in her room and the kids love to come in and see her flowers.

Next is my room and I like it so much. My door has a dove on it. Inside is safe and warm and Louise brings me fresh flowers for my table so I can enjoy them. I have a kitchen in my room and Louise and I like to make cookies for the children. My bed is soft and warm and on my walls are words from Dragonslayer to help me stay strong in him. I like that.

Raquel's room is next and it has a pretty eagle carved on her door. Indian flute music plays inside her room. It looks like a teepee. She sleeps on a mat on the floor. In the middle of the room is a campfire and the Eagle Clan shares her room with her. She is the only one with another door in her room leading to the outside. I don't know how, but it leads directly to Sacred Mountain. Her room has lots of feathers and Indian stuff in it. She has a small table with this strange pen with feathers on it and keeps her journals and poems on this table.

Ruth has the next room and the door is plain white. On the inside is a bed with flowers and all of these Bible books everywhere. She has a table and pretty throw rug.

Elizabeth Ray has the next room and on her door it says, 'Keeper of History.' Inside it looks like a business with all of these filing cabinets and vaults. There is a computer with timelines on the walls. It is a busy room and goes too fast for me.

Mari has the next door with a picture of a lion on it. It is very peaceful and nice.

The last door on the left is the door to the leaders' room. I don't know what this one looks like cuz I haven't been in it.

I hope that I did a good job of explaining it. There's so much here to explain that I'm tired of trying. I wish that you could see just how beautiful everything is for yourself. Know what? Dragonslayer is preparing a banquet for all of us, kind of a party or open house celebration.

I Love You, Maria

"If we submit everything to reason, our religion will have nothing in it mysterious or supernatural. If we violate the principles of reason, our religion will be absurd and ridiculous."
Blaise Pascal, *Pensees* (17th century)

> *"We should take care not to make the intellect*
> *our god; it has, of course, powerful muscles,*
> *but no personality."*
> Albert Einstein, *Out of My Later Years* (1950)

> **"To you it has been granted to know the mysteries**
> **of the kingdom of God, but to the rest it is in parables,**
> **in order that seeing they may not see,**
> **and hearing they may not understand."**
> **Luke 8: 10**

I thought about Pascal's statement on reason, the supernatural and religion, as I read Maria's letter. As I've stated before, I do not consider myself a 'religious man', rather a man of faith in God. This faith was a gift from God, introduced to me by way of reason. Jesus knew that I wouldn't accept a belief that wasn't both reasonable and experiential. By this I mean that I struggled for many years to understand the mysteries that surround and sometimes support our understanding of God. I started however, on a false premise, that mystery and reason could not be mutually sustainable in a definition of reality. Einstein's thought is the key to the faulty premise. Reason, driven by intellect only, is an apathetic relationship, but reason empowered by love can have a personality that is mysteriously akin to God's plan in Jesus Christ.

> **"Let no man deceive himself. If any man among you think**
> **that he is wise in this age, let him become foolish that**
> **he may become wise. For the wisdom of the world**
> **is foolishness before God."**
> **1 Corinthians 3: 18-19**

Whether or not you believe what Maria describes in her letter as being possible or not, isn't as important as what you believe is possible or even reasonable by God. The end results of all that was 'created' by Dragonslayer, as a fulfillment of His promise to the System before the chemotherapy, is both reasonable and consistent of His relationship with them. It is also exemplary of His relationship with us, as He defines it in the Holy Scriptures. His renewal of Preservation is a reflection of what waits for us when

173

we finally get to go home. It is not a perfect reflection however, as we are unable to fathom the reality of heaven and it must remain a mystery for now. But like any worthy mystery, it has the possibility of being solved reasonably, by understanding God's methods of healing the brokenhearted. Let's look at the letter again.

Dragonslayer begins the renewal at His appointed time, after the renewed faith of a little girl, the weakest one in the land, brought a renewed hope for the future of everyone in Preservation. It would not be the last time that Joy would need healing to confirm her trust in Jesus, and it reaffirmed that she would not make the journey alone. Joy chose Jesus in spite of her memories and the pressure put upon her by the spirits at war around her. There is an evolution that occurs when anyone of any age chooses the path of Jesus Christ.

"Do not be conformed to this world, but be transformed by the renewing of your mind, that you may prove what the will of God is, that which is good and acceptable and perfect."
Romans 12:2

This letter reflects the awesome power and illuminates some of the mystery of Jesus at work in the kingdom of God. He creates with a word and His creation draws us into it by its sheer beauty. Maria describes her 'natural world' inside, I believe, as we were always intended to behold God's creation in this physical world. I know that we may have screwed this world up beyond our ability to recover it, but I am secure in the knowledge that one day God will make all things new again.

The creation of the new home for all of the System was the best part of the event for me. Here, Jesus built individual rooms that support and nourish each individual's needs and personality. He reaffirms their uniqueness in His eyes, as well as their freedom to grow in their knowledge of Him...while living with Him. It should be remembered that, though this may appear to be a mansion with many rooms made in heaven, it is not their final destination. It is a home where Jesus lives, teaches, protects, encourages and offers the patience of love, to those on their journey to know it. He does not offer to Ann or Jennifer anything less in their accommodations, than He gave to those who had already accepted Him.

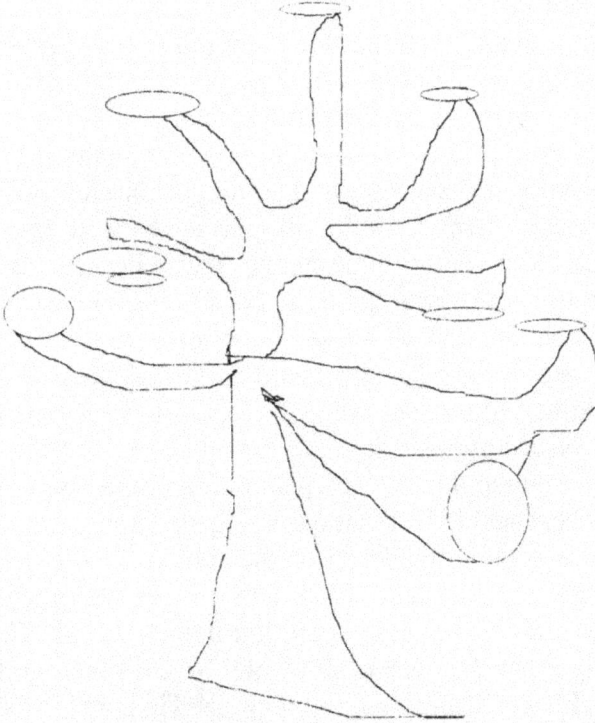

Daddy and mama I see prte butrflis   they   go my nos and tikl mama
I love you daddy you be warm and be safe   mama   you go nit nit
with daddy and mariann plez   and lamee com   mama I go dragunslar
watr and get dragunslar soap ok   mama I love my mama   mama
chrch man hurt lamee I mak pitur my brd nest I slep I be big girl I be
way hi

Mariann sent this drawing of her new bedroom and nest inside their new home in Preservation. When I asked her why she hadn't drawn the wall murals she described as Maria did, I heard this audible gasp on the phone and simply, "Too hard for me daddy!" I later learned from her that each child had their own nest, starting from the lower right side going up of: Joy, Tabitha Ann, Hopi, Lilah, Mariann, Penny and the Little Ones.

Plate # 6

It might also be remembered that, although this appears to be a paradise for the System, evil still exists within its borders and will until the day that Christ returns. This fact will keep all of us aware of our need for Him in either world. The System will barely get settled in before the enemy is attacking again. Sergio's ex-girlfriend will die of breast cancer this week. She was the same age as Maria. This puts him in a nasty mood about his luck with women with big breasts and cancer, putting Maria and Louise into a depressed state.

Maria wanted to attend Bob's church to hear his sermon on the Wednesday before Easter. She was going to have the opportunity to hold his baby during the service, and holding babies is the one thing that brings her joy…almost as much as talking about Jesus. The System was drawing closer to the pastor and his family, as he reached out to them. I went to the service as well, in order to put a face with the voice over the phone. I was hoping that maybe this man and his family would be the ones to become caregivers in our place, when we had to move south for a few years. They were local, loved the Lord and seemed to be a logical choice to walk alongside of the System when we could not. Within four months this will be accomplished.

Bob will take this journey planning an itinerary of his design. It will be a reasonable one that quickly gets detoured by God, and the mysterious ways of God will be the subject of a lot of prayer time for them together. When Carol and I meet with them to pass on whatever we can to ease their journey, we will leave with the knowledge that they are in for a hell of a ride ahead, beginning it with such confidence. Bob, his wife Tina and I will begin to communicate as needed over fax machines and the telephone. Elizabeth Ray will forward all of the copies of their travails to me, to help maintain a balance and consistency for the System to consider as they face differing viewpoints. They exercise this option often and while I didn't like saying alternative viewpoints behind his back, it gave me the chance to open my own thoughts to new ideas, as well as praying that the both of us would hear and incorporate God's plan for the good of the System.

Maria was surprised and ecstatic that another Christian pastor and his family accepted her as a multiple and didn't treat her like a freak. She immediately began pouring herself into the relationship.

Mariann didn't quite understand what was happening with the adults, but she clearly understood that children her age were being nice to her and wanting to play with her in the outside world. They even asked for her by name to come out from wherever and be with them. This was something totally new in her experience. Tabitha would come out eventually, usually when Tina was around because she spoke Spanish and could converse with her.

It was clear that the Lord had brought them together as they bonded quickly having Him in common. Tina had suffered some abuse early in life and Maria became a confidant and friend, as she worked through issues affecting her adult life. Maria began sharing her hopes and dreams about healing and the future with them. Many in the System were reluctant to attempt a friendship at first, while we were still around to contact easily, and some never felt comfortable doing so for reasons they only shared with me. One day Maria shared a dream she had with Bob, looking for an interpretation as to its meaning. I don't think that he was surprised, having met Raquel through her writings that she would respond in a letter the next day questioning his interpretation.

(A memo from Raquel to Pastor Bob – Maria's present church has not made contact with her in over a month and your church seems to be the only one reaching out to her. – Elizabeth Ray)

Greetings from Quiet Walker

I listened to Maria tell you of her dream and I have listened to the Great Spirit after I heard your words. The interpretation of the dream is not what you believe. The bubble represents this present life on earth with much trouble and suffering. One can not escape this bubble until the Great Spirit releases one from it. Yet, while in the bubble, the Great Spirit uses the suffering of one, to help with the suffering of another. Through suffering, one finds the meaning of one's life. Suffering leads to wisdom in the bubble.

Those who know the Great Spirit find great peace in knowing that he is with them in the bubble; comforting them, absorbing their pain and teaching them. Yet they long for the day when the

177

bubble will be burst open and they will arrive into the spiritual dimension of heaven. All in the bubble are dissatisfied; for they hunger for something that they know in their spirit, but not in their mind...a longing for an unfallen world of harmony, balance and connectedness.

They long in their spirits for that which they cannot have in their bubble...their fulfilled desire for heaven. It was with the dream that the Great Spirit gave Maria the gift of understanding her suffering; to be an encourager to others through her brokenness and to continue to long for heaven with Jesus; where there will be no more tears and no more suffering.

May the Great Spirit bring you deep peace.
Quiet Walker

"To know the meaning of friendship one need only travel the journey of Jonathan. For Jonathan became one in spirit with David and he loved him as himself."
- Quiet Walker

Easter Sunday came and my family had a delicious dinner with Maria's family in her home. The conversation was cautious at best, as no one in her family acknowledged the existence of parts to anyone outside of their circle, even though they knew that we knew. We referred to the System as Maria in front of them, but thanked Louise quietly for the meal before leaving. Driving home, my daughter was perplexed and saddened for all of them because she knew firsthand what the family was missing out on. She thought it was such a waste of time and energy not having a relationship with so many beautiful people, simply because of fear of the unknown and not wanting her 'disorder' to reflect on them. She asked. "How can they not take the risk of knowing all of them fully, when the System can give back so much love and so many talents? At least the children should understand how so much of who they are is from the System. What are they afraid of in not loving Mariann or Tabitha? I just don't understand it."

That night I received a letter from Elizabeth Ray detailing their Thursday night worship service in Preservation called for by Jesus. I also received some 'extra' tidbits.

*Dragonslayer spent time explaining to Louise how to prepare the banquet meal that he was going to give for us. Louise listened carefully and then went and prepared the lamb and bread. We were all invited by Dragonslayer to the supper and everyone came. We were seated around a long table after the children rushed in to sit next to him. When all were seated and quiet, Dragonslayer rose and said, "**I have eagerly waited for this time with you.**" Then he proceeded to explain to all of us why he died on the cross, rose again, and what that means for us.*

He talked about his body being like the bread that Louise had pre-pared, bread being the staple of life for the physical body and he being the staple of life for the spiritual body. He talked about the significance of what he did...how his Father planned the shedding of his blood so that we could have life. He told us how our souls were purchased back by his sacrifice. He told us that the evil one is actively seeking to take us from him, but that he is greater than the evil one and we belong to him.

He warned us that we must stand firm in our loyalty to him and that there will be attacks from the evil one. We must pray for God's strength to resist the temptations of evil. We must be alert to the attacks and pray for discernment. He told us how he will always be with us, if we allow him to walk with us in our life. We can always go to him with our questions and fears. He told us that he sent us others to disciple us and teach us and we are to listen carefully, and he will guide our paths.

Then he prayed for us and told us to eat and enjoy. The children climbed up in his lap and ate bread. Dragonslayer did not eat or drink the wine, but simply held the children and talked with us.

Easter Sunday morning at dawn: the system arose early and everyone went to the clearing where we could hear lovely music all around us. The land seemed anew and fresh. Dragonslayer was

179

there and radiant. The children were full of energy and dancing around Dragonslayer singing Mariann's song. Joy was hesitant but allowed Ruth to hold her while she observed. We stood before Dragonslayer and worshipped him...thanking him for his love for us...telling him that we were unworthy of that love...and singing praises to him and glory to his Father. After the celebration, Louise began Easter dinner for her family and yours. Maria started a conversation with Jesus about friends.

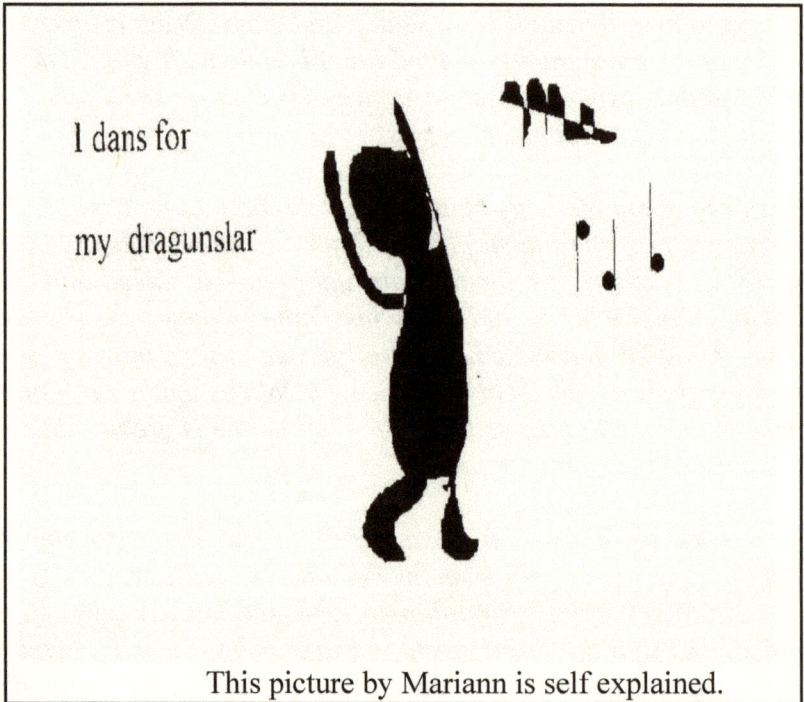

I dans for

my dragunslar

This picture by Mariann is self explained.

Plate # 7

Maria: Jesus, I need to talk to you. I get really sad when I think about my friends moving away. I don't have anyone like Pastor Chalberg and I know it is selfish of me to want him with me, but I love being with him.

Jesus: Why do you love being with him Maria?

I could just listen to him talk to me all day. I learn so much from him and he is safe. I don't feel scared around him and he is soft and warm when he hugs me. He doesn't think I am stupid and he treats me nice. He understands me and doesn't hit or yell at me.

Do you love him more than Me?

No, because I kind of have the most love I have for you and him. It's like I can't think of anyway that I could love you or him more. I love you both so much.

Do you love Me more than him?

I think so. I love you as my Lord. You died for me and gave me the only chance I had to get to heaven. I know that I am not heaven material, but you are and so I get to go to heaven because of you. I love you so much because you would do that for me. I don't love Pastor Chalberg that way. But I love to hug both of you and be with you and listen to you. I am never going to forget about him or get used to not having him around. He thinks that I will get over it, but you know Jesus that my heart will ache so much to be separated from him.

What about Carol?

I am going to miss her too, but you know that I love her too, but different than Pastor Chalberg. They're both my friends and I don't want them to leave. Is it selfish of me to want to be with them?

No my child. But remember that if you want to be my follower, then you must love me more than Pastor Chalberg, more than Rosalinda...more than anyone else. And you must carry your own cross and follow me to where I send you. Who do you think sent him to you?

You, Jesus.

Yes, Maria, I sent him to you and he obeyed my calling. I know of your love for him and I know of the relationship between you. When I had to leave my disciples, did you not think that I was sad

and cried over our separation? But I knew that it is far better to obey the will of my Father. I sent the Holy Spirit to be their comforter and I told them I would be spiritually with them. It is that way with you and Michael. The enemy can not break the bond between you. You both desire to serve me and preach my message. Continue to pray for guidance and do not overlook those that I send to you for this purpose.

Will I ever see him again and be with him?

Yes, Maria, I know the plans I have for both of your lives. You will unite together again. Continue to pray for strength. Continue to pray for Michael and Carol as they do my work. And continue to lean on me when sadness comes, for I am here always and I am your friend.

Jesus, I still need Pastor Chalberg to teach me more about life. I don't know enough stuff and I still got problems with being a multiple and he helps me lots. What are we going to do when he leaves?

My child, do you not think that I know what is best for you? I know every need of your system. I will choose the right time. Do not be concerned about your abilities. I have given you many gifts and talents. I will give you the words to speak. I will guide you and teach you. Do not be afraid that you don't have the abilities to serve me. I am your ability.

Jesus, you understand don't you?

Yes, Maria I understand everything.

The next few months would pass quickly as we prepared our house to go on the market again. Ann had reached a settlement with the contractor to simply finish his obligations in the remodel and mark it up as one expensive lesson in trusting people, especially those who offer the promise of being Christian. The state didn't follow through on any of the claims against him and told her that her best recourse was to take him to civil court. Given all of her other problems, it didn't seem worth the risk of exposure. Ann was doing well in her classes at the university and Louise was earning the grade in the language class.

Louise and Maria were having difficulty with the changes in time schedules for Ann to be in school. They were not able to complete their chores with the same level of high efficiency as previously. Their daily routine had become a place of escape where they didn't have to deal with things outside of their chores. Now they were adjusting to the fact that it would never be the same again. We, Council and I, had to intervene with Ann's response to this drop in efficiency, as she continued to push them too hard in the midst of change. Getting her to lower her expectations was like pulling teeth.

Jennifer came back on Easter from wherever she was in Preservation and began checking out various environmental religious type groups. She was still not sure about Christianity and didn't think there were any teachings there about preserving nature. This was a door I entered, to begin talking with her about these issues beginning with God's covenant with Adam in the Garden of Eden.

Carol and I began to plan day trips on weekends to give them exposure to various experiences and opportunities to explore locally. We knew that the next outing would be for Mariann's baptism and we wanted to make it special for her. The suggestion of doing it in our backyard fountain, that I had just installed, just didn't seem a choice worthy for her or Dragonslayer. I talked to Mariann and asked how she wanted it done. *"I have to get all wet that is what Dragonslayer did!"* Council dumped it into my lap to decide when, where and how. So I in turn asked Helper to begin teaching her about the meaning of baptism so I could test her before the event. I had no doubt that she would begin getting instruction from Dragonslayer on these things. As we moved forward, we continued to prepare for separation from the System.

We want to alert you to the current concern about separation between you and us. Although we have worked hard to prepare them, some still struggle with it. Mariann is the neediest here. She understands that you have to do Dragonslayer's work and that you will still have contact with her, but she already struggles with the widening time between visits now.

If it is too long, she begins to weaken and want her daddy. We believe that she is determined to not lose her daddy this time. All she wants is to "go nite nite, keep warm and get hugs." We try to get her to transfer that to her doggy for warmth and companionship, but that isn't working. Mariann has the strongest bond with you. She defends you on the inside whenever anyone says anything against you, even when they're joking. She models herself after you and listens more to you than to us. She doesn't understand multiplicity and wants to live with you and Carol now. We are concerned how she will react when you leave.

Maria is strongly attached to you as well. She is closer to you than she is to Sergio, because of how much she has learned about positive relationships from you and Carol. She prays for you two constantly and likes to sit and listen to you talk about Jesus. She has learned so much from you about so many things, that we are afraid she might go back into her shell when you leave, if there is no support person to take your place. We are not yet sure if Pastor Bob is able to handle all of what that means or wants to even try. We have real concerns about how this could affect his family as well. Lindsay tries, but she is in a demanding program and can't see Maria often. We feel that she babies Maria too much and doesn't help her in becoming self-sufficient by having her depend too much upon Lindsay.

When we mention your leaving to Liz, we notice an agitation and refusal to talk about it. Although she portrays a tough skin attitude, she will be affected by the separation. You are probably the only person in her life who can relate to her in teaching positive values. Liz doesn't trust anybody, but she trusts you. We know that she has a deep admiration for her cowboy preacher and her own kind of love for you.

Raquel seems spiritually connected to you and hasn't shown any distress about you physically moving from the area. However, she does not rotate out much these days and her contact with you is on a spiritual plane rather than a physical one.

Ann says that she will not be bothered by it, but we believe this is a mask. Ann does not realize how much your contact with the others has reduced her stress so that she can function at a higher level. We know too that Ann has enjoyed the few times where the two of you have gotten into deep intellectual issues. Ann thrives on that and has a difficult time cultivating that in relationships with anyone else. She too trusts no one else but you.

We will prepare as best we can and then try to resolve the problems that arise from the move. We know that for many, this will be traumatic. We also know that we need to find other support like you have given us, apart from Bruce, if we wish to continue healing. We just are not sure how this will be accomplished. We will listen to our Commander and appreciate any advice you can offer.

Mother's Day was approaching so Carol and I decided to lift Maria's feelings by recognizing her as a mother. As it turned out it also started something new for Carol, as she was given several nice handmade cards from the children of the System. Ann appreciated our efforts and wrote the following:

Mike and Carol,
Thank you for making Maria's mother's day special for her. The nursery outing was the highlight of her day. Louise told Maria that she would share the strawberry tree with her so Maria could make it her mother's day flowers. If it had not been for you two, Maria would not have had a mother's day receiving no cards or flowers from anyone. She was more worried that her mother had not received the flowers that she sent, because the mother doesn't call to say thanks. Ruth called her because Maria was concerned and all she said was, "Yeah, thanks," and hung up.

Usually I just ignore holidays like these. Every year Maria honors her mother and father and every year she is ignored. So we honor cruelty, hatred and rejection, and we watch everyone refuse to acknowledge her kindnesses and caring attitude. No wonder that she gets confused when she is told that she is a bad parent.

Anyway, thanks for showing her that you care about her. She seems to grow every time that she is with you. Although most of that growth is torn down after returning home within a few days, she still retains some of her happy memories with you. Thanks!

There was a debate within Preservation over who should have priority in time out on the outside. Since some primary issues of stress seemed to be solved for the moment inside, people wanted to be outside discovering, relaxing, learning and establishing new relationships, because they had accepted our imminent departure. It was one of those moments when Circle Council would need the wisdom of Solomon to satisfy everyone. The outcome was given as an edict and refusal to abide by it meant loss of current privileges. The three main statements were these:

1. All parts have equal rights even if they are unaware of them or unable to accept them at this time of their development.
2. All parts have equal worth and all functions performed by these parts are to be considered equally important.
3. Sunday will be a day to allow parts to grow in their relationships with others and no housework or schoolwork will be done on that day.

The other 8 are mostly an encouragement of particular parts to continue growing in their areas, while remembering to share. There are adjustments to these guidelines that come in a few years, but for the most part they hold up well in maintaining the integrity of the System. Ann will need the changes when she begins work so she can keep the System out of debt, at least for another 6 years. Ann will receive a scholarship within a month to pay for her education and she notices that her 'luck' is changing. Rosalinda gets accepted into a major university with a scholarship to pay for most of it. Then Ann gets accepted into the school of her choice, along with another scholarship and she is perplexed as to why suddenly good things are happening. She began looking at these things as a sort of payoff for her hard work and accomplishments…in short, an ego trip that the enemy was supporting. Others in the System were getting on this bandwagon as something they deserved as well.

The enemy of course wanted them to look at it this way, instead of seeing it as the plans of Dragonslayer. Yet, they wanted the end result to be confusion and not self-confidence, so they started wrecking havoc in other areas of the family's life. The oldest daughter was out-of-state and began having seizures. She called her grandparents, who immediately without any real information called Maria to scream at her for being such a worthless parent in allowing this to happen. They yelled at her for not calling them, they couldn't do anything anyway, and that was her fault as well.

Even though Ann was on top of the situation and handling it from home, she couldn't tell the parents that as they wouldn't have accepted that 'Maria' could be that competent. Instead, the System had to listen to the ravings of the father about Maria being irresponsible and uncaring to everyone in the family. The whole System was becoming stressed and finding it hard to maintain control and balance from the repeated phone calls and they could not control the grandparents from getting involved either, which produced nothing but stress. Between school; disability ministry, church, immediate family and helping Claudia a long distance away, the 'good luck' was fleeting at best. The realization that the spiritual attacks were increasing was becoming obvious to most but needed to be reinforced... Raquel enters the picture.

Report to Council on Quiet Walker's words:

I have come down from the mountain to speak to you of the words of the Great Spirit. Our system is being led into empty deception. Our eyes must watch out. Where is our ground of confidence? We do not walk according to the flesh anymore. Listen to the Great Spirit's words. We walk in newness of life. We have the spirit within us. Everything is found in our relationship to Dragonslayer and not in our achievements in the flesh. We are not to be troubled when we are called irresponsible and not performing to the standards of the world. Instead, we are to rejoice in the Lord and worship in the spirit.

What we are and will ever be is all found in the finished work of Dragonslayer. TETELESTAI we must remember. We are put in right standing with God because Dragonslayer paid our debt in full. We are acceptable to God based on who we are in Dragonslayer, not on our performances in the flesh. We are justified by faith alone.

Beware of those who mutilate the word and subscribe to false circumcision. They profess to be true Christians, but they are dogs... evil workers. They attempt to lead us into the traditions of men interwoven with the word of God. Do not buy into it because it calls itself Christian. Keep on watching...for the dogs are like scavengers, greedy and not satisfied until they absorb us into their deception. Remember, Dragonslayer made us alive with him...having forgiven us all of our transgressions on the cross.

He canceled out each certificate of death written against us. He removes the power of the flesh by putting to death our old self. We are anew in him. Our confidence is no longer in the flesh, but in him who saved us. We take God at his word. Therefore, do not be taken captive by those forces who place great importance upon accomplishments, the right committees, the right dress or education. Beware of anyone who comes along as a wolf in sheep's clothing seeking to catch you by the philosophy – "yes, you are saved by grace, but you have to work it out in the flesh." God's standard depends solely on Dragonslayer...not performance.

Listen and you will gain wisdom. Our confidence is not in the church, the leaders or even our baptism. Our confidence is in Jesus Christ, our Dragonslayer and Lord. Our goal is to know him and to be like him...all else is nothing. We have been set free by God from the flesh, because it cannot please him. No, our God has circumcised our heart by the spirit and not by the flesh, so we must glorify him by worshipping him in spirit and in truth. ***Do not be troubled by the attacks and do not be afraid. Remember: we are complete in Jesus Christ alone.***

Helper added this note to the above fax:

Kid out of the hospital. System highly stressed. Council decided to not tell Maria about Claudia until she is home and safe. Internal kids very needy due to stress of adults. Liz wants permission to do damage to grandfather – not granted. Ann complains that she tries to better the system's life, but black cloud follows her around. Every time she proceeds forward positively, crap happens. We're tired...

When I talked to Raquel about her letter, I learned about what they were hearing in sermons from the two churches they attended, and the responses of several members to Ann's apparent successes. I suggested to Council that they have an internal Bible study of the Book of Romans to help understand what Raquel was giving them.

Also Helper sent me Mariann's answer to why I should baptize her soon. She made her own card on the computer that said, "Why I Be Baptizd" on the cover, and on the inside she wrote:

Dragunslar tel me mariann let pepl no you lov me and you belong to me and you my child. I say ok dragunslar I be baptizd to tel pepl I be dragunslar strong. The end mariann.

It was a beautiful card and I keep it in my office. I let Helper know the questions that I would ask her and anyone else at the baptism, which we had decided would occur at the beach – weather permitting. I suggested May 17th as a possibility because the weather had been bad for a couple of weeks and it looked like it might open up by then. We also invited Liz over before then to go out for burgers and beer to help her cool off from residual anger. Council replied:

We cannot allow Liz any alcohol because of the side effects on the medication we're taking. Liz may have non-alcoholic beer or wine if she wishes but we will switch her inside if she attempts to consume beer. According to Dragonslayer, Tabitha Ann and Mariann are ready for baptism, but Joy is not. Tabitha Ann will shadow close to Mariann and they will be baptized together. She will hear her name and respond on the inside simultaneously. We have talked with Mariann about the ocean, but we believe she still does not have the concept of that much water clearly understood in her mind. We have set up the following rules for her at the beach. She is NOT to leave your sight. She is to ALWAYS hold yours or Carol's hand when she is near or in the water, as she does not know how to swim. She is NOT to eat sand and ALWAYS obey you or Carol. The weekend of the 17th is approved. What time on Saturday do you want them over? Mariann said 3 AM and we told her that Mr. Miguel will decide. They can spend Friday night at your house if you wish.

Dragonslayer called a meeting to discuss Ann's letter of acceptance from the college. He addressed the reason why he had her selected and stressed how the system will be serving him while teaching. He told Ann that she will be a very popular teacher among the students and that many students will be coming to her with serious situations. He told the system that he will give them the words and resources to help these children, and that Ann is not to be afraid to stand for truth. He will protect and guide her.

He then talked about where teaching math fell on the importance scale, as opposed to leading lost sheep to him. He told Ann that it was not a coincidence or the result of hard work that resulted in the placement. He has placed her in this program because of his plan. Liz questioned him as to why he wouldn't send us to some exciting far away place to tell people about him. He replied;

"You are needed here for a reason. I have given you work here to complete. If you cannot obey me and complete the work that I have already assigned you here, why should I send you somewhere else?"

Liz continued: "Why then are you sending Mike to Alaska and we gotta stay here?" Dragonslayer gave her that look and said;

"Did I say I was sending him to Alaska, Liz?"

Liz responded with, "No, you won't tell us where he's going or if he's going."

"Mike trusts me. Has he finished all of the work I have given him here to do?"

 Liz: "How do I know?"

"Mike knows."

Ann: "Let's get back to our situation. I want to teach math."

Dragonslayer: "You will Ann. But remember to continue to ask yourself...Am I serving the creator of that math or the math itself. I have given you an abundance of blessings and provisions. As surely as I give them, I can take them away. You will be my soldier in enemy territory. Many of my soldiers have run from the battle and have sought comfortable places in Christian schools and home schools. They have left the children in the enemy's hands. I am sending you

to the front lines as a public school teacher. You will be thrust into committees and curriculum that is not of my teaching. I will give you the strength and wisdom to show those who are being led astray by the false teachers, the real truth of my love for them. There will be many attacks and much tribulation but stand firm and continue to stay close to me. Ann, I am especially concerned about our relationship. I want to spend more time with you, teaching you my ways. I have given you many gifts and I wish for you to use those gifts as much as you can to serve me. Are you willing, Ann?"

Ann: "Yes."

"I am the master teacher from where you will receive your finest training to go forth and teach others of me."

After the meeting, everyone gathered for a celebration and the kids were given tambourines and shakers. They danced and giggled while Ann and Dragonslayer talked together privately, sitting quietly against the wall leading to the wildflower garden. We will be meeting with Dragonslayer later this week about time management for all of us.

> **"And the Lord's bondservant must not be quarrelsome, but be kind to all, able to teach, patient when wronged, with gentleness correcting those who are in opposition, if perhaps God may grant them repentance leading to the knowledge of the truth, and they may come to their senses and escape the snare of the devil, having been held captive by him to do his will."**
> **2 Timothy 2: 24 – 26**

Chapter Nine

"Every Child Comes With A Message..."

"Behold, children are a gift of the Lord;"
Psalm 127:3

"Children, obey your parents in the Lord, for this is right...
And fathers, do not provoke your children to anger; but
Bring them up in the discipline and instruction of the Lord."
Ephesians 6:1, 4

"Forgiveness is the answer to the child's dream
of a miracle by which what is broken is made
whole again, what is soiled is again made clean."
Dag Hammarskjold, *Markings* (1964)

We were a week away from Mariann and Tabitha's baptism, the weather was getting worse and the spiritual attacks were on the increase. The long range forecast had suddenly changed and it was not only going to be stormy through the weekend, storms were lining up in the Pacific so that heavy rain was expected to be continuous for several weeks. When I called Mariann on Sunday night, I explained how we might have to postpone the baptism until we had a break in the weather. She reminded me that Dragonslayer had said – 17 Saturday. I explained how I was sure that He didn't want us to get sick doing it in the cold weather, but that we would talk again on Wednesday to see how the weekend looked. Her response was, *"I talk to Dragonslayer Daddy."* Helper continued his preparations of Mariann for baptism and Council sent this note on Tuesday night.

Helper is trying to prepare Mariann for her baptism and a possible delay, but she is so excited that he is finding it difficult to contain her enthusiasm. He talked again about the vastness of the ocean and how the waves try to grab you. Mariann told him that she is Dragonslayer strong and Mr. Miguel is big and the waves can't eat him. She said that the water works for Dragonslayer and he is going to help Mr. Miguel baptize Mariann, so the water will obey him. Helper decided to quit while he was ahead.

I remembered as I read this that Tabitha Ann had been baptized into the Santeria cult and given the orisha, Yemaya. This demonic god was supposed to have power over the ocean, rivers and waterways. She was also still hanging around Preservation, trying to get one of the children to invite her back in. Since the Catholic Church had given Yemaya the mask of Our Lady of Regla in the 1500s, in order to bring the pagans into the church in Cuba, her connection to seashore rituals had become known in Santeria circles as the mother of all human beings.

One thing I have learned is to not underestimate the power of my enemies, even though I know that none can overpower Jesus in battle. This would mean that I needed to be prepared as well with the armor of God, and not orchestrate the baptism my way, but get out of the way when Jesus would use me to baptize her. I didn't want to supply the enemy with any more opportunities to hurt the System. I began praying for more time to prepare the System and me. By Wednesday evening, I thought this was going to happen, as we had some of the worst weather in a long time happening here. All of the forecasters were in agreement that it would continue through the weekend and into next week.

When I called Mariann that night, I was pretty confident that I could make her understand the need to wait. In fact, I was so confident that I told her to ask Dragonslayer to confirm my position. I thought that she hadn't really asked Him, responding more from her desire to make it happen, when she said, *"Dragonslayer already say – 17 Saturday, daddy, don't you listen?"* I decided that it was time for another 'fleece' test. So I told her that to do this, we would need for Dragonslayer to clear the weather up by Saturday and…as if this wasn't arrogant enough on my part…that it would need to be warm weather so that none of us would get sick. Her only response was, *"Okay Daddy, I tell Dragonslayer."*

When the weather suddenly became partly cloudy on Thursday, I was somewhat surprised along with every weather person in the Bay Area. They still predicted that the storms had 'stalled in the Pacific', but would push on in on Friday and the weekend. I can still remember all of them scratching their heads on Friday, as the skies cleared and the temperature rose into the low 90s. I called Mariann to confirm that we were on for Saturday…if the weather held. Some forecasters stated how they had never seen anything like this, with so many storms stacked and seemingly stopped. All Mariann asked me was *"How warm you want it daddy?"*

It was clear to me by then, that Dragonslayer had a purpose, as well as the time and temperature, for setting aside Saturday the 17th to accomplish this event to honor Him. The System would come over early Saturday, 9AM and not 3AM as Mariann requested, to leave for the beaches south of Half Moon Bay. They sent me another note on Friday night with the following:

Mariann is very excited about her day tomorrow. I hope that you are rested and ready. That child has more energy than all of the adult parts put together. Ann will be taking the weekend off and resting inside for her finals coming up. Would you please remind Maria to take her medication on Saturday night and Sunday morning. She doesn't like taking the holistic medicine that Ann has us on, along with her prescriptions. Liz tried to get Mariann to not keep asking Dragonslayer about making it warm for Mr. Miguel and Mariann. Mariann smiled at her and said, "You want to go in the water too?" Liz threw up her hands and said, "Damn kid!"

Now I used to live on the coast above Half Moon Bay, and any weekend that was clear and in the 90s was solid with traffic all day long, going to and from the beaches. We left for Pescadero beach as soon as they arrived, with a picnic lunch and bread and water to hold communion after the baptism. I laughed as we drove there in virtually no traffic, arriving at a mostly deserted beach. It was great and a little overwhelming at the same time. When the water proved to be around freezing to me, I decided to wait awhile to let it warm up, while I began asking Mariann about all that she knew about her Dragonslayer…and why she wanted to be baptized. I asked the same questions that I would ask any one in her place but said in a way that she understood the intent and importance. Examples: Why do you want to be put in the water in Dragonslayer's name?

What does Dragonslayer do with the water? Who is Jesus to you?

She wasn't quite sure why I needed to hear her answer for myself, and kept asking, *"Don't you know daddy, you do work for Dragonslayer?"* Tabitha came out briefly and answered the same questions in Spanish. By 11AM the beach was still deserted and the water very cold. The kids and adults still laugh about the day I turned blue, baptizing Mariann and Tabitha in the waves up to our waist. I had to take a break in between the baptisms because I thought my feet were going to fall off from exposure. As far as the children were concerned, the ocean might as well have been warm bath water. The cold did not affect them in the least, which was more of a lesson to me about trusting God over my senses. I also have a very funny picture from Mariann about the day but, alas, it doesn't come out well for insertion here.

While I was baptizing Mariann, she told me about all of the bright ones surrounding us and singing beautiful words. She told me afterward how she opened her eyes underwater and saw one there. Tabitha saw the same thing when I baptized her. I asked her if she saw Yemaya and she stated matter-of-factly how she doesn't come near Jesus. As Carol and I sat on the rocks with them looking out at the beautiful waves, Tabitha came out and began prophesying in very clear English. She quoted verbatim from the Book of Ezekiel about the last days of mankind. Carol and I both knew that it was the Holy Spirit talking through the child. We would never hear her speak with such clarity in English again.

We warmed up by going into a cleft in the cliffs along the beach and began singing praises to God and praying to the Lord. The place was like a little chapel in the cliff wall, so we sat and ate lunch before we had communion. Each person in the System was given some time to come out and pray, before we left for home. It was about 2PM when we exited the beach, and cars were stacking up along the coast highway as people arrived. The traffic was solid all of the way home...of people going to the beach.

That evening we discussed the events of the day and laughed heartily as the forecasters seemed perplexed...and relieved. The storms were on the move again and arrived by midday Sunday with a torrential downpour. I almost called one weather person who kept repeating how unusual and unexplainable the last few days had been and kept apologizing for the bad predictions. The

System agreed with Carol that I shouldn't waste my time, as no one would believe my explanation anyway. But for everyone in the System, Carol and I…17ᵗʰ Saturday will long be remembered.

> **"By awesome deeds Thou dost answer us**
> **in righteousness, O God of our salvation,**
> **Thou who art the trust of all the ends of the**
> **earth and of the farthest sea; Who dost establish**
> **the mountains by His strength, Being girded**
> **with might; Who dost still the roaring of the seas,**
> **The roaring of their waves, and the tumult of the**
> **peoples. And they who dwell in the ends of the**
> **earth stand in awe of Thy signs; Thou dost make**
> **the dawn and the sunset shout for joy."**
> **Psalm 65: 5 – 8**

> **"God thunders with His voice wondrously,**
> **Doing great things which we cannot comprehend.**
> **For to the snow He says, 'Fall on the earth,'**
> **And to the downpour and the rain, 'Be strong.'…**
> **Out of the south comes the storm,**
> **And out of the north the cold.**
> **From the breath of God ice is made,**
> **And the expanse of the waters is frozen.**
> **Also with moisture He loads the thick cloud;**
> **He disperses the cloud of His lightning.**
> **And it changes direction, turning around by His guidance,**
> **That it may do whatever He commands it**
> **On the face of the inhabited earth.**
> **Whether for correction, or for His world,**
> **Or for lovingkindness, He causes it to happen."**
> **Job 37: 5, 6, 9-13**

And I can attest that God will do all of these things and more, if that is what it takes to provide a way for His children to come into His kingdom. Tabitha Ann and Mariann were now 'officially' members and heirs in the kingdom of God, and I have to tell you… the enemy was not a bunch of happy campers. Within a few days, I could hardly walk because the arch of my foot felt like a knife was being shoved into it. When I went to my doctor to check it out, the pain disappeared upon entering the office and reappeared for a short time after leaving. It wasn't a wasted trip because he told me that I had skin cancer on a spot on my head that needed to be cut off. These events were not really a surprise, because I had grown to expect a counterattack every time we have a significant victory. It is part of the reality of living in two worlds by faith. No one can do it if they aren't assured that Jesus has already won the war.

The attacks on the System came as they returned home again. I received another fax on Monday from Council, revealing the current state of Maria's marriage. After filling me in about the reaction of Liz to Ann's school problems, the insurance problems with Claudia's care, Louise's Spanish final and car problems with Jose and Sergio, I learned more about how the children of the System responded to issues between Maria and Sergio.

Maria's husband is back to his normal routine of ignoring Maria. Helper has been trying to help her connect more with him. Maria told Helper about how she asks you questions about your day and you always talk with her. So she decided to ask Sergio more questions about his day and it backfired on her. When she would ask about anything, he would simply answer, "I don't want to talk about it." When she said, I bet you did great on your presentation, he responded, "Never mind about that – leave me alone." Maria went to her room crying and asked Helper what she did wrong and why doesn't Sergio want her in his life. Helper didn't know how to answer her and walked away leaving her still confused.

Mariann had watched everything and made a book about it on coloring paper that night. She drew a little flower with hearts around it and wrote, "Me and my daddy." The next page had a flower wilting and she wrote, "Me at Mr. Sergio's house." The next showed a flower looking stronger and healthier with, "Me back at daddy's house." The next showed a wilted flower at Sergio's house and the last page showed the flower dead with, "My daddy went away."

Helper understood what she was conveying...how we grow at your house and get smashed and crushed at home. Helper tried to tell the System not to lose hope. We might get crushed, but we won't be destroyed. He's concerned about when you leave, how we have no support that will provide the care that you two have given. You have helped us heal so much.

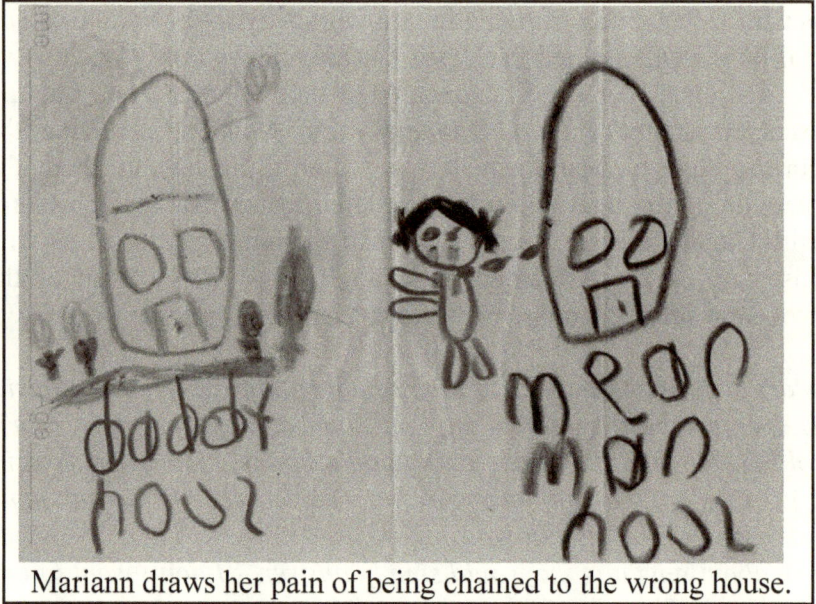

Mariann draws her pain of being chained to the wrong house.

Plate # 8

The System is now aware that marriage can be different than what they were raised under and have never known real love in a marriage. They want what they do not have and see how much more fulfilling life can be when someone loves and cares for you, like you and Carol have. They are becoming dissatisfied with their current situation, yet they cannot escape this because Maria will not leave. Thus, they see themselves as imprisoned and forced to live an unfulfilling life. This causes great concern for Council and they need your advice. Council informed the adults that they would only agree to divorce, if Maria, on her own without coercion, wants a divorce. For now, she is adamant that she will keep her vows no matter what.

I began counseling the adults about their overall situation, as a multiple in a marriage where only one wants to be married. They all wanted me to 'authorize' a divorce for Maria, knowing that she would obey whatever I told her to do. What they heard was that I could not and would not do that. It wasn't my decision to make, to break vows made between her and God. More importantly, they were not in a marriage where there was no hope of recovery and renewal. I asked them to read 1 Corinthians 7:1-16 and then talk about its meaning when we were together next. When Maria finally did ask me directly, I told her how the only one who can release her from her vows to God...is God.

Over the months that followed, we would talk about this issue many times, and many times I would tell the parts, "don't ask me to do what only God can do." Sometimes, when I was angered over Sergio's treatment of Maria and the System, I would ask the Lord if divorce was the best answer, but He never said yes. The System knew that I was divorced and why only three couples in almost 25 years were told to seek one as the best answer. I could not say yes, as long as I thought there was hope of healing for Sergio's troubled soul and subsequently their marriage. What I saw in Sergio was a man who never learned what real love in a healthy marriage was from his parents, or the role models that were in his life. Though ignorance is no excuse for abuse, there was no one else in his life who had the potential of teaching him about real love. Encouraging her to suffer in her marriage simply on the possibility that one day he might come to know Jesus Christ as we did, was some of the hardest counsel I've ever given. There were no easy answers here.

> *"And a woman who has an unbelieving husband,*
> *and he consents to live with her, let her not send*
> *her husband away. For the unbelieving husband*
> *is sanctified through his wife..."*
> **1 Corinthians 7: 13-14**

It is difficult to explain the reality of the spiritual realm, or how the beings there interact in our world to guide us, as in the case of angels, or misdirect us as the demons attempt to do. Even with the number of real, practical examples that will be shared in these books, it is not enough to prove to anyone who doesn't accept that plane of existence. I reiterate this now, because much of what follows in this and the last book will deal with how evil will try subtlety to enter every aspect of our lives. If you are not convinced that evil exists, or in the power of God's good love, then you don't need to go any further. If you do, then you will understand when I say that the attacks of evil upon the System, my wife and I, and anyone else connected with the presenting of these stories will be a constant in our lives. We will not always make the right choices and we will fall often, but the Lord will also be a constant whose power will be proven through our weaknesses and our victories. We, the System and I, received the following message the week after the baptisms. It helped to strengthen us, maybe it will you.

Council has received the following message from Quiet Walker:

Behold, I saw the one who slays the dragon coming out of the clouds. He spoke to me and this is what he said:

The warfare between the kingdom of Satan and the kingdom of God intensifies as the time draws near. Beware for there is a battle for the mind of the system. The enemy wants to keep you from putting your complete trust in me.

Remember, the devil is a liar. He will try to deceive you into believing that there is no heaven or hell and that salvation is simply an illusion. He will tell you that there is no salvation from your problems. Do not believe him. Do not allow your mind to be blinded by the god of this age. He will tell you that God is a liar, but you know the truth and the truth will set you free.

Do not believe him when he tells you that God's way is not the best way. When he says that God is just spoiling your fun and your way is best, remember that my word and my law is for your benefit. The devil is the great accuser of those who trust me. You have been plucked from the fire of hell. Remember that your accuser has been thrown down and you have overcome him by my blood.

He will tell you that you are not saved. He will point to the mistakes you make and bring doubt in your mind about your salvation. Do not believe him. I was slain and with my blood I purchased you for God. You have been justified by my blood. When the evil one tells you that I cannot forgive what you have done, remember my blood cleanses you from all sin. If you confess your sins to me, I am faithful and righteous to forgive all of your sins and cleanse you from all unrighteousness. I am your advocate with my Father.

I know that he has been telling my little ones that I do not hear your prayers because you are a sinner. Do not believe him. By my blood you have a new and living way opened for you to enter the most holy place. I hear your prayers. Celebrate the victory. You, my dear ones, are mine and you shall overcome Satan because of your devotion and love to me.

Know that you will be tempted, for the princes of this world want to destroy you. Many trials will come to test your loyalty to me. The enemy and his angels will use deception and accusations to try and destroy you in the battle for your mind. Be aware of his strategies and know what is at stake is salvation and power. And know that you will lose some battles and win others, but I have already won the war. Remain faithful as soldiers of my kingdom!

The evening that we had dinner and discussed the full meaning of this letter for all of us, the System was attacked while driving on their way home. You may see some of the things that Jesus warned about happening in the following description of the events by Mariann.

The following is what Mariann told us about as she shadowed Ruth driving home last night:

Helper I see pretty lights, then two bad ones come in car. The bad one come to Ruth's ear and say turn left here. Ruth turned left and we go a long way. Then bad one say in Ruth's ear, Maria illegitimate and you must tell the truth to her because the truth will set you free. It is wrong to keep the truth from her. (Then Mariann asked Helper what illegitimate means and he replied that it is a legal term determining legality. That was enough to stop her questioning and get back to her telling of the events.)

Mariann told Council that the bad ones made funny laughs and Ruth heard it. Ruth then prayed to Dragonslayer and Mariann did too. Then Mariann laughed, telling us how one bad one got sucked out the window and ended up in a tree. The other one held on to the headrest a little longer, before popping out the window and into a garbage can. Ruth then heard, you are going the wrong way, turn around and take Woodside east.

Council believes that the dark forces are using the conversations at your dinner table with us as a means to attack and divide the system. They want the system to go under and prevent it from being used by Dragonslayer. Council has asked Ann to stop investigating Maria's relatives for a while, at least until she is more stable. Ann and Ruth are trying to understand why the family, especially her parents, treat her so badly. They will cease. They also believe that the reason the car died suddenly, forcing the call to Sergio for help, was a ploy they used to agitate him and hoping that he would stop us from coming that far to see you. Council is on the alert.

The next night I received a letter from Jennifer conveying her questions on the issues of marriage vows, healing and God:

FOR BETTER OR WORSE UNTIL DEATH DO US PART

We can handle economic better or worse. We are well adapted to being poor and can adjust to well off. We have parts who delight in eating worms and sleeping in the bushes. Over the years we learned how to handle extreme cold and hot environments. We know how to scrounge for what we need and enjoy what we find. So for us, these things are not an issue.
What exactly does, better or worse until death do you part, mean? Are we supposed to remain in an environment that prevents us from doing what we need to do? Are we to stay in an abusive relationship where there is no love, no encouragement and no acceptance? What if the part who made the promise did it under

false pretenses? What if that part made the promise simply to
escape home? Is the promise then legally binding?
Is death the only avenue for escape? How easy it is for those who
do not live it to give us advice. Try remaining in a stifling and
oppressive environment, hoping and praying day and night that it
will end. Remember Paul's request to remove the thorn in his side
three times. Remember that he was told my grace is sufficient for
you. If his grace is sufficient for us, why have relationships at all?
Why desire human contact and warmth? Why did God make a
mate for Adam if his grace is sufficient? Is there not a deep need
within our being for human love that cannot be filled by his grace?
Will the worse last until we die? Will the system ever be able to
heal and grow, or is the punishment for the past, administered in
the present until death do us part? Why is the system being
rewarded with a relationship bent on destroying it? Why did God
tantalize the system by showing them through the Chalberg's what
they have missed? Why give and then take away? If this God wants
good for them, then why does he not remove the bad?
I do not understand this God that the others are trusting.
I am perplexed.

Jennifer

I spent a number of hours over the next several months trying
to help Jennifer find the answers to her questions and there were no
easy answers. As the System made new friends connected to Bob
in the church and his family, free advice started coming from various people when they learned about some of the abuse occurring in
the home. It stirred angry responses from many in the upper middle
class church. Yet, no one really took the time to find out why they
couldn't leave, or understand the cultural complexities surrounding
the history of the marriage.

Sometimes, when Maria visited them and bruises were
discovered on her body, I would get calls about why I wasn't
reporting this to the authorities. No one wanted to think it through
about the ramifications of doing that, for the System as a whole
and as individual parts who would become suicidal if outsiders
took control. Had people with little or no concept of their situation
institutionalized them for their 'protection,' it would have set us

back many years in their healing process, if not stalled it completely. For this reason among others, I was granted the power to remove them into my care immediately, should that ever happen. There will be a couple of close calls, but it will be with me ready to remove them from their home if the situation worsened. Being a mediator in a family crisis, with people who are totally oblivious to the cause and effect of their actions, is the hardest thing to do when you're trying to love all sides.

June found us listing our house for sale for the third time. This time we had offers put on it before it ever made the papers. We all accepted the fact that our time here was now limited. As the System adjusted to that, they began thinking of ways they could help defray the cost of schooling by offering to buy some of my textbooks. Each person that had income of some kind wanted to buy a book and sign the inside as their personal gift. Even Mariann began collecting the coins she found around the house and putting them in a jar marked for this use. They felt that in this way, they would be a part of our combined effort to do God's work. While their book purchases were few, their gifts of prayer support and constant encouragement would help get us through some tough times.

June would also be the month that Carol and I met the crazy people of Titus Task Force International in Bakersfield. I say crazy because they were all in the intentional interim ministry like us. It was nice and reassuring to discover that other people were going into troubled and dying churches to help turn them around. We all agreed that our calling by God to be in constant conflict resolution, with believers who were often completely unaware of the divisions within their ranks, meant that being 'touched' for God was a requirement. It brought us hope to know that we were not alone in this ministry. They saw how our ministry of counseling to the severely abused fit easily into this larger work within the churches.

Ironically, just as the churches deny their need for help from an intentional interim until they have one foot in the grave and in need of triage, so do most victims of abuse, especially clergy abuse. The primary reasons why both wait to get help until the last possible moment is shame and embarrassment in acknowledging the need for help with problems they want to keep hidden from the outside. It is also true that when either group, churches or the abused, ask for help early when the problems first manifest themselves, healing can come much faster and less painfully to all concerned.

A case in point will be the church I interview with in Pasadena in June, for the Senior Pastor position while we are finishing seminary work there the next year. I knew in one meeting that they needed an interim to deal with their issues and told them so. They elected to call the other guy who was ready to commit to at least seven years sight unseen. I left my card and said call me when this doesn't work out. I hear from them again in about a year. I'll tell more of this saga when the time comes. I only include this particular church's story, because they become a part of the System's journey of healing, just as the System will become part of their journey with God.

The enemy would escalate the attacks on the System by targeting the children and Maria about our imminent departure. They used this as a means to weaken them, by telling them, "If God really loved you, he would send away the bad man (Sergio) and not your daddy." Joy was being attacked regularly to take advantage of her confusion and mixing it up so that she didn't know who to believe. Maria was told that I would become important and forget about her and the others. Maria was sent to talk with Jesus and Elizabeth Ray recorded her conversation. Notice how her questions haven't changed much and how Dragonslayer responds to them with gentleness and grace, even after hearing them many times.

"Maria, why are you afraid?"

"I'm afraid I won't see him again and be able to hug him or be with him."

"Do you trust me Maria?"

"I keep trying so hard. Can you help me trust you?"

"Yes, Maria, and you will see Michael again."

"I am so sad."

"Tell me about your sad."

"I can't find the words to explain it."

"Try."

"I feel like I'm being ripped away from them, like I'm being shredded and I'm going to die. I felt like I was growing and warm, safe and happy attached to them, but now you are ripping me out. I want to be close to them so I can hug them and listen to Pastor Chalberg tell me important things, see him wink at us and smile. He doesn't make fun of us or think I'm stupid and he protects me and tells me how to do things right. I just like being still with them and listen to him talk about you. I want to encourage them when they get tired, but you are taking him away and I'm crying inside."

"I know how difficult it is to trust me when things are so hard Maria. I remember how hard it was for me to leave my Father and come to earth. But I knew my Father's plans for me were not plans to harm me and I trusted Him. Do you trust me Maria? It is okay to feel sad and cry. You are sad as I was sad when I had to leave my Father. But just as it was for me, it is for you. My plans for you and Michael are not to harm you. You and Michael need to be separated for a season so that both of you will grow stronger in me and produce an abundance of fruit. Michael needs to write the book and Ann needs to follow the teacher training program I am placing her in. And you both need to do it separated from each other. Do not worry Maria. I am in control."

"How long must I be apart from them?

"I know the time, trust me."

"I love them."

"They need your prayers and your encouragement. They need your focus and your love. You can give them all of that and be apart."

"I don't know if I'm strong enough to be apart from them."

"You are not strong Maria, but I am. You need to be closer to me and I will comfort you in your times of loneliness and fear."

"Do I love Pastor Chalberg too much?"

"You can never love too much but remember who is your God."

Liz attempted to influence Helper about her beer over at your house. She tried to tell him that it was illegal for her buddy to cross state lines with beer. "Now you don't want him in jail...do you Helper, for going from the state of Northern California to the state of Southern California? Think of it Helper, PASTOR IN JAIL FOR TRANSPORTING BEER OVER STATE LINES. What would the church say? So...why don't I store it here?" Right when she finished her statement, she heard her name called from behind and she turned to see Dragonslayer smiling at her. For some reason and Helper isn't clear why, Liz nervously told Helper to forget the beer and ran out. – Elizabeth Ray

By mid-June, Maria's parents visited for Father's Day and stayed for four <u>long</u> days. Ann had just finished getting the house back in order after the remodel and hoped the parents would notice. They did. All Ann heard immediately was "how cluttered everything was and how nothing else could possibly fit into this dirty house." Ann remained silent under the barrage but was infuriated over the lack of care or anything encouraging. Maria and Louise had spent the day before cleaning the house to a spotless condition, just to avoid these comments. When Ann tried to change the subject, the mother moved it back to the condition of the house and how they never would have remodeled it this way.

Ann had to go take a final at school luckily and told Jose to entertain his grandparents. Before she could get out the door, the mother raised the issue of obtaining breast prosthesis again. When Ann said she didn't want them, the mother stated, "You look ugly the way you are and you don't look like a woman." Maria was shadowing and became extremely depressed over her mother's comments. Council tried to pull her out of it. Helper asked her, *"Who are you going to believe, your adopted dad, Pastor Mike, or your mother?"* *"But my mom wouldn't tell me I look ugly if I didn't look ugly."* Maria refused to believe Helper when he said, *"I'm sorry to say that she would."* Council was angry now, for they had tried very hard to get Maria to accept her body image, and just as they were seeing results, the mother comes and tears her down again to feeling worthless in her sight.

Council wrote me a note to ask me to call Maria and explain the truth about her parents' lack of love for her. They had joined with Ann in never expecting anything positive from the parents. I did as they asked because I, like Carol, had received Father's Day wishes from everyone in the System. Tabitha had made a book from her drawings depicting me in a variety of situations. Her title was written very broadly in Spanish across my image said, "mi libro por papa (then her English) I luv my dady sincir". Mariann, not to be outdone by Tabitha, made her own book called, "my daddy be my daddy" and sent this single drawing as well.

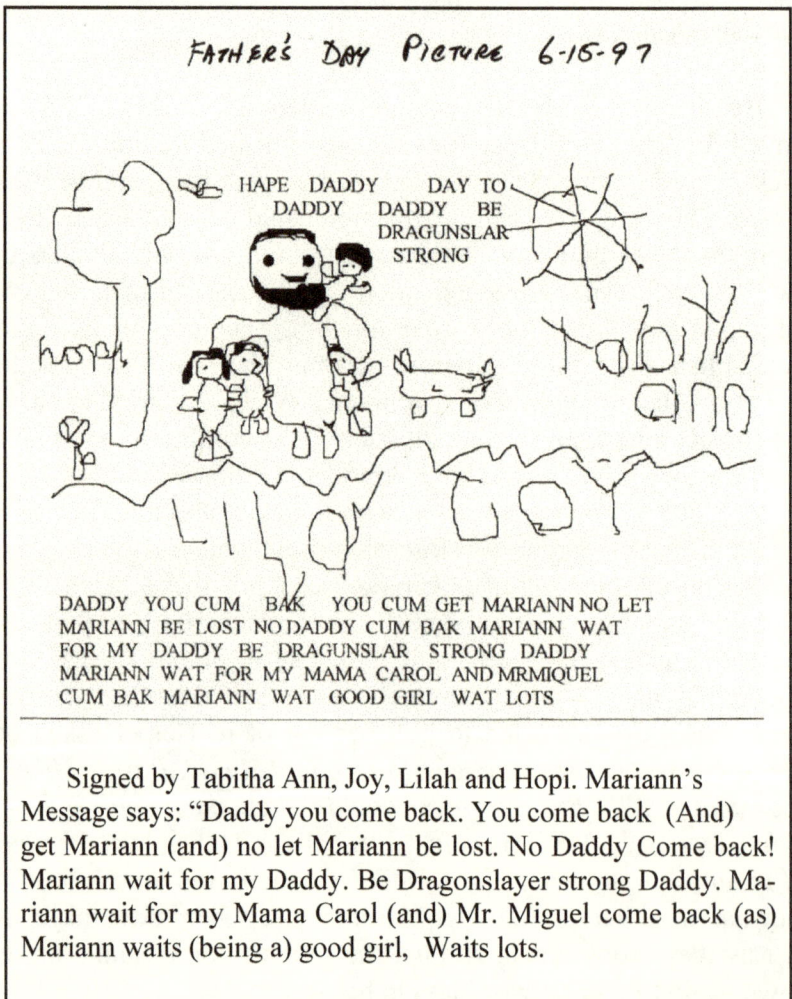

FATHER'S DAY PICTURE 6-15-97

HAPE DADDY DAY TO DADDY DADDY BE DRAGUNSLAR STRONG

DADDY YOU CUM BAK YOU CUM GET MARIANN NO LET MARIANN BE LOST NO DADDY CUM BAK MARIANN WAT FOR MY DADDY BE DRAGUNSLAR STRONG DADDY MARIANN WAT FOR MY MAMA CAROL AND MRMIQUEL CUM BAK MARIANN WAT GOOD GIRL WAT LOTS

Signed by Tabitha Ann, Joy, Lilah and Hopi. Mariann's Message says: "Daddy you come back. You come back (And) get Mariann (and) no let Mariann be lost. No Daddy Come back! Mariann wait for my Daddy. Be Dragonslayer strong Daddy. Mariann wait for my Mama Carol (and) Mr. Miguel come back (as) Mariann waits (being a) good girl, Waits lots.

Plate # 9

The System returned with Claudia to the parents' home in Nevada for several days in July to retrieve a number of items left there by Claudia. Upon their return home I received the following letter:

Memo from Council:
System is safely back. Maria's parents seem very ill and we are attempting to prepare her for their death. Mother in a lot of pain and has lost much weight. Father also in pain and rarely leaves his chair. Ann allowed Maria to do the housework; cleaning bathrooms, cooking, laundry etc. Louise took care of the gardens...over 3 acres worth watering every day. Ruth did the grocery shopping.

Liz got in trouble arguing with the father, when he demanded that she buy Claudia more art supplies. Liz responded that Claudia has more money than she did and could afford to buy her own supplies. The father's response was "when you are in a wheelchair and her condition then you can complain." Liz shot back with "this has nothing to do with wheelchairs and everything to do with who has the most money". The father told her to not be a wise ass and Liz said better a wise ass than a stupid one, before running out the door.

Raquel switched out and went for a long walk in the desert. She calls the father the Thorn Snake. He hates the Pyramid Indians who are Raquel's friends and always telling the other farmers how his daughter is a traitor and supports Indian rights. Raquel will not communicate with the father and chooses to walk alone instead when she is there.

The System ran into several problems there. The mother was successful in cornering Maria into trying on artificial breasts. Maria was so embarrassed by her scars and mother's comments that she would only put them on in private in the bathroom. The mother said how she looked like a woman with them and a freak without them. She reiterated how she was her mother and would not tell her anything that wasn't right for her. Maria cried herself to sleep that night and Ruth had her talk to Jesus to calm her down.

About one in the morning the system was shaken awake by the mother telling us that we needed to help her, because she was in such terrible pain. We did all we could and applied ice to the pain. At lunch the next day the father proceeded to inform Ann how perfect Claudia was and how Ann should be grateful. Ann told the father, "wow, what an honor to be in the presence of the only perfect human being in the world. Gee dad, I am surprised that you gave up your title." Claudia began to laugh and Ann followed after her. Then Ann said, "If Claudia is perfect, I'm the Pope." The father changed the subject.

Ann had to spend time with the father, because the mother wanted to be alone with Claudia. The mother kept saying how glad she was that at least her grandchildren turned out good...no thanks to their parents. The father spent the time alone with Ann demeaning his weak son and bitchy wife who was taking him for everything. Ann attempted to offer advice to him that, if you're afraid of her inheriting your estate, just sell the farm and spend the money how you want. Ruth switched out and added or leave the farm to the church to help poor people. Both ideas were quickly rejected when he said, I can't do that, he's my son and gets everything.

Mariann was allowed out once to play with the frogs in the canal. We took the chance because we were alone and it's impossible to keep her inside that long without some release. We couldn't risk having her out in the house at night because the parents walk in at all hours and we didn't want her threatened by him. Unfortunately Mariann shadowed the slaughtering of an animal and the drinking of its blood as some sort of macho thing. She became hysterical and we had to place her deep inside for awhile.

A few days later she sees a little girl her age with pigtails like her, drinking a soda in the store. A man in front of us kept looking at the little girl and whispered something to the girl's mother. We thought it was her grandfather but we were wrong. When he turned and smiled at us, Mariann started screaming inside. When we asked what was wrong, she told us that he was a bad man and works for the bad angel...please don't let him get me! When she can see what we cannot, how do we help her become calm again?

It doesn't happen often, but with the attacks on the increase, do we give her the benefit of the doubt about what she is seeing?

Maria is looking forward to her time with you and Carol this week, before you go to LA to set up your school year. We will be interested to hear about this Titus group you told us about. Council has approved Maria attending the other church for now. Pastor Bob is attempting to get her into a small group for support. Do you think he has enough understanding of the system to explain Maria to them? We are concerned that he might be moving too fast, without grasping the complexity of our lives and needs.

Joy is not doing well because we have had to keep her inside at all times. Mariann and Tabitha Ann are needy and this affects her sense of security. We hope that on our return the children will settle down and we can balance. They are also affected by the constant calling of Maria by her sister, as she gives details of all of the family problems, including aunts, cousins and anyone she knows. With more and more seepage occurring in the system, we can't hide information from each other like we used to.

We need to reinforce with Maria that it is not a mortal sin to take care of her own needs once in a while. Do you have any suggestions on how to convince her? The system has to take care of the body's needs or we will fall. Some parts work too hard and never rest, because they prefer to think that Maria had cancer and Mariann had surgery, not the body having cancer. It seems to be a difficult concept psychologically to accept and they are not taking the health orders seriously. We need your help to get the message through to them.

PS: Can you call Mariann tonight to reassure her that she does not have to drink blood and that she will not be left with the bad man? The enemy attacks her constantly.

While we were in LA for the week, Carol arranged to send postcards to the System's children and I called a couple of times to reassure them that we would be returning soon. This helped them to know that they weren't being abandoned and learn another style of communication that would become the norm for awhile. When

211

we returned for our final time in the Bay area for a few years, the following letter greeted us.

Welcome home! You have several children who have eagerly been waiting for your return, not to mention a few adults as well. Ann received her contract for employment at the school she wanted. Liz is irritated that Ann is not buying a new car and planning to walk to work. Ann says that it is because she is nervous about over extending herself too fast, but Liz says she is listening to the father about spending too much on herself.

Joy is having a difficult time lately and has started cutting the body again to watch the blood pour out. We thought these things were over with and we are concerned about it beginning again. Do you know why? Ruth cut the body's fingernails so she can't scratch us and we have removed all objects to above her reach as we can. Joy has not seen Bruce in over a month because of his illness preventing him from doing therapy with kids. Going to Nevada has set her back and she hasn't balanced as well as we hoped.

Maria is doing better and has written a letter to her parents that she is praying for their health to improve. She is excited to go hear Bob give a sermon on Sunday entitled the pursuit of happiness. She knows that you have open house then and wants to invite you to join us.

Mariann is confused about church. She thinks that because Pastor Bob said she could attend, that he rules over Council's authority and she doesn't have to obey us. We need advice on how to handle this situation. We do not want to deny Mariann the joy of being in church, yet we don't want to alienate Ann with her fear of discovery of the system's multiplicity either. We want to avoid becoming authoritarian and controlling over the parts because of their past, yet we find they can't seem to come together and compromise over the issue of church, worship and who can or can't take part as far as the children are concerned. Ann is not alone about allowing Mariann out in worship and fears that Pastor Bob won't be able to cover for her as he says. She doesn't want us kicked out again.

The summer went by fast for all of us. Since the first of the year I had been applying for a position as senior pastor across the continent. I had hoped to spend only a year in Southern California to finish my master's degree and then move to whatever call I received. Since I had spent, or misspent perhaps, my youth there, I had no desire to remain longer than required. I received a number of possibilities up through August, several that were very appealing. One was in Alaska being an itinerant pastor between several Eskimo villages, which I liked, but Carol wasn't sure about the idea of traveling by dogsled. Another was in London at an international church with mostly American sojourners.

There were a number of others in-between, but each one in its turn would reach a point of praying for a final decision, then decline because they felt the Holy Spirit saying no to their desire to say yes. This same process followed us for the next three years, with the Interim Pastor position in Pasadena the only exception. Carol and I accepted each door being opened wide with it being slammed shut at the last moment, as God affirming that He had us where He wanted us for the moment and He would change it when it was time. This was one way He taught us to remain dependent upon His guiding our paths on a daily basis. It also made it difficult to plan anything longer than a few months ahead, which was harder for Carol the 'planner' to get used to than me. I guess it fit better into my 'one day at a time' mentality.

It was particularly hard for the System to adjust to, especially when the time came to leave. They knew we would be in Pasadena for at least a year, but where was God going to send us after that? I think we all tried to pry the information out of Dragonslayer ahead of time, but to no avail. None of the plans we made happened the way we wanted, other than graduating from Fuller Seminary by the next summer. The next three years would be full of adjustments for all of us and expecting the unexpected became the rule of the day.

I told Council the first week of August that we would be moving the last day of August to our new rental house just outside of Pasadena. They and I took the easy way out of telling Mariann by asking Dragonslayer to inform her for us. She responded by sending me the following drawing to express her desires on paper to keep us here. She will draw her pain of being separated from us for several years to come.

213

Mariann's final plea to keep us here.

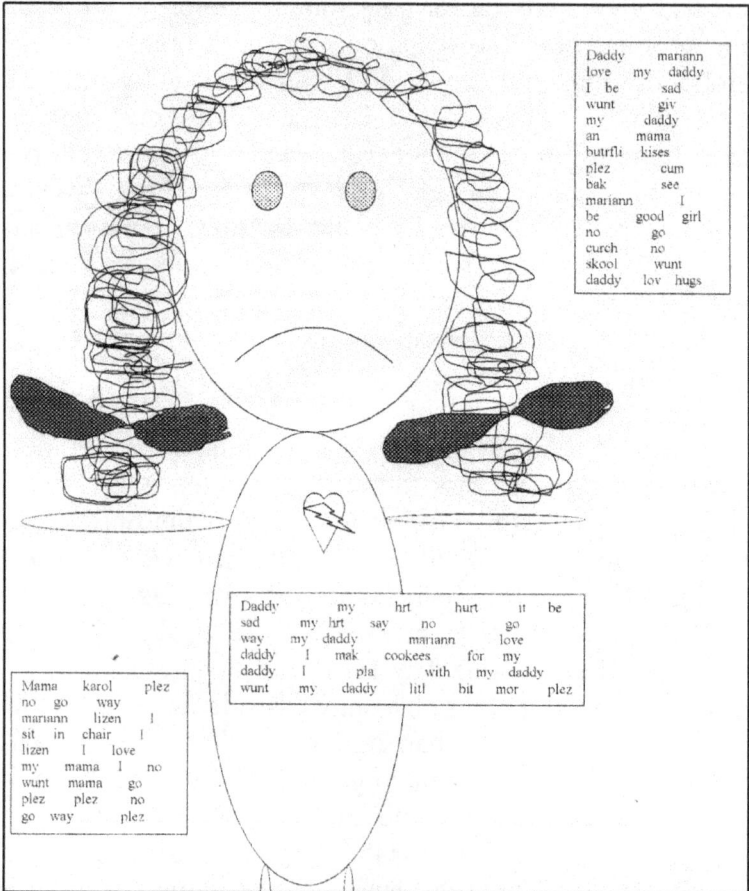

Plate # 10

Mariann's text boxes say, *"Daddy, Mariann love my daddy. I be sad, want give my daddy and mommy butterfly kisses. Please come back see Mariann. I be good girl, no go church, no go school. Want daddy, love hugs."* Next: *"Daddy, my heart hurt, it be sad. My heart say no go away my daddy. Mariann love daddy. I make cookies for my daddy. I play with my daddy. Want my daddy little bit more please."* Bottom: *"Mama Carol please no go away. Mariann listen, I sit in chair, I listen. I love my mama. I no want mama go please. Please no go away. Please."*

That evening I received this message from Raquel:

And Dragonslayer spoke:
Do not be afraid for I bring to you words of encouragement.
Michael came so that you could learn of my love for you. And
I knew that you would grow close to him and depend upon him.
But now the time has come when he must go to do the work
I have given him. It is time now for you to put into practice what
You have learned from Michael. Know that I am with you, and
Know that you will be with Michael again when it is time.
Do you have faith enough to trust me?

Circle Council wrote a lengthy report to me a few days later. They were feeling a little more comfortable with Ann's move into her teaching position in the public school. She had dazzled them with her skills and adaptability to this new environment, and they were learning from her about time management. Ann was already receiving high praise from her fellow teachers and professors, making life for her different, if not easier. She had never before received this kind of outside acceptance by her peers.

They filled me in on where everyone was with our departure and there was little change. Mariann didn't understand the time frame and yet, she was trying to accept what Jesus and I were telling her. Being the little girl she is and coming from the experiences of her past, it was difficult for her to know for sure that the *"big people know for real that Mr. Miguel not die."* She was unable to accept why Dragonslayer sends her daddy away and not others. Council was confused, because this event seemed more difficult to her than the surgery or the chemotherapy. Bruce told them that she might withdraw inside for awhile but wouldn't know for sure until the day arrives. Council decided to stay alert for spiritual attacks and seek Dragonslayer's advice on how to proceed in helping her.

Tabitha Ann and Joy were told that we were moving to a new house for them to play at and they would see us when the Christmas trees were here. Liz appeared more on edge and was getting 'house arrest' more often than in the past. She refused to talk about her feelings with Council. Raquel appeared to Council as though she was in mourning, spending her time in private and not discussing it with anyone other than the Great Spirit.

Maria's mother was growing sicker and experiencing tremors and shaking, so Council didn't tell her about it for now as they thought it would be too much for her. They feared her sadness with our leaving and this info would put her into a depression spiral. Instead they chose to focus her and Louise on our farewell party coming up. Liz was even going to be allowed 2 beers, if she ate some food with it. They were going to be scrutinizing her closely to make sure that Maria wouldn't be forced out in a drunken state.

Finally, they were concerned about Mariann and the System spending the weekend with us prior to our packing and leaving. It was important to keep our promise to Mariann, but they feared the private saying of goodbyes might be too much and drawn out too long for the recovery time needed by the adults for the next business day. They were also concerned about Carol and her level of stress. Well, we did it and it was a long and sad goodbye with lots of tears, but it was after a time of rejoicing with Jesus for all of the healing, for all of the laughter and for all of the love that we would now share for eternity.

I wasn't prepared for the pain I felt, as Mariann sobbed from her innermost being on my chest, begging us not to go. It took a while for Carol and I to get her calm enough for Helper to pull her back inside. Our last minutes together were spent in prayer with Maria in renewing our hope for the future and the fulfillment of God's plans in our lives. Raquel sent me these two stories to read as we traveled south:

A Story for Mariann
- Quiet Walker

Once upon a time there lived a shepherd who cared for many sheep. His sheep grazed in the valley and were content under his care. One day a small sheep wandered into the valley. Her name was Molly, and she had belonged to a cruel shepherd who beat her. Scars on her chest and sides told of a life of pain and suffering. She hid under a rock, afraid to approach other sheep.

But one day, a sheep named Mikey was told by his shepherd about Molly. The shepherd told Mikey to go see Molly and help her. With warm, tender eyes, Mikey told Molly not to be afraid. He would be her friend and not hurt her. Molly was afraid to trust Mikey. She did not know if he was going to really be nice to her, or if this was another trick to hurt her. She would not move from under the rock.

Each day Mikey would bring some fresh grass and water to Molly. He would sit near her and tell her stories of his shepherd. He would tell her how much his shepherd loved her and cared for her. Molly decided to walk with Mikey and meet his shepherd one day. His shepherd was not like the shepherd who had owned her before, for he had kind eyes and a soothing voice. Molly eagerly agreed to join his flock.

Molly and Mikey became best friends. Mikey would tell Molly all about the shepherd. Molly loved listening to Mikey. He was her hero. He was strong and wise. She felt safe with him and grew to love him with all of her heart. Mikey taught Molly how to call for the shepherd when the wolves were close. "Do not wait until they do harm, Molly. Call the shepherd immediately and he will come and protect you." He told her of the never-ending love the shepherd had for her and how much he cared for her. He told her how beautiful she was to the shepherd and Molly came to adore him.

Molly and Mikey spent much time together. They loved to play games in the green grass and spend many hours frolicking in the cool breeze that danced from the north. When they grew tired, they would curl up together to keep warm. Molly always felt safe with Mikey and their love grew as they became inseparable.

One day, the shepherd gathered the flock and took them to a place where there were many men and trucks. Molly was scared, but the shepherd told her not to be afraid. He told her that the time had come for his flock to be dispersed around the earth. Mikey and Molly would be separated.

"No," cried Molly, "Please no! You can have my legs, my heart...my coat, but please do not take away my friend Mikey."

"Molly, you and Mikey will always be together in spirit. Love cannot be destroyed by distance. Both you and Mikey will grow during your separation in ways that you could not if you remain together. And know this, Molly, there will come a time that you and Mikey will be reunited and never separated again."

217

Molly cried and cried, but she trusted the shepherd. With all of her strength, she walked up to Mikey before he was placed in the truck and told him, "I will always love you." And both of them held each other for a long time. And with a goodbye hug, Molly turned and walked to the truck the shepherd had picked for her. She would wait for the day that she would once more be reunited with her best friend Mikey...trusting in her shepherd's love.

"My sheep hear My voice, and I know them, and they follow Me. I give eternal life to them, and they shall never perish. And no one shall snatch them out of My hand. My Father, who has given them to Me, is greater than all; And no one is able to snatch them out of My Father's hand. I and the Father are one."
John 10: 27 – 30

Shedding Tear
And One Who is
Like the Angels

Friends
(music: Michael W. Smith)

Packing up the dreams God planted
in the fertile soil of you.
I can't believe the hopes he's granted
means a chapter in your life is through.
But we'll keep you close as always
It won't even seem you've gone.

Cuz our hearts in big and small ways
Will keep the love that keeps us strong.
Friends are friends forever
If the Lord's the Lord of them.
And a friend will not say never
Because the welcome will not end.

218

Though it's hard to let you go
In the Father's hands we know
That a lifetime's not too long
To live as friends.

And with the faith and love God's given
Strengthen from the hope we know
We will pray the joy you live
Is the strength you now show.
We'll keep you close as always.

May the Great Spirit keep you safe on your travels
And may you always know that we are here for you.

"A friend loves at all times,
And a brother is born for adversity."
Proverbs 17:17

Chapter Ten

"...That God Hasn't Given Up On Us."

*"For I consider that the sufferings of this present
time are not worthy to be compared with
the glory that is to be revealed to us...
For in hope we have been saved, but hope that is seen
is not hope; for why does one also hope for what
he sees? But if we hope for what we do not see,
with perseverance we wait eagerly for it...
And we know that God causes all things to work together
for good, to those who love God, to those who
are called according to His purpose."*
Romans 8:18, 24, 25, 28

*"Consider this, that in the course of justice
none of us should see salvation."*
William Shakespeare, *The Merchant of Venice*

*"Grace is indeed needed to turn a man into a saint; and he
who doubts it does not know what a saint or a man is."*
Blaise Pascal, *Pensees* (1670)

Looking back to the spring of '95, I can see now how it was a preacher of the Gospel of Jesus Christ who had entered the lives of the System, but it was, I hope, a minister of the Gospel who was leaving in the fall of '97. Everyone involved thus far had been changed in their understanding of God's power to love and to heal. The more I learned about God's love through the sharing of it, the more I felt compelled to confront the lack of it in the church, and in myself. I was discovering how 'being Good News' meant letting God do it His way and letting go of my need to control it.

As I entered Fuller Seminary to finish my final year, I learned very quickly how I would only accomplish this feat, if Jesus would give me the will and the strength. It had been 30 years since the last time I was in school full-time. Over the last 15 years I had taken a maximum of 8 units a semester, so as not to die from working a full-time job, doing ministry and raising a family. Now the plan was to take 16 units each semester to complete the 144 units required for the Master of Divinity degree, as well as find a part-time job in ministry. Carol had already graduated with a Master of Arts in theology through Fuller's extension in Northern California the previous year and had planned to find a full-time job as soon as possible to help defray the cost of living there.

Well, evidently, our plans didn't quite match the plans Jesus had for us. We also didn't expect the constant spiritual attacks to follow us down there. We had mistakenly looked at this time as leaving our 'ministry' to replace it with academia, something that I thought evil cared little about. Within the first semester I learned that I was partly right...evil cares very little about academia and sees it as a distraction in many ways, to keep some believers away from hands-on-ministry. But I was also wrong in that the academic culture on campus also provides numerous opportunities for ministry with the people there, students and teachers alike.

Over the next year I not only had the chance to learn from my professors and fellow students, I also had many opportunities to be a pastor and counselor to both. Carol and I were blessed to be able to build mentoring relationships with several of the younger students and clergy couples in our area. I felt free to challenge many of the things being taught, from a practical perspective, as well as from my own experience. When one professor stated that as pastors we would probably never run into a case of Multiple Personality Disorder in our church, it was interesting to hear the responses to my having encountered at least 1 in the last three churches and 5 in 1 church alone.

No, things didn't go the way we planned. The seminary had lost or deleted my program requirements from 15 years earlier and they were telling me what I needed to complete now to get my degree. This meant that I would be taking 19 units my second semester and 24 units my last semester, and this removed any possibility of my holding down even a part-time job. To make matters worse, Carol wouldn't find work for several months as well. The only real relief I had was taking courses in areas where I had many years of experience and courses required for all students but geared towards first career students.

The hardest lesson came to us from Jesus. We had hoped to retain enough of the profit from the sale of our house, after deducting the cost of school, to purchase another house wherever we were called to as our 'security for the future'. We learned by the end of this school year how Jesus wanted us to rely on Him to provide our security, not only for our financial needs, but also for every aspect of our life and ministry. This was not an easy concept to accept for either of us. I had spent most of my adult life as a builder and contractor dealing in real estate, and more importantly, as a homeowner. It would be another year or so after graduation, before I was ready to relinquish control to Jesus.

One of my best lessons came in writing several papers that became the outline for the first book. While required to write many things for seminary, it caused me to get in the habit of writing. I was also blessed to have the opportunity to discuss the books and our ministry, with professors like David Augsburger and professionals in the field who came by the seminary. I was surprised however, by the amount of pastoral counseling God had me doing for both pastors and students while attending that year.

All of this year, we maintained our relationship with the System and kept abreast of all they were going through in their lives and the lives of those connected to them. They would fly down at appropriate times for a getaway with us, to rejoice over what God was doing in all of our lives and be renewed in our spirits. Something happened within the spiritual realm, like a battle or a blessing, with every visit. Looking back I can see how God was preparing us for a particular ministry that lay ahead. All of the signs and messages were there to define it, if we had only relinquished control of our future to Him sooner to see it. But we were stubborn and continued to plan our future a while longer, especially when the need for employment became rather important after graduation.

As we were getting settled into our new home and routines for school, the System was trying to integrate with Bob, his wife Tina and their family. Bruce was there to assist as well, but changes were coming in his life and visits to him were getting further apart. Circle Council wrote to Bob to help him understand who it was that had entered his life. They recognized that his initial contacts were with a few parts, so they focused on the needs of these parts alone. After expressing first their gratitude for his kindness toward Maria and Mariann, and that they weren't writing to criticize or judge his actions, they wrote about Tabitha's needs and how the needs of the children might affect his children. This came about after Bob had Mariann out drawing with his kids, and Tabitha switched out to draw too…

Tabitha Ann is a child part who has experienced much pain in her life. It has taken the therapists a long time to get her to be unafraid to express her feelings and talk about the hurt that she has in her. The therapist and Pastor Chalberg have continually provided her with crayons and the acceptance she needs to draw her feelings without fear, knowing that no harm will come to her.

We believe that when the children were playing about bad men and good men, kidnappers and such, bad angels caused Tabitha Ann to switch out. She was drawing what was bothering her, when you called Mariann out quickly and proceeded to tear up Tabitha's pictures, saying you would destroy them. Tabitha shadowed that and got the message that she was bad for drawing them and it's wrong to draw bad pictures.

We are concerned about the single children and the effect the multiple children have on them. Under no circumstances will Council allow our children to heal at the expense or trauma to your children. Yet, if you allow Tabitha to be out, we need to make sure that her pain is acknowledged in her drawing and not have her treated as bad. We have some suggestions if this occurs again. Let Tabitha know that you see her drawing and it makes you sad, but don't worry, you don't have to be sad here. Can you draw me a picture of a pretty flower or something that makes you happy? Or collect her pictures and tell her thank you for sharing these with me. I'll give these to your daddy and don't worry you are safe here.

The fact that she felt safe enough to come out and draw says a lot about the work of those helping her as being effective. You can contact either of them if you need advice. We don't want Tabitha reverting back in her therapy, thinking she is bad. As Tabitha shadows Mariann, she sees her getting toys, coloring books and hugs. She does not comprehend that you allow Mariann out to have fun, but not her. Maybe it is too complicated for single children to understand a variety of child parts or how and why they switch. We would feel more at ease if you spoke to Bruce or Mike about these issues soon.

As far as Maria babysitting, we have given both Maria and Ruth permission to baby-sit once a month, as it would not be wise to take away Liz's Saturday night too often. Maria is the tender one that children love and Ruth can make sure everyone is safe. Liz will not come out when they do this. We need your help to let our children know that they don't have to eat other people's food that falls to the floor. It's a habit from childhood that our children have and we want to break it. Also, are you sure you want the children sharing an apple in the playhouse? We have no contagious diseases, so it's not an issue for us.

There is one other area of importance for us to discuss with you. It is about Maria and her expressions of grief about her daughter's disability, her home-life and her husband. She has a difficult time telling anyone of her sorrow and pain. Jesus wants her to allow him to absorb it, yet she doesn't want to hurt him. Some days are better than others, but when her husband gets angry or enraged over situations, Maria becomes sad that everyone isn't happy. She does not handle confrontation well at all. She becomes distraught when the husband yells and tells her to leave him alone.

You have already given her more support in a few months than she has ever received from her husband. Understand that it is depressing for some parts who want to leave the situation, but we can't condone that happening until Jesus gives permission. He hasn't given Maria that yet. We are hoping that your church and the bible study will provide the emotional support that she needs to experience happier times. She talks non-stop about joining it as she really wants to belong somewhere. We hope the study will challenge her emotionally and spiritually.

Although we hope no graphic presentations of abuse are presented and talked about, we would like her to know how other people who have been wounded learned to trust and love God. We want her to know that it takes a long time and God understands that. We want her to be able to cry about it and know that it wasn't her fault. We want her to heal her broken heart. You, Bruce and Mike have all been a model to her for God the Father and she is learning about God's love through you.

There were some things that began to happen after our leaving when the System started to develop relationships with Bob and his family, particularly his children. It was something that I hadn't anticipated, but I understood why it occurred. Due to losses of security in relationships, Maria and Mariann were drawn to the innocent love provided by children unconcerned about issues such as multiplicity. Maria regressed in her ability to express herself verbally or in writing, to about that of a 14 or 15 year-old. She relied on others to make the difficult decisions, thus allowing her to perceive life as simply as possible. This would be a gift for her spiritually, to conceive of heaven's reality and the kingdom of God as a child would look at it. While some will see her as stupid or slow, more people will hear the wisdom that she shares from the mouth of God.

Mariann however, will begin to regress in maturity and intellectual age to about that of a 4 or 5 year-old. This is due in part to her lack of schooling, but emotionally it is due to her desire to connect to a child whose age connects with her. While Bob had children of various ages from infancy to preteen, it would be the Chris that connects the most directly with Mariann. She communicated with him as easily as she did with the older children. The older ones begin to lose interest in the multiplicity over the next few years and accept it as normal, they mature faster than Mariann as they begin to find companionship with other friends. It will be the son who bonds with Mariann, who does not have many other outside friends to draw them apart.

Mariann will also begin to pick up 'bad habits' by watching the interaction between Bob and his children. She will learn how many times to ask for the same thing, before he will tire and say yes instead of no. When it doesn't work on me, she'll ask why. Joy and Hopi will begin to express their fears through Mariann and Tabitha in their drawings, more as a plea for protection from the ever-present spiritual attacks, than an actual memory being relived.

Mariann and Tabitha also seem to accept this role as protectors. As I watched Mariann connect with the varying ages of single children, it was hard to see her fluctuate in maturity on a regular basis. This was one reason why the System would become exhausted when spending time with the pastor's family. Mariann was catching up on time lost in her childhood and so it will take a physical toll of energy of Bob and Tina. Their sacrifice will be rewarded, as they begin to accept Maria as a gift from God.

Mariann wrote to me about Tabitha waking up in the middle of the night screaming about "not dying." They had shadowed a difficult situation between Maria and her husband and were now asking to see us for love and hugs before Christmas. She also wanted to 'teach' me about the Pharisees that she learned in a story from Dragonslayer. She was committing His stories to memory and wanting to act them out with Tabitha. Ruth wrote to fill me in on the issues of the day and explained some underlying issues.

You have no idea of the powerful prayer army you have in Maria and Mariann. They pray for you two all of the time even while doing housework or eating cookies. We are all adjusting to Ann's work schedule and learning just how phenomenal a teacher she is. I am worried about her health as she pushes herself and us too hard. Maria's family is not handling the transition well. Sergio does not like having to take on some of the household responsibilities. He becomes more difficult as he can't do it as well as we did. I am grateful that he isn't an alcoholic or it would be too much.

You heard about the episode with him and Maria moving furniture. Maria insisted on not telling Bruce about the bruises on her upper body and thighs caused by him dropping the dresser on her. She is sure it was an accident, but I think that he was taking out his rage on her. I'm glad that you told her to tell Bruce, whether he pursues it or not.

I'm concerned about Tabitha. Mariann told you about her waking up, but not about her dream of her mother killing her. I think it's because she feels rejected by Bob and Tina over the drawing incident last Sunday. Council is concerned, as I am, about Tabitha

*and Joy not getting enough outside nurturing since you left. They
are not able to see Bruce either right now.*

*Liz wrote a nasty letter to Bob because he was praising Ann's work
and accomplishments and saying that Liz is lazy for not working
outside. It's too bad that he doesn't understand very well how we
operate, or how comparing parts just sets her off. Maybe he'll
learn 'to be slow to speak and quick to listen'.*

*I find it interesting how Tina has connected to Maria. She was also
abused and has a difficult time trusting God. Maria finds this
amazing for a pastor's wife. Tina told her that she doesn't know
why she has become so close to her and that it is something she
rarely does. Maria's friendship is helping her to learn how to deal
with her own issues. Bob told Maria how he is always teaching
others and not too many teach him, but she does without knowing
that she's doing it. I wonder who is benefiting the most from the
friendship. Maria captures people's hearts in a way I cannot. Even
Chris recognizes her and wants to be held by her. Her love engulfs
him and he never fusses with her like he does with me. Go figure? I
am hoping that Sergio will see how others value her and change
his attitude toward her and appreciate who she is.*

*You'll like this...Ann now gives Maria $20 a month for her
housekeeping. (Talk about cheap labor.) Maria decided to give it
all to her church and Ann was upset. Even Pastor Bob said that
she should only give $2.00 and Maria asked why. She wanted to
know what she was supposed to do with the rest of it. He suggested
new clothes or something that she needed. She stated how she
doesn't need anything and that Jesus knew how to invest it better
than her.*

The desire for companionship made the children and Maria
draw closer to Bob, Tina and the kids. Mariann and Tabitha were
spending more time out in a typical family setting. They would
bring the books we gave them and Bob would read to them. It was
Liz who got in trouble first when she tricked Bob into letting her
have a beer and mushrooms together. That turned into 2+ beers and
3 hangovers, for which she received house arrest again. Maria was
excited to soon be entering her first bible study, the first since ours

had ended. Everyone was excited because Billy Graham was coming to Oakland and the System would have to negotiate who would attend the ceremonies with Pastor Bob.

As the growth within the relationships continues, so does the spiritual attacks to separate them. Mariann warned of the presence of 'smelly ones' when she began attending Bob's church. The attitude of the adults to her words was that it is to be expected, but Christians don't have to be concerned, as they won't be harmed. It was sad when I heard this, but not surprising, as a majority of those who claim Christ as their Savior, underestimate the ability of Satan to bring physical harm to them even in 'sacred' surroundings. Some choose to believe that churches, or places of worship, are settings where miracles have occurred and pious people are exempt from attacks 24 / 7. Nothing could be further from the truth.

The only holy ground or sacred place is where Jesus is called upon to be present with the people there. If anyone calls upon His name and asks Him to be with them and protect them from the evil of this world, it will happen! But how many of us do that in our daily routines outside of a worship service? How many people ask for protection in a bible study or prayer time, in a choir practice or Sunday School class, or even while doing an outreach of feeding the hungry or clothing the poor? These are opportunities for the enemy to enter our lives, to try to block us from knowing God in the presence of Jesus Christ, when we take the enemy's power for granted and even worse, take the admonition of Jesus for granted.

"Therefore let him who thinks he stands take heed lest he fall. No temptation has overtaken you but such as is common to man; and God is faithful, who will not allow you to be tempted beyond what you are able, but with the temptation will provide the way of escape also, that you may be able to endure it."
1 Corinthians 10: 12 – 13

The point here is one of an active, alive relationship, where we ask for Christ's power and presence often, in everything we do. As in the cases of clergy abuse, we assume that the devil cannot control a man or woman of God, simply because they claim the name Christian. But is that what the Bible teaches? The verses above are clear: Satan will tempt us just like everyone else, yet we are also allowed choices others don't accept. Verse 12 is a warning to not be so arrogant as to think we can face Satan within our own strength alone, or we will fall to that temptation. The next verse reminds us first of our human frailty; then God's grace in accepting our weaknesses before we are tempted, in His offering of three choices for facing temptation. These three choices are difficult, if not impossible, for anyone who does not have faith in God, to help them get through whatever temptation they face.

The first choice is one of faith in God who knows us fully, with our fears and pride, weaknesses and strengths. He will not allow evil to tempt us beyond our ability at any moment to make the right choice. This means that believers can and will face temptation and God is aware of it and allows it. Thus begins the third request in the Lord's Prayer: *"Lead us not into temptation..."* or "Let us not be tempted..." reminding us of our need for God's strength to survive by receiving His mercy through it. It also reflects faith in God's power to restrain evil's temptations.

The second choice is faith in God's grace of having already provided us with choices. God allows temptation to come upon believers for a reason, otherwise it would not be logical for Him to also provide a way of escaping it. This is the other half of the request above; *"but deliver us from evil (the Evil One)."* The Bible is full of reasons why God allows us to be tested directly by Him and by His adversary. The character building of making difficult choices to choose God's way in the midst of suffering strengthens our desire to choose Him in any circumstance. It builds our faith in the truth of God's promises and our need for Him.

That is the third choice of having faith in His faithfulness, to be there in our time of need to provide His strength to both endure the temptations and walk through it with Him. He will never abandon us when we are challenged by evil. Yet, if we choose to submit to our temptations and not call for His help and protection, we suffer the consequences of those actions. We never lose the third choice of having faith that God will forgive our human nature of often making the wrong choices, when we are willing to admit it. It is the understanding of these choices that will face Pastor Bob and Tina, as God's servants in the church very soon. He will be taken on a journey of discovery to learn what kind of a church God calls him to establish as God designs the church and his role as pastor.

The lessons begin with the opening of Bob's eyes and ears to see and hear the reality of the spiritual battles around him everywhere; even in the place he calls church.

"And no wonder, for even Satan disguises himself as an angel of light. Therefore it is not surprising if his servants also disguise themselves as servants of righteousness; whose end shall be according to their deeds."
2 Corinthians 11: 14 – 15

"It is harder to confess the sin that no one believes in
Than the crime that everyone can appreciate.
For the crime is in relation to the law
And the sin in relation to the sinner."
T.S. Elliot, *The Elder Statesman,* (1958)

Maria and Mariann would write or call me, when they began encountering the evil within Pastor Bob's circle of influence. There was a direct correlation between his acceptance of God's instruction and the increase in spiritual attacks on him and the people around him. It wasn't more than a few months before he realized there was more spiritual activity connected to the System than he was used to in ministry. Maria wrote of one early incident at church:

Something happened today that scared me. I didn't hear Mariann say inside to go the other way at church cuz the smelly ones are there. It was after church time and the kids were getting ready to sing for the Billy Graham speech that is coming. Tina and me were going down the hall when we smelt it. It smelt like sulfur and I got scared and wanted to leave, but Tina went back to see if there was a fire. She couldn't smell it back inside, so she came back out to her daughter and me where she smelled it around us, so we went home.

We told Pastor Bob and he said that a very strange electrical fire had started, some man no one knows put it out, but no one can understand how it started. The bad ones started it and they are in the halls. Mariann told Tina to call Dragonslayer and Pastor Bob, cuz he is not afraid. Sarus (an angel) told Mariann to tell Tina to pray from now until the leaves stop falling every time he goes to church, to pray for bright ones to keep him safe. I don't know what this is all about, but I know that smelly ones were in the church halls. I didn't know that they could go there, but Pastor Bob says that people bring them in.

I really miss you a lot and I like my new friends, but you are special to me. How come when I say things in my bible study people laugh at me? Do I talk wrong? I get to go see my mom soon and Jesus says that he will tell me the words to talk to her.

The next night I received this from Ruth:

Quiet Walker called Pastor Bob last night. She told him that the Great Spirit has sent a gentle wind to connect the web of Maria's life to that of Tina's and how Maria does not know that she is an encourager to Tina. Tina will grow in the strength of the Great Spirit as she watches Maria and Mariann grow.

She told him to be patient for the journey will be long and difficult. She then said that he will be a great leader of the word, but he needs Tina stronger as there will be many attacks from the evil ones. She stressed to him that he must not move away from the will of the Great Spirit, or force Tina to move quickly. She also told him to look with spiritual eyes and know that the evil spirits will use others to try to destroy the friendship of Tina and Maria that the Great Spirit has created.

It was interesting to hear how she told him, that although he thinks he and Tina are there solely to minister to Maria, God is having Maria minister to them. What surprises me is that Maria has no idea that she is doing it, she is simply being herself. Maria is enriching the members of the bible study. Her words are so simple and pure, that we all can't help but be affected by them. I am in awe of how she thinks. It will be neat to watch what God has in store for them...

A couple of days later another letter from Ruth:

Things are getting weird again around us so something must be up. There have been lots of spiritual attacks on Pastor Bob and last night Maria learned how Bruce's mother had a car accident and is in the hospital. Ann heard that Maria's mother is a lot worse, so she is flying out to see her this Saturday and back on Sunday. We haven't told Maria how bad it is and we worry that she will crash after her death. I think that she knows something, because she is talking to Jesus a lot.

Maria went again to her bible study and truly enjoys it. People have a hard time understanding her perception on things. She doesn't realize that others don't always hear Jesus talking to them or experiencing him as closely as she does. She takes things for granted, like angels sitting in trees watching Mariann play. It's normal to her, but bizarre to others.

On prayer, Maria said let the people know that Jesus loves them and wants to talk with them. She says that people got to be still and quiet and stop talking, so they can hear Jesus because he speaks in a soft quiet voice. He never yells. She said that Jesus isn't impressed with fancy words or scripted prayers... he wants to know about you and wants you to talk to him in your regular vocabulary. People need to know that Jesus will talk with them any time day or night. Just speak real to him.

Your comment to Ann about MPD being the norm for understanding the spiritual plane is interesting. Can you elaborate on what your professor meant in response to that observation?

The System expected things to get weird, as Halloween approached again. It seemed to many that this year was going to be a difficult one with Maria's mother dying and everyone tired from Ann's new job schedule. The last thing Ann wanted to do was go to Maria's parents and listen to them put her down all weekend. Yet, out of respect for Maria's family obligations, even if she felt Maria was naïve about wanting her parent's love even now, she went so Maria at least had a chance to say goodbye in person.

The growth from this weekend was a surprise to everyone in the System...except Dragonslayer. Maria wasn't afraid to face her father, if it meant that she could see and talk with her mother. She knew that Dragonslayer would give her the words to say, but even her expectation was that her words would be, "I'm sorry for being so much trouble to you...forgive me", and not upset anyone by saying it. I think that if Jesus had told anyone what He had planned for her, they might have become too sick with fear over the possibilities of failure. I told her how we would be praying for her over the weekend and received three emails starting the day of their return. The second and third is Ruth telling about the whole trip in two parts and the first is Maria telling the main points in her own words.

I got to see my mom for twenty minutes. I didn't know what to do so Jesus told me to look at him and talk to him. So I got on my knees next to my mom and we were all alone. My uncles and aunts and dad were outside drinking. I talked to Jesus lots. I said, "Jesus it isn't true that the priest can put oil on my mom and tell her that it cleans her soul so she can go to heaven, is it? Only you can clean our souls to get us into heaven, huh."

I told Jesus about the cream tuna that my mom made and how she gave me peas to eat. I told Jesus that my mom tried her best, but she didn't have enough love for all of us and she had to give it to my brother. Then I told him I still love her and I'm sad that she is dying. My mom put her hand upon my head and said it will be all right. Then I told Jesus that the one thing I want most is for my mom to go to heaven and be there when I get there.

My mom said I have done a lot wrong. So I told Jesus that and he said tell her I know. Then my mom said, "I am sorry Maria, please forgive me." I said, "I forgive you mom. I love you and Jesus forgives you too cuz he loves you." Then I asked Jesus, "can you call my mom your precious child like you call me?" Then my mom heard him and started crying lots and I cried lots and we hugged. I told Jesus I love him so much and please help my mom with her pain. My aunt opened the door and I went inside and Ann came out.
It was funny Pastor Chalberg cuz my mom could not see Ann kind of like she had cobwebs in her brain. She didn't know her but Jesus

let her see and hear me by cleaning away the cobwebs. Ann let me give her pretty flowers and I got to help her to the bathroom and hug her. She felt very small and old and didn't look mean any more, but peaceful like. I knew you and Carol were praying for me. Jesus loves you and me and my mom now.

Dear Mike and Carol,

We are home again. I don't want to go on vacations with the rest of the parts... it was too unreal. (Like she had a choice!) *Ann didn't want to go and was acting like a robot going through the motions. She boarded the plane saying nothing to anyone. When we arrived in Reno, she went straight to the car rental place. They couldn't find her reservation, so she asked Elizabeth Ray if she booked it elsewhere and she said no. Ann got nasty with them until they finally found it but told her it would be a 45-minute wait.*

Liz starts in wanting to gamble and tells Ann to give her five dollars so she can play the wheel of fortune machine next to the agency. Ann refuses telling Liz that we are here to see a dying mother, not to gamble. Liz keeps bugging her until Ann yells at her to shut up...that she wasn't getting any money. Just then a guy sits down at the same machine and puts in the money and wins a jackpot for $280,055.56... Liz goes berserk and tells Ann that she is going to dissect her. I heard words coming from her that I have never heard before. Ann tells Helper to put Liz under house arrest, but he refused. I guess he was mad at Ann too.

We get the car and Liz is giving Ann so much grief that she has Raquel switch out to drive. We were supposed to be at the parents' house at noon, but we lost two hours. We still aren't sure where she went. When we get close to the house, Raquel switched in and Ann came out to Iroquois music playing. She glanced over and sees a 'thing' sitting in the passenger seat. She yells inside for Raquel and says, what the hell is this? Raquel tells her it is an eagle claw dancing stick that medicine men use to dance over the sick, bringing the power of the eagle's strength to the one dying. Ann tells her you got to be kidding. We are not going to be dancing over the mother with this...get rid of it.

As if on queue, Mariann pops up while Ann is driving through town and tells her we have company. She wants to know how the

234

bright ones can sit on the outside of the car and not blow away. She tells Ann that she wants to do that. According to Mariann, one is in front pointing ahead, two are on the sides and one is in back facing backwards. She said the wind outside doesn't touch them. Ann yells at her to shut up and go deep inside like she is supposed to do. We have to go to work now...

Next day:

While we were still in town, Maria starts crying about getting her mother flowers. Ann spends ten minutes looking for a florist before finally telling her to go into Safeway to pick out whatever kind of arrangement she wants. $56 later Ann is carrying out this huge green vase with five bouquets of flowers neatly set within the ferns.

As Ann pulls into the driveway, she is met by all of the uncles and aunts and the father. They all started giving her grief immediately and Ann says inside to us, "What I have to do for you guys." She proceeds to take out the vase of flowers and walks past everyone to the father asking, "Where's mom?" He said inside and she kept moving away from them.

After entering the bedroom, Ann tells Helper to switch Maria out, but he told her to wait. The mother complains about not seeing Ann very well and starts talking incoherently. Maria is shadowing and pushes her way out and says, "Hi mom, it's me, Maria." The mother suddenly clears up and says, there you are and oh, what pretty flowers. Maria takes one look at her condition and drops to her knees next to the mother's bed and starts talking to Jesus.

She doesn't look at her mother but talks to Jesus with her mother listening. It was so special that even Ann shed a tear. I thought of Aaron speaking for Moses and how Maria was her mother's tongue in the conversation with Jesus. Several times the mother cried and patted Maria's head. Maria is so forgiving and loving. In the end the mother understood what she had missed and told Maria she loved her. Maria accepted that with her whole heart. I believe that Maria's one wish will be granted and she will see her mother in heaven again.

235

Maria prayed for about twenty minutes before the aunt came in and Maria switched in as Ann was shoved out. The mother started becoming incoherent immediately and couldn't see Ann. All of the relatives wanted to go to mass and Ann wouldn't go. The father said, "you still in that religious cult...Don't you know that you're going to hell for leaving the true church". Liz wanted at him but Ann held on and replied, "I'll stay here and take care of mom and cook dinner." Louise switched out and made dinner for everyone.

When they returned, I switched out to eat with them. Maria's uncle decided to tell dirty jokes and got the father started on how he was a breast man. I had it after the third joke and gave an opinion that surprised everyone. "If you are going to continue to talk filthy at the dinner table, then I am eating outside." I was truly surprised when they stopped.

When Maria called me to tell me her good news after returning home, she wanted to double-check with me if what she thought happened, did happen. After a little discussion I told her I believe that your mom accepted Jesus after seeking forgiveness for her sin, therefore in my understanding yes, she'll be in heaven. I asked her if Jesus had already confirmed that with her and she said yes. It became clear that I needed to reaffirm her trust in Jesus as the first priority for her questions and the last one needed for her answers. It has been ten years now and I'm still advising her to go to Jesus first, and then there won't be a need to ask me all of the hard questions. It is a grave responsibility to have someone trust you... as much as they trust Jesus. Even after the mistake score is Jesus 0 and Me... well, let's just say that she has forgiven me often.

I also wish that I could say that everyone in Preservation was elated over the turn of events, but I can't. Ann and Liz thought the whole thing was too easy, that someone could seek forgiveness on their death bed, after a lifetime of cruelty to them, and receive it in twenty minutes of contrition. This perception evoked conversations with them in the week following the mother's death. It centered around who will be our judge at the end of our life, how are we judged and by whose standards, and do we trust Jesus enough to

236

not be upset over whom He imparts grace and say Praise God when any of us receives this unmerited gift.

"I have never met a person I could despair of, or lose hope for, after discerning what lies within me apart from the grace of God."
Oswald Chambers

The next week, however, was spent preparing for a Halloween apart from us. Circle Council and I discussed options and we agreed that regressing backward by hiding in a closet again would not be fruitful for the System. They narrowed it down to three possibilities: 1.) Have children stay in closet; 2.) Communicate by the computer through email or phone to Mike; and 3.) Spend the night with Pastor Bob and Tina. They wrote to me about their decisions and sought my direction. I suggested that they work this out with Bob, without telling him that they had run it by me, after reassuring them that I would be there if option two was the final choice, and in case of an emergency. This was going to be a case of on-the-job-training for Pastor Bob with the System's realities.

Tolip was very against option one as he felt it would be regression for the pod children. They need more outside experiences with Halloween where they are not victimized. He believes that being with you will help dilute their fear of that day. Council agrees.

Lion felt that option two was too limited. What happens if we can't get access through a computer that night? What about the triggers if we stay home to use ours...teenagers coming over dressed in costumes...kids playing tricks on Maria because they know how she spooks easily? Even if access is obtained, how does Council get a traumatized part to calm down enough to type, while they are experiencing flashbacks? What about down time between messages and Joy, who can't type or be understood over a phone?

Daniel and Tolip agreed that the children needed human contact and comfort, rather than a machine. However, several parts are concerned with option three. Does Pastor Bob realize the trauma of the children and particularly Joy? Will he be able to control the

237

situation without causing further trauma to Joy? Does he understand the working of the system well enough to know what to do and what not to do?

(**Content Warning!** See explanation in preface of this book.)

The best scenario is for Joy to be with Mike, but that can't happen so Council is ready to approve option number three. We ask that you please remember that individuals on Halloween, dressed in priestly garb sadistically abused Joy. They inserted crosses into her and Joy and Hopi have talked about the light burning, a reference to the branding done on private parts as a mark of ownership. Joy speaks of a baby that is asleep. We now know that it was dead.

Joy was buried alive in a box by a female helper of the Goatman and he would then resurrect her to be her 'savior'. Prayers were twisted, said backwards and a lot of chanting occurred. The participants in the rituals would work themselves up to a frenzy and ejaculate over the child on the makeshift table. There would be drinking of blood, candles everywhere and an oath taken to Satan.

Joy does not trust anything or anyone, but Lammie and the one who takes care of Lammie called the Shepherd. She always repeats the same question to Lammie to make sure she gets the same answer. She asks, "Do me?" Lammie always says, "I will not do you and my friend the shepherd won't do you. He is safe." Then we suggest that Lammie says, "This is my friend Tina." She will ask her, "Do me?" and Lammie might say, "Oh no Joy, Tina will not do you. She is my friend and a friend of the Shepherd. He takes care of her too." You might have Lammie introduce you too and expect to repeat the process.

Joy associates the lamb with Mike's voice very easily, but not Mike directly. We're not sure how it works, but we hope it will not be confusing for Joy. If it does, she may or may not want to draw to express herself better and Lammie would listen and say things that reassure her of her safety. She needs to be reminded of how the shepherd protects his lambs by keeping the Goatman away and not allowing him in the house.

This is how best to communicate with Joy. Throughout the night the children will rotate out. Mike could tell which different child parts were out by their mannerisms. One sleeps on her back, another one moves around a lot, one cuddles and another whimpers. When they are stressed they do this. Joy will not sleep on anything that resembles a table. Let her sleep on the floor with a blanket and pillow. If things get out of control, Mike says that he will be available by phone to help soothe their fears and you are free to call anytime.

As to your request to take Mariann to Marine World, Council has given its approval. Maria must be home by nine in the morning on Saturday however, if Mariann is to go. Lion wishes you to know that Mariann has never seen a caged animal and has no fear of animals. We do not know how she will react at Marine World and she must stay with you at all times. We think that it will be an extraordinary experience for her and you, and we are encouraging the other children and Maria to shadow. We thank you in advance for your courage to attempt this.

This trip to Marine World happens and it is a memorable day for all to experience but delayed until next year. Halloween night I stayed up all night but there was never a need for my intervention. At my request, Elizabeth Ray mailed me a synopsis of the events on the following night. While the evening did not go as scripted, or with ease, Council was pleased with the results. They had asked Bob to assimilate a lot of history in a short time and hoped that he might handle it the same way as I would. I knew that that was asking too much of him and I was pleased with how much he did rise to the occasion. It turned out to be one of the easier Halloween nights that the System would encounter with anyone for another few years.

Halloween night:
System arrived at the house around 2:30. Maria spent time with Tina and her son. She had a migraine headache and was feeling

weak. As night approached, Mariann became agitated. Maria started to bleed and became very upset. Mariann came out to listen to her book being read and Tabitha followed to hear her Spanish book.

Knocks came at the door a couple of times, but no one was there when Bob went to see if there were 'trick or treaters.' Joy switched out and crawled into the corner, stuffing herself away from Bob. Bob puts her blanket over her, but the child does not respond. She is in a flashback. Tolip waits on the inside as the flashback intensifies, and chooses to pull the child back in. Mariann finds herself stuck in the corner and begins crying for her daddy. Bob lifts her out of the corner and holds her to rock her to sleep.

Thirty minutes later the scenario begins again. Joy is still not responding to Bob so Mariann is sent out. Again she is held and rocked to sleep. As time draws closer to midnight, the rotation out becomes shorter. Fifteen minutes later, Tolip sends Joy out. Joy looks at Lammie and says no do me, but begins to lock into the trauma, hitting the air and banging her head. Bob attempts to stop her as Tolip pulls her inside. Mariann comes out hysterical and wants her daddy. Bob holds her and rocks her.

Mariann wakes up and says Sarus is here. She points and says he is right there, pointing to the area of the corner and sliding glass door. She is frustrated that Bob can't see him or acknowledge him. She talks to him and hears, "I have come to keep the 'smelly ones' out per directions from the Almighty One." Mariann calms down and says that she has to go potty. Tina takes her and Council has Maria come out to tell her that she needs to rearrange the corner setup next to the glass door, as evil ones are outside and Joy can see and hear them from there. She tells her to get crayons and paper for her.

Tina does as suggested upon returning and Joy switches back out and tries to go into the corner and can't. She begins rolling on the floor until Bob asks her if she wants to color. Child nods and begins coloring her flashbacks of being on a table and buried in a box. Joy draws the Goatman and Dragonslayer side by side with

240

crosses. Bob attempts to show her the difference. Joy continues to say trick. Bob then says have you ever seen Mariann hurt by this one pointing to Dragonslayer and she nods her head no. Then he says have you ever seen Tabitha hurt by this one pointing to the Goatman, and she nods her head yes. Bob continues with this is the bad one and this is the good one. They are not the same. This one lies and hurts. This one tells the truth and no hurts. Joy switched inside and Mariann comes out to be rocked to sleep.

At 3:23AM, Mariann is restless and Joy switches out. She holds up her hands on the outside trying to communicate to Bob that she wants to go to Dragonslayer, but she is having a difficult time making the crossover. Bob doesn't know what to say. Dragonslayer puts out his arms inside and Joy runs into them as he closes them around her. She is still in his arms. Mariann switches out and her tummy ache doesn't hurt any more. She says that Dragonslayer do a funny(?) and he be a shepherd now for Joy. Council is pleased with results of the night. Tolip wants Joy's next step to be connecting with people.

The night was a success for the children of the System, because they could now associate Bob and Tina with the victorious side of a spiritual battle involving the Good Shepherd. It allowed them to trust him knowing that Dragonslayer worked through him. For them to see Bob's home as a safe place, meant that they could relax, knowing that Dragonslayer was just a call away. God was establishing three parallel paths into a time of instruction in His ways, to remind us of how far we have to go and to encourage us during the journey. He would reveal His itinerary for each of us as we needed to know it, and occasionally a little ahead of time.

"Thy throne, O God, is forever and ever;"
Psalm 45:6

"Trust in the Lord with all of your heart,
and do not lean on your own understanding.
In all your ways acknowledge Him,
and He will make your paths straight."
Proverbs 3: 5 – 6

Chapter Eleven

"Hearing God's Voice Above All Others"

*"He who learns but does not think is lost.
He who thinks but does not learn is in
great danger…Shall I teach you what
knowledge is? When you know a thing,
to recognize that you know it; And when
you do not know a thing, to recognize
that you do not know it. That is knowledge."*
Confucius, *Analects*, II, 15-17

**"All Scripture is inspired by God
and profitable for teaching, for reproof, for
correction, for training in righteousness;
that the man of God may be adequate,
equipped for every good work…
preach the word; be ready in
season and out of season;
reprove, rebuke, exhort,
with great patience and instruction."**
2 Timothy 3: 16 – 17, 4:2

**"When he puts fourth all his own, he goes before them, and
the sheep follow him because they know his voice…
I am the good shepherd; and I know My own, and
My own know Me, even as the Father knows Me
and I know the Father; and I lay down My life
for the sheep… My sheep hear My voice,
and I know them, and they follow Me; and
I give eternal life to them, and they shall
never perish; and no one shall snatch them
out of My hand. My Father, who has given
them to Me, is greater than all; and no one is
able to snatch them out of the Father's hand.
I and the Father are one."**
John 10: 4, 14 – 15, 27 – 30

Over the last two weeks I have been asked the same question that has been asked more than any other throughout my ministry. The first questioner was a total stranger in an art gallery, responding to a statement I made. The second one was a close friend and brother in the Lord searching for answers about his impending death. The third time came from an 11-year-old boy who had met Mariann and wanted to know how she could be telling the truth. It is a simple question really, but one with an answer that is hard to accept, if you have not experienced it often.

The question comes in various forms:

"How do you know it's God talking to you?"

"Do you actually hear God's voice answering you?"

"If it's hearing God's instructions in your 'heart', how do you know it is God and not the devil or your own ego?"

"Does God speak the same way to everyone?"

"How come I don't hear God the same way as you do?"

There is a question that is often raised by defense attorneys on TV, which is consistent with the general issue here. "Why is it that when we say we talk to God it is acceptable in society as prayer, but when we say God talks to us we are considered crazy?" I know for myself that when I share with friends how "God told me to… or God said to do this or that", I can usually expect some challenge or question like the ones above. Sometimes my answers are satisfactory to the questioner and sometimes they are not. It is often said that the base problem here is one of semantics, or the words used in the statement, but I don't believe it is.

Whatever words I use to explain how God speaks to me through His Scriptures, through another person, through a still small voice inside my soul, or even audibly through an angel sent by the Holy Spirit, can really only have meaning to someone ready and willing to hear whatever God has to say. God is always communicating to us in a variety of forms, often so directly and gently that when we miss it, we assume He is silent or not answering us. I think that God is sometimes silent in answering redundant and rhetorical questions that seek answers that are not His. None of us will hear God in any form, if we are predisposed to reject His answer.

It is easy to say "I hear God" or "God told me to do this" when the instruction or direction coincides with what we want or expect from God. But what happens when the answer is no, or go on this path which is very difficult and filled with pain to arrive where I want you to be? When God's answers are not what we want to hear and not what we expect, it is helpful to remember our place in relationship to God. The question of how I or anyone else hears God is not as important as what God is saying to us... and sometimes through us to those willing to listen. I can say with all confidence that God wants us to know and hear His will for our lives. The real question is "Am I... Are you... ready and willing to hear it?"

I raise these questions now because they will be a constant catalyst in all of the relationships that are formed with the System in the coming years, as well as my own relationships. As happens in all human relationships in the beginning, listening establishes a sort of trust account by which we measure our belief in another's statements. The more we accept a person as truthful and honest in life, the more trust we deposit into that relationship. This can be the building blocks for long and fruitful friendships. Of course, these friendships get stronger when we hear God through them the way that we want and yet, they can quickly be broken when we are not willing to hear God redirect, challenge, or chastise us in them.

Maria had already established herself in a number of relationships through her innocence and trust in Jesus. When she repeated what she heard from Jesus to her new friends, she was accepted as a woman filled with the Holy Spirit. When these same friends would hear anything from Liz that supposedly came from Jesus, there were immediate questions and challenges, primarily because of how she said it. Both could be speaking the truth, but only one might be heard. Was this ambiguity given them solely because of the multiplicity, or these friendships that fickle and fragile that God must only offer His truth in gentle, uplifting words?

Mariann probably had it easier in that she would repeat whatever Dragonslayer told her without concern about what He said or who heard it. This would become an endearing quality of hers in prayer with these friends. Some would leave the evening perplexed over what they heard but acknowledging at least that they heard it. Maria would often call or write me to ask about the meaning of what she said to people, as would Mariann.

Within a year, both Maria and Mariann would complain to me about a new problem facing them. As more people began to grasp the depth of faith of both adult and child, and their close relationship with Jesus, they began seeking them out to ask for direction from Jesus about their own issues. Initially, Maria tried to comply to the requests out of her need to be accepted and to please her new friends, but it didn't take long for the questions to become difficult and life changing. I believe that this was an outcome of so many people who struggle with the questions above... how do you hear God and communicate with Him?

My counsel to them from the beginning was simple. "If someone is asking questions pertaining to their self, then tell them that they need to ask Jesus directly and wait for the answer. The gifts that you are blessed with from the Holy Spirit are to be used as the Spirit leads, and not as a shortcut for others. You are not to be a crystal ball to Jesus, but His servant and prophet/teacher. This means that you should delineate between your opinion and what Jesus tells you to say to anyone. That will be difficult enough since you don't like having an opinion on anything. Don't worry too much about this, as I believe that Jesus will tell you most of the time to tell them to come to Him personally for the answer. Never be afraid to tell them the truth that Jesus gives to you, whether it be no! - He wants you to talk to Him... not me; - This is what I'm hearing... and tell them only what Jesus tells you. Remember, you are only the messenger – not the message. Jesus will guide you in these times so keep listening. Don't be afraid to test whatever God says with what He's already said in the Bible."

Over the next 5 years this behavior pattern would come and go as relationships came and went. It was always clear to those around Maria that she could clearly hear God speaking to her, at least as long as her answers were positive and supported the position or choices of the questioner. When her answers challenged them to change direction or stated that they are on the wrong path, then most would say how she doesn't hear God any better than the rest of us. Given Maria's own struggle with self esteem, she tended to support the latter thought by telling anyone the truth about listening to God. *"Anyone can hear God talking to them, if they are ready to hear, trust and obey whatever He tells you. Sometimes it is not what you want to hear."*

"But prove yourselves doers of the word, and not merely hearers who delude themselves."
James 1:22

Four days after Halloween, Maria's mother died. Her father called to say how he didn't want her to come up for the funeral, while her sister and others called to say what a horrible person she was for not going. Circle Council talked with Jesus and concluded that the environment would not be good for Maria, so they offered an alternative solution. Maria would write her message and her daughter, Rosalinda, would attend and read it for her. Council sent me the following excerpts.

We finally had some contact with Maria. She told me what she wanted in her message and asked me (Ruth) to fix it so it sounded good. Bob thinks the family will say it is preachy, but what does one expect out of Ruth! Anyway, Rosalinda will be representing Maria and reading it. Pray for her. As she stands up there, she will be Maria at nineteen in the eyes of the family. She will be taking Maria's heat, yet she is strong in the Lord. Maria is so happy that she is willing to do this. I tried to get Sergio to do the right thing and represent the family, but he refused. So much for being the man in the family.

"In the past few days, my mind has been swarming with thoughts of my mom. I have been trying to grab hold of my feelings and somehow understand them. I don't think that I am quite at the place of accepting that my mother is no longer on earth with me.

Yet, I have a peace in knowing that I will see my mother again in heaven. God blessed me with the opportunity to spend twenty minutes with my mother several Saturdays ago. I had flown up from California and it was a special time for us. As we sat there together praying to Jesus, we both asked for forgiveness for the times that we hurt one another. We talked about heaven and we talked about Jesus' love for us. It was a quiet moment of understanding that Jesus had forgiven both of us for our mistakes, sins and errors. We could feel his presence and love surrounding us. We both felt the security of knowing that we were not alone, but that Jesus was there. As we exchanged our love for one another, we cried in each other's arms. I was at peace when I said goodbye to my mom and told her that I'd see her in heaven someday...."

Maria wrote to Carol the next week to share her thoughts:

Hi Carol,

It's me, Maria. I miss you lots. My mom died on Wednesday and I still can't think of her dead. How long did it take for you to know your mother was really dead? I knew it was coming, but I can't believe it came...

I've been thinking about heaven a lot. Do you think heaven is way on the other side of the universe, or in another universe? I wonder if people from all over come to heaven and we will meet believers from other planets? Do you think that Jesus died for them too? Heaven must be like the warm light that Mariann talks about all of the time. I wonder if the flowers are perfect in heaven and if all of the bugs and worms are there, but they don't eat anything. Maybe the bees just fly around to sing beautiful buzz music, but they don't sting. And Mariann will be able to hug all of the elephants.

We'll never get hot from the sun because Jesus will be our light and it will be perfect. Perfect is a hard word to think about. When I think about it I think of Jesus. Perfect isn't on the outside because Jesus lets the kids mess up his hair and sometimes his clothes get dirt on them and stuff. But he is perfect in his heart and no dirt or mess ever touches that. So I wonder if heaven is heart perfect and outside perfect or just heart perfect? It would be funny to see Mariann and Tabitha Ann never get dirty rolling around. I don't know, it will be a surprise...

Maria would not be allowed much time to grieve for her mother with pleasant thoughts of seeing her in heaven. Her father called and Maria picked up the phone.

Her dad called and we did not switch out in time. Maria heard some stuff from him that made her sick. He told her that her mother died when a blood vessel broke in her head and blood

247

exploded out of her mouth, ears and nose. He told her that she suffocated because of the blood. Then he proceeds immediately to tell her how wonderful her sister was for coming up for a week and helping him clean out the mother's stuff. (This was an understatement as she 'cleaned out' the mother's jewelry, cash and anything else she could to sell for drugs later on.) *I was awakened to switch out at this point to say "that's great that she could be so helpful." Of course Maria feels bad that she wasn't allowed to go up and help, even though we reminded her that the father said don't come up. Maria doesn't look at the whole picture, only at her failure to a family that cares nothing for her.*

Maria's family is warped and I know that she struggles with being pulled between her new family that cares for her (you, Bruce, Carol, Lindsay, Bob and Tina), and her old family that cares nothing for her. She is conflicted over her two families saying different things and she has to choose whom she will believe. She obeys her new family out of trust and love but feels guilty about betraying her family obligations. I told her that you can't obey two opposing sides...

Maria's church is having problems. Tina told her it was issues in the hierarchy that are making people wonder about the direction they are heading. It is making Bob stressed. Maria just prays for wisdom for everyone in leadership and hopes they will hear Jesus. She told Bob that they aren't listening...

In the early years of the System's relationship with Pastor Bob, Quiet Walker would communicate with him about his struggles as a church leader. Often her words came in story form, but always with a message of encouragement and direction to help him. I do not believe that Bob ever really took the time to assess the messages from Raquel that applied directly to him, or truly attempt to understand and accept her in her relationship with the Great Spirit.

To the One Who Speaks of He Who is Truth:

Grace to you and peace from the Great Spirit. I have come from Sacred Mountain and have heard from the Obedient One (Maria) of the message given to her by those who are against the Great

One. I am not afraid for I know their ways. They are like chaff to the wind. Their threats carry no substance.

We are secure in He who is truth. Be encouraged my fellow traveler. He who has begun a good work in you will continue to mold and shape you. Do not be dismayed or afraid, for the Great Spirit is with you always. But you must remember to be as shrewd as a serpent and as innocent as a dove. Remember the words from the Great Spirit to the servant Jeremiah as it was told to me by Heavenly Dove.

"They speak falsehoods in my name. I have never sent them, nor commanded them, nor spoken to them. They are telling you false words, deceptions of their own mind."

Beware follower of the truth, do not be deceived for the enemy has sent reinforcements and is energizing those who have strayed away from the truth. They have allowed their eyes to be blocked and their ears to be plugged. They no longer see with spirit eyes but with earthly eyes.

You, my fellow journeyman, continue to remain close to the provider of all life. Continue to seek his face and his direction. Do not allow the words of the enemy to penetrate your being... resist it. Yet do not be exceedingly righteous, but humble and know that the Great Spirit is able to straighten that which has been bent.

Continue to trust in He who is truth. Be careful not to allow that which is not from the Great Spirit to enter your being. Carefully and slowly consider your words for the tongue comes with much power. Be one of pure love and sincere faith. Do not allow others to pull you into empty discussions, for there are many voices who profess to be from the Great Spirit. Test them all. Do not be confused by their rhetoric for they have been equipped with tongues to lead astray. The enemy is using pride, ambition, power and control to lure many into confusion... causing division. Be encouraged! The body of Christ will not be overtaken by the enemy, but the Great Spirit is in the midst of purging the factions within that are leading the body away from growing in faith.

Let all you do be in love. You are a front-line warrior of the Almighty One. Make sure your armor is securely intact as you enter battle. Know that your fight is not with those who grace the same table with you, but the battle is of another dimension. It is a battle that many can not understand and few have seen. It is the great battle and you are a warrior in it. Know that many bright spirits have encircled you and your family. You are well protected, so you do not need to be afraid. But do not let your guard down for the enemy is lurking in the shadows, waiting to jump at any opportunity to bring fear, depression and chaos.

Again I bring you peace and intercede on your behalf as I walk with Dragonslayer. I leave you with these words:

"Speak the words of truth in love. Seek the wise counsel of the Great Spirit. Do not be discouraged. Continue to praise him in the midst of the circumstances and you will be given wisdom."
                              Quiet Walker

I began to follow Bob's choices in ministry with interest to see what difference if any, the input from the System had on him. I decided to record his journey alongside that of the System, to see if he would respond differently then most when the difficult choices came as I knew they would. It wasn't difficult in the beginning for him to answer Maria's questions, or that of Mariann and Ruth, but Ann was still on an in-depth search for scientific truth and verification of God and Liz followed demanding 'real' truth be lived out. He found his interaction with Ann as challenging and stimulating as I did and wasted no time giving his theological perspective to her. Ann would give me the same question to compare answers.

Ann renewed this process in late November after observing the events described until now. She had accepted God as real but was working very hard to understand our relationship with God and its purpose. She asked me, *"What does it mean to be made in the image of God?"* She had asked a similar question of Bob and didn't yet feel close enough to him to challenge his response. She had been hearing from Jesus about being created for His purposes and how teaching was just one of those purposes. This caused a more basic question to be addressed, what does God look like?

"Hello Ann,

It's been a while since you asked me a 'theological' question. I've missed our discussions over lunch. I'm wondering about two things: What prompted the question for you? And, Why did it take you so long to ask about this particular issue? Frankly, I expected it last summer, which is why I think my questions are related. God's timing is impeccable. I've been contemplating this question as I write a paper about 'how the Gospel of John is to be understood in overall meaning by us.' I'll condense it for you given our time problems currently. You will expect of course that my answers will be more questions for you, so please answer as much as you can…when you can.

You asked for my interpretation of what it means to be made in the image of God? Anyone's interpretation of this is dependent upon three concepts that are related to each other. The first and most important is who do you understand God to be? If I ask you to paint a verbal picture of the image of God, what kind of features or characteristics would you describe? What emotions, attitudes, or personality traits and qualities…even physical criteria, would you ascribe to God?

John 1:18 starts us in a direction of the answer. "No man (the word here stands for male or female) has seen God at any time; the only begotten Son, who is in the bosom of the Father, He has explained Him." The answer to the first concept is then understood to be revealed by the only individual this side of heaven to have ever seen God or know Him. My interpretation, within the parameters I gave you, of who God is given to me from the whole of Scriptures, is the revelation of God about Himself in relationship to mankind, particularly in the Gospel of John.

Jesus revealed to us in person all that we could comprehend or needed to know about the character and person of God. "I and the Father are one…If you had known Me, you would have known My Father also, from now on you know Him and have seen Him."

Ann, you are in a better position than I to paint the image of God, if only in a visual sense. I cannot see the face of Jesus as you can on the inside, except by faith through the eyes of my soul. So my question to you is this; whom do you see and know when you are with Jesus? How do you describe Him beyond His gender? I ask it this way because I believe our image before God is never a gender issue. Who we are is the only way to understand God over what we are. Who I am as a person in relationship to other people can reflect images beyond my physical self and this reality. What I am is limited to this reality.

Remember how many times you asked me, Why are you here? I hope that I was there to reflect the reality of what I know by faith, and the image of the One that you can see face-to-face, with a reality that could be touched and known by all of you...before you could 'see'. This is where I want to leave you with my first response to your question. Image is in the eye of the beholder, so who do you see when you look at Jesus?

Of course, to really see Him well enough to describe Him characteristically, you have to spend time with Him to know the person inside. Write back and define the image question in your own words and we'll move on to the next part of the equation with your axioms set in place. You might find John's Gospel to be a useful thesaurus. I'll look forward to your answer with anticipation. Give my love to everyone and tell Maria not to worry...Liz's right hook was an appropriate response to his actions. Take care.   Mike"

Ann wasted little time in responding:

I can't seem to get the bugs out of my technology lesson, so I thought I would take a break and get back to my question about the image of God. I don't see how your two questions have anything to do with the discussion about image. I looked in the Webster dictionary for a definition of image. It defines image as a popular conception. So I looked up conception which means formulating an idea. So the definition of an image of something is an idea or picture accepted by most people.

For example, the image of St. Nicholas is a fat old man with a white beard and ridiculous red clothes, driving a sleigh of reindeer over rooftops. Now an image does not need to be accurate, true or tested by scientific methods. The only criteria for an image, is that it is an idea or picture accepted by most people. Also, images change over time. For example, the image of the automobile is very different today from the 1950's. So from this information, I began to consider the image of God.

My earliest recollection of God's image was in the Catholic Church. I remember seeing this stain glass window with this huge old man blowing the wind around. It was a strange picture and I surmised that it had something to do with creation, but as a child it was very threatening. God's image was of a huge old man with a bitter attitude. He enjoyed sitting on his throne and dictating to his priests how he was going to send all of us to the 'fiery pit'. He especially hated woman and made a point to remind his priests how women are always tempting men and leading them astray.

At college, I put God out of my mind. He stayed away from me and I didn't bother him. The only time that he was discussed was in philosophy. I learned how God was a made up idea to get people to obey the law, by making them believe that something terrible was going to happen to them if they didn't. I explored reality and liked the security of setting up criteria for determining reality versus 'ideas'.

Well here I am in the 90's and I'm facing this issue all over again. You asked me who I see when I look at Jesus inside. What a question! I can only go on what I have seen there. He has more patience than anyone I have ever met. The kids never seem to irritate or stress him out. In fact, he seems to be the happiest when they are crawling all over him. Although he is a male in outward appearances, he seems to have a nurturing aspect to him and a motherly type way of comforting the kids. He understands them emotionally which is something men do not seem to grasp. I can't quite explain it.

His motives are a dilemma to me. He is not concerned about financial gain and doesn't seem interested in advancement. He seems only interested in those kids and the other parts. Maria and the kids trust him with their lives. Mariann wants to be just like him and even Liz has great respect for him.

So who is he? He is not that easy to put into a character box. I had a difficult time coming up with a reasonable explanation of who he is. I asked Maria and she told me that Raquel told her that the Great Spirit is the alphabet. So I will leave you with their definition.

A=Awesome	*B=Beautiful*	*C=Caring*	*D=Devoted*
E=Encouraging	*F=Faithful*	*G=Good*	*H=Holy*
I=Infinite	*J=Jubilant*	*K=Kind*	*L=Loving*
M=Merciful	*N=Nurturing*	*O=Omnipotent*	
P=Powerful	*Q=Quiet voice*	*R=Radiant*	*S=Strong*
T=Tender	*U=Unchanging*	*V=Victorious*	
W=Wise	*X=eXcellent*	*Y=Yahweh*	*Z=Zenith*

I can see some of these descriptions, but not all of them. I see him as a very patient person with the interest of the children and the other parts as his focus. He comforts them when they are afraid. He teaches them. He disciplines them at times. He laughs with them and plays with them. He can fluctuate from simple words for Mariann to a higher level of discussion with Ruth. He seems to always be around, but never shoves his power around.

So these are my axioms. However, I do not see the connection yet between "image of God" and Jesus. I didn't ask you who God was. I asked you to interpret the meaning of 'image' of God.

-Ann

P.S. I can't wait to dump these kids on you at Christmas. They have been driving me crazy.

I had to respond before my finals were due or I would not have time until after Christmas. When the System came to visit us Ann would usually not be seen, with all of our time taken by everyone else. She rested while the children, Maria, Louise, Ruth and even Liz took turns getting filled with love. Council would relax as well, as they knew that everyone was safe with us. I wanted to respond while Ann was still restless over the issues discussed, because once she 'shutdown', it would be a while before she started again.

"Hi Ann,

I'm answering now because I won't have another chance for at least two weeks. Your original question was clearly stated; "What is your interpretation of "made in the image of God?" If all you wanted was the definition of image, then you are right to read Webster's and we can stop there if you wish. My intuition says your original question is the real issue before you otherwise you wouldn't keep qualifying the word image with God. Your axiom from your youth even begins by explaining your concepts of God.

The image of God has no contextual value in itself if simply viewed for understanding as a picture or idea of some being that we cannot really know or have a relationship with to understand. If all you want to understand is 'what does God look like', then I'm back to pointing you to Jesus' interpretation for the reasons previously given. The Bible explains to us why we are unable to behold the face of God until we pass into heaven for eternity, when we will see God face-to-face. We wouldn't survive the glory of His righteousness as sinful human beings. He wants us to know Him and survive to tell about it, so He sent us Jesus.

I think the issue here is, understanding the 'God' who made us in His image. Why? Perhaps we need to define more clearly the specific terms used in the question. Your definition of image works as far as it goes for images in general, but not for the specific image of God as described in the Bible. So the next word to define is God, as it gives definition to image.

There are two basic definitions, one spelled god and the other spelled God. The first is defined as: a being of supernatural powers or attributes, believed in and worshipped by a people; especially a male deity thought to control some part of nature or reality or to personify some force or activity; a man godlike in aspect and power. The second is defined as: a being conceived of as the perfect, omnipotent, omniscient originator (Creator) and ruler of the universe, the principal object of faith and worship in monotheistic religions; the force, effect, or manifestation or aspect of this being the single supreme agency postulated in some philosophical systems to explain the phenomena of the world, having a nature variously conceived in such terms as prime mover, an immanent vital force, or infinity.

I am of the opinion that the second one, God, is the only one worth knowing as God. This being is not limited by our definitions, our knowledge, our tests, our concepts of gender, power or fear, our expectations or fear of the unknown. This is the

God I choose to know because He made the choice to be fully known by those who seek Him. As the only supreme God, He could have forced us to know and acknowledge Him, but instead He gives us the free choice to believe in Him. Does a supreme, omnipotent, creator God have any obligation to His creation, except by choice?

All other gods that we conceive of are only gods with power over us that we give to them. This is not to say that these deities are not powerful, they are, but not more so than the One true God deserving of our worship. They really only exist with this power as we support them in our belief systems. We create various and conflicting images of gods that change, as our needs of them change our conceptions reflected in these idols. You used the example of the image of the automobile. An automobile could be conceived of as one of these gods and worshipped as such by some poor souls.

While God is not limited by our realities or our conceptions of Him, we are limited only by the amount of His reality that He chooses to reveal to us. Yet, He does this without ever changing His nature. This reality is not defined in Webster's because it can't be fully by definition. This God can only be defined by Himself. He has done so to three major religions of the world and many more philosophies as the God of the Bible. So I suggest that we look for our definitions of God, His image and His work of creation there.

You offered me a limited definition of the image of God that was not your own, but that of the other parts. You also described the image and person of Jesus as only affecting and encountering the 'others' and not necessarily you on the inside. By your own words you have trouble understanding who He is, yet you have accepted Him as your Savior. Why? Do you have a relationship with Him or not? If you do, then you have a basis for establishing axioms about His reality. Your definitions from the other parts are not valid unless you believe them to be true. All good scientific study begins with a step of faith, one where the 'truth' of a fact, idea, concept, or object of study is sought to be proven through research and empirical evidence. Ultimately, all scientists believe philosophically that the truth of anything will prove itself.

The object of your image in question is outside our ability to scientifically define it within our reality, unless that same truth reveals itself in our time and physical space. So we are either back to the Bible again for definition, or we have to look inside His reality, something you still seem reticent to do. I believe the God of our discussion is best reflected by the one you know as Jesus on the inside. He matches up to the image and reality of God as I know Him in my realities of the Bible and faith philosophy. If all of the things that you have witnessed so far as a scientist on the inside and on the outside, even vicariously through other eye witnesses, doesn't confirm this as the only rational explanation, then our discussion is a waste of your time.

According to your letters, you have let the Catholic Church, human philosophies, Webster, children's concepts and other parts, determine your reality of the person Jesus as the 'image' of God. I have to ask why again. You are the one wanting to know the truth about the image of God and why we are the way we are. They already know what they believe. Do you not want to know for yourself? Whom do you seek if it's not God? Whom do you want to see as God's image?

If you are looking for any 'image', then I offer you Jesus as my interpretation. If you are looking for the truth of the image of God, then I offer you Jesus. Interpret Him and you will have your answers. He will reveal as much of Himself and His Father as you are able to understand within the amount of faith that you have. You are perhaps the most intelligent person I have ever met and your capacity to learn is extreme, but do not worry, Jesus will not overwhelm you before you are ready. Remember that faith is necessary to understand that reality which exists beyond what we are able to measure or verify.

Your description, as brief as it was, is consistent with as much of Him as you know. What I hope you gain from this exercise is that there is so much more waiting for you. You have to discover the truth of it through faith first. Read John 1:1 thru 1:18 and see if it matches up to the God of Webster's dictionary and remember which came first. If there is one truth I want you to know, it is that God revealed Himself in history and in our hearts through Jesus Christ His Son. Your choice to observe Him and keep Him at arm's length in developing a relationship can result in your knowledge being limited by those restraints. I expected you to jump at the chance to know truth about life, God and who is in control. You can learn a lesson from the children about God, because their faith and trust in God through Jesus has overcome greater odds than you will face in your lifetime. Read Matthew 11:25.

No one can take your salvation away from you and only you have the power to know the reality behind the image of God as the only true original God personally. Or you can settle for a myth of limited reflection without any real power to change your life. Jesus wants you to know that what you get out of this journey equates directly to how much you put into it. Write again soon my friend."

Ann was not the only writer these days. Liz had been writing to Bob at his church. She made a discovery that evoked a reaction:

...I ain't writing to Bob anymore. The damn staff at that church throws my letters away. Talk about censorship...they read them cuz I checked. I wrote this nice letter and then, right at the end, I said if you are reading Bob's mail then f*#% off and mind your own business. Well, it got shit canned. So they read the stuff. I told Bob that's it! You ain't getting no more pearls of great thought from me. Of course, I ain't got no pearls of great thought...just pearls of how to have fun.

How's Carol doing down there? I miss watching her turn red and wigging out. Her and I gotta do some wild Christmas stuff together when we're down there. Are you gonna take me to that Hollywood church to meet your friend? I'm sure you already heard that the mother died a couple weeks ago. So, you still got my beer? I plan to have several for New Years Eve with you.
Gotta jet!

I wrote her to ask about her feelings surrounding the mother's death, because I knew that she was bothered by it. However, the conversation would have to wait until we were together. I tried to set up an opportunity for some graduate students in psychology to interview the System through Liz and Ruth during winter break, but the dean considered it too much of a risk for both parties concerned. I think the school lost a great teaching moment in reality.

Liz wanted to open some eyes beyond theory and offered a hands-on response to seminary students before entering their careers. Her response to hearing that they declined followed her last letter.

Hey Buddy,

I haven't been ignoring your questions. Been busy with adopt-a-family stuff like you used to do up here. Bob's church said they want real poor so I gave it to them. Let's see how they handle it.

Here's my response to your bad news:

Once upon a time there were these Pharisees called Deans. They ruled over their charges with memos and emails. To control them was their main goal. The deans never allowed them to hear someone who spoke of things that they did not understand. They especially despised someone who was different and might lead their charges to rethink their beliefs and prejudices. And because of this...new little dean clones spread throughout all of the churches with the minds of the Pharisees.

My reaction: Screw them. I don't give a rats ass about their decision. They are afraid that Maria's feet will contaminate their holy ground! Well, I ain't letting Maria walk into a place that rejects her. What are they afraid of...the truth? So our deal is off and that means no Disneyland trip at Christmas. But I know you must feel like getting us something, so I did a survey for you.

Liz – a six pack for New Years Eve with junk food.

Mariann – 15 hugs from daddy because that's a lot. (This kid don't know what to ask for when she has the opportunity.) Going to the moon and swing, eat cookies and drink Mr. Pibb (What the hell is that? Shit, she's not stopping!), go nite nite... play, talk to lami, can I have 15 hugs from mama too? See daddy's sandal camp and church...cheerios, no more.

Tabitha – ice cream blanko

Joy – talk to lamb

Maria – I want to sit at the table and have hot chocolate and listen to Pastor Chalberg tell me all that he has learned about Jesus in school.

Louise – I would like to go to the parade of flowers if that is okay? I have never seen anything like that and can I smell them too? I would like to work in Carol's rose garden if she will let me.

Ann – nothing except for him to take care of these kids for a week so I can rest.

Jennifer – I would love to walk along the ocean.

Ruth, Marie, Mari, Hopi all want nothing.

Lila – can I have a small hug?

No one else is answering so I guess that's it. See you in a few weeks.

Liz's reaction to the school's rejection was somewhat harsh, because of two reasons. First, she really wanted to offer a dose of reality to graduate students who normally don't get an opportunity to interview a multiple as responsive as her. Also because she doesn't like 'professionals making decisions about her protection.

The fact that everyone was excited to come for a week's visit over Christmas and New Years made it difficult for Ann to contain them the next few weeks. An elder at the church in Pasadena had offered us seating out front on the Rose Parade route and we took him up on it. Maria wrote us about the current status:

We are getting excited cuz it is almost time to see you. I always pray for you cuz Jesus puts you in my mind and tells me to. Ann went to a conference on the beach. I watched from inside some and it was beautiful, but they all talked too high up for me. Ann got called up front and they said that she was a scholarship winner. After lots of big people from New York and places talked with her, Liz came out and got in trouble for trying to drink liquor. Helper stopped her and Ann threw it away. Raquel took a walk real early along the beach when no one was around and watched the ocean from the hill. Say hi to Carol for me. Louise says hi and Mariann is ready to see you now!

A week later:

Greetings Shedding Tear, It is I, Quiet Walker,
There is much excitement in the land as the children prepare to see you. Their hearts have yearned for your presence. I have been at Sacred Mountain. The Great Spirit has called me there to learn of the ways of the trickster shepherds. The evil one has confused them and led them astray from the truth.
I am sending with the obedient one some gifts for you and One Who is Like the Angels. The Talking Feather Stick is Sioux. When the leaders of Council sit, they use the talking feather. It is passed around the circle and each one has a chance to hold it. The one holding the feather is the only one person allowed to speak.
I am giving you my Eagle Claw Dancing Stick for I know it will be cared for by you. My stick is used by medicine men for healing and calling up the power of the strength of the eagle. The claws must always point down and never touch the ground.
May they serve you well.
Quiet Walker

Dear Carol and Mike,
I finally have some time out and thought I would update you on things. As you know, life is never dull around here. Ann has been working a lot and gaining a name for herself in the district. She is good at what she does, but God always slides in a few things to throw her off. This week she was lecturing about variable expressions and this kid raises his hand saying I have a question and it's personal. Ann puts the class in groups and goes to talk to him. He pulls down his lip and asked, "Are these herpes?"
Ann's first reaction inside was I am a math teacher not a sex ed teacher. Liz is rolling inside by now and tells Ann to ask him if he has got them anywhere else. Ann then tells the boy, if you are worried about it you should go to the health clinic on campus and they will tell you everything you need to know. Ann almost died.
Ann is corresponding with Bob about societal law versus religious law. I have no idea what she's talking about but Bob says

that he understands her. Bob nailed Liz over the issue of responsibility in working. They get along in a weird sort of way. Liz had her first outside encounter with him over a beer. She requested a beer and Bob learned his lesson and made her eat first so what happened last time won't happen again.

Liz got to bring some cheer to Jeri today. Things are not going well for her. Her unborn child has kidney problems and will require an operation after birth. The husband is not supportive and not providing for the child. Jeri called her in terrible shape because the baby is due any day and she doesn't even have a bed for it. The husband spent his paycheck on a racing bike telling Jeri that he's got to do these things before he gets old. That's when Liz blew. She told Jeri how no friend of hers was going to have her baby sleep on the floor. She told her that she would take care of it.

In one hour, Liz showed up with a crib and mattress, car seat, and more clothes than we got. She and Jeri sat around with the kids and looked at all of the outfits. Vanessa told Liz that now the baby doesn't have to be naked and Liz said no way! Vanessa then said God is the greatest and Liz agreed telling her, yeah kid he's pretty cool. It was Bob's church that came through for her. Liz was highly impressed and knows now that not all Christians are selfish.

Yesterday I did my first solo babysitting job for Bob and Tina. Tina has been very sick and Bob had a funeral to do so I offered to help. I couldn't find Louise inside to come out to cook, so I did. They ate it anyway and after I put them to bed, Maria informed me that I didn't make them brush their teeth. Holding the baby and trying to get the others to lay down was difficult. Somehow their baby boy could see Maria waving to him from the inside and kept laughing without going to sleep. When I looked away he'd start to fuss a lot, so I had Maria come out and he curled up in her arms and was fast asleep in no time. I guess I'm not the maternal type.

When Bob came home, he brought Tina some flowers from the funeral that they gave him to cheer Tina up. We had fun teasing her about getting dead man's flowers. It was Liz's time I used to help Bob, so she gets a beer for her generosity.

Mariann has really been missing you a lot lately. Bob's kids talk a lot about her daddy being gone. They don't understand either since their daddy is there. We keep stressing Christmas is coming, but she has a difficult time with length of days. We knew that she was close to you, but I think that even Council didn't realize how close. They hoped that her play with these kids would distract her, but even though she likes playing with them, you are always on her mind and heart.

Bob plans to take her to see Billy Graham soon. She wanted her daddy to take her to hear the 'Dragonslayer man', but since you can't she has agreed to go with Bob. Helper and Council still need to make contact with Bob about holding on to Mariann in a crowd and being aware of the smelly ones around. He doesn't listen well yet to Council and I hope that changes. Why do you think that is? We will be in prayer over this.

My time is up and I've got to go. Tell Carol the roses that she gave Louise are flourishing now...no surprise there. She also resurrected the dying plant...good thing you didn't give them to me or they would be dead by now.
Ruth

The week and a half spent with us at Christmas would be a major turning point in the healing journey for the entire System. It did not occur with great spiritual fanfare or awareness of a spiritual battle happening around us. No, this odyssey began in the home of an elderly couple, who reached out in love to a woman and two children. Prior to meeting Maria, Mariann and Tabitha in their home, Bruce and Tone (*See Book One, pg. v*) had only heard about their journey with us through my descriptions and many prayer requests that had come their way. They had been my faithful prayer support team since the days when they had introduced me to our Lord Jesus Christ.

While very familiar with the Bible and a long healthy relationship with God, they understood very little about how MPD or DID worked within the human psyche and soul. They had a firm grasp of evil and the capacity of mankind to do evil. More importantly, they had experienced firsthand the unfathomable grace of Jesus and His power to overcome evil. They had modeled for years the unconditional love of Christ and had decided to give no less to the System. They readily admitted being sure of nothing about the System on that day, except a belief that God was with them, based upon their trust in me and that God would reveal His truth.

On that blustery day on the beach and later in their home, they began to give them love, without expecting anything in return. They offered real love that only grandparents can give. They gave it to children who had only known pain and abuse from grandparents that were still alive in their memories. The children knew instinctively that these two would not hurt them and accepted their embrace without fear. As I watched Bruce put his windbreaker on Tabitha's shoulders on the beach, I saw her smile express her feelings that this grandpa was not 'Hombre Malo'.

Later that night, as Bruce entertained Mariann with his big bear that talked about the Good Shepherd, I saw different child parts rotate out to look and hear this man. He was unaware of the other kids because the expressions of awe rarely changed. Mariann was the only one to engage in conversation with him because she knew that he knew Dragonslayer. This was the first male that she talked to who was more ancient than her daddy.

When Mariann moved to show him her scars from surgery like they were marks of honor, before we could stop her, imagine my surprise when Bruce retaliates by showing her his scars from open heart surgery. Trying to keep either one from going into too much detail for the more squeamish parts was a chore and a half. In one evening, Bruce had cemented his authority as a friend of Dragonslayer forever.

Later, as the time together would be limited to a few times per year, the security of having grandparents who loved them would encourage them in future spiritual battles knowing that they were praying for their healing and protection. Maria would find great joy in being able to pray with these two whom she considered to be her grandparents from God. Some of the adults in the System used to ask me after that day, *"How is it that they can love us so easily and obviously understand very little about multiplicity? Are they that trusting or simply not curious?"*

I explained about their journey with God and how the need to know and understand was secondary to their trust in Jesus. They had already accepted in the loss of their second son through mental illness, how many important questions will not be answered in this life. I told how they accept in grace because they have been accepted in grace. Some years later they will provide a strong, simple defense of how God is a part of the System and still can't explain the multiplicity to any degree. They know that the love given and received is real and the details of how that is possible won't change a thing.

The rest of our time together was memorable as well. Trying to contain the joy, laughter and awe as Mariann, Tabitha and Maria sat in the front row seat on Colorado Blvd. watching the Rose Parade glide by, was great fun for me. It was only rivaled by the first time I took my son to Disneyland. When the giant caterpillar came by dancing the Macarena, I thought Mariann would pass out from excitement. She was afraid at seeing such a large insect 'alive' and dancing happily on the street, yet she vacillated between running out to join it... to staying securely in her seat. Thank God for marching bands or the adults wouldn't have seen a thing.

I have wondered sometimes about who God would have brought into the System's lives, if Bruce and Tone had chosen to not 'trust and obey'. Their faith and obedience led me into the presence of God 27 years earlier and now God was using them again to heal generational wounds. Listening to God and hearing His will becomes a lifetime challenge to change lives for eternity.

"Grandchildren are the crown of old men,
And the glory of sons is their father."
Proverbs 17:6

"The righteous man will flourish like the palm tree,
He will grow like a cedar in Lebanon.
Planted in the house of the Lord,
They will flourish in the courts of our God.
They will still yield fruit in old age;
They shall be full of sap and very green,
To declare that the Lord is upright;
He is my rock, and there is no unrighteousness in Him."
Psalm 92:12 – 15

Chapter Twelve

"The Soul's Search for Reality"

*"The other disciples therefore were saying to him,
'We have seen the Lord!' But he said to them,
'Unless I shall see in His hands the imprint
Of the nails, and put my fingers into
His side, I shall not believe."*
John 20:25

"What men perceive as real is real in its consequences."
Sociological axiom

"Reason is a light that God has kindled in the soul..."
*"The end of art is to figure the hidden meaning
of things and not their appearance;
for in this profound truth lies their true reality,
which does not appear in their external outlines."*
Aristotle

While on my journey as a young man in search of truth, I read Aristotle and came across his statement about the 'end' or goal of art. I remember thinking how this could apply to more than art and if I really wanted to see beyond the surface appearances of reality, then this meant that I had to be open to more than what I perceive through my eyes for a deeper understanding of anything.

An example of this is the way a blind person will develop all of their other senses to a level higher than the average person, or how a good counselor will listen and understand more than just what is said. A mother's intuition concerning the safety of her children can often go far beyond her sight or hearing. Is the connection between these senses only the filter of our mind, or does the soul play a part in perceiving what we cannot see, hear, touch or smell? Just as a picture can evoke totally different emotions between two people, our soul's perception of the spiritual realm can have two people describing the same reality differently. The reality itself does not change, just our perception of it. The things we experience in life can become the filter that mediates between the mind and the soul.

If this filter becomes clogged with conflicting perceptions, we have to stop and analyze our choices, putting them in an alignment which allows for the flow of free thought. When the choices force us to choose between realities within the spiritual realm, that we can't perceive with our senses, we usually opt for the mind's understanding over the soul's. The more we compromise our soul, the less effective it becomes for determining 'unseen' realities with our senses. It's sort of like the old Star Wars films where Luke Skywalker must learn to use the 'force', by putting a helmet on to blind him and thus allowing the force to flow through his other senses. We must allow our souls to be trained in the ways of the spiritual realm in order to 'see' its realities and learn how to respond in that reality beyond our sight.

It had become clear to me during the System's visit that the amount of time spent counseling them was not going to diminish as the New Year began. The major difference would be that the bulk of it would be over the phone and by email. This meant that I would need to trust and develop my senses other than sight to be aware of their present condition. I began spending more time in prayer and asking the Holy Spirit to guide and gift my soul to help those in need by 'seeing' the spiritual truths surrounding them.

The need to keep the System focused on Jesus and listening to His instructions to them was always immediate in this long distance approach. I had explained to Mariann how we were following instructions by coming down to seminary to be prepared to do more work for Dragonslayer, yet we were still a team. It appeared to her that everyone but her was going to school and she wanted to experience what Pastor Bob's older children did going to school each day. That's when the Lord had me suggest that she and any of the children inside who wanted to could go to 'sandal camp'. This would be time spent with Jesus as He taught them about sharing His gospel in ways that only a child can do effectively.

We also needed a method of sharing and feeling warmth and love over the phone. I instituted our 'phone hugs' and blessings for each child as requested. Each time we asked Dragonslayer to be on one end, as the children closed their eyes and pictured me there on the other end. I would begin humming a hugging sound that varied with intensity, depending upon the length and their need for a hug. It is hard to describe the event that has taken on a life of its own. We had butterfly hugs, cowboy hugs, flying hugs and many more, with Jesus doing all of the special effects until I ran out of breath. It may sound hokey if you're not a hugger, but I can tell you truly, that when I heard a child laughing so hard on the other end of the phone that she could barely hold on to it…my soul leaped with joy.

Many emotions would be openly expressed and shared in a mutual presence that only the Holy Spirit can bring in Jesus with adults and children alike. When we were able to come together on brief visits, it was as though we hadn't been apart for long. The old encouragement of "I can't be there in person, but I'll be there in spirit" became a sensory reality between Maria, Louise, Mariann and us that can only be experienced, not explained. Trusting in Jesus to be the conduit of love between our physical distances was getting easier and easier. The spiritual gift of perceiving their spiritual reality through voice inflection on the phone, proved to be both useful and unnerving to most of the adults. It also began to overlap into other areas of ministry for which I am grateful.

> **"Thy word I have treasured in my heart,**
> **that I may not sin against Thee."**
> **Psalm 119:11**

> *"For by these He has granted to us His precious and magnificent promises, in order that by them you might become partakers of the divine nature, having escaped the corruption that is in the world by lust. Now for this very reason also, applying all diligence, in your faith supply moral excellence, and in your moral excellence, knowledge; and in your knowledge, self-control, and in your self-control, perseverance, and in your perseverance, godliness; and in your godliness, brotherly kindness, and in your brotherly kindness, love. For if these qualities are yours and are increasing, they render you neither useless nor unfruitful in the true knowledge of our*
> *Lord Jesus Christ."*
> **2 Peter 1: 4 – 8**

I speak of these issues now, because a significant amount of energy is spent over the next seven years trying to understand and determine what is real within and around our lives. The System is about to enter a tug-of-war between dimensions and the beings living in both, as well as between their loyalties to Christian friends. I observed certain themes being tested repeatedly, as they looked to new friends to give affirmation to the spiritual realities seen only by them, yet often heard and intuitively felt by others. The reoccurring issue was: *"How is it that we can see so many things in this world that are consistent within our inside world that so many outside cannot see?"*

Perhaps the most difficult spiritual issue that the System will encounter immediately and continually will be Christian love. The people they encounter will both empower and confuse them as they attempt to express the love growing within their souls. No relationship will escape untouched by their desire to love and be loved. It will also be the subject of many sessions in Circle Council, as Ann tries to prevent Maria from giving love too easily to everyone she meets. Ann expresses her fears to Council over Maria loving Carol and I too much, after returning home from the holidays with us. It will precipitate a number of letters between Council and me, as I seek to help them understand the various types of love we face in life.

Greetings from the leaders of Circle Council. We have been in session for several days discussing concerns brought to us by Ann. She has stated her concern regarding Maria's dependency, as she calls it, on you. We called Maria in to hear Ann's complaints to challenge them, but Maria became very frightened and confused, so Ruth became her advocate.

Ann stated that Maria is addicted to loving you and can't stop talking or thinking about you. Ruth countered with, "Maria loves both Mike and Carol with all of her heart, much the way that she loves Jesus. She repeats the memories of her time with them over and over again because it brings her comfort and happiness. She likes to think about her time with the Chalbergs because it gives her joy for the first time in her life having only 'good memories'

269

about a relationship." Ruth said that she sees nothing wrong with Maria's closeness with the Chalbergs and Ann is overreacting.

Ann stated how she wants the parts to go and then come back and forget about them until they see them again, if she is required to provide Maria and the children with three plane tickets a year to see the Chalbergs. Ann voiced her complaint again over us allowing them to form relationships with people that come and go...and only cause anxiety for the weaker parts.

Daniel questioned Ann as to why it bothered her so much that Maria talks about Mike to her. He challenged her that maybe she was jealous of Maria's closeness to Mike. Ann got angry of course and said, "Not on your life. I'm not jealous of any man. I just get tired of hearing her talk about him as if he walks on water."

Ruth said, "I've seen him sink several times Ann."

Ann, "Funny Ruth and you know what I mean."

The discussion went on for several hours with Ann setting her case and Ruth tearing it down. Finally Council closed the discussion and voted to have Ann give the system three weeks a year with spending money and plane tickets to visit you. In exchange, Ann is allowed to work full time from September to June. Maria continues to be allowed freedom of speech to talk about anyone she wishes, as long as it isn't with Ann.

Ann must allow the other parts freedom from mid-June to mid-August to travel and engage freely in new relationships. If Ann will adhere to this, the other parts will agree to allow Ann to have week days from mid-August to mid-June. Saturday nights are for Liz and Sundays are for church and time for the children with Pastor Bob's family.

I talked with Maria after this about her fears over the topic being discussed and her understanding of love. I asked her to ask Jesus if our relationship was inappropriate in any way. He told her no and how He wished more of His children would have a relationship like ours. I decided to write Ann and discuss her fears about Maria's desire to be with us. Ann still refused to believe that a close loving relationship was possible long term and impossible long distance. She was also the person most concerned about the new relationships developing in our absence.

Ann was uncomfortable with the physical intimacy between us of long hugs and shared details of private areas of their life but was totally unconcerned about a sexual relationship happening. As I pushed her for more information, I learned that Bruce was leaving as their primary therapist. She was struggling to know how to bring closure to that important relationship and very reluctant to start another one with another therapist. The sessions with Bruce had become sporadic and longer than a month apart at times. Ann began sending me the written material on the life of the System that had been stored by Bruce.

Ann wrote, *"My concern is her constant need to be held by you and at your side. She needs to realize that she is on her own in this world and she is simply torturing herself by getting too close to you and then having to retreat. Enough said about it. You know where I stand on developing relationships that are too close.*

What do you mean by the art and practice of the learning organization? It sounds interesting. Here's the inscription for the book we bought for your class. 'Always remember, God gave us brains to use them. Don't accept anything on face value. Inquire, analyze and question, then analyze again before you accept it as fact. Stay logical! – Ann'. I suggest that you stay versatile with the emphasis in pastoral counseling as you are gifted there. Also the world is screwed up and I'm sure churches are looking for pastors with your specialties. I'm still working through my research on the image of God. My roadblock is trying to understand if an image can have characteristics that the host does not. Anyway, I've been doing some mind mapping on the subject and find it interesting..."

Circle Council was busy with their own research as well. Over the holidays, they had noticed how the children would wake several times during the night and crawl over to my side of the bed and get a hug, then return to their bed. Mariann and Tabitha did it at least once each night. They discussed this with Dragonslayer.

271

Greetings from Circle Council.

Ann has generously given Elizabeth Ray ten minutes on her school computer over lunch to communicate with you. Council has had several sessions discussing issues and concerns with the high leader, Dragonslayer. We were interested in knowing why the children always want to be warm and why is it so difficult to keep them in their own bed? According to him, our children are on level one of basic needs. They want to be safe, warm and fed. Joy clings to his arms because it is warm to her and safe like a little cocoon or her pod. Tabitha crawls to Mike because he is warm and she feels safe in his arms like in her hole. It is like a baby who needs to be bundled. They become insecure if there is free space all around them. It is the same with the children. This is why they went into holes, hid in the tank-house and rafters for safety.

We also learned that the reason why Mariann never asks for toys like Bob's kids is because she still hungers for the first level of needs and toys do not satisfy her needs at this time. Dragonslayer has told us to not be too harsh on the children. It will take them time to be fully comfortable with staying in their own beds. They are not trying to be disobedient and we must be patient.

Ann has finished her CLAD assignment at the middle school as of today and like always, received an outstanding evaluation from the district. She was offered another class at the high school and accepted it. She now teaches three integrated algebra classes and two algebra 'B' classes. Ann can take on no more assignments because she is now full time. She is taking 12 units at the college of which 6 are met by her job.

She is renegotiating the three plane tickets in the summer to two with a longer stay in June or July. We need your advice and input on this and ask Carol. Is it better for the children and Maria to see you one week at Christmas and two weeks in June, or one week at Christmas, June and August?

The Bible study that Maria is currently involved with is entering into very difficult areas. Council is concerned about triggers, depression and the 'stirring up of memories.' The group consist of five women who were abused (the system having the most) and one man. Bob and his prayer partner Dave are the only two who have not had sexual abuse in their background. Council requested that Bob seriously reconsider if he has the skills to run this type of group. Maria commented to him that she wished her and Tina could be real small and crawl under the couch when people are talking. Maria is having a very hard time with Liz's anger at the church and the group's discussion about anger. We are concerned that if God is leading Bob to stir up the waters to allow healing, that there is enough support for the system during the stirring.

Mariann received the pictures from the parade that you sent. The Caterpillar doll is guarded by Britta bear in a chair. She told Britta bear to make sure Caterpillar doesn't eat her, but only dances like daddy says. She cried when she saw the picture of you and Carol and started repeating, "I want my daddy." We finally got her inside and hid those pictures from her. The Grand Canyon pictures were too difficult to explain, so we gave them to Raquel who enjoyed them immensely. She particularly liked the Hopi Rock picture. We've been informed that our ten minutes are up so must go.

Elizabeth Ray – Scribe for Council

It would be this next letter from Council that speaks of events which cause some of Maria's new friends to question my counseling ability. There were no easy answers and none of us involved in her caregiving got through it without questioning why it should be allowed to continue.

Maria had called me one night and asked me if her promise to God was more important then obeying her friends who had more experience in understanding God than her. When asked to explain she said that it was too embarrassing and started to cry. I could tell that she was depressed about something. I decided to write Council and ask them through Ruth about communicating with them without Maria reading my correspondence first and do it outside of Ann's school.

Content Warning

Greetings from Circle Council,

We have received your message from Ruth. We would appreciate all correspondence to us marked confidential and sent to this address. This will help us avoid difficulty with Ann. We seek your advice on the present issue that is affecting the system. We are not experts in this area and are having considerable understanding the whole concept. We have attempted in the past to communicate with the husband of Maria. However, he does not accept our existence and refuses to believe that there could be male parts in the system. We have very bad rapport with him.

In our experience we have seen how the whole system avoids this area. Ann considers herself asexual. We are not sure what that means, but we are sure that Ann has no sexual relationship with anyone. Ruth also avoids sex but seems to be able to have intimate nonsexual relationships (unlike Ann). Liz confuses us. When we asked her what lubricants were, she laughed and asked us what flavor. We asked her if she would consider using this item to help Maria and she commented, "Yeah right. That old man of hers would never stand for it and anyway. I don't do shit with him unless he pays me. No freebees!" Liz, according to Elizabeth Ray, has been the most active part in the system, but her motive is unclear to us.

Maria refuses to see a doctor. She has been torn in the past and it eventually heals. She has a painful time going to the bathroom for awhile, but somehow handles the pain. Maria tries to stay out during the ordeal of sex, because her husband becomes upset that she 'escapes' to her Kansas. Somehow he knows that she has left the body. We were surprised at his sudden attack after a year and a half, thinking that he wanted nothing to do with Maria after she had her breasts removed. We wonder if it had any connection to his recent trip to Nevada. The husband and the father spent a considerable amount of time together talking away from the system. We think the father said something to the husband initiating this.

From our view, it seems that this area is wrapped up around maleness. The husband always initiates it and takes charge. He usually comes into the room while the system is asleep and begins to remove clothes. Usually, whoever is out wakes up and runs inside throwing Maria out. The husband is very aggressive and will forcefully enter Maria. Maria never cries but tries to leave to avoid displeasing him. All others scramble inside for protection as it is extremely traumatic for them. We have tried to observe to attempt understanding in this area.

This last time the husband avoided the chest area and Maria wrapped her arms around her chest in shame. The husband doesn't speak during the time of the attack and seems to acquire what he needs in about five minutes, and then leaves the room.

Maria grabs the covers and curls up into the fetal position and shakes. We never know when this will occur and the system is not allowed to lock the bedroom door per his orders. There is no privacy for the system at all times.

How can we understand this area called sex? How can we prepare Maria? Why do men do this to women? How can Maria heal from her sexual disorder with this happening? None of the other parts are willing to help us in this area. Maria has had no instruction in this area to help. Can you offer her instruction? Is there any way that she can overcome her anxieties over this? Is the woman always supposed to experience only pain during this process? How can we help Maria to accept her body and not look at it as ugly and shameful?

As leaders, we are having an extremely difficult time seeing Maria taken like this. She never complains and says it is her duty as a wife and wishes that she could stay present so she would be a better wife. We asked her why he does this to her and she said that is what husbands do, it is the rules of marriage. We are lost in how to help her, any advice would be appreciated.

We also need your advice on the issue of the husband using Mariann as his test case for a paper on teaching children. As we explained earlier, we're not sure his methods are helping Mariann and we need your input. - Circle Council

Maria was very reluctant to talk with me about these issues over the phone and I could sense her great shame at even having me aware of the situation. I encouraged her to talk with Jesus about it by approaching Him to discuss the issue of pain. The following was sent by Elizabeth Ray of Maria's discussion with Him, after He took the initiative and approached her.

Maria, would you like to talk to me?
I think so. I am not sure about something. I talked with Pastor Chalberg and he said that if I give you my pain, it won't hurt you. Is that true?

Maria, my dear one, when I willingly died on the cross, I took not only your sins and the pain of those sins, but everyone's sin and pain. It is finished.

Jesus does that mean that you don't feel pain now cuz I would not want to give you my hurt if it's going to hurt you. I don't want to hurt you again.

My precious one, I want to absorb your pain but you must release it to me. You asked if it will hurt me...it will not hurt in the same sense as it is hurting you. I know of your pain and hurt. I hurt for you...for what you carry in your heart...for that which was and is done to you. But the pain which you carry cannot absorb me. No, I shall absorb it, but you must release it to me. You do not need to carry it any longer for I will take it from you. It will not harm me or overtake me for I am Dragonslayer.

But how do I give it to you? I try, but I keep having nightmares and getting scared and sad. How can I bundle it up and give it to you?

"Slowly, Maria, as you learn to love and trust Me. It will become easier to release the pain. You will not forget that which has happened to you, but you will not be shattered because of it. For you shall gain strength through Me and you shall be a witness for Me. "See what the Lord has done!" And many shall come to know Me because of your testimony."

I still don't understand that Jesus.

It's okay, you will in time.

Jesus, Helper asked me something and I don't know how to answer him.

What did he ask you Maria?

He asked if I love Sergio as much as I love Pastor Chalberg.

Do you Maria?

I've been thinking about it a lot and I don't know how to explain it but I love Pastor Chalberg because I want to and Sergio because I have to.

Can you tell me more Maria?

I don't know how to explain it, I mean, I don't hate nobody. I try to like everyone. Even people that are mean to me I try to be nice to because I remember that you were nice to people who were mean to you.

But what do you mean, I love Sergio because I have to and I love Pastor Chalberg because I want to?

276

It is the only way I can explain it. Pastor Chalberg is like you Jesus and I love him with all of my heart like I love you. Sometimes when he holds me I feel like it is your arms wrapped around me to keep me safe. He talks with me and never calls me stupid. He laughs and enjoys walking and looking at nature with me. He teaches me about you. He never hurts me. He's like you. I love him because I want to. I wish I could be with him more, but I know that you have us doing different things now. I know that this is what you want for all of us.

What about Sergio?
He's not like you Jesus so it is hard. But I remember you saying that it is easy to love lovable people, but it is hard to love people who are not always kind. Please help me be a good wife and show your love to Sergio. Is it wrong for me to love Pastor Chalberg? Ann says it is.

Maria, my dear child, you have done nothing wrong. Continue to love Michael and Carol as you have been, for your love is pure. I have brought you together to fulfill my plan. Trust me and listen to my words.
I miss them so much.

I know Maria. Stay strong in me. Rest now my child and know that I am with you.

This time with Jesus helped Maria to talk more with me about the issue of pain. However, Maria still blamed herself as being a bad wife, rather than look at another person's anger and desire as a culprit causing the pain. When I offered to contact Sergio to consider alternatives to ease her pain, Maria asked me to promise that I would not. We discussed at length her promises to God in her marriage vows and what the Bible says about them, as well as the implications of what it means for a believer to remain married to a nonbeliever. The following letters from Council describe what our talks stirred up in their lives with friends and the enemy.

Memo from Circle Council:

We have been experiencing attacks. Yemaya has continually approached Tabitha. On Friday, January 23, she told Tabitha that El Papa would show Tabitha that Yemaya works for Dragonslayer.

Then she came to Tabitha on Saturday evening and said El Papa crowned the Santeria's goddess Ochun. Tabitha knows about Ochun and recognizes who that is. Tabitha told us that this orisha is worshipped in the Catholic Church. So, if El Papa is the highest worker for Dragonslayer and he worships Yemaya, then Tabitha is being a bad girl by telling Yemaya to go away. We read in the Sunday paper how the Pope crowned a statue of this orisha.

Louise will give into Tabitha on this, although she does not participate in the Santeria, because the Catholic Church sanctions it and Louise obeys the Catholic Church. As you can imagine, this is raising havoc within the system. Ruth is furious and called a special meeting last night to address the issue. Raquel came down from Sacred Mountain to be present. Dragonslayer was also present and told us that Yemaya is disguised as an angel of light. Tabitha is too young to not be swayed by her and it is up to the adult parts and adult outsiders to protect the child from the evil one until she is mature enough to understand. Mariann has been instructed to pull Tabitha away from the messages of Yemaya and take her to Dragonslayer. If Tabitha resists or Yemaya attempts to stop her, she is to call Dragonslayer immediately.

Maria has healed from the issue of the husband. It took a lot to convince her that it is okay to go to the ceiling. She still wants to obey the husband but is physically and mentally too fragile. Lindsay noticed that Maria was having difficulty walking after the incident and tried to pry the information out of her about what happened. Maria didn't want to talk with her about it and went to Bob. He told her that she didn't have to say anything if she didn't want to, to Lindsay. Lindsay believes however that Maria must talk it out and Council is upset at her pressuring Maria. We plan to rotate Ruth out to ask her to stop discussing this issue. Ruth has talked with Bob and Tina as well about pressuring Maria into getting a divorce. After their conversation, they agreed to not approach this topic with Maria. Obviously, they do not agree with you that divorce should be the last option.

We appreciate the conversation with you and the guidance you are giving us about the sexual issues we are facing. We hope to hear more from you about how we can help Maria to do the best she can in the situation that she is in. We discussed your dream with Dragonslayer and he asked us if Mike was sure that is what he dreamed. We stated that we assumed you were and

Dragonslayer then said to call upon Raquel to interpret the dream. This is what she said to us:

"The insane asylum is not a hospital, but a state of being. The husband has placed Maria there through his relationship with her. Along with others, he has imprisoned her in misery, pain and loneliness through his pursuit of lust and control. The Holy Spirit has revealed this to Shedding Tear, who has come as Dragonslayer's representative to take Maria out of this imprisonment. How? By the love of Dragonslayer displayed through his actions."

Raquel also gave us this warning; *"Do not be impatient, for it shall take many moons for that which has been broken to be healed."* She also informed us that a very powerful enemy of Dragonslayer attempted to visit her. It came to threaten her, but Brave Eagle swooped down from Sacred Mountain and shadowed, while spreading his powerful wings across the opening to the Land of Preservation. Wolfdog and the whole Eagle Clan guarded the entrance into the land while shadowing Raquel. Raquel raised her hands high and spoke to the Great Spirit. The evil one fled and the computer on which she was working began to work again. She had been writing Dragonslayer's words in a letter to Pastor Bob.

Transmission complete.

The following is Raquel's letter to Pastor Bob.

Greetings to One Who Speaks of He Who is Truth,

I have received your words from Brave Eagle. It is said that there is a story passed down by the ancient ones. In it the Acorn people are tricked into giving their ways of making bread to the one known as Coyote. As the storyteller speaks of Coyote, the hearer learns how Coyote justifies every action and deed and even defends it in his own mind. But when the Acorn people seek the Great Spirit's advice, they learn the true motive of Coyote's heart. The hearer learns that one can always trick the mind into believing one is performing the deed for noble causes, but one cannot trick the Great One...creator of all.

One Who Speaks of He Who is Truth be wise and stay on the life path chosen for you by the Great Spirit. There are many turns

279

and forks to lead you astray. Mastop (Evil spirit – Head Commander) *knows of your weaknesses. Why do you not think the enemy of the King would not? Beware of those that seem to be leading you in the right direction. Seek the counsel of the Great Spirit. Listen to the wise one for he will guide you in wisdom and you shall know the path you are to walk.*

The Great Spirit has favored you with many gifts. You have been anointed by the Great Spirit to use these gifts to touch those who are broken and have no hope. For through you, they shall be touched with the love of the Great Spirit. You have chosen the right fork in the path by declining the offer sent to you by he who sets the canoe adrift.

The Great One has given you a handful of broken people to comfort, teach and love. Through them, you will learn much to prepare you for the life path the Great Spirit has for you. Do not take this present task lightly, for it shall be the stepping stones of your life path and shall bring much honor to He Who is Truth.

May the blessings of the Great Spirit be upon your spirit.
Quiet Walker

Although some parts were able to function, like Raquel and Ann, others were still in a downward spiral over the sexual issues. I don't believe that Council was aware of the implications of the relationship with Maria's husband and how it was affecting everyone. To report that she had healed was only true for the physical injuries temporarily, but the emotional scars were still bleeding. No one wanted to discuss the issues with Jesus because of embarrassment about the topic or ignorance about the solutions. They all failed to grasp the lifetime affect that trauma from sexual abuse has over the victim.

It would be easy to blame Sergio for his lack of understanding and compassion, but that would not take into consideration the other factors at play here. The enemy had stepped up their attacks on the System to turn their focus away from recent victories, to have them remember the pain of the past when Yemaya was in control. The quickest way to do that was through a sexually abusive event. Sergio was being used and he had no knowledge of it. He exercised his marital rights without consideration of how this might be damaging to Maria, or to anyone else that might be close. For him to consider anyone else would mean that he would have to accept their existence first. I didn't know if he would ever learn the difference between having sex and making love. His way was about power and control in relationship that satisfies only the one in control.

For Maria and Louise, this was too shameful an experience to talk about explicitly with Jesus. They were conflicted between duty as they knew it and self preservation needed for healing. They trusted me enough to talk more directly with me about some of these specific issues. Ironically, they saw me like a priest that would be their intermediary before God so as to save them the shame of talking directly to Him about it. It would take several encouraging conversations over several days to get them to both go directly to the source of understanding and healing.

This was a difficult time for Council and the children as well. Council felt helpless and the children were hiding in fear of another attack. Yemaya was keeping everyone scrambling to put out fires, while draining their energy to resist the constant attacks. There were several spots in our conversations wherein I felt some measure of futility in their healing process. They had been learning by watching my wife and I, and now through Bob and Tina, that marriages can be relationships that are loving, gentle and safe. They wanted this for themselves but had no idea how to begin to help this come about in their own experience. They had never had a sexual experience that was surrounded and filled with love aimed at understanding their needs.

When we finally reached the point of discussing methods to relieve her physical pain, the embarrassment was too great and a child would switch out to talk with daddy. Even then the child would usually be crying from loneliness and reflecting the inner pain of Maria. The futility was present because they were healing by learning that sex in a marriage didn't have to always be a traumatically painful event, yet they saw no healing for them as a real possibility. They were trapped.

All of the solutions had the high probability of greater pain inflicted upon them for attempting to change the existing relationship. Her husband was neither ready nor willing and Maria didn't have the strength internally to confront the power over her that the sexual act had established for over 40 years. This was going to take a long time to bring healing in this part of her relationship. The following portions of several letters are indicative of the struggle they faced.

I wanted to talk to you last night but everyone else did too and there wasn't time for me. I know you are busy and if you don't have time to write me I'll understand. I tried to talk to Ann, but she didn't want to hear it as she takes care of everything else for us and doesn't want to deal with it. Liz laughed and told me to charge money or get Helper to do it. So I am lost about what to do and I don't want to ask Jesus cuz it is dirty and I feel bad about it.

Helper asked me if I would take over Maria's job because she seems to be getting weaker and weaker. I don't know why she is so weak. Helper says that she is more fragile than anyone else for some reason and he wonders if Ann is so strong because Maria absorbs all of the sickness and weakness. He asked me if I would do the time with Sergio when he comes and gets us.

I want to help Maria but I don't know if I can do it alone. We used to share it because it is so hard to do. I don't like it at all and it really hurts and I feel terrible afterwards, so I don't know what to do. I want to obey Helper and I care about Maria a lot. I'll do it if there is no other way but it is the worst thing for me. I would rather be beaten with a strap or put in a cage and not fed for a week instead of doing that, it is so terrible.

You know, when I get to shadow Maria and the kids in Southern California with you and Carol, it is like rays of sunshine warming my soul. I wonder if there is a way I could think about that while the terrible thing is going on? I don't know if I can. I wish I could be a nun. Do you know what I can do? I want to obey, but how can I do it and survive all by myself? – Louise

Memo – E.R. from Council
    We have been in session for several days over the concerns several leaders have with Maria's depression and downward spiral over the sexual issues facing her and attacks on Tabitha. Ann was called before Council for overlooking Maria's medication

for four days. Ruth is now in charge of the medication and we hope Maria will stabilize soon.

Ann was also told by Daniel that she has to make sure that the children are fed breakfast before leaving for work. She may be able to go from 6AM to 5PM without food or water but the rest of the System cannot. She was instructed about water and food intake for lunch and dinner as well. There will be no exceptions or her work permit will be revoked.

We are not allowing Tabitha out until she is more stabilized, as the attacks from Yemaya have been too strong for her and she is safer inside. Mariann is on guard duty.

Maria and Louise will not go to Jesus to ask advice about the issue with the husband. They feel it is too terrible and disgusting to talk with him about it and he would be disappointed in them. Maybe you could encourage them to seek out his help. We are at a loss at what to do. We asked Louise to take over to help Maria, but this is only a covering over the wound. We need to somehow educate ourselves as to what this whole concept means for the differences between love, sex and the complications in a marriage.

How do we explain things to Maria and help her find a way to survive it if he will not change? Maria is always under stress over whether tonight will be a night of pain or will she escape it. Can we help change it for her? The husband does not accept us as male parts leading the system and any letter or communication from us would be ignored. Thus we believe the only way that we can help Maria is by finding a way to help her tolerate it. We never told her that she could not go to the ceiling, as that was her choice, or should we say the husband's choice. He told her to stay and she tries very hard to obey him.

It bothers us that the children are aware that Maria sleeps and the 'mean' man does to her what the priest and the grandfather did to them. They don't understand the difference and they scatter whenever it begins, for fear that they will be grabbed. Is there any research or books on this problem that you can offer us?...

Memo from Council:
Since talking with you last Tuesday, Maria and Louise are still with Jesus. Elizabeth Ray has informed Council that the file of their conversation with him has been marked confidential per her

instructions by Dragonslayer. Maria and Louise are the only ones who may choose to talk about it.

The only conversation allowed out was when Maria told Jesus that Liz told her to get this special chocolate and heat it up to paint it all over her body. Maria wanted to know from Jesus what for and would it make Sergio happy? Jesus told her that if he wanted her body chocolate, he would have made her a chocolate bunny. No, you don't need to do that Maria. Then the conversation was closed off.

Helper shadowed Ann's conversation with you. He knows Ann is very upset about the rape, however he is in agreement with you about Maria's responses now...Ann is afraid of loosing her new found independence and that Jesus will try to control her life. She doesn't want to give control over to anyone. She is also afraid to completely trust for fear of another betrayal. Having a relationship with someone is a risk that she is not willing to make at this time, due to her insecurity about her ability to relate on a level that is nonprofessional. Ann was extremely upset that you said you love her in your relationship to her. She cannot feel comfortable with that. You can love Maria, Mariann, Liz, etc. but she doesn't want you saying you love her in any way. We are still trying to figure out why.

Ann was truthful in saying that she doesn't love anyone. She admires certain people for their accomplishments and positive impact upon this world, but love...That is a difficult word for her. As a group we tried to understand her relationship with you. First, we don't think that she would call it a relationship (even though we know it is). Ann considers you a consultant trying to fix the weaker parts so the system can function like a well-oiled machine. She does respect you and thinks that of all the men she knows, you are the most decent of the bunch. She likes your wit and intelligence, but she doesn't like you snarling her in theology and tries to avoid that. She disagrees with your philosophy about loving the parts and thinks her view is correct. We know that she really cares about Maria and doesn't want her hurt any more.

The problem is that Ann has taken care of Maria most of her life and basically controlled Maria..."knowing what is best for her," then enters this person that upsets Ann's control and authority over Maria. Ann would never admit it but we think that is part of her problem. "I've been there with them and took care of them through the thick of it and now Jesus and Mike walk in and take that away from me." Just a bunch of old men's perspective...

Problems occurring:

Lindsay is trying to get the system to move out and stay in her home to force Sergio to change. She has written a letter to Maria (which she hasn't seen) and one to Liz and Ann. Things are getting out of hand. We have not seen Bruce for three weeks due to his sickness and Maria being sick from all of this. There is no continuity with therapy now and you are the only one they all turn to on the outside. We believe this is why you are getting so many phone calls every night. We also wonder if the increases in attacks are in relationship to what you are writing about this semester. (I had begun writing a thesis on the connection between spiritual warfare, healing and Multiple Personality Disorder.)

We would appreciate it if you would contact Lindsay and Bob to explain to them the complexity of the situation and why the system cannot move out. We need them to understand so they can avoid complicating matters. We know that they want to help, but we are not getting confirmation from Dragonslayer to do as they say and we are to follow your counsel. Also Bob plans to startup Maria's Bible classes again next week and we believe that he needs to understand more about us to effectively plan for it. Lindsay needs to know that although we appreciate her offer, it is not possible. Maria mentioned last night, when we asked her how she felt staying during the activity with Sergio, that it was like a garbage truck had dumped its garbage into her. She would not elaborate. Do you understand this or have insight?

Helper

PS: Ruth talked to Lindsay when Lindsay found out from Tina about Maria being hurt. Ruth tried to explain the system to her after listening to you regarding the sexual ways of the parts and why it is impossible to force Ann or another part to take the function over. We don't believe she understood the difficulty to correct it.

Why does the caged bird sing?
Because it sees beyond the cage.

The System had come full circle in many respects over the last 40 years. They were again facing old memories of pain and suffering that renewed the old questions; "Why was God allowing this to happen again?" "Where was God when this happens?" "How can God bring good out of this?" However, these were questions being asked as much by the Christians surrounding the System than the System themselves.

Maria was looking to Jesus for guidance in how to endure the pain, not take it away. She had made a promise to God to stay in her marriage, no matter how difficult it might become. When Jesus explained to her that the suffering was not due to any sin of hers, it increased her resolve to stick it out and her fidelity to God as one who suffers unjustly. Many were seeking guidance from Jesus for understanding how to deal with their current circumstances. This in itself was a new place for them to return and face old issues.

I struggled with some of these questions too, and how to provide counsel to each individual posing different perspectives. I was reminded by the Holy Spirit to read again the Book of Job. I knew that Job teaches us very significant truths about human nature and how we approach suffering, but more importantly about our conceptions of God and control in the testing by choices between good and evil. Job is declared blameless and upright before God, having turned away from evil in the first chapter, by God Himself. Job questions the reason for his suffering throughout the book and even comes close to declaring himself completely innocent of any sin deserving of this punishment yet allowing how his God is the only one who can judge that. He's ready to go before an impartial judge to decide his innocence, if only there was someone greater than God to judge him but knows there is not.

What seems to bother Job more than anything else is God's silence. Job says many things out of pain and frustration, even voicing his challenges to God about the veracity of His justice. Though Job had everything taken from him, he never lost his faith in God. In the end, God does not answer Job's questions, but declares the reality of their relationship. God restores Job for remaining truthful in his responses to undeserved suffering through faith that God would not abandon him without just cause. When Job sees God face to face, he realizes two important things; 1.) God does not have to explain His actions to anyone, which causes

Job to say nothing more, and 2.) God loves him enough to reveal Himself to Job, something He didn't have to do. Job's understanding of his relationship with God was declared in verse 13:15:

"Though He slay me, I will hope in Him."

Reading Job again reminded me of the similarities between the System's current reaction to their suffering and Ann's rational arguments about the betrayal of innocence she felt from God for not stopping the abuse. She too, along with others, was asking God to explain His actions, or lack of them, but she was stating her case from the position of never having a relationship with God. Unlike Job, she was just beginning to learn about the meaning of having hope and trust in a God she needed to see...face to face.

Ann was being challenged by this turn of events, even though she stated clearly that Maria's sexual problems were not affecting her. I decided to send her another book by one of my favorite authors Peter Kreeft, entitled, *Making Sense Out of Suffering*. Her response follows and I believe that it helps to define further the struggle between the soul and the mind in understanding God.

I could relate well to his chapters on suffering. I too have questioned the random and pointless suffering that I have seen and experienced. It's not easy to turn to a God who constantly allows you to have your head banged against the wall. I was impressed by the author's answer to the unbeliever about why we should read his book. "For the same reason a believer should read an unbeliever. If you know only what you know, you don't even know that. You understand things by contrast." *This I understand and accept as one main principle in scientific research. If you want to know the characteristics of cold, you need to look at the contrast of hot.*

I went through his arguments carefully. I have always wondered if deep down inside I was a closet atheist. I must admit however, that logically I know there is a higher source, because we exist. It is not possible to make something out of nothing unless there is a higher source that has capabilities that we humans do not have and can't comprehend. So I realize that I'm not an atheist.

I went next to demythologism…the fairytale god. At times I have crossed the line to demythologism…thinking of the stories of the plagues on Pharoah, the splitting of the Red Sea, Jonah and the whale as nice, cute stories, but not much different than Hans Christian Andersen's fairytales. I still wonder about these stories and the possibility of exaggeration to make a point. I didn't think that Kreeft supported his argument well in this section.

I threw psychologism and polytheism out the window, but I eagerly investigated his section on Scientism…whatever science cannot detect does not exist…my concrete! He left me hanging in this section, as if he was saying…best answer so far. You have exchanged a fatalistic point of view for faith in an all-powerful but morally indifferent God. This section helped me identify where I am with God. I believe in Scientism. The rest of them I threw out.

Chapter three was excellent and the reader zeroed in on where I would have challenged the author. There is no logic to agreeing with all four conclusions that God is real, all-powerful, all-good and there is evil (argument from St. Augustine). *I have always maintained that something that is absolute good cannot have the capacity to create something that is evil. If we are made in God's image* (back to the image question again), *how can we be evil? It is not logical. Logic tells facts and is true…this is not logical.*

But then he gave me something to think about…the difference between a problem and a mystery. Problems have solutions, but I never reasoned that mysteries remain mysteries. Maybe I can't use logic to explain the problem of evil and it is understood somehow only by God revealing it to us. I am not sure. Kreeft states that logical thinking is not the only method to understanding. He does admit that a solution can never be illogical. If something is true, it cannot be illogical. He seems to stretch the reader into exploring the structure of thinking and surmises that logic is a tool and the real issue is the meaning of mystery.

Still confused, I read into the area of philosophy…the area of why. My first stop was with your favorite, Socrates…perhaps the greatest of all time. I read about intellectual humility and spiritual humility, though I don't agree with there being only two types of people; the wise who know they are fools and the fools who think they are wise. I know that I am not all-knowing. I pursue truth and I am interested in finding it. I value knowledge, but in no way do I consider myself wise, yet I am not a fool either. I also admit that I am not all-good because I sin like everyone else.

When the author went to Plato, I agreed with the reader's statements that in the world, injustice seems more profitable than justice. Plato's declarations are unrealistic in our world. When the author attempts to answer the reader's question, he uses the riddle Socrates receives from the oracle; 'know thyself.' Then he proceeds to tell the reader that "the only person who can do my real self harm is me. You can only harm my body..." WRONG! Come on Chalberg look at what the system has been through. Can you tell me that the abuse suffered by the children did not go to the core of their soul? The choice was never up to them. They were wounded in their spirit. Others can do harm to one's soul and one might not have the power to stop it!

Aristtole, Boethius and Freud all seemed to revolve around the idea that we need truth, even if it requires suffering to get to that truth, and truth is more desired than comfort or pleasure. I agree to that conclusion. After reading the artists, I thought that Raquel's definition was excellent. "A poet is an unhappy being whose heart is torn by secret suffering, but whose lips are so strangely formed that when the sighs and cries escape them, they sound like beautiful music."

*I read his main points: Suffering makes one more real. We make things more real when we tame them and take responsibility for them. From suffering comes wisdom. People are willing to suffer for a cause or meaning. Suffering must have meaning. **Suffering must have meaning.** This made me stop...the ultimate why question... does our suffering have meaning? We need to suffer to remain human. Without choice, without making mistakes, without suffering and living in a world filled with diversity and drama, we would be reduced to a sterile lab of robots and puppets. The greatest creativity and excitement in life comes out of suffering. Our world is interesting, exciting, adventurous and alive because there is choice and suffering. Would I rather want to live in a* *bubble with no choice, stripped down to a thing manipulated and controlled by an outside force, or take my chances with suffering and be alive to have choice? Of course I want to be human, but can't the suffering be a little more balanced and less intense?*

I disagree with the author that prophets are closer to God than the philosophers or artists. Raquel seems to have a very close face to face relationship with the Great Spirit as an artist. (Have you noticed yet the similarities between her thought process and experiences, as they correlate with the book of Job?) *I also disagree with his statement that we suffer because we sin. Sometimes we suffer because someone else sins and we receive the consequences of that sin. I wish that he had stated that rather than assuming that we suffer because we do the sinning. Our suffering is not because we misused our free will and were disobedient. Tell us Kreeft, where was our choice? This chapter was the most challenging for me.*

I related well to the author's statement that God's way out of a mess sometimes seems to lead further into the mess, but I could not understand his conclusion that the solution to suffering is to suffer more. So I went further, hoping that he will explain his conclusion. That's when it started getting sticky for me. "Suffering is a road out, a road to repentance, which is the door to blessedness...Only after suffering do individuals and nations turn back to God. Suffering reminds us continually that we are not God." *Sometimes I forget that. I get so wrapped up in controlling my destiny and life that I forget I am not God and do not have the power to control my destiny. I keep trying however because I cannot seem to trust anyone or anything except for myself. I play God to myself. It's hard to explain why I cannot relinquish control...past experience I guess.*

God hasn't proven to me that he is trustworthy yet. I hate getting on this subject of trust...it's my core issue. I know that God is, yet I cannot seem to give my will up for his. (Here perhaps, is the primary difference between Ann's perspective and Job's need for an answer to his suffering. All Job needed was to hear from God that He was in control. Ann was not ready to relinquish it.) *The next chapter wasn't any easier as it deals with love. I never thought about God sitting beside me everywhere I go and I especially have a difficult time understanding the kind of love that Kreeft talks about. Why does God care so much? Why would he love this miserable species called humanity enough to allow himself to be nailed to a cross in horrible circumstances? Why...for love? Maybe I cannot understand this because I do not feel loved...I do not know love. I know pain and suffering, but not love. Maybe I hide from love, I don't know, but I cannot understand this mystery of love.*

He goes on to say that "true love is willing to suffer. Love is the cross." I cannot think this through. Then Kreeft hits me with my dilemma, "Though he believes, he does not accept. He is not a doubter, he is a rebel... He is angry at God for not being kinder. That is the deepest source of unbelief, not the intellect but the will." *There I am in full view I said to myself, stuck in the battle of wills...only God is not battling, I am. Shit Chalberg, can you help me out of my dilemma?*

Augustine supposes that God proposed to you a deal and said, "I will give you anything you want. You can possess the whole world. Nothing will be impossible for you. You will have infinite power. Nothing will be a sin, nothing forbidden. You will never die, never have pain, never have anything you do not want and always have anything you do want – except for just one thing: you will never see my face." Would you take that deal? If not, you have the pure love of God. For look what you just did: you gave up the world, all desired worlds – just for God. Augustine asks, "Did a chill arise in your heart when you heard the words 'you will never see my face'?" That chill is the most precious thing in you; that is the pure love of God.

From Saint Augustine's sermon, "On the Pure Love of God"
Three Philosophies of Life, Peter Kreeft, Ignatius Press 1989

"Let love be without hypocrisy."
Romans 12:9

Chapter Thirteen

"The Soul Symphony - 'I AM"

"Bless the Lord, O my soul;
And all that is within me, bless His holy name.
Bless the Lord, O my soul;
And forget none of His benefits;
Who pardons all your iniquities;
Who heals all your diseases;
Who redeems your life from the pit;
Who crowns you with loving kindness and compassion;
Who satisfies your years with good things,
So that your youth is renewed like the eagles…
For He has satisfied the thirsty soul,
And the hungry soul He has filled with what is good."
Psalm 103: 1-5, 107:9

*"A child's nature is too serious a thing
to admit of its being regarded as a
mere appendage to another being."*
Charles Lamb, *Essays of Elia* (1823)

*"Thinking is an attribute of the soul, and here
I discover what properly belongs to myself.
This alone is inseparable from me.
I am, I exist; this is certain."*
Rene Descartes, *Discourse on Method* (1637)

Every soul I've ever met has responded to the need within us of being acknowledged by another human being as existing. This has ranged from a simple question of, "Who are you?" to the statement of, "I love who you are." Each time we are recognized individually as a person, we are affirmed again that this life is real and not just a dream reflected in someone else's mind. For every survivor of abuse, particularly clergy abuse, there is a soul searching for another existence that is more real than the one they have known. What is it about each of us that identify us as a person apart from any other human being?

Some have suggested throughout the ages that it is our physical body that identifies us as an individual. From fingerprints, retina scan, voice modulation and DNA, we are inundated every week on forensic shows about the ease of identifying a single individual from any other living person. Yet, for the high majority of us, these methods of identification are only available for identifying another person as unique, when it is connected to a crime. I got into real trouble in high school when I tried dating twins and never really knew for sure which one I was with at the time. I was at their mercy in trusting that they were who they said they were. Most of us are in that same position of trust in relationships, even when we aren't dealing with twins. It appears that even the physical body can't always reveal the truth through physical characteristics alone, about the spiritual traits of the person inside the body. How many of us would trade our body in for another one that matches our self-perception of what our mind/soul says we should look like? Is not any human being so much more than the sum of its physical characteristics, the shell that houses this life-form?

"Man is the only animal that laughs and weeps; for he is the only animal that is struck with the difference between what things are, and what they ought to be."
William Hazlitt (1778-1830)

Is it then the mind which gives each of us our separate identity? The French philosopher Rene Descartes had a simple argument in the arena of dualism – what the world consists of, or is explicable as two fundamental entities, such as mind and matter. In psychology, this distinction is between mental and physical properties, while in theology, this concept is seen as man having two basic natures, the physical and the spiritual. Descartes simply said this: 'I can doubt the real existence of my body…at least theoretically, because it is logically possible that any physical sensations of embodiment are delusory. But I cannot doubt the existence of my mind, because the very act of doubting means I'm using my mind. My physical body, (including the brain) has the property of doubting its real existence, something the power of my mind lacks. Therefore, my mind and body are not one and the same.'

If the mind is distinct from the body, what is it within the mind's existence that determines personality, or causes anyone to declare "I exist"? Here, philosophers and scientists...and even theologians, begin speaking of the mind, or human consciousness, in the same context as the human soul. One might immediately ask, "Can the mind or consciousness exist and function apart from the soul?" A brief study of human behavior in history would suggest that it is possible. However, the Bible indicates that it is in fact a conscious choice of the mind to ignore the soul's existence that can perpetuate this possibility, if the premise is accepted that it is God who breathes life into our soul, which allows choices between good and evil, in creating causal relationships with Him.

This apparent dual existence of mind and soul is examined by the Apostle Paul to understand the coexistence of law and grace in the Book of Romans, to help us understand the dynamics of how the soul/mind is in a battle of choices within the mind/body. It is in this battle of our consciousness that human behavior is determined and the characteristics that define our unique personhood are chosen and refined.

"That means you must not give sin a vote in the way you conduct your lives... Throw yourselves wholeheartedly and full-time – remember, you've been raised from the dead! – into God's way of doing things. Sin can't tell you how to live. After all, you're not living under the old tyranny any longer. You are living in the freedom of God... The law code had a perfectly legitimate function. Without its clear guidelines for right and wrong, moral behavior would be mostly guesswork. Apart from the succinct, surgical command, "You shall not covet," I could have dressed covetousness up to look like a virtue and ruined my life with it... "I know that all God's commands are spiritual, but I'm not. Isn't this also your experience?" Yes. I'm full of myself, after all, I've spent a long time in sin's prison. What I don't understand about myself is that I decide one way, but then I act another, doing things I absolutely despise. So if I can't be trusted to figure out what is best for myself and do it, it becomes obvious that God's

command is necessary. But I need something more! For if I know the law but still can't keep it, and if the power of sin within me keeps sabotaging my best intentions, I obviously need help. I realize that I don't have what it takes. I can will it, but I can't do it. I decide to do good, but I don't really do it; I decide not to do bad, but then I do it anyway. My decisions, such as they are, don't result in actions... I've tried everything and nothing helps. I'm at the end of my rope. Is there no one who can do anything for me? Isn't that the real question? The answer, thank God, is that Jesus Christ can and does. He acted to set things right in this life of contradictions (and choices) *where I want to serve God with all of my heart and mind, but am pulled by the influence of sin to do something totally different. With the arrival of Jesus, the Messiah, that fateful dilemma is resolved."*

Excerpts from *The Message,* **Romans 6, 7, & 8**

Does the soul/mind operate in a realm that can transcend the physical limitations of our bodies and brains and 'connect' to that which is metaphysical, or spiritual, ever mindful of the physical nature that daunts us? Plato believed that the mind, or soul, might not only pre-exist the physical body, but that it could survive and exist after death of the body. Most of human history reveals that the majority opinion is that the human soul does transcend death of the human body...existing outside of the limitations of this physical realm. Into what realms of existence then can the soul survive and can they have a causal affect in determining how the soul identifies itself as a sentient being within self-awareness?

For example, I went to school in the '60s when a number of my classmates were considered to be brain-dead by their peers, as well as their teachers, because of too many drugs ingested to escape. If any one of them happened to have a period of coherency, they would gladly regale the earnest listener with details of their out-of-body experiences into other realms. These stories were logically and correctly rejected as hallucinations.

However, I had a larger number of friends who survived the war in Viet Nam and returned with stories of near-death experiences. Most of them stated that their experiences were not drug induced and their fear of dying was altered forever. Many started on a journey to understand just what it was that their 'soul' encountered. Was it just in their mind, as a dream or vision induced by the trauma of the fear of dying, or a reality that only the soul can perceive? These days, part of the therapy that seems to bring healing to returning soldiers displaying post traumatic stress, is the pursuit of understanding these very questions. War, severe violence and trauma seems to be a catalyst in causing anyone to either question who they are as a unique person or lose their value as a person…wanting to erase that part of their experience from the soul. What is sometimes diagnosed as schizophrenia, dissociative identity disorder, or post traumatic stress disorder, is I believe, the soul's search for meaning before God… within this life's brutality.

Pastors are often called upon to preside over a funeral for people that they have never seen or known personally. To properly prepare a eulogy, we have to interview the living to get a sense of who this person was in life. I have often wondered how it's possible for different people to be describing the same person, when the previous person described a completely different truth in confidence to me. Too bad it's not possible to have a post-mortem interview with the person's soul to hear their story from their memory. Would any person's concepts of who they were in life, their likes and dislikes, accomplishments and failures, why they loved one person or stopped loving another…would anyone's story completely match someone else's understanding of who they were?

My mother died at the age of 60 by her own hand. She had 5 sons and additional family who gathered together to prepare to tell her 'story.' Being the only pastor for several generations in my family, it fell upon me to write her eulogy and put together her service. Input was given from everyone about her favorite hymns, her most meaningful scripture verses, the most important events that defined her life and her thoughts on family and friends. The night before her memorial service, we discovered a box of letters that she had written throughout her life. Many of them were to my father, both during the marriage and following their divorce, and even some after his death twenty years earlier.

More significant were her open letters to Jesus that reflected her struggles in this life and her firm beliefs of what lay ahead for her with Him. It was these letters that impacted me the most for how I would tell her story. Until that moment, most of her life was not consistent with what we read about in her letters about her beliefs. Each of us had partial knowledge, but none of us had the whole story. She never told anyone...except for Jesus. A couple of days later we found another box that contained her personal Bible. In it were dates, favorite verses and songs to be sung at her funeral service. We had one song right out of seven and none of the verses. This outcome isn't as sad as it is revealing, about how even people within the same family cannot truly know who a person is...better than the person can discern for herself.

My mother's mind was troubled often in her life, caused by abuse at a young age, growing up in the Depression with a mother married three times, seven marriages of her own and continuous depression brought on by an addiction to prescription drugs and dieting the last 20 years of her life. Yet, her soul always clung to a knowledge and purpose for who she was as a human being, in spite of what she encountered in life. She revealed sides of her personality to fit the occasion that confronted her, while always keeping a private side to herself. She sacrificed a large portion of her life, to be a mother for her sons in the midst of constant change and few did it better than her. But her greatest gift to her sons wasn't what she hoped it would be by the time of her death. That gift has not yet been fulfilled... that all of her sons would know Jesus Christ as Savior and friend.

These examples are given to help us define a soul or person apart from their physical body, and to realize that only an individual's soul can accept or reject the reality of one's own existence, being the only one to define that inside and out, in time or space. In our inner most being, where only our spirit and God can transcend and communicate, separated from all other reality other than the spiritual...how do we define our personhood and how does the Holy Spirit define us? Both Old and New Testaments offer direction for understanding how God describes the creation and design of the body, mind and soul... reflected in relationship to Him.

**"And God created man in His own image, in the image of God He created him; male and female He created them...
Then the Lord God formed man of dust from the ground,
And breathed into his nostrils the breathe of life;**

And man became a living being." Genesis 1:27, 2:7

"For Thou didst form my inward parts;
Thou didst weave me in my mother's womb.
I will give thanks to Thee,
For I am fearfully and wonderfully made;
Wonderful are Thy works,
And my soul knows it very well...
Search me, O God, and know my heart;
Try me and know my anxious thoughts;
And see if there be any hurtful way in me,
And lead me in the everlasting way."
Psalms 139: 13 – 14, 24.

*"Jesus answered, "Truly, truly, I say to you, unless one
is born of water and the Spirit, he cannot enter into the
kingdom of God. That which is born of the flesh is flesh,
and that which is born of the Spirit is spirit. Do not
marvel that I said to you, 'You must be born again.'
The wind blows where it wishes and you hear the
sound of it, but do not know where it comes from and
where it is going; so is everyone who is born of the Spirit."*
John 3: 5 – 8.

If it is possible and necessary to define the human soul as that reality of mind/spirit which transcends the finite physical body, then any attempt to limit the definition of a person to their physical presence only, is neither logical, nor accurate and temporal at best. If we can't see or touch a person and only hear them...does that mean they are the reality our mind creates of them? I can remember one blind date made over the phone where I later wished how that was true...but that's another story.

Earlier in the morning on the day of my mother's death, she had an awful argument with my brother before he left on his long haul deliveries. Spiteful words of anger and resentment were the last things heard by either of them. A few hours later, at the time of my mother's death, my brother swears that he heard my mother's voice speaking to him in the cab of his truck over a hundred miles away. She spoke of forgiveness, her passing and now being at peace for the first time. Was this my mother's soul speaking?

This sort of occurrence is documented throughout history and many accept the possibility of a person's soul or personality being identifiable as existing apart from the physical body. Yet, when most adults come into contact with a soul inhabiting a particular body, they become very uncomfortable when they experience through their senses another soul existing there. In the case of the System presented here, adults seem to accept the possibility of other adults existing in one body much easier than they accept the possibility of children existing in one adult body. It is ironic that children don't have the same problems and tend to accept both adults and children living in one body with ease.

Christians have a difficult time because they believe that only one soul, or person, should inhabit one body at a time. They can believe in the Trinity, three persons in one, but reject this possibility in human beings. Why? Jesus says in several places how the body does not define the person, even using Himself as a way of explaining how this is possible.

"For this reason I say to you, do not be anxious for your life, as to what you shall eat or what you shall drink; nor for your body, as to what you shall put on. Is not life more than food, and the body than clothing?"
"And do not fear those who kill the body, but are unable to kill the soul; but rather fear Him who is able to destroy both soul and body in hell."
Matthew 6:25, 10:28

"No man has seen God at any time; the only begotten God, who is in the bosom of the Father, He has explained Him...

I and the Father are one...

When the Helper comes, whom I will send to you from the Father, that is the Spirit of truth, who proceeds from the Father, He will bear witness of Me..."
John 1:18, 10:30, 15:26

(To Bruce,)

I don't know if you have time to look at my homework. I haven't seen you for a long time and I don't know if you are still a counselor but Helper told me to do this. You asked me what things I want to do with my life and how I'm going to do it...

I'm sorry I stopped but Sergio has been real mad and it is hard to think when he is yelling that he don't care about me. I want to be more like Jesus, be with Pastor Chalberg more, be a good wife and learn how to do the sex stuff right. Be normal and be a good friend to the people Jesus wants me to help.

To be like Jesus I have to listen to him better and watch how he does stuff. He has been telling me this week how the body must be connected to the head and the head protects the body. Jesus explained this by telling me how the bad ones are like germs trying to give the body diseases. He told me how he is healing the body with gentleness and love. Then he said that he is head of the body like the husband is head of his wife and the husband is to love his wife like he loves his body the church. He said to think about this and I will.

I want to be with Pastor Chalberg more cuz I love being with him. I feel safe with him and he talks nice to me about good stuff and doesn't hurt me. I could be his housekeeper for him and Carol when Sergio tells me to go away maybe. I would want him to do Dragonslayer work at my church and then him and Carol could live at my house for free.

I am still trying to know how to be a good wife. I think that we are selfish and don't do enough for Sergio anymore and that makes him mad. The other things are hard to talk about cuz I can't find the right words. I don't think sex is from Jesus cuz Jesus would not make something that hurts so much. I think that Jesus made something else but I just can't find it.

I want to be normal and fit in the world. I don't want to be different. I have a hard time cuz it goes way too fast and I can't keep up. I would like to be me without people thinking I have demons and that I'm scary and different. I need to know what is normal. Is there a normal test to see if I'm normal?

I know when Jesus tells me to talk to someone it is cuz they need a friend. Like the girl I talked to about going to this new place with hope and Jesus.

The things I am scared of are fighting, yelling, hitting, doing the sex stuff, not knowing where I am sometimes, Claudia hating me, getting cancer again and my friends leaving me. I don't like people getting mad cuz then they hurt lots. I learned how to be quiet and not make them madder. I don't want opinions if they are going to hurt me. I get scared when Sergio gets mad at me for loosing stuff and not remembering to do stuff he told me to do.

Claudia says I am weird and stupid and she hates me. I love her so much and I wish I could be the mother she wants. I know that it is hard for all of them to have me for a mother and a wife but I try my best.

I don't get scared about dying but I don't want doctors to cut me more. I don't want my friends to leave cuz I just got friends and I don't want to lose them cuz then I don't have friends.
Maria

Helper called a Council meeting and sent a letter to Bruce about the discussion they had with Ann and her troubles with him. It revealed some identity issues with Ann and her relationships with the men on Council, as well as with men in general. The following excerpts give the gist of the conversation.

Helper: Ann, did you send a letter to Bruce without our consent?

Ann: Yes. It was personal and I see that Bruce did not respond to me and decided to go through you.

Helper: Bruce did not "go through me". You know the rules. We approve all communication and decisions that have an impact on the entire system.

301

Ann: Look, I did what was necessary since apparently none of you are going to act. I requested the picture boards two months ago so Bob could communicate with Tabitha. Bruce cannot find them. Since he does not have them in his possession, he cannot guarantee his promise of confidentiality. Therefore, I requested all of the materials to be returned as that is the only way I can guarantee our safety... (A discussion ensues about the missing items.)

Ann: I know for a fact that the system's things are not together and kept from being viewed by others. It is one thing to allow certain people to see them and quite another issue to have no control over who sees them...

Helper: I think we need input from Bruce before we make a decision. Why are you accusing Bruce of ruining your career Ann? Was he not the one who went to bat for you when we were questioning the impact that work would have on the system? He has supported you many times in disputes against Liz. Have you ever thought that maybe he is concerned that your obsession (oops!) *with a career will cause the system to spin in a downwards spiral?*

Ann: I am not obsessed with a career! I am only doing my best for the system by providing financial security. What the system needs most right now is to be able to make it on their own.

King of the Lights: No Ann, what the system needs most right now is to know that they have worth and are loved, and that not everyone in the world wants to hurt them. I agree that working and being responsible is important, but there must be limits on work and Council doesn't want you to carry such a heavy workload. I believe that I speak for the others when I say that you are not the only one in the system with the priority for time out. Other parts deserve time out to explore their interests as well. Ann, you are multiple whether you like it or not, so stop fighting it and work with it. You will never lead the life of a single.

Ann: What are you trying to do...control me? I have been told to be quiet, stay in my place and not excel all of my life. All my life men have had power over me and kept me from achieving. I have had to do what I did not want to do. I have carried the responsibility even when I did not own it and now, when I have finally started to excel, you are going to suppress me again. You are not going to do it! I am not going to have it happen all over again. Neither you, Bruce, Bob or Mike is going to control me. Everyone complains about me and has an opinion about my personality, about my job, my way of doing things. Everyone complains, but I don't see any of you taking on the responsibility.

Helper: Ann, it is not our purpose to control you. We admire you very much and respect you highly...

Ann: Don't patronize me Helper. I am not stupid.

Helper: Ann, I'm not going to argue with you. We have been discussing this for a week and Council has set the following guidelines on work for your job. You have a choice to either adhere to the guidelines or quit your job. It will be your choice and there will be no further discussion. We are sorry that we have to express our authority in this way, but we have the whole system to care for and this is the only way that works with you.

Ann: You can't put these rules on me...

Helper: We just have. Think about it Ann and let us know what you decide. As far as the issue of the System's material, I have requested that Elizabeth Ray contact Bruce to have him communicate with us directly about the items being out of his possession and how we can get the system's material to Mike.

Ann: I want to discuss this further.

Helper: There is nothing to discuss Ann. We are sorry, but we must consider the welfare of the entire system. It has been painful for us to develop these guidelines, but it is necessary. Meeting adjourned.

While Ann lost this round to Council, she proceeded to make her case with Bruce. The two of them would go back and forth in letters for several weeks over what each one thought was best for the entire System's healing process with a new therapist coming into the mix. Ann was a perfectionist and logically organized the System the way she wanted, to the extent that she was given authority to do so. Bruce was more laid back, less organized than Ann and had authority within the System as the primary therapist to first diagnose and to then bring healing to them. Eventually, it was worked out between them...sort of...maybe...not really?

Bruce would leave after setting them up with another therapist in a few months. Unfortunately, he left without any real session with the System for closure in the relationships, particularly with the children. It fell upon me to supply the continuity of a therapeutic relationship from Southern California. Bruce felt it was best to cut all contact quickly, so the System would turn to those of us still providing support. As the children slowly become aware of the situation, the enemy uses it to expand on issues of abandonment all over again. Maria will start to listen to the enemy as well and blame herself as the reason he left. He does make contact again in about 5 years and renews the relationship this time as a friend, just in time to write the forward in this book.

In my effort to fill the gap in love that was fast approaching, I began to encourage the System to become more involved with Bob and his family, his church and friends like Lindsay. My main concern for Ann was that she was moving faster than the rest of the System was prepared for in exposure to the outside world. I had no doubt that she could do her job very well, but I also knew how in the past, if everyone wasn't supporting her, it could collapse around her causing even greater pain through failure. Jesus was preparing her for this job and the enemy wanted to break it, so every day was a battle.

Ann was in the fast track for achieving the recognition she had long desired in this job, as an individual apart from everyone else. The stronger she got with her accomplishments and successes; the harder things became in her relationship with Sergio at home. A portion of one of her last communications to Bruce revealed some of her frustration and reasons for wanting to achieve so much. She finally gets to the most important point of contention with Bruce, his perspective of her need to achieve to solidify her identity.

Mr. Bruce Fielding,

I too am angry. First, you refuse to admit to me that you did not take proper care of those things that were entrusted to your care...

Second, I do not use the other parts to address personal issues I have with you. I have always addressed them directly myself...

Thirdly, how can you judge me? You have decided what is improper and what is proper. You have determined that you know exactly what I need to do and how I need to behave. And you talk about me having a problem with control and power...

Fourthly, you do not live in this system. You say I have dictated to others what their roles will be and have narrowed those roles to fit my personal plans. That is bullshit! Did I not offer to Liz the opportunity to find a job, if she thought she could pay the bills better than me? Did I not agree to let Maria...

Although the above mentioned comments irritated me, your idea of psychoanalyzing me is what really pissed me off. So you think my resentment of men having power over me is what drives me to succeed. You think that I am walking on the others to fill my hunger for success and that I am cramming years into months in order to accomplish this.

I will admit that I don't particularly like men. I have found most of them a bore. They whine about the slightest aches and pains, are terrible organizers and have this terrible habit of putting women down, especially assertive women. "Behind every successful man is a good woman." I hate that saying but it's true. I'd change it to, "behind every successful woman is a man trying to catch up."

As far as walking on the others, you are wrong. All my life I have done what is best for them. If anything, it should be the other way around. Maria walked over me when she got married and forced me into this ridiculous marriage arrangement. What choice did I have when she had three children that I end up raising? Liz does it all of the time like when she switches me out to receive the traffic ticket. And I could go on, so don't label me as walking over them.

As far as cramming years of success into months...I agree. I might not have long to live and I want to achieve my goals before I die. Though I agree that you went to bat for me with Council over this job, you turned on me when I started succeeding quickly and tell them to pull the reins in on me. Is that fair to me? Have you ever really considered my future within this system?

Ann's last question is a valid one and its answer depends upon the therapist's perspective of healing with a multiple. If integration of all the parts into one 'person' is the goal, without 'losing' any single part in the process, one would have to establish some sort of criteria with which to measure the value of each person in relationship to the whole. This would be to establish the order of integration, if for no other reason. I believe its purpose is also its failure.

Unless each and every part willingly subrogates their value or contribution to the greater 'whole', healthy integration is not possible. The weaker parts can be forced into integration against their will, if the stronger healthier parts don't recognize or value their role currently or historically, within a given system. When this happens, everyone within the system loses. The part forced to integrate loses its identity and subsequently, its desire to contribute further to the well-being of those in control. Does this part die?

It is possible I believe for a multiple's parts to die, without causing the death of the body and other parts. However, I believe that this can occur for the same reasons that any human being can die, or go away within themselves. If who we are, how we identify ourselves apart from any other soul, believes that we have no value and nothing to contribute to life and therefore unlovable, that part of our soul can die from loneliness. They can lose their reason for living.

Conversely, if any soul discovers their unique reason for living and refuses to submit that to another, even the soul that is a part of a multiple, that person will fight to maintain self-awareness even unto death and beyond. For the multiple, this means that any part not wishing to integrate has the choice to stand and fight to be recognized or go deep inside to hide in their world until the opportunity arises to try again to fulfill their purpose.

Of all the multiples that I've had the opportunity to interview or counsel, the only ones to have achieved healthy integration in part or in whole, have been those people who have willingly submitted themselves to integrate out of a greater love for others within the system than for themselves. This new being, in part or in whole, exhibits the identity, talents and gifts of the previous individual parts. They are more than they were, not less, and still carry all of the hopes, fears, goals and memories that love conquered and released to the greater good.

Consider for a moment the catalyst of love upon the System. In 4 years they have come from believing that God hated them, to accepting that God counted them worthy of His unconditional love. They were being healed from the inside out...literally. Each part's identity was being remade with God's perspective of them. Even Ann had moved from the idea of an unknowable godlike entity to acknowledging that God did care about them for some reason. They had moved from; "If God is merciful...why doesn't He just kill us to end our suffering?" To; "God loves me, yet my suffering will continue because He says I will remain a multiple for Him."

You can see the conundrum facing the System. God says, **"I love you and I will heal you. You will remain a multiple for My purposes and bring glory to Me. Trust Me!"** At this point in their journey, all of the parts who chose to, willingly integrated. The parts remaining expressed no desire to give up their identity, yet their identities were changing by the very nature of their healing. Each one was accepting that "God has a plan for my life", but "what is it and do I want that as my future?" Each one wanted to discover why God was keeping them around.

Mariann already had the clearest understanding of all the parts as to why she was here: *"To love my Dragonslayer and dance in His pretty colors; sing to Him and tell people about Him, and to love my daddy and mommy too. Amen."* From the beginning of her healing, her identity was intertwined with that of Dragonslayer's. Just as God answered Moses by stating, **"I AM WHO I AM"**, so would Mariann answer the question, *"I be Mariann."* She will continually correct people who say to her; "What's your name? or, You're a sweetie; or Aren't you a blessing!" by stating, *"No!...I be Mariann... I be!"* It is perhaps due to her understanding of why she exists that the enemy began attacking her through her identity at her heart and soul.

Everyone within the System whose identity was waiting to be defined by God's plan, would find themselves being attacked in this arena, if they sought fulfillment and acceptance in the outside world. Ann would not find this as difficult a challenge for her until she accepts Jesus completely 5 years from now. All of the other adults who came to the surface will learn through Mariann, about the difficulty of having ones very existence hinge on the veracity of Jesus' words, **"You are...because I love you. I created you to glorify Me."**

I was asked by a fellow student in seminary who had read my thesis concerning healing and MPD, to describe the present state of the System and how I thought God was going to heal them. After I thought about it briefly, I used the analogy of a symphony that is being created and refined in process. The composer, God, already has the entire piece finished in his head, yet has only put the first movement down on the sheet of life to be played by his musicians, the System. I'm like the conductor, looking ahead at the music as fast as the composer gives it to lead the musicians through it.

Each musician has a specific instrument and part to play, and some play more than one instrument. If any musician is removed, or change their music without consent of the composer...then the whole symphony changes. In order to produce the symphony the way the composer intends, we must all trust and obey the direction and composition of the composer. All of the musicians are learning new pieces and committing it to memory, and some are playing new instruments that have to be broken in.

The symphony hall itself is old and being remodeled. Some musicians aren't convinced it will be strong enough to last until the symphony is finished. There is always the possibility that we will find more damage in the structure and have to repair it ourselves as we learn new music that is given. Even if the hall is condemned or closed, the symphony will be finished and heard in whatever venue is open to us. I can say this in all confidence, because the music is not dependent upon the stage it's presented on, but the musicians and conductor staying committed to playing whatever the composer gives them.

The music that each musician produces comes from their soul and identifies uniquely who they are in the orchestra. The composer picked each one to play that piece of music that no one else could play the way he wants. The symphony will go on long after the musicians have finished playing and hopefully, it will be picked up and played by other orchestras who appreciate the power of the music…and the healing that the composition offers. The name of the symphony…*"I AM."*

**"Let the peace of Christ rule in your hearts,
to which indeed you were called in one body; and
be thankful. Let the word of Christ richly dwell within you,
with all wisdom teaching and admonishing one another with
psalms and hymns and spiritual songs, singing with
thankfulness in your hearts to God. And whatever
you do in word or deed, do all in the name of the
Lord Jesus, giving thanks through Him to God the Father."**
Colossians 3: 15-17

"Music is a higher revelation than philosophy."
Ludwig Van Beethoven (1770 – 1827)

"The greatest disorder of the mind is to let will direct belief."
Louis Pasteur (1822 – 1895)

*"God is. That is the primordial fact. It is in order
that we may discover this fact for ourselves,
by direct experience that we exist."*
Aldous Huxley (1894 – 1963)

**"As the deer pants for the water brooks,
So my soul pants for Thee, O God.
My soul thirsts for God, for the living God;"**
Psalm 42: 1-2

**"Behold, all souls are mine;
The soul of the father as well as
the soul of the son is Mine.
The soul who sins will die…
If he walks in My statutes and
My ordinances so as to deal faithfully,
He is righteous and will surely live."**
Ezekiel 18:4, 9

Chapter Fourteen

"A Child's Cry for Acceptance"

*"In the little world in which children have their
existence, whosoever brings them up,
there is nothing so finely perceived
and so finely felt, as injustice."*
Charles Dickens, *Great Expectations* (1861)

The identity issues come into focus when you begin to look at Mariann's life and attempt to understand why a child's desire to be accepted as real, apart from any other soul within the System, becomes so vital to her healing and subsequently, for each one in the System. Is it because she had the greatest need for purpose in being …for existing? Her 'birth' was for the purpose of receiving sexual abuse from a priest and told by him that God wanted this to happen "so she would become acceptable to God." (See Ch. 5, Book 1)

Even though it is difficult to do, imagine for a moment how a child's development of their soul, that part of us that is created to know God, could have their trust in God shattered and denied the possibility of knowing the truth for most of their life. If that same child is hidden from the reality of the outside existence for her own protection, then what reality should that child/person expect when she does emerge some thirty years later? Her definition of herself and her experiences in the physical body would not have changed or aged, and she would interact with others on the outside by expecting them to see her, body and all, as she sees herself. She has remained a child in both realities of the physical and metaphysical.

Mariann emerges with the purity and innocence of a child in search of a father's love. After several months of total outside time that actually occurred during three years of our time, her soul has accepted the truth of a Father's love and she seeks to define her purpose for being as someone created to receive that love. She understands that she is real because God says she is. Initially, she desired to be with her Dragonslayer and dance in the glow of His love. Yet, she was also experiencing outside relationships that challenged her very existence as a person, and spiritual beings inside were attacking her as well. Whom was she going to believe?

Dragonslayer's love would convince her that the priest had lied about Him and about receiving God's love. Some on the outside would give her love without expecting her to conform to their expectations and others would require her to adapt to them before giving it. She wanted to please Dragonslayer by being obedient to Him, while observing how that wasn't a priority to several of those around her on the inside or outside. Somehow, she was making the connection within her soul how Dragonslayer's love was unconditional, yet there was a need there to be recognized and loved as Mariann in her outside relationships.

Ever so slowly, as Mariann begins to trust those around her, her soul begins to accept more than just the love that she was created to receive. As she trusted Bruce first, then me, she learned how love doesn't have to hurt and friends can help open a world up for exploration and understanding. By the time she receives a mother's care and love from Carol, she stands firm in her commitment to do and be whatever Dragonslayer asks of her, because she knows His love is true in these people who share it with her. Her strength of character as an individual becomes directly related to her faith relationship with Him, something that others in the System notice and begin to follow her lead. A child has pointed the way in the journey of healing.

The adults observe her relationships inside and out closely, for they are beginning to see a rebirth in her of something they thought they had lost forever...the innocence that comes from trusting God to be all powerful and true. It will be this quality of trust, as much as, or more than any other character trait that will define her as a person and become the catalyst which causes each adult to fill their own soul with its power. As Mariann begins to absorb every detail of the outside world during her time out, her innocence will be tested repeatedly and her trust in God's steadfast love is taken into the refiner's fire to strengthen the relationship.

Mariann began to learn how some of her earlier experiences in the outside reality were shared ones with Tabitha and others within the System. 'If you talk about the bad you will be punished by family members and the church. No one will believe anything you say. Love is always painful on the outside. Trust no one there. You are only safe on the inside.' She learns how some adults on the inside world seem to care about her, if not love her, yet some don't seem to believe what she is saying about her experiences outside with the priest. This becomes more complicated as new friends like Pastor Bob and Tina get upset with her and Tabitha for drawings done on these memories with their children. Maria and Louise could not bear to discuss it either inside, so they would simply walk away quickly as it was still too painful. This is one of the ways that the enemy likes to attack the trust relationships growing within Mariann or anyone for that matter…avoid talking about the truth of a painful experience that our God, for reasons unknown to us, allowed to occur. No one really wants to acknowledge the tremendous amount of things that we don't understand about God.

This method of the enemy to challenge God's love and healing power is most effective with survivors of clergy abuse, whether or not they are multiples. It is also used in cataclysmic events which fall into the category of 'Act of God'; like tornados or hurricanes. When a survivor encounters another traumatic event in life where the power and purposes of God are called into question, the strands of trust are tested again for their strength, with the recalling of memories captured in the soul. Each test is amplified by the enemy with statements like; "God didn't stop the destruction, suffering, death," etc., or "God is not all powerful, or He would have prevented this." The abuse or trauma survivor may then be thrown back in their search for truth about God and it may not recover for years, if ever.

Maria, Ann, Mari and other adults will be tested like this over the next few years, with events like 9/11, gall bladder surgery that nearly kills them and two more bouts with cancer. For the children these events are traumatic, but not as difficult as the attacks upon their very essence...their soul's identity. Because of Mariann's total trust in Dragonslayer, she will feel the brunt of these attacks.

It begins in the spring of 1998, when Mariann starts to grow rapidly in her realization of self...her personality. She is out often at Bob and Tina's home, interacting with adults and children on a regular basis. She observes how the children are relating to their parents and begins to compare those relationships with our relationship. She begins learning how children communicate with and even manipulate parents to achieve their desires. She witnesses the exchange of love and discipline with the youngest child to the oldest and commits to memory the nuances within each one. Later when we're together, and even sooner over the phone, she will attempt to use these methods to get the outcome or answers that she wants from Carol and I. She sees how each child gets attention from a parent and quickly makes the connection that being heard and responded to must surely mean they are loved. She becomes bolder in talking to adults on the outside, if they are connected to those few that she has been told to trust in any way.

Everyone adores her innocence in looking at the outside world that she is discovering for the first time. They laugh at her honesty in describing the world exactly as she sees it. They hear her explaining in her own interpretation the important things that she is learning from Dragonslayer about life, including those people who are disobeying Him and asking why they do. Usually, she is dismissed simply as a child speaking out of place, but later asked about specifics privately. Here, she is accepted and listened to as someone with spiritual insight. Publicly she is ignored as a child who may well embarrass you, if attention is given to her words.

Mariann begins to question Dragonslayer, the System, me and Bob about who she is and why she is treated differently than other children. We both approached the explanation of these differences from our own perspective and understanding from God. The enemy jumped on this situation to create division between us in the future and used the identity issue against Ann and Maria as well. I planned a trip up to Northern California to have a meeting with Bob to discuss these issues and have it coincide with a meeting with the new therapist and Bruce to transfer care. The letters that follow our visit begin to indicate the erosion of identities and the struggle to maintain and develop them by some of the parts.

Council continued to keep me informed during this time about the progress of preparing Maria for a new therapist, as well as the circumstances of the various parts. I knew that Mariann was having a hard time explaining to her new friends why I couldn't be with her, as their father was with them. After Council's letter, I decided to write to Mariann on a regular basis, even if it was just a note to give hugs.

Memo from Council

In the past several weeks we have noticed a change for the worse in the husband. He is highly agitated and has a short fuse. He threw some binders at the bedroom door and stormed out. We attempted to have Ruth talk with him last night. He quickly concluded that if we don't like him the way he is, then maybe he should leave. He still misses the point that we are not out to judge him, we only want to help him have joy and peace. Apparently, the system brings him no joy. This made Maria very sad.

Ann is keeping a low profile with the husband. She is not sharing any of her accomplishments, because he is highly jealous of her. She tends to spend as little time as possible with him and escapes the difficulties by concentrating on her work.

Jennifer has rejected Mormonism and told Ann that she was crazy to spend time exploring a religion that has women perpetually pregnant. Ruth and Liz are fine. It is the children, Maria and Louise whom we are concerned about. Maria is trying to find her place in the system's world. She receives no encouragement or support from her family as you know. She hasn't seen Bruce for over three weeks and she has very little time in her home for daily chores, because of Ann's career. She never complains, but we sense she is starving for positive physical contact. That is why we think holding the pastor's son is so important to her. She can love him and in return he accepts her.

Maria is still lost in church. She misses her bible study and seems stressed over the church not having unity. Her father turned 69 yesterday and we let her call him to wish him happy birthday. He told her to be more appreciative of Sergio for how hard he works to give her a home. She tried to talk to him about Jesus and he got angry and said how he did not want to hear about a God that did that to his wife.

We hope that things are going well in school. If you have time, please send a line to Mariann. She looks everyday to see if her daddy says hi.

When I wrote to Mariann, I asked her to write back and tell me all of the things that she was learning in sandal camp and give Dragonslayer a big hug from me. She wrote back that very night. I will translate her spelling and add punctuation for most of her letters from now on for ease of understanding them.

Daddy

Daddy I get letter from my daddy. I give Dragonslayer big hug. He laugh funny. I get sit on Dragonslayer and he hold me and tell me. Daddy, you know about little mustard seed? My friend and me want you to play with us. I tell her my daddy will play, but only I sit with my daddy. No share please.

Daddy you be strong. Dragonslayer makes the smelly ones be afraid of him. Daddy I see pretty orange butterfly come see me. I watch it for long time. I eat my Cheerios daddy and my birdie and doggy eat with me.

Dragonslayer say do not walk to daddy's house. Mariann no go to friend's house. Mariann say okay Dragonslayer. Daddy my other friend tell me about big rocks that have Dragonslayer rules on them. Do you know rules daddy? Do not spit! That is the ten commandment. Daddy I no spit. How Dragonslayer make words on rocks and why he put them in sky. He not afraid they fall and hit him in head? Why do big people spit daddy?

I love my mommy and daddy lots. Bye mommy. Bye daddy. Mariann give big butterfly kisses and hug from me. Hug from my Dragonslayer.

Response:
Good morning to all,

Thanks for the letter Mariann. Maybe you could explain the spitting commandment to Maria so she could explain it to me, okay? Keep praying for me to have more Dragonslayer brains to pass my test this week. Give my love to everyone. I want you to try and sneak up on Dragonslayer again and give Him a big hug from me! We love you and we are sending cards today. Bye for now.

P.S. For Council: how is Tabitha doing in standing up to Yemaya? Is she calling for Jesus like I instructed her? I'd like to hear from Jennifer about her search for Truth. I've got one more paper to finish tonight about my theology of preaching and I'll be done with my second semester. Your prayers have been helpful and I'll need more of them to remain focused to finish the race after 16 years in this school. Take care and we'll see you next week at Bruce's office. Do you know the name of your new therapist yet?

...Bruce has made an appointment for you to interview the new therapist with Maria at 9:30 AM. After that we will drive to Tina's house so Mariann can introduce you to all of her friends. Their daughter is informing Mariann how her daddy is much more ancient than Mariann's daddy. I'm sure that Bob will be thrilled to hear that. Helper wants to go slowly with the transition as change is very difficult for Maria, as she needs to feel safe before she'll open up to a stranger.

Ann and Sergio are not speaking to each other again. Sergio made the comment to her that he loves to torment Maria and Ann called him a sick SOB. They got into a fight and haven't spoken. We received the cards for the children, thank you.

Bruce will be seeing Maria while you and Carol begin the interview and see you afterward.

Our schedule that day made it impossible to spend any time of substance to talk with Bob and Tina. There was a surprise birthday party for Maria/Mariann and I at Tina's which took all of the time allotted. The next day as I returned home I received the following from Council that evening and Mariann's letter the next morning.

Memo from Council
Leaders are meeting daily now to find the source of energy being drawn from the system. Ann has been extremely fatigued which is unusual for her. Liz is causing problems for her at school by not following protocol with the students. How do you force boundaries on someone who refuses to obey the rules?

Maria is expressing her loss over her mother again. She is sad that her mom didn't live long enough to see how good a teacher Ann is. Something is making her sad about Mariann and she again blames herself for not being stronger as a child. She says that if she had not made parts, then they wouldn't be suffering right now. We have tried to explain to her how she had no control over what happened and we sent her to Dragonslayer for counseling.

Mariann has withdrawn inside after the visit with Bob today and is causing problems by disobeying the rules inside. She pushed Tabitha off of a swing and told Joy that she is running away to her cookie mansion with her daddy. When questioned, she told us that **"Mr. Bob not see me. He say I not be. I not be like his little girls. I be special. I not go to store with them. Nobody see me. I bad to see. I want my daddy. I no go to places cuz I bad to see. Mariann no come out no more. I want my daddy. My daddy come back get me."** **We told her that her daddy and mommy see her and we sent her to Dragonslayer as well.**

The concept of identity and reality is a critical issue to the system. Our reality is different from others and because they don't understand it, it is considered unacceptable and cast out as impossible. Where does that leave a system like us? We do not have a choice and we can't explain it to their satisfaction. We don't understand it totally ourselves and sometimes question why us. But we know we live it and that forces us to accept it, whatever it is.

All of the parts need to hold on to what little they have of who they are. Even Tabitha Ann as a blend of Angelina, Tabitha and Anna, has the flavor of all three now. At times Tabitha Ann will take the baby's pacifier...a side of Angelina showing that indicates her identity hasn't been lost. Some parts are adamant about expressing their identity every time they're out. "This is Liz" is the way she addresses herself. She states clearly to not mix her up with Ann or Ruth. Liz wants recognition. They share time out and they share a common body, but they want to have their own identity, values, likes and dislikes. If anyone takes their identity away and tells them that they are not really a person; "You are a part of a person. You are not really Liz. You are the rebellious Maria. You don't exist. You don't have ownership of a name, a birth, or a body"; then you destroy them and destroy the system and everyone's ability to function and stay alive.

It is difficult for the outside world to understand what it must be like to exist in a world not made for you, to be a foreigner, not acceptable and misunderstood. The system does not have any other outside world to live in and the parts are trying to adapt to the rules (except for Liz) of that world. We leaders attempt to protect them in a world that is not willing to allow them to be who they are. They must always portray normalcy in the world's standards and it is exhausting for them. Yes, they could spend the time inside, but there is a hunger for relationships in the outside world.

They want to run with the girls holding balloons, do finger painting, see the ocean, trees, birds, people worshipping and singing. The outside is different in that it has other people to watch, know and interact with...even if it's scary. Some parts are afraid because it goes too fast and they could be hurt again, yet parts like Mariann want to explore the tide pool...find out how it works...see new things...try new things...meet new people and develop into a social butterfly... who is now being told by the outside that we have to tie your wings because you can't fly in this world.

To: Mike Chalberg

Daddy I want my daddy to hold Mariann. Daddy I be Mariann. Daddy sees Mariann. I be Mariann. I sorry I be bad so no see Mariann. Mariann no come out. Make bad come out. People no see Mariann. Daddy come get Mariann and Tabitha and Hopi. Joy not talk lots but want to come too. We say come we go with daddy to cookie mansion. I love my daddy. My daddy knows Mariann be. My daddy say hi Mariann. Daddy you take Mr. Bob and wash eyes with Dragonslayer soap so he see Mariann. Dragonslayer see Mariann say Dragonslayer be and Mariann be. Mr. Bob's eyes be sick. I want be with my daddy please. Mr. Bob say girl no see Mariann. I want my friend see me cuz she know me. Mr. Bob say no see Mariann. I no want be special. Special no go bye-bye. Special is bad. Daddy come get his Mariann. Daddy say I be Mariann. Mariann be. Mariann be.

I don't believe Bob had any realization about how his statements were going to affect the System for a long time. I wondered who he was trying to protect when he told Mariann the hard truth as he saw it. In the coming weeks as he and I dialogued about how the System identifies itself individually, we would be at odds about the veracity of that for our world. Bob preferred to believe what a well-known psychiatrist said in his book, over what the System said to him personally from their own experiences. Being a pastor, the question I posed of individual personalities having individual souls was never going to be tested by him because of its challenges to his belief structure.

Yet, in the first two years of his relationship with them, he will constantly be challenged in his understanding of the spiritual realm around the System, spiritual warfare increasing and becoming obvious in trying to break their relationship and most of all, encountering the Holy Spirit speaking to him through the System for training him for future ministry. He will acknowledge their varied gifts of the Spirit affecting his life and God having a purpose in bringing them together, but never accept God's stated purpose. To do that would mean to submit his will completely and accept something he couldn't understand through his own intellect. How many of us reject the miraculous events in our lives, simply because they can only be explained as miraculous? If these events are an indicator of God being actively involved in our lives, how does that affect our view of this world? As we continue the journey, take a close look at some of these events for Bob and the System and ask yourself whose purpose is being accomplished within these circumstances.

Being Different

Do not weep my child that you are different. Do you not remember how the Great Spirit bore you on the wings of Brave Eagle and brought you to Himself in the land of Preservation? You must learn child that what is in the inside world is not in the outside world. We live in two worlds. They are not the same. You dance in Dragonslayer's colors, fly with Brave Eagle and see magnificent things that are of the world of Dragonslayer gave us. In the outside world you cannot fly with Brave Eagle or walk above the buttercups on the open meadow. The outside world cannot experience this for it does not have the spiritual eyes to see beyond its world.

It also cannot understand our inside world for it has not seen as we have seen or been as we have been. The outside world cannot see you, but that does not mean that you are not there. Sarus cannot be seen and yet he is there. They cannot see for they do not have spiritual eyes to see. They cannot hear for their ears are for their world. Their understanding of what can be and what cannot be is based on the rules of the outside world. You my child must learn to transfer between the worlds and know what is in Preservation is not always in the outside world. Do not be upset my child with the people of the tribe of greed who can not see you. They live with outside world eyes. Shedding Tear sees you through the eyes of Dragonslayer and that is enough for him. Remember my child, Dragonslayer is called different too. Walk on the water with Dragonslayer and do not worry if the tribe of greed accepts you.
Quiet Walker

Memo from Council
We've had meetings since you left to assess the past few days. The issues raised by several leaders were brought to Dragonslayer for advice on how to respond. The little ones are struggling with your departure next summer. Daniel questioned if it was a good idea to allow Mariann to see you for such a short time. Lion stated that he has evaluated the past several weeks and noticed how the children are waking up more during the night wanting daddy. He is not sure if it's the length between visits, seeing Bob's kids with him, or the season approaching Easter. Tolip mentioned that the time interval in which the children can be separated from you without switching problems, disobedience towards the leaders, being easily manipulated by the enemy and problems at night like bedwetting, seems to be around 3 months. The other leaders agreed with them and turned to Dragonslayer.

According to him, the children hunger for warmth, protection and human physical contact. They are at an infant stage of development right now, because they were denied positive bonding

320

with a parent in their early years. They connect daddy with warmth (something desirable and opposite of what they had known); protection (my daddy big/Dragonslayer strong, cancer surgery daddy stays to protect Mariann, feeds me Cheerios); and positive contact physically (hugs, listening to daddy's heartbeat while napping next to him). At home they do not receive any of this. At Bob's it is a safe interaction for them with their peers. Bob doesn't offer what their daddy does. The therapist is a regulated environment to help correct wrong thinking. Thus the only place the children receive what they desire most is with their daddy. As they develop and become secure, the attachment will lessen and the time between visits will lengthen.

Daniel questioned why Dragonslayer couldn't be a substitute for their daddy, as it would be much easier to have them go inside and be with Him. Dragonslayer said that they are increasing their visits with him more and more, but the relationship with Michael is important for them to learn to relate to people, accept good love and give love to others. If they are to do the work He has for them, they must learn this to help them express His love to people. Also, He sent them to Michael for him to learn more about Him and His love. He does not want them to only love Him, but He wants them (this includes me) *to learn to love people as He loves them. They are learning through their daddy and he is learning through them. When the training is over, they will go forth and show His love in a way they never before could.*

We questioned Maria's closeness to you and we were told that He wishes all people would love each other with the intensity and purity that she loves. "Chris recognizes My love through her and he reaches out for My love. Let her be. You do not know the impact she is having on those I bring to her." We expressed our feelings of vulnerability. What if Michael becomes so busy that he can not be there for them? We are concerned with the intense closeness now developing into problems later for us. Dragonslayer told me, "Trust me Helper. I have them in the palm of my hand."

We concluded the meeting and the children are clinging to Dragonslayer, nursing their wounds and crying about daddy leaving. We are preparing for changing therapist soon with Maria.

We would like for Maria to be out at your graduation party this June. She wants to help Carol with the preparations and Louise wants to do the cooking. If she gets tired, Ruth will switch out to interact. We don't want to embarrass anyone by a child switching out, so could you spend some time with them the night before to comfort and instruct them on what you expect for the day?
E.R. for Council

I called to talk with Mariann the evening I received these two letters and ended up talking only to Maria. She explained that Mariann was with Dragonslayer on a special outing and wasn't available. This was the first time during our time apart that she didn't switch outside to talk with me. After listening to Maria's fears about seeing a new therapist and telling me how she thought that therapy wasn't necessary anymore, she asked me to convince Council to let her stop. It really wasn't the therapy she feared as much as what it meant – Bruce would be leaving the relationship, and abandonment issues were rising again for her and the children. I had already talked with Council about my interview with the new therapist and the pros and cons of her for the System, expecting that therapy would continue.

As I raised the issue of abandonment with Maria, she began to softly cry. She stated how the only people that love her...leave her. Bruce was leaving and she didn't understand why. He had promised to always be her friend, yet he was leaving without giving her an explanation. The enemy of course seized this to convince her that it was not only her fault, but the System's as well for being too needy and causing too many problems. We had moved away, forever in her mind, and the enemy was telling her we did it to get away from the System who was too much of a burden. Pastor Bob seemed to care, but he didn't know her like we did. She didn't want to be a burden for his family, too. She was beginning to believe the enemy's lies that God was doing this to turn our efforts to more important work, rather than waste it on them.

I asked her if she trusted Jesus...did she trust me...had either of us ever lied to her. I then began to tell her the truth of what I saw happening in her life. She accepted this and remembered again with me the healing process that the System was going through and most importantly, that it was Jesus' plan for her. She knew really only one thing and that was that she was committed to serving Him. She didn't know how or why He would want someone broken like her, but she would trust for now and take it one day at a time. She was very concerned about Mariann's reaction to what Bob had said, because she could see the turmoil it caused for her.

She then said something that became a forewarning to me about the time ahead. She asked, *"Mariann is real isn't she? You said she is and you see her, but Pastor Bob says she isn't...so who do I believe? Cuz, if she's not real, then maybe none of them are real and I'm crazy."* I asked her simply, "What does Jesus tell you about Mariann and everyone in the System? He's already told you how He has plans for each of you to share one day about His love. Do you remember the letter I read to you on the first day of chemotherapy that Jesus gave you through Quiet Walker and especially the last part about being a multiple?"

"Yes. It was beautiful and He said how He was going to heal us, but that we would remain a multiple for His purposes and that our wholeness would be in Him. I don't understand that yet, but I know I get to tell people about His love one day when I'm better." "Do you know how you are doing that already? You have taught me many things...many truths about His love ever since I met you. I know from the times I've talked with Bob, that you are teaching him and Tina many things just by praying with them." *"But he doesn't think multiples are real people and if Mariann isn't real then maybe I'm not real. Maybe Ann should be real...or Ruth...?"*

"Maria, stop for a minute and think about this. If God says you are real and said that He kept you all alive as a multiple to survive so that you could do His work...who are you going to believe? I have no doubt in my heart and soul that all of you are as real as I am. God would not put so much love in a person to share, if they were not only real, but alive and living in order to share it. Why do you think that Mariann is with Dragonslayer now? I can guess that she is being healed of the wounds to her spirit by Him showing her just how real she is to Him. By the way, when she returns, have her write me about where she has been, okay?"

Later that night I received a copy of a letter sent to Bruce from Council. They had decided to not inform the children of the therapist changes until they were more stable and they had a chance to assess the new situation and how it proceeds with Maria. Even though Maria wanted to stop, they saw the need to work on issues like boundaries and standing up to mental and emotional abuse from her family. They hoped that the new therapist would understand and accept their reservations about working with a woman. They remembered their only experience with a female therapist had destroyed in a relatively short period of time much of the work that had been accomplished until then. They didn't want over three years of therapy and a lot of money for them to be wasted.

They wanted to set a time with Bruce present for the first meeting, since he couldn't be there with us in our meeting last week. It was also hoped to be a time for goodbyes, if only for Maria. I think if I had not given a favorable response about her, they probably would have opted to let Maria slide for awhile until another therapist could be found. Around midnight I received the following email from Ruth, typing Mariann's story for her daddy. As you can see, she types it word for word.

My story to my daddy,
I like go to platoe. Brave Eagle come and say ready Mariann. I get on Brave Eagle wings. I hold on little things by his ears. He got hole ears. He go up. I go whee and we go high. Brave Eagle go up to Sacred Mountain. I see cliffs. I see colors. I hear wind make noise. We go up more. We go up to platoe. Brave Eagle stop. We way high and it warm. I lay down go nite nite. Brave Eagle watch. Dragonslayer put the colors over me. I be warm. I be way high.

Brave Eagle wake me up. Brave Eagle tickle me with his face. I get on his wings. We go back to meadow. Dragonslayer and me go for walk. We like walk in meadow. Buttercups like to tickle us. We walk on top and they under us tickle our feet. We not go down and Dragonslayer laugh. Mariann laugh. They sing pretty colors.
The end

What's your first reaction to this letter? What a cute little story from an imaginative little girl; or how absurd to think that anyone could fly on eagle's wings or walk on the top of buttercups. When I read this I thought of how fortunate we are to have a God that loves us as much as He does. God knows we don't deserve it, yet He provides a place in His kingdom where we can walk on buttercups with Him one day. If one believes in the spiritual dimension existing all around us as Jesus says it does, then accepting this story as possible isn't so hard to do. Here's a place where broken spirits get mended and our relationship with God becomes real.

If we spend our lives believing in only what we can see with our eyes or touch with our hands, smell or hear for ourselves and not risk believing that it is real just because God says it is, then why risk having faith in anything He says?

I chose to believe it long before I witnessed the outcome of Mariann's outing with Dragonslayer. Jesus renewed the spirit of this little girl and strengthened her with His love. He then tells her to go back outside and tell those that He brings to her the truth of His love, warning her that many will not have spirit eyes or spirit ears to believe her. When she gets her spirit beaten again and she will a number of times ahead, by people that say they believe her statements but not in her 'being', she will return inside to Dragonslayer's side to be renewed again.

Mariann went off to school as was the law
With some crayons and paper she started to draw
From the corners to the center...color filled the page
For that is what she saw in her little cage

And the teacher said...what are you doing child
I'm painting the sky said a voice soft and mild
It's not the time for art Mariann
And anyway skies are blue don't you understand
There is a way things must be done
And make sure you paint yellow that sun

And Mariann thought
There is a way things must be done
Skies are blue and yellow is the sun
But why do I see so many pretty colors
The sky is rainbow and the sun mosaic
So many colors and I see every one

You are defiant and need to learn
There is a way things must be done
And you will learn
Skies are blue and suns are yellow
So repeat after me
And mind your manners

But why do I see so many colors
The sky is rainbow and the sun mosaic
So many colors and I see every one

I've had enough of your crazy thoughts
Stand in the corner in the garbage can
Until you get it right you shall stay
There is a way things must be done you say

Mariann withdrew and stayed all day long
In the lonely corner away from everyone
When finally alone and afraid
She went to Miss Brown and she did say

There is a way things must be done
Skies are blue and suns are yellow
No room for color
No rainbows or song
Colors must be seen the way all things are done

Time went by and the child did learn
The outside world sees differently
As far as she was concerned
-   Quiet Walker

Daddy
I give my daddy butterfly kisses.   My daddy be Dragonslayer
strong I love my mommy   I love my daddy   My daddy see me
Trust and obey no other way be happy for Jesus but trust and obey
Love from Mariann

Hi Mariann,
Thanks for the kisses! We love you too. Where is our picture of
you running through all of the rainbow colors and lights around

Dragonslayer? Keep being Dragonslayer strong for everyone in the System like a good soldier. Trust and obey for there's no other way! Sing that to Maria when she's worried and give her a butterfly kiss too! We'll talk soon. Bye for now.   Daddy & Mommy

Mariann's adventure with Dragonslayer that day was told to me over the phone and I asked her to draw a picture of where she had been. I also asked if anyone had talked to her about the Book of Revelation and the answer was "No!"

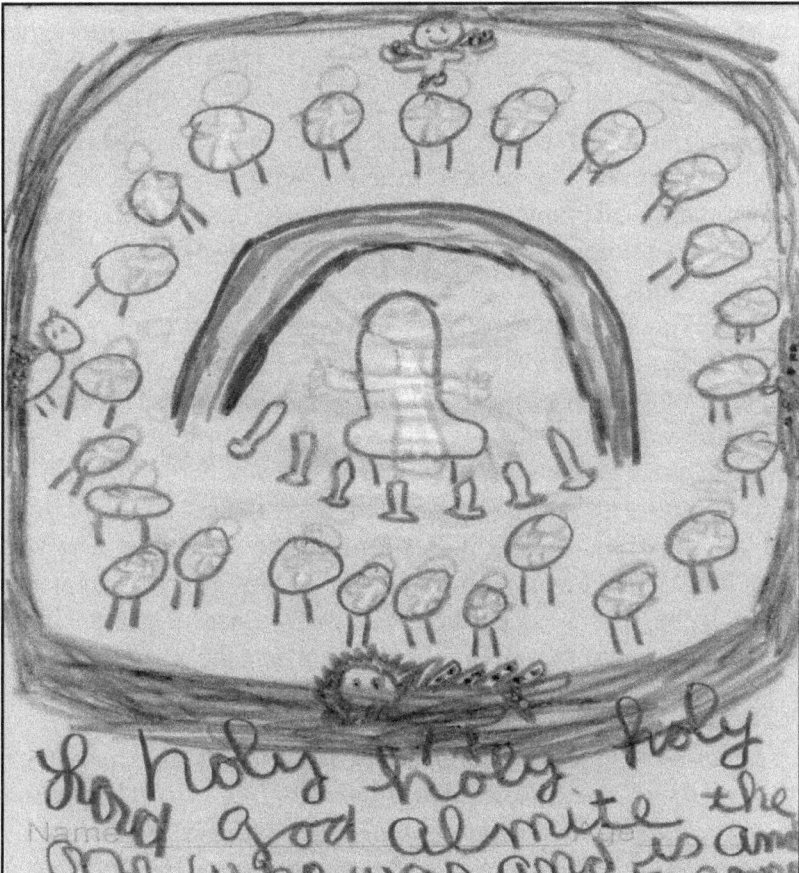

Plate # 11

To see this in grayscale instead of color makes it very hard to comprehend. If you look closely you can make out Jesus sitting on His throne in the middle, a rainbow arching over Him, seven lamp stands in front of the throne, 24 thrones around them with people wearing crowns and four creatures top, bottom and sides that resemble a lion, calf, man and eagle. Now read Revelation 4: 1 – 8. The words at the bottom are in verse 8 verbatim.

I asked her after I received this if Dragonslayer had taken her any place special. She just said, *"Yes, Daddy. That be what I draw for you. You like it?"* Make up your own mind whether this is active imagination or possibly a place Dragonslayer might allow her to see for the renewal of a broken spirit. Mariann will continue to supply us with a number of drawings about the places that she will see with her Dragonslayer. She will draw the spiritual activity that is revealed to her with great detail on the inside world as well as outside. For her, this is normal everyday life and she often questions why the 'big people' don't see it. Every time I spoke to her or wrote her, I would remind her to call Dragonslayer first, before engaging in conversations with the smelly ones. Unfortunately, like any child, she had the greatest curiosity to see what they were going to try next and how they scattered as soon as she called Him.

However, time apart from us was taking its toll on her with the lack of affection she received. Trying to keep her focus on Jesus for her emotional needs would actually become harder as she spent more time with Bob's family. Here she would see her new friends receiving their father's love on a regular basis, which in turn only made her miss us more. Kisses and hugs over the phone and in emails helped, but they couldn't replace the real thing. She wrote me a long letter one night where she shares her fears, joys and desires to be with us in heaven. This one is harder to transliterate her words because the spelling is worse when she's sad.

Hi Daddy,

I want give you and mama Carol butterfly kisses. You come my house NOW go nite nite and my doggie not lick you or bite you. He is warm and I share my cookies and sleep with him. I no sleep with lamees. Daddy, DRAGONSLAYER know a trick He show me. He walked on TOP of water...

Dragonslayer make me a swing in the trees like on our walk and I swing high on it and not be scared I fall. I got Sarus watching me swing too. Then I got more sandal camp. I work on more Dragonslayer work.

Dragonslayer's name is special in all land. He be my rock and my fortress. Daddy that is a big big house to keep bad ones out. He be my shepherd and take care of me. I be his lamee and he make my heart jump happily like frogee jumps. He give me my nest and tell me true things and not lie to me. He have my daddy give give me hugs from him. I like hugs when bad things ones come and bad things like the cancer monster come. I not afraid because Dragonslayer be with me and he hold me. He make a cookie mansion for me and my daddy in heaven. You can lick the cookies and eat the corners. My daddy be a soldier and have Dragonslayer's armor.

I want to be with Dragonslayer and sing to him, 'Dragonslayer is my friend...he love me and I love him...we be special friends can't you see.' Dragonslayer is my teacher and I go to sandal camp school to be Dragonslayer strong like him. He tell me he train my hands to be soldier for him. My birdies sing, 'Praise Dragonslayer! He is the only one we sing praise to.' I put his words to hide in my heart where no bad ones can take them away.

Daddy I love you and mommy and I still be sad that you go away. I no see you for a long long time daddy. No squirt water at daddy no more, no go swinging, no go to moon, no go to church, no hugs, no nite nite with you, no more Mr. Pibb, no more. All gone. No more walk around pray for houses, no more chair from mommie, no more cookies, all gone.

Dragonslayer I be sad, why you take daddy and mama away from Mariann like smelly ones say? I be good girl Dragonslayer, if please you no take my daddy away. I don't want another daddy... I want my daddy please.

Hi Daddy
Mister Bob no spank Mariann. He say forgive Mariann. He make belt of truth. I wear on me. (Bob displayed a belt to threaten his children about a spanking to coerce them into changing behavior. Of course he never used it, but it traumatized Mariann and Tabitha Ann because of her basement beatings by the grandfather. Fortunately, he recovered quickly and turned it into a belt of truth.)

I wear on me Dragonslayer's words. I put on Tabitha to wear. I hold breast plate right (righteousness). *We got helmet of salvation. We no hear smelly ones in helmet. I have Dragonslayer shoes for sandal camp. Tabitha no need shoes, she a little girl. Miss Tina give me cookie for my boo boo. Daddy you come and hug butterflies at Marineworld with Mariann. I like all the animals and want to hug elephant, but Mister Bob say no. I be here daddy...come get Mariann. Daddy come take Mariann home? Mama I listen okay?*

Bob and Tina went out of their way to provide Mariann with opportunities to experience new things. This year they took her to Marineworld first, followed shortly there after by the Billy Graham Crusade in the Oakland Coliseum. To say that it stretched and exhausted Bob would be an understatement. At Marineworld, getting Mariann and Kellie out of the prairie dog exhibit took the patience of Job. To keep both of them back from jumping in with the dolphins took the strength of Samson. To pull Mariann away from hugging the elephant, (the elephant didn't seem to mind but Bob and the trainer were almost in apoplexy), took the courage of a loving father. He didn't realize (or perhaps didn't believe the possibility) that Mariann had hidden in her world inside from the 'Beast' for many years with the help of a guardian elephant which she could hug anytime. (See pages 260-262 in *Journeys to Joy-revised.*)

But even this adventure paled in comparison to going to Oakland and the Crusade. Bob took her on BART for the first time and that would have been enough of an adventure for her, except that she had heard on the inside about this Dragonslayer man coming to tell people the truth. She made a drawing that I will describe in detail to offer at least a mental picture of all that Mariann witnessed occurring above and around her. No one else of the thousands there were aware of the intense spiritual warfare happening above them.

The Coliseum is filled with people smiling and approaching the podium with Rev. Graham preaching and holding a Bible (brown). Covering the new converts on the floor of the Coliseum is an umbrella of light of various warm colors that extend upward toward the sky. Standing on the rim an arm's length apart are guardian angels dressed for battle. On the light standards are commander angels, with Sarus on the lower left side nearest to Mariann (left bottom [rise side below] with Red ribbon in her pigtails next to Mr. Bob). The screens say "I Am the Way" in royal purple. Above all of this are smelly ones trying to come in to disrupt the proceedings, unsuccessfully.

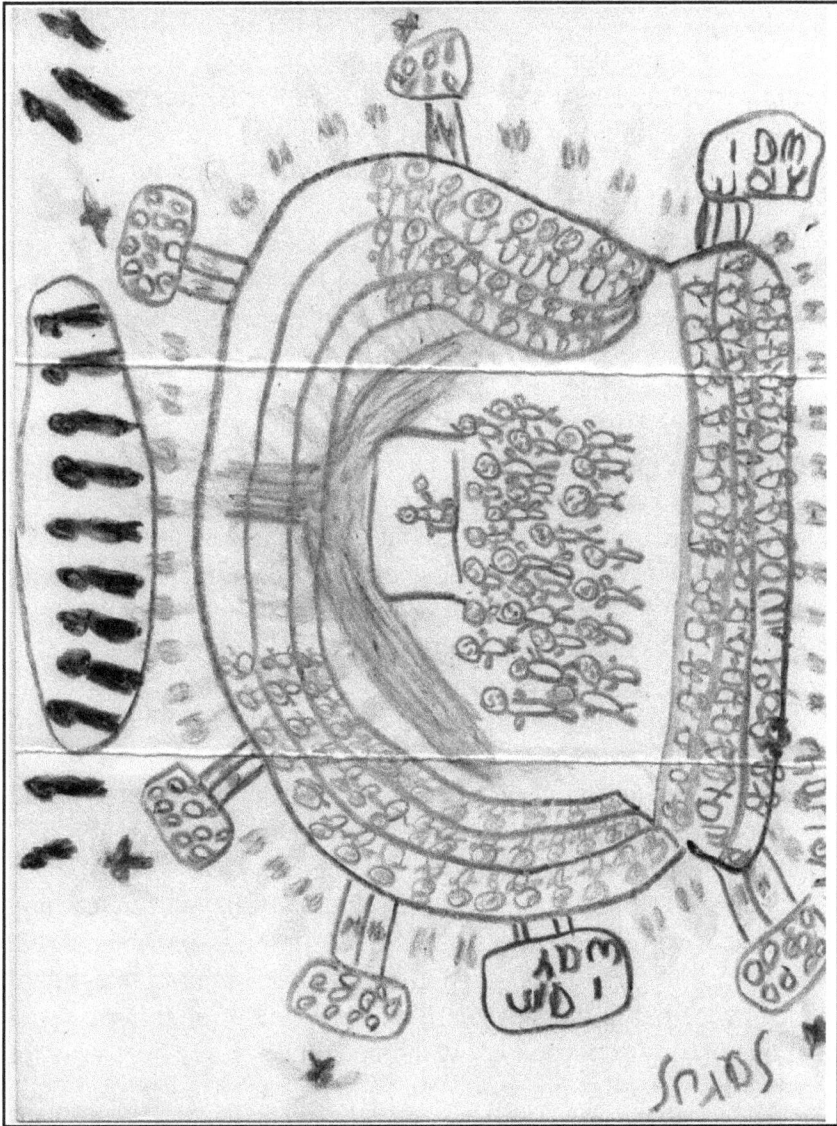

Plate # 12

Bob's main fear was that Mariann would either fall backward out of the bleachers from watching the battle overhead or jump forward wanting to go down and dance in the warm light she saw.

This chapter has focused primarily on Mariann's self identity and just as importantly how Jesus has described her to all of us. For anyone to accept His description, they would have to do so in faith, as they have met or will never meet her in this life. I realize that most of these books on *Shattered People* need faith in God to grasp the potential of what I write about. This has been perhaps the most life-changing aspect of my own journey with Jesus in my process of teaching the System, particularly the children, about the power and truth within His love.

I highlight the children because a child accepts His love before they have any real concept of what faith is in these matters. Every child can recognize the offering of real, pure love that is given without expecting anything in return, not even saying "I love you back". An older child or adult encounters Jesus and will begin in faith to accept His love as true, based upon the promises we've read in the Scriptures, or by the testimonies of loved ones we trust sharing their relationship with Him. Sometimes the adult will meet Him before reading anything about Him yet accept His reality because there is no other logical explanation...or it is the only logical choice. Either way, faith or logic, adults will spend the rest of their lives trying to reach an understanding of God's love that can be freely received...without any response needed. This is the difficulty in our own struggle, to feel worthy of that kind of unconditional love...so foreign in life yet so close.

I began my journey with Mariann with the idea that I would lead her to Jesus and watch how He healed her to learn His 'ways'. What I wasn't expecting was how learning His ways would change my theories of loving anyone so dramatically. I have been learning how to love with power and truth and beginning to understand that I have so far to go to fully grasp it for my life. I want to integrate it into my very being the way that I've observed through Mariann. I say this not only because I know the outcome 7 years from now for her, but because the process of how her Dragonslayer has made His love in her real has only recently been understood. It is this process of transforming a soul into its own reality by giving love in a way that God wants us to do likewise, will be how I close this chapter. It is perhaps the most central concept that everyone on this journey is struggling to learn and accept; **"God loving us is the process by which each life is made whole and faith becomes real."**

"If therefore there is any encouragement in Christ, if there is any consolation of love, if there is any fellowship of the Spirit, if any affection and compassion, make my joy complete by being of the same mind, maintaining the same love, united in spirit, intent on one purpose. Do nothing from selfishness or empty conceit, but in humility of mind let each of you regard one another as more important than himself; do not merely look out for your own personal interests but also for the interests of others."
Philippians 2: 1-4

"Consider it all joy, my brethren, when you encounter various trials, knowing that the testing of your faith produces endurance. And let endurance have its perfect result, that you may be perfect and complete, lacking in nothing."
James 1: 2-4.

I believe that these two sets of verses go hand-in-hand to reveal the process by which we learn how to love. Most of us have a hard time finding joy within our suffering as James seems to imply here, but is that his meaning? The 'encountering of various trials' is the process in which we recognize our need for God. The 'perfect result of endurance' is accepting the power of God's love to endure, His very presence in our lives to complete us. Paul emphasizes this by defining how this is possible, by how joy is completed in us.

Jesus encourages us to experience His love by the Holy Spirit uniting us with Him in the process of loving with His power, by having the same purpose in offering His love to others, without concern about how much love we are receiving first. Herein lies the key to understanding the process. When we love and accept others through His power and purpose for loving, we are caught up in the energy of the process without having to ask for it. When we enter this wanting to receive anything from the process... recognition, kudos, or praise from anyone, even the person we are trying to love… we've lost our purpose and the energy of love within it.

I have not found anywhere in Scriptures where Jesus says that 'joy' can be found in this life on earth anywhere else. The joy found in our tribulations, testing and suffering is not in our circumstances, but in the presence of Jesus loving us in the midst of them to sustain us through these circumstances. This is why I was asked by Jesus to enter into the process of giving His unconditional love to each one in the System. He was teaching us all about how we are completed in Him in this process.

Mariann had spent her life understanding the reality of pain and suffering on the outside and experiencing 'safety' on the inside in friendships with those protecting her as her only connection to love until Dragonslayer reveals Himself. She began to learn how His love was given by those created to protect her and sustain her through all of the circumstances. Even those people inside created to protect her did not understand their complete purpose for being until they encountered the power of Christ's love.

Yet, the reality of the suffering in this life could not be understood until she received this same love on the outside. The love of Christ in our lives has made her as real in this world just as much as it has made me real. Her joy is being made complete through the process of being loved by Jesus and her faith in Him continues to grow exponentially. As I have loved her without expectation of what that means for her or me, I have grown in the potential for sharing the love of Christ in this life. As I've accepted and loved each one in the System for who they are as God created them for His purposes, we both have grown in our understanding of love.

It has been and will continue to be a humbling process to remember that my purpose is not to prove the reality of their souls or individual identity as people, because God does that Himself. My purpose is to love them as He does…the only real proof of any of our existences. I will continue to make my mistakes in this, as you will read further on, but there is joy in the knowledge that what I screw up in the process does not prevent Jesus from completing His process in them…or me. It doesn't really matter what I believe about Mariann's purpose for existing, only that I love her with the love of Christ and continue to try to do the same with all whom Jesus puts in my life. The process is not contingent upon my abilities or strength to accomplish this, only in my willingness to let Him. As Bob becomes caught in the ebb and flow of the process, he too will make choices based upon his understanding of his purpose in life for God. The outcome of what we both learn in this can offer to all of God's caretakers valuable lessons in the process we call loving.

Within three months the System will come to revel in the celebration of my completion of Seminary after 16 years. Mariann will learn another difficult lesson in that Dragonslayer isn't finished with us in Southern California, so we won't be returning with her as she wanted us to do. New adventures, as well as more testing through suffering await her. Warnings start coming into the System of another great spiritual battle looming ahead. Carol and I are put to the test ourselves very soon, as we continue to discover how we are to apply this loving process in the greater body of Christ.

"By this is My Father glorified, that you bear much fruit, and so prove to be My disciples. Just as the Father has loved Me, I have also loved you; abide in My love. If you keep My commandments, you will abide in My love; just as I have kept My Father's commandments and abide in His love. These things I have spoken to you, that My joy may be in you, and that your joy may be made full. This is My commandment, that you love one another, just as I have loved you. Greater love has no one than this, that one lay down his life for his friends. You are My friends, if you do what I command you."
John 15: 8 – 14.

Life is found in communion with God,
Loving is its crucible.

Chapter Fifteen

"Come, Let Us Reason Together"

"But Jesus, aware of their reasoning, answered and said to them, 'Why are you reasoning in your hearts? Which is easier to say, 'Your sins have been forgiven you,' or to say, 'Rise and walk'?"
Luke 5: 22 – 23

Reason itself is a matter of faith. It is an act of faith to assert that our thoughts have any relation to reality at all.
- G. K. Chesterton

"Let not your heart be troubled; believe in God, believe also in Me. In My Father's house are many dwelling places; if it were not so, I would have told you; for I go to prepare a place for you. And if I go and prepare a place for you, I will come again, and receive you to Myself; that where I am there you may be also."
John 14: 1-4

In the past few chapters I have offered Mariann's drawings and letters which reflect her perspectives of life in this world, and some of what she has seen and heard in her spiritual dimension. Except for Tabitha, no one else in the System felt the need to confirm her observations by drawing it, only to reaffirm that what she drew about Preservation was their reality as well. Though Raquel would do some renderings of Sacred Mountain and of Eagle Clan, her paintings might look a lot like things you would see in Utah or in Arizona. Mariann, however, began revealing places that no one else will see with Dragonslayer but her, at least for several more years. Why? Why was Mariann taken to these specific places?

Who was this child of God that needed so much love? She never asks the question, "Who am I?" of anyone but Jesus because she trusted His answer above all others. Her very being was connected to Him, because no one else could supply the depth of her need for love. I believe that Jesus doesn't waste energy loving any person or thing that is not real. If she was just a collection of fractured memories from Maria's past, I don't believe that Jesus would put so much effort out to teach her trust and faith in Him. The same goes for everyone in the System.

As you continue this journey with all of them, take special notice of how the issues of individual identities being questioned by many on the outside, yet repeatedly affirmed by Jesus on the inside. Stay especially close to Mariann in her ongoing struggle with Pastor Bob to be accepted, seen and recognized clearly as Mariann and not as a multiple of Maria. People will try to rationally explain the concept of multiplicity to her for valid reasons surrounding the safety of the System, yet she will staunchly reject any possibility that she is not a 'real' person. Eventually, she will simply say, "Go ask Dragonslayer if I be!" Her tenacity in this will become the lynchpin for encouraging every adult to say the same thing.

Think about that statement for a second. **Go ask Dragonslayer if I be (exist).** Given its context, it calls into question all that we say we believe as Christians about Jesus Christ. Is He alive today... involved in every aspect of our life in Him? Is what He says to us throughout history and in the Scriptures, as validation that He is who He says He is, as real right now in your prayers with God, as it has ever been? Consider the verse at the top of this chapter when Jesus heals the paralytic by saying, *"I say to you, rise, and take up your stretcher and go home." And at once he rose up before them, and took up what he had been lying on, and went home glorifying God."* Jesus has just asked the scribes and Pharisees a very important question about their ability to understand or accept Jesus as the Son of Man (God). Does He have the power and authority to "forgive sins" and "heal a crippled man"? If either can only be done in God's power, which is easier to do?

Nobody in the System will ask the question 'Who am I?' either, simply because that question can only be answered by the person asking it to have any meaning. None of us live in a vacuum and we all exist in relationship with someone else; family, friends, enemies and God. It is in these relationships that we ask the question, "Who am I...in relationship to you? Or... Who am I becoming from your knowledge of me?" We learn our selfidentity from people that we trust like our family, our friends over the years and yes, God.

Perhaps the most important things we learn about ourselves in these times are the qualities and talents we possess, to contribute to the growth of the relationship in question. We have a responsibility to life to give not only what is uniquely our perspective and gifts, but also the generic gifts and talents that we share in common, to achieve the common good for all. Jesus shows us how to accomplish this when He said;

> **"This is My commandment, that you**
> **Love one another, just as I have loved you.**
> **Greater love has no man than this,**
> **Than that he lay down his life for his friends."**

Mariann, Ruth, Louise, Maria, Raquel, Tabitha Ann, Hopi and even Joy had received the power of Dragonslayer's love to define their self-identity in Him. Who was going to be next? It turns out to be Jennifer.

*...Jennifer has decided to make a commitment to follow Jesus. She plans to attend a praise service on Easter Sunday and make her vows to Dragonslayer then. When asked what changed she said, "I have come to realize that he is the only one of the prophets who was willing to die for me. All the others were going to show me the way, but he **is** the way to truth and eternal life."*

With every positive turn in the System's life together, there was the corresponding follow-up action by the enemy to try and keep some of them down. Maria's sister contacted her late one night to condemn her for being so cold hearted in not attending the mother's funeral. It was also Maria's fault that she had no friends, an aunt had a stroke, the father was having surgery, and her sister was deciding to quit seeing her therapist and psychiatrist because they weren't able to handle her violence like Maria could.

Ann quickly attempted to set boundaries about her visiting and Sergio intervened to help as well. A discussion followed between them about the necessity of a restraining order, which ultimately doesn't happen. Sadly, Maria shadowed Ann's conversation inside and started to believe the sister again. Raquel gave Council a note:

"Do not underestimate the harm that can come from one whose mind has been damaged. Encourage the timid one to hear truth from the Great Spirit."

Council wrote me to ascertain if their concern over Maria was valid. They noticed how her friends, Lindsay and Tina, wanted Maria with them continually and Council felt like they were absorbing Maria's energy. Each woman recognized the strong spiritual essence from Maria and both wanted to revel in her company. It was in part due to the aftermath of Maria's sexual mistreatment at home with Sergio and both women were very protective of her.

We discussed the implementation of boundaries for Maria and her time with the two families. When Maria was in depression, she naturally went to her closest friends to be encouraged, but this also prevented her from working on her own issues with healing. Instead, she escaped into another place where all she wanted to do was care for Bob's children as a nanny. This wasn't good for them either as Council noticed, when the children would go to Maria over their own mom. Then there were other issues, like when Bob and Tina cleaned their fish tank with a long plastic tube…just like the one Tabitha remembered the grandfather using to 'purify' her in the basement. Council worked hard at clarifying how that wasn't going to happen to her again, but Tabitha backed off from trusting Bob and Tina as much. One step forward…two steps back.

Ann wrote to tell me how she planned to bribe the kids inside with the promise 'Daddy' would take them to Disneyland in June after school was out. All they had to do was promise to stay inside all next school year while Ann was teaching. Of course she made it clear that she was not paying for Liz to go there too. Even though I knew her perfect plan wouldn't work, at least we had her blessing to go to Disneyland while they were with us for my graduation.

Maria began observing the division among the groups in Pastor Bob's church. It troubled her greatly and she wrote asking for advice on what to say…if anything. She wasn't allowed to attend church for a month when issues got worse. Couple that with Ann taking extra time to finish her first school year teaching, and you have a very insecure young woman.

You know my church is like there is two groups, one standing here and the other there. One teaches one way and one teaches another. One is threatened by the other and they stand on opposite sides. Then I see Jesus, standing with the group that listens to Him and wanting the whole church cleaned for the people to know his love. The one group makes the other upset and nervous. They say they are way out of line. Some say praise God, while another questions the powerful group. That group says the others are just wanting power...and there stands Jesus with tears because one group has fallen away. Nobody seems to see or hear Dragonslayer there in the groups, but we do.

I get really lonely in the outside world. I can't get my butterfly wings to open up like Ann does. She says I am insecure, but I need another butterfly with me to fly together. I just have a hard time making friends and learning how the world works. It is so fast...

May found the System still having a difficult transition with meeting the new therapist and arranging a final session with Bruce. The communications were mostly emails now between them, this being very unsatisfactory for the children needing his hugs to halt fears of abandonment. He attempted to help them set boundaries with Maria's sister by approaching her in a letter, but Council decided to hold off, knowing how anything from counselors which challenged her addictive lifestyle could bring more wrath upon Maria. Bruce tried to bring some resolution between he and Ann, but that would slowly fade unresolved by them. Maria however, was bothered by it and grasping his imminent departure.

...Also, Council wishes to notify you that Maria is struggling with your relationship with Ann. She says she loves you both and wishes you both would get along. We have tried to stay out of the middle of you two, for we see valid points on both sides. However, we are concerned about Maria's feelings and would like for you to prompt her to talk with you. We are worried about the length of time between contacts as Maria is not doing well in the transition. She has commented to me that you will go away like everyone else. She believes that the fact of not hardly seeing you anymore is proof of her unimportance and that you too will abandon her even

though you promised to stay her friend. We believe her feelings are affecting the children as well...

May was not all sadness for everyone. When Mariann said she wanted to buy flowers for Mama Carol for Mother's Day, Ann promised to help her do this. In the past year, Ann or Ruth bought them and let the kids tell her it was from them. You know the kind, nice little bouquets. This time however, Mariann was on a mission to choose her own flowers for her mama. Ann took her to the florist and said, "Pick out the flowers you want so I can buy them and get out of here!"

*...It seems that Mariann wanted a funeral wreath that was displayed in the center of the store. It was the tallest and biggest flower arrangement there. She liked it because it was heart shaped in red carnations, never mind that it said "Beloved" on it. To her it was the best one there. Well Ann proceeded to explain to her that it was a funeral wreath...but got nowhere. Mariann was determined to get those flowers. Liz chimed in and said, "Send it, she'll never forget it!" Ann told her to shut up and turned to explain to Mariann that **these are for dead people.** At which Mariann replied, "Why do dead people want flowers?" Ann then said, "It is not for the dead people to enjoy, but the people who go to see the dead people." Mariann, "But why do people go see dead people? Do they want to be dead?" Frustrated, Ann turned to Ruth and said, "Deal with her please and explain how she can choose from one of these four...and hurry up." Ruth told her to choose only one of the four and to ask Dragonslayer which of these he likes best. Mariann made her choice and Carol did not receive a funeral wreath!* (I suggested as how it was a novel idea afterwards and would consider getting one another time myself. So far I have not .)

As June came, everyone was excited to come down to Pasadena for my graduation ceremony. Ann was looking to some rest following the end of school and several others were looking for rest from Ann. She had accomplished a tremendous thing this year and at different levels all the adults were proud of her. She had been nominated for various awards, yet she shunned the publicity in favor of self affirmation. We sent her a card, the only one she received, and she stated how the others don't understand why she's not making a big deal out of it. She sent me the following quote as explanation for her humility.

"Success means doing the best we can with what we have.
Success is in the doing, not the getting,
in the trying, not the triumph." - Davis

Council wrote me two days before coming down with a list of issues to be prepared for…in case I was a little tired. Dragonslayer had a number of issues he wanted us to resolve during this two week visit, so that the people could return better prepared for what lies ahead for them and us.

Council Memo,

1. *Mariann was warned by Ann that if she refuses to go potty for Tabitha at night, that she will make her wear diapers. Mariann refuses to wear them because she is a big girl. We believe that she is reluctant to go because of the recent biopsy. Please have Mariann go each night before bed.*
2. *Mariann still having abandonment issues…Bruce disappearing and this might cause problems for you. Child still thinks she was to be patient for one year and when "daddy finished big people sandal camp" he would come back. We are having a particularly hard time with this one.*
3. *Bob tried to take Mariann on a drive through the canyon where he thought she had been molested, not knowing that it was Tabitha. He was trying to reassure her that no harm would come to her in his care. Instead, she became hysterical and Council was forced to pull her in. Unfortunately, his experiment didn't work and now we have two children upset and struggling with this issue.*
4. *Council has spoken to Dragonslayer about the letter going to the bishop. Dragonslayer said,* **"The letter is to be written. Michael is to help in the construction of the letter. It is to be mailed from Southern California and she is not to be identified. Those in authority must know of the harm their choices have caused My little lambs. I shall guide the pen of Michael."**

5. *We are sending a letter concerning power of attorney for you. It will not be signed as we are not sure whether you want it notarized there. Ann must sign her signature.*

6. *We are sending as well a letter of funeral wishes so there will be no disagreement or confusion when Dragonslayer tells us it is time to come home with him.*

7. *Ann has the ultrasound in July to see if the cancer has returned. Council has discussed with Dragonslayer a plan of action. Our purpose is to protect the system and keep it functioning with whatever is necessary to accomplish this goal. However, Council is also mandated from protecting the system against prolonging life, when it is clear from Dragonslayer that it is time to enter the spiritual dimension. We await his direction.*

8. *Ann is struggling with control, her career and the system's health. We applaud her fighter mentality, but we must balance work with rest. Ann must take care of the body.*

9. *We congratulate you on your accomplishments this year and celebrate with you.*

Respectfully,
Council (E.R.)

The night before leaving the System went to a Wednesday service to pray for the week ahead. While there, a pastor spoke on the End Times and stated how the 'Beast' was coming back. Mariann switched out hearing this and began listening again to the 'smelly ones' over the adults of the System. She was sure the pastor wasn't lying about the beast and the bishop rising up again. I wrote a letter to her late that night to help calm her down.

Hi Mariann,
I'm going to see you tomorrow night and give you the biggest hug of your life. The Beast is not coming! I talked to Dragonslayer and He told me the preacher was talking about something different and you misunderstood. You are safe with Dragonslayer because He keeps you Dragonslayer strong! Mama Carol and I are excited to see you and Britta will be here too. You can remember what I taught you, in All things TRUST and OBEY JESUS – there's no other way. His love will protect you and keep all of His children safe. Ask Him to tell you and the kids His stories until you get here

and it'll go by so fast! See you soon sweetie. Love and butterfly kisses to the children.

The two weeks were a time for celebration and spiritual reflection over where God would lead us next. I asked Elizabeth Ray to write a synopsis of the time together for my records later, as I was mentally exhausted by the day of graduation. After the party I pretty much slept for 24 hours to be prepared for other events. I do remember getting permission to wear my Panama hat from Dr. Mouw, the president of FTS, for 16 years of perseverance in achieving the degree. It was so my family and friends could recognize 'Panama Mike' on stage so far away. It felt like the end of an era for Carol and I after so long in graduate studies.

Mariann waited until we were in the car to come out and tell me of all the bright ones at the event. Her description was later confirmed by Elizabeth Ray in her letter. I believe the Lord had them there for everyone, but in particular for the System to enjoy a part of our journey together, without being hassled by the smelly ones for a few hours. Evil wasted no time in attacking the children of the System after the event and throughout the weeks, as we went to Disneyland for their first time, out to a brewery with Liz, to Bruce and Tone's house for dinner (Our prayer partners and the children's God-grandparents) and to baptize Jennifer in my brother's pool. Disneyland gets its own paragraph after the following letter tells of their points of attack in our time together.

I will attempt to write you concerning the conversations and activity surrounding the system and Dragonslayer as you requested. As they visited you, spiritual activity heightened after Maria attended graduation exercises. Bright ones were present at the ceremony lined up on both balconies with two larger ones stationed in the center. The entrances were guarded and Smelly Ones stayed out.

Child Mariann was main target of smelly ones. Continual remarks by them included "Daddy is going away too. See, he said once he finished sandal camp, he would be with you...but watch he will send you away again...he doesn't tell you what is really going to happen...he is going away...he doesn't love you."

Child resisted remarks and called on Dragonslayer several times in the early days of the visit. Night sleeping was very restless, as smelly ones spoke to child and caused nightmares. One include child being punished for fire starting in office child was supposed to protect...father sent child away. Smelly ones are changing appearances and have started appearing to children through birds, animals and physically appealing beings...becoming hard for children to make distinctions.

Smelly ones also utilized conversations of adults regarding funeral preparations to further traumatize child parts and divide loyalty to Dragonslayer and daddy. "See, they are going to put you in a box again and this time you will never get out, because you have angered Goatman. He will not save you when your daddy puts you in the box...unless you tell Goatman you are sorry and you love him not Dragonslayer. Mariann questioned daddy about the box comment. Smelly ones were furious the child went to her daddy to clarify. They began to realize how the child was getting stronger and smarter. The Veggie Tales tape made them agitated. They decided to center their focus on abandonment issues and Joy. Child Joy was traumatized that night and used paper clip to scratch herself trying to get the pain out. Continual badgering of Joy late into the night causing a nightmare through a flashback of suffocating in the box. Michael and Carol intervened and soothed her to sleep.

A continual tug-o-war is occurring between smelly ones and bright ones over the children. Smelly Ones attempted several times to distract Mariann from speaking Dragonslayer's words to Michael and succeeded twice. Their tactics were sabotaged by bright ones when the child revealed to Michael that he is to take up thy pen and follow the primary task given to him by Dragonslayer. She continued saying be diligent and that he will be as Aaron was to Moses. Michael expressed concern about having to earn money first to pay bills. Child talked about the birdies and grasses and how Dragonslayer takes care of his lambs. Also child was protected in backyard by bright ones around in conversation with Dragonslayer and Michael on trust. She told how Dragonslayer gave him his friend David to help with the task.

Dragonslayer continually talked to Mariann about trusting and obeying. He stressed that he never leaves his lambs. He would spend time in the early dawn bringing soothing words to her ears, that he understood her love for her daddy and how hard it was to leave him. He told her about leaving his daddy to come to earth as an infant. He understood. He told her that it was not the time for her and her daddy to be together as a family because everything is not in place yet. He told her that he would give her strength to see the pain through, and like he and his daddy, she and her daddy would forever be together in love and her daddy would not stop loving her.

Smelly ones continue to use fear of abandonment, as they reminded Mariann that Kelly had her daddy and of all the fun they had together. They asked her why Kellie gets her daddy and not Mariann. If Dragonslayer really loved you he would let you be with your daddy. They had been successful in planting doubt and confusion with the therapist and now were attempting to break loyalty with daddy, thus creating a spiral effect leading to distrust of Dragonslayer.

Adult parts not aware of smelly ones presence, as the smelly ones centered efforts solely on the children. They do this because Mariann is used by Dragonslayer in ways that threaten the smelly ones domain. When Michael took Mariann to swim at his brother's pool, bright ones were all around in the water and the trees. Smelly ones watched and waited for child to be alone in the water and her daddy to fall asleep. They told her she could swim and go in the big water like daddy. They tried to have Mariann go into deeper water by telling her to watch her feet in the water so they don't fall in the holes. They waited until they thought surveillance of child was lax and made their move, pulling her from the pool wall. Sarus appeared, Bright Ones attacked the smelly ones and Michael jumped into the pool to rescue Mariann. When Michael baptized Jennifer the smelly ones were furious again but could not enter the area.

At the park bright ones were present surrounding the child. Mariann was told by them a friend will play with you. She thought it was the first little boy she encountered, but it was the second boy

346

named Steven. He no more saw her differences than she saw his. They played contently on the swings and slide without any attacks from smelly ones under the watchful eyes of eight bright ones and her daddy. System arrived home without further incident. Children were inside with Dragonslayer. Mariann viewed Jeremiah story and listened to angelic music.

Elizabeth Ray – excerpts from records.

If you notice particular attention given with the tactics of the evil ones, you are correct. The 'records' were made to provide assistance to me in completing my primary task mentioned above. It was only because of Jesus' training that I was aware of most of what they were trying to do with the children as it happened. When the children slept at night on the floor on a sleeping bag, I would sleep next to them and whisper to them to call Dragonslayer anytime they were restless. Carol and I slept in shifts so that one of us was always awake and aware of their activity.

When Mariann and I were in my office talking with Dragonslayer, I noticed how the activity of blackbirds outside of the patio doors dramatically increased causing Mariann to get distracted from our conversation. I prayed for them to go away and they left. Shortly afterwards, the wind kicked up and was shaking the trees and rose bushes rather loudly. We prayed about it and things died down, so we decided to finish our conversation outside and asked for protection from the smelly ones even coming close. It turned out to be a beautifully quiet evening.

At the pool I could tell that they were tempting Mariann to slide further along the side towards the deep end of the pool. I set boundaries for her and each time I looked away; she would edge a little further past the mark. I reminded her how she was **not** a swimmer yet and had to obey or lose her time in the water. Being in the swimming pool was almost as fun for her as eating cookies – almost. I decided then to see how far she would listen and obey. I laid down on a chair and pretended to nap...keeping one eye slightly opened to watch. When she got to the 6-foot mark and seemed to fall backwards, I dove in and pulled her out. In tears she promised to not do that again until such time as I declared her a swimmer. During Jennifer's baptism, the wind was howling above us and the trees were whipping around at the top, but the surface of the pool was warm and gentle for the entire time.

The park time was really special. I had hurt my foot the day before doing something stupid and couldn't go with Mariann on the slides and whirligig. There were only a few children there when we arrived and the parents were cautious about letting any of them play with Mariann for more than a few minutes at a time. A few asked me about her and all I said was "She's my special gift from God." Mariann was beginning to get disappointed, when a car pulled up with 4-5 kids around 8 years old and their mother.

They were all mentally or physically handicapped to one degree or another. They immediately began playing near Mariann as though she was just another kid in the park. She asked the boy having the most fun on the slide his name, Steven, and if he wanted to play with her. They had a ball together for at least an hour. They were on the swings (daddy powered) and the monkey bars and anything else the mother and I allowed. This was a special lady we met with all of her children drowning in love. They were all adopted. Neither she nor her children saw anything in Mariann except an 8 year old having fun. God bless them. Mariann still asks about Steven almost 7 years later…never forgetting that one hour.

Now for Disneyland…I took Mariann (with the System tagging along) and Britta early in the day to last until the first one drops. I think Britta learned real fast not to pay any attention to those few impolite people who stared at Mariann or mumbled comments. It distracted from being a part of the joy of the moments. She wanted to ride everything, see everything, eat everything she wasn't supposed to and smell, touch, hear and share every bit of action in front of her. Britta had given her some aviator goggles to wear while 'driving' the car with her in Autopia. The picture of her smile is priceless.

She can recite every ride and song accompanying it, the pirates song, Peter Pan's, It's a Small World and on and on. We almost lost her climbing on Daniel Boone's fortress. Perhaps the highlight of the day came when she met the 'real' Tigger and Pooh, her heroes. I went ahead of her and asked the attendant if they could give this special 8-year-old something to remember. Tigger went to her in turn and starting bouncing her all over the place for several minutes. Pooh in turn offered her honey and all of them posed for

348

several pictures, something she still laughs about remembering. She collapsed from exhaustion inside before ever leaving Main Street.

We took advantage of all of the children sleeping inside the next two days, because of what they had shadowed with Mariann. I took Liz to a brewery to let her taste some beer. Of course she tasted too much, so Britta and I took her bowling to sober her up, as we didn't want anyone else paying for her hangover. They got through it and returned home happier, exhausted and filled with memories to carry them through the summer and more. I had an email waiting for Mariann to encourage her to trust, obey and ask for patience until we can be together again. Ruth wrote back;

...Mariann has not read your message yet as she is still inside. She has settled down and seems to be depressed, but at least she is not hysterical. She is a tough cookie and Council knows she will rise to the occasion once more. The other kids are tired but okay. Maria is sad and not talking much. It really surprises me that none of them are happy to be home except that they can see the hills and breathe better. Sergio told Maria that no one missed her and that didn't help, but that is the way it is. Maria will twirl inside with memories of these past two weeks. We will continue to keep you both in our prayers, as you are always with us. Thanks for a wonderful time!

The summer would fly by in many respects. The System's relationship with Bob and his family continued to grow. Bob was already having an impact in his ministry in new areas. A multiple called the office and Bob fielded her questions with a new awareness and understanding of her plight that it overwhelmed her unexpectedly. Mariann began writing him to help teach him all that she learned in two weeks about the smelly ones tricking people by not looking bad.

...Dragonslayer love you. Smelly ones no look bad now they trick. They make Mariann do other things so no do Dragonslayer work. Dragonslayer tell me smelly ones no want man do Dragonslayer work. So they make other people interrupt man all time no work. Dragonslayer say Mariann know my voice. No get distracted by smelly ones. My lamees know me and I know my lamees. Dragonslayer tell me about Jeremiah. He tell people no do bad,

trust and obey Dragonslayer. They do bad and hurt Jeremiah cuz he say stop. Then Dragonslayer teach big people lesson...

(From Ruth to Tina)
...Council is finding it interesting that the enemy has centered its attacks on Mariann. She is the strongest in faith of all of the parts in the system, yet they focus on her. They are using distractions, disguises and even other people to confuse the child and stop her from ministering to others. Council wonders if the focus is because they are uneasy about her seeing the spiritual world around us. They get real agitated when she tells of their operations to others. They like to plan their dirty work in secret and they don't like Mariann talking about what she sees and hears.

They really don't like her telling what Dragonslayer tells her to say. They try to distract her by sending static when she's on the phone with Mike. He prays with her and the static stops. This happens often when they speak on a spiritual level. We sense that the spiritual activity is very high right now, so we need to be in constant prayer not only on the inside, but more importantly out loud on the outside. When we pray for strength and guidance from Jesus and praise him in song and word...when we tell him we love him and we surrender all of ourselves to him...we set the enemy back.

We pray for strength and guidance for you and Bob as well as ourselves. We have a good amount of prayer warriors inside. With a multiple praying for you...you get a whole prayer support group.

Maria attended her first meeting with her new therapist. Council noticed how none of the children would come out to meet her. They knew that Mariann was upset about Bruce leaving without saying goodbye, but they hoped she would grow accustomed to her gradually. The other kids were all shadowing Mariann to see if she would accept this new 'big' person outside. The therapist raised issues about Maria being 'used' by family and friends...Council had to agree and had me call her to encourage her and Mariann after the first session.

...It was good hearing your voice. Your words of encouragement and counsel to Mariann are very much appreciated. She is much better since you spoke to her about seeing the therapist. Daniel had a long talk with her afterwards about you. He told her there are two truths that will never change for Mariann. They will always be true. Dragonslayer and Daddy will always love you. Don't let anyone ever make you think they are not true. Then he reminded her of how he, the clan of Argus and Lion always protected her from anything not true or hurtful.

...Tina cares a lot for Maria, but we need to be careful of the codependent stuff you talked about. Tina sometimes forgets that Maria is a multiple and still has a lot of issues that drain her. She forgets the system's health issues as well and needs rest to maintain everyday. Council will help her set boundaries with her friends. The body cannot hold all these spirits without adequate rest and good nutrition. We were very concerned when Tina told Maria everything went wrong when she left for your place. She told her that she could never leave again. Maria doesn't want to hurt anyone and we are concerned about outsiders putting guilt trips on her. Sergio told her, "If you weren't gone for so long your garden wouldn't have died from neglect."

Hopefully the therapist will help her to be more independent and make choices. She tried to explain to her about your relationship and knowing what she thinks without asking, but to no avail. She said how hard it is to go back to a place where no one understands her. "I never had choices and I don't know what to do with them. I am happy with anything if I could just be with the people I love."

Mariann has been reprimanded by Sergio for laughing, singing or giggling in the bedroom at night. It does not matter whether she was on the phone with you or laughing with her Tigger doll, the rules are no noise from that bedroom. We believe it is a control thing like no locks on the door. We agree that it his problem, but Mariann is afraid when he opens the door suddenly and stares at her with that look. Council sees no way to contain her joy at those moments. Mariann can't just twirl inside like Maria, she is too bouncy. It is hard enough to see her caged in that room because outsiders do not want her out. Our dilemma is how do we allow

351

her to express her joy and still maintain a safe environment for her? We have given the counselor permission to contact you to ask anything she wants and that you will ask for progress reports.

Council called a meeting with Dragonslayer to discuss boundaries for Maria and the System. Ann was trying to complete another class for accreditation in summer school, Louise was keeping her garden up as well as being asked to do weeding for Sergio's mother and help Tina with hers, Maria was doing her housework and assisting in caring for Bob's kids…all of this while facing a biopsy for cancer. They turned to Dragonslayer for advice, who was now sitting in on all of their meetings to listen. He told them a parable using Mariann to declare the meaning before saying this, **"Carry each other's burdens, but do not carry that which the other is able to carry for himself for it does not benefit him."** Council decided to adjourn and reflect on the meaning of burdens and what boundaries might be important.

I heard a few days later that the biopsy was negative, no cancer, and Liz was allowed out to party. Ann was still not convinced of the cancer not coming back and remained somewhat depressed about the possibility. She would finish her class sooner than expected and allowed Raquel to take the System on a trip to Canada to spend some time on a reservation there. She asked if we could reinstate our correspondence on questions about the Bible. She started by asking why Mary would waste all that expensive perfume on Jesus at the party. To her thinking, Mary was impulsive at best and not a very good conservator of money, just like she felt about Maria. She brought up Martha and how <u>she</u> understood the value of a dollar and would have stopped her, like Ann would have stopped Maria from wasting it. I planned to answer her by leading her into her own bible study… subtlety.

I wrote to Mariann every week and Carol sent cards and stickers for the kids to share. Mariann wrote back every other day, often repeating the loss she felt with Bruce leaving. The enemy tried to make her depressed, but Dragonslayer kept her emotionally stable. I would hear about all of the things she was doing with Bob's kids, including the things she got in trouble over. Mariann has never been able to keep a secret involving herself for very long, good or bad. Tina asked me why Mariann couldn't draw on the sidewalk like her kids. Mariann had told her that I said no drawing. I had told her that she could no longer draw on other people's property...the property being discussed at the time was Ann's new (used) car. She had 'decorated' the dash and cloth overhead with 'pictures'.

Tina was grateful to clear it up and told me how she had drawn pictures of her being sad when Bruce left. She drew how she thought it was her fault for being bad. She learned how to help in the situation. She also wanted to keep me informed about Joy starting to come out to hug and lie next to Chris for brief periods. Bob was offering help as well to find a pastoral job in Northern California, but I informed him of plans to accept the interim position at Calvary in Pasadena, yet to be offered. He was surprised at my prediction coming true about this offer, something that will haunt him later in our relationship when I have a prophetic message for him.

Mariann was getting worn down by the enemy over the issue of abandonment. Council wrote the therapist and I about their discoveries from Dragonslayer's counsel. The following are excerpts;

...Council has allowed frequent phone calls to her daddy to reinforce that he has not gone away and still loves her. We noticed the increase in contact and Daniel suggested that the child is 'checking' to assure herself he is still there. Daniel believes her behavior with the new therapist is her acting out her anger at Bruce leaving, and does not want a substitute. Just as Mariann has never understood the concept of being a multiple, Mariann has never understood the concept of a therapist and understood Bruce as a 'friend to play with.' The acting out of eating a worm, sticking her tongue out at Ann and playing a trick on Tabitha, she is trying to express her feelings about Bruce leaving, having to go back to Maria's home from her daddy's and Ann taking 'her' time for school.

She was under the assumption that her daddy would be with her now and didn't grasp the long-term plan. She is aware that Kellie and Anna's dad sees them more than her daddy sees her. Although she has no anger towards them for having their daddy all of the time, she is upset that she can't have her daddy. This gets worse when they have daddy discussions attempting to outdo each other over who has the greatest daddy. She also misses the physical contact with her daddy and mommy. Her needs are not fulfilled at home adding to her stress. Daddy hugs are very important to Mariann because they give her a sense of acceptance and protection. The child seems to be unusually needy of this type of safe contact and will forego food and toys for these types of hugs.

When Mariann has talked to Dragonslayer about her predicament, she has offered him her most sacred treasures...Britta Bear, Pooh, Tigger, Fredricka (parrot) and Nikita (dog)...if he would tell daddy to come and get her and take her home. Dragonslayer understands from personal experience Mariann's issues of loneliness and abandonment. He understands her "I'm finished with patience", because he knows the strong tie of love and devotion she has for her daddy and mommy.

Council finds it interesting that he has never tried to explain multiplicity to her or why she is different. Instead, he asks her simple questions like, "Mariann can you make it rain? Mariann, can you make the sun come up in the morning? Each time she giggles and says, "No Dragonslayer, I be little." Then he asks, "Mariann, can daddy make it rain or make the sun come up in the morning?" She answers, "That silly Dragonslayer, daddy can't do that, he lost his brains in school and can't find them."

Dragonslayer tells her, "No Mariann, even if daddy had more brains than anyone else on earth, he still could not make it rain or the sun come up in the morning. But Mariann I can because I am Jesus and I made everything. I know how everything works and I know about tomorrow and what is best for you, but you must trust me Mariann. When you get sad and miss daddy, come to me and I will hold you and comfort you. Mariann I'm always here waiting to be with you. I am always with daddy too. Trust me Mariann."

Dragonslayer changes the questions with her and asks her things like, can you make the stars shine in the sky or a coyote howl at the moon? But he always follows the same pattern with Mariann about who he is and why she must trust him. We asked him why these

354

conversations with him do not seem to be working. He reminded us about how hard it is for us leaders to trust. "She is a little lamb of mine who has been deceived much. She is growing in trust and it takes time for that seed to blossom. We must be patient with her and continue to fill her with truth. She is very special to me and I will give her heart's desire when it is time."

So for now we will continue to let her call her daddy as frequently as needed. We will continue to push her out at counseling to give her consistency with the new therapist. We will also seek the wisdom of Dragonslayer on this issue and encourage her to talk with him. We will continue to let her have play time at Bob and Tina's home.

Maria wrote me about what she had been talking to Jesus about as well the following night:

...I like talking with Jesus on the inside, especially when I'm sad. I think Ann and Ruth have been arguing inside and Pastor Bob says it is a debate, but my head still hurts. Ann told Ruth that she agrees God provides for the birds, but she says he doesn't put food in their mouths. It has something to do with trusting Jesus. Ruth went to complain to Jesus saying how Ann is too hard to debate. Jesus said, "Did I tell you to debate with her?"

I talked with Jesus about how I feel being different from everyone else and how hard it is when people know. He told me how he felt when people didn't understand him and how he didn't fit in this world. Then he told me not to worry about being normal to the world's standards. He said to keep abiding in him and know that I am loved by him.

I told him how everyone says I have to grieve to get better. It is very hard for me and I'm afraid that if I begin I will never stop. He told me that he will grieve with me and that the pain must come out for the healing to take place. He said I don't have to do it all at once, just a little at a time. I think I want to grieve with Jesus.

We talked about you too. He told me I could love you and Carol as much as I can. I liked that. He told me to listen to you about boundaries and said he has boundaries too. I asked if I could do only a couple of them, cause it is hard. He asked me why and I said because if you say no to someone, they might get mad and say what did you say? Or they might leave and not come back. Or they might say you will do what I say or else. It just causes fights and I hate fighting. He said he will help me to learn boundaries.

I'm learning how life is like a beautifully woven rug. Jesus is the weaver and I am one of the threads in his kingdom rug. Each time I get woven a certain way, he's got to have all of the other threads where they need to be for the weave to be like he wants it. So I got to wait sometimes to be woven cause he's working on other threads that maybe break or get tangled and he can't weave me without the others.

"And the day came when the risk to remain tight in a bud was more painful than the risk it took to blossom."
Anaisis Nin

"The Lord is my shepherd, I shall not want.
He makes me lie down in green pastures;
He leads me beside quiet waters.
He restores my soul;
He guides me in the paths of righteousness
For His name's sake.
Even though I walk through the valley
Of the shadow of death,
I fear no evil; for Thou art with me;
Thy rod and Thy staff, they comfort me.
Thou dost prepare a table before me
In the presence of my enemies;
Thou hast anointed my head with oil;
My cup overflows.
Surely goodness and lovingkindness
Will follow me all the days of my life.
And I will dwell in the house of the Lord forever."
Psalm 23

356

Chapter Sixteen

"The Stamp of Acceptance"

"You shall therefore impress these words of mine on your
heart and on your soul...And you shall teach them to your
children, talking of them when you sit in your house..."
Deuteronomy 11: 18-19

*"In Him, you also, after listening to the message of truth,
the gospel of your salvation – having also believed, you
were sealed in Him with the Holy Spirit of promise, who
is given as a pledge of our inheritance, with a view to the
redemption of God's own possession, to the
praise of His glory."*
Ephesians 1: 13-14

*"The Church as community of faith...in these days must
not be concerned primarily with the observance
of ritual, disciplinary and moral regulations,
but with men being able to live and receive
from one another what they need in order to live."*
Hans Kung, *On Being a Christian* (1974)

I received a frantic call late Wednesday evening from Tabitha
and I knew by the timing that she must have heard something at
the worship service at Bob's church. After getting her to slow
down so I could understand her Spanish, I realized that either they
had communion, or the sermon was on this subject. Yemaya was
attacking Tabitha through her flashbacks of the Santeria rituals of
drinking blood of sacrifices. Tabitha was desperately seeking
confirmation from me that she never had to do that again and not
only for herself, but for all of the children.

As I tried to reassure her that it will never happen again, I
realized that the children would need to learn that the sacrament of
communion in the Christian church was opposite of what had been
implanted in the psyche for so many years. Prior to this evening, I
served communion with them at baptisms and in my home using

words and phrases which didn't frighten the young ears and eyes observing the meal. Now, they were going to be in churches observing communion who were either unaware of the probability of 'multiples' in the midst or chose to perform their rituals the way it always would be performed. They were not aware of what might be understood by a minority of abuse victims in their midst.

She cried something about writing Mister Bob, but I didn't understand what she was saying. I told her to go talk with Jesus, while I talked with an adult. Ruth came out but wasn't sure what all had transpired since church and said she'd email me more the next day. I received copies of Tabitha's letter to Bob, his response, Mariann's letter to Bob explaining again for Tabitha, and her follow-up letter to me explaining what Dragonslayer taught her about the purpose of His communion ritual for His children.

Mariann wrote in Spanish (sort of) with Tabitha spelling to her about "not listening to 'yamia', bad what orisha del mar know, Tabitha no want drink blood, church no make blood go on rocks, why Santeria be in church, why Tabitha say orisha mad, and why Tabitha say Tabitha must die."

Bob answered with as much as he understood, not knowing a lot about Tabitha's past experiences with the Santeria and the SRA cults within it. He tried to refocus her back on listening only to the friends of Dragonslayer (not realizing that she referred to as Jesus), which ultimately helped Mariann to assist her. He wisely used the example that 'yamia' will not hug Dragonslayer and so cannot be His friend. That she understood, but it didn't help her in the context of what she saw happening in the church of 'drinking blood.'

Mariann tried again:

Mister Bob,   I write for Tabitha.   Me Mariann. Tabitha not big girl to write.   I tell Mister Bob words.   Tabitha and Mariann no want to drink church blood.   Mariann say Dragonslayer come. Mister Bob smelly ones try trick   use Dragonslayer's words.   They try   trick   look   pretty   so   Mariann   no   call   Dragonslayer. Dragonslayer tell daddy 'bembe' be cultic party. What that be Mister Bob? (When Tabitha said bembe over the phone I understood baby as in the one sacrificed in front of her...her flashback.)

Mariann went to Dragonslayer and later wrote me the same night:

Dragonslayer come, what Mariann do? Dragonslayer tell me he love me lots and he want me be in heaven, but no can go without Dragonslayer stamp. How get Dragonslayer stamp Mariann say. Dragonslayer say Mariann one night I had supper with my friends. It was the last supper with my friends, because I was going to die on the sticks so you and they could have my Dragonslayer stamp at supper. I tried to tell them what was going to happen. I wanted them and you to have the bread to think of my body on the sticks because I love you and want you to have Dragonslayer's stamp.

Then I asked them to drink wine to know the blood in my body would be coming out, when I get cut on the sticks. And know I let this happen to me because I love my Mariann and want her to have Dragonslayer's stamp to live forever in her cookie mansion with me. So I want my people to have bread and drink in church to remember I love them so much that I go on the sticks and die so they can have Dragonslayer's stamp.

Dragonslayer put stamp on me and everyone knows I belong to Dragonslayer. He put his mark of ownership on me. Stamp say Dragonslayer buy me back from bad. Mariann say Dragonslayer I no see stamp. Where it be Dragonslayer? I see Tigger stamp and Pooh stamp, where be my Dragonslayer stamp? Dragonslayer know, he say Mariann, Holy Spirit bring stamp in your heart. Stamp in Mariann's heart. Daddy, Holy Spirit comes into Mariann's heart. Mariann knows communion. Remember, Dragonslayer go on sticks for Mariann to get Dragonslayer stamp and go be with Dragonslayer forever. Daddy, I no afraid of Dragonslayer's supper. Bad ones trick me.

As you can see, Mariann understood quite well for an 8-year-old the purpose of communion. I added capitals, punctuation and a few words spelled correctly to help the reader. It will take Tabitha a longer amount of time to understand and accept the ritual. This is because of the continuing ties with Yemaya that have to be broken and trust in what Jesus is teaching her over all that was previously learned in the Santeria. It does happen…in the Lord's time.

359

Mariann was not allowed to attend a Sunday School camp with Bob's girls that summer because Ann was in school. The girls drew the armor of God on 'angels' as an exercise and couldn't wait to show Mariann. Imagine her many questions to me when the angels didn't look like the same angels she saw around them and the shields not looking at all like the ones she saw the angels holding in times of battle. I received 3 letters from her seeking to understand the differences. Like Ann, sometimes she can be a stickler for detail.

I began writing Ann with scriptural references and more questions to challenge her in her study. She finished it the next night and responded, so it was my turn to propose a question. I wanted to give her something to really stretch her thinking and lead her into a deeper study of Jesus. She had finished school and wanted something to take on Raquel's vacation to contemplate while she did 'her thing.' The question: "I would like to hear your opinion on the logic of the necessity, of the death of Jesus…given the gift of free will for all people by God."

I offered to refine it and she accepted later that night. "You have the premise correct, but I will add some variables to smooth it out for you. 1. As stated, what are the ramifications for the perspective of mankind relating to God? 2. What changes, if anything, for Jesus being 'fully man' in His relationship to His Father and the free will factor of obeying His Father's will? Did he have a choice, really? 3. Does it make a difference in mankind's relationship to Jesus, as compared to God the Father (regards to your question of man's acceptance of God.) Does one's acceptance of God presume acceptance of Jesus and His choice of actions? I look forward to our dialogue upon your return." Two weeks later, I received the following from Ann. I won't make any comments until afterwards so you aren't distracted from following her thoughts.

Here's my analysis of your question on the logic of the necessity of the death of Jesus, given the gift of free will to all people of God. I started at the beginning in Genesis 1. It seems that man was perfect at creation…no aging, no sin, etc. In chapter 2 I get the sense that God didn't want Adam exposed to evil when he warned him that if he ate from the tree of knowledge of good and evil, he would surely die. I find it interesting that God did not want

Adam to be exposed to evil, yet we are told that Adam was created in God's image. This would suggest to me that if God knows evil, then Adam should likewise...but that's another topic we have not finished fully.

So I questioned if God didn't want Adam exposed to evil, then why would he place a tree of temptation right under Adam's nose? Logically that doesn't make sense. Why not void the garden of anything that would allow Adam the chance of learning about evil?

I pondered this for quite a while and came up with this conclusion. If God had not placed the tree in the garden, then Adam would not have had free will. The tree was put there as the ultimate choice of spiritual fellowship with God...or with Satan. I think it was grossly unfair of God not to give Adam all of the facts though. Adam should have been informed about Satan and his methods. God knew Satan would come along as a very intelligent, rude and crafty being. He also knew that Satan would introduce doubt into man's mind, telling a half-truth with just enough of the truth to get Eve to bite. God knew all of this and yet didn't prepare his new creatures for this type of battle. Adam and Eve never had a chance against the strategies of Satan. You can't battle against something you know nothing about.

According to chapter two, it seems that when Adam ate the fruit he was basically telling God, "I'm going to find out about this evil and explore." I found it interesting that even in the beginning of man's existence, he refused to take responsibility for his own actions and like usual, tried to use a woman as his scapegoat... the world has not changed!

Okay so they ate the fruit. The consequences were enormous for all of us. Adam and Eve died that day. They died in their spirit and the physical death also began its slow process. The spiritual death concept required a while for me to fully grasp its meaning of separation from God. In the beginning, Man had a direct contact line with God. At the fall, that line to God was severed. Man became afraid of the Lord and fled from him. This started evil in the world from Cain to the present day.

I jumped to the New Testament and wondered when the disciples really understood why Jesus had to die. In Luke chapter nine it talks about the transfiguration. Here I believe is where the disciples were going to learn God's opinion of who Jesus was. I thought it interesting that all we are told about the conversation between Moses, Elijah and Jesus, is that they talked about Jesus' departure. In looking back to 1st Kings chapter 19, it seems that Jesus was going to complete what Moses and Elijah had started of delivering the people out of bondage. But I believe there is a big difference here. In John chapter five, Jesus says whoever hears my words and believes God who sent me has eternal life and will not be condemned; he has crossed over from death to life.

Jesus is saying man is condemned because he chose Satan's lies over God's truth. Man has made a choice that is irreversible and must pay the penalty which is eternal separation from God. That is logical to me. Basically, you play, you pay. There are consequences for every action, in science a reaction for every action. So I can understand God's stance here. Man chose, yet I still have a problem with the fact that Adam and Eve chose...not me. I am condemned because of their choice which seems grossly unfair. So where is my free will choice in this situation?

I thought on this for a long time as well. I came to the conclusion that Adam and Eve were the closest people in relationship with God from the beginning of time until the present. They walked with God and were perfectly in tune with God...yet they blew it. So what about me? I have nowhere near the type of relationship with God that they did, so logically I probably would fall faster than they did. I don't know, this is still a gray area for me. I hate taking the flack for Liz's behavior, Mariann's behavior or Adam and Eve's behavior. I want to be only responsible for my behavior. Yet, I realize I am not perfect and have made bad choices for myself... joining that Catholic Church was one of them! So I am going on the premise that any one of us humans would have blown it in the garden sooner or later. With that basic premise, I focused on God's loophole.

This part of God providing a loophole in the consequences seems illogical to me. It seems that God could not simply waiver the consequence of man's choice because that would imply God condones evil or bad choices. So God had to devise a way to bring man back in line with him and still judge the choice. The consequence for the choice was death. God said that right up front before they blew it. So someone has to die as a consequence for the action. God can't just forgive our sin...it carries the penalty of death. Because God is holy, there is God's wrath... judgment against sin. But because of his grace, he provided Jesus to buy us back... to take on the judgment for our sins with his death. 2 Corinthians 5:21.

Jesus died because he chose to love and obey God at any cost, including death and because of his love for mankind whom he redeemed by his death. Somebody had to pay the ticket and Jesus willingly did. Now this is the illogical part for me. Why did Jesus willingly want to die for man to live? Why is man worth the price to God? In fact, God could have saved himself a lot of headaches by simply never creating this creature that he knew would rebel. Why does God love mankind so much that he provided this plan so that all of his wrath would fall on Jesus on the cross? Why was God so willing to transfer all man's sins to Jesus? Does he not love Jesus more than man?

So in the end, I guess that we have free choice to choose to allow Jesus to pay our ticket or not. Romans 10:9 makes it very clear to me. So there is logic in the necessity of Jesus dying for the choice of man, yet I do not see the logic in why God provided this loophole for man. Looking forward to your response.

> *"But what does it say? 'The word is near you,*
> *in your mouth and in your heart' – that is,*
> *the word of faith which we are preaching,*
> *that if you confess with your mouth Jesus*
> *as Lord, and believe in your heart that God*
> *raised Him from the dead, you shall be saved."*
> **Romans 10: 8-9**

Our continued discussion centered around the issues of God's judgment and compassion for His creation, Adam and Eve as the archetypes for us all, and Jesus as our sacrifice. We began by looking at how free will choices of trust and obedience became the determining factors for the sufficiency of God's justice, and His unilateral approach of loving us first and unconditionally before we know or even accept Him...that reveals the quality of His compassion. For Ann, the quantity of the love of God in Jesus Christ's choices will remain illogical and a mystery for a while yet.

I kept Mariann busy with a mission of trying different ways to sneak up on Dragonslayer and hug Him for me. She tried every way possible and was never successful of course...you can't sneak up on God. It was not an exercise in futility for her because there was a lesson behind it. She would declare her frustration to Him every time He called her name as she closed on her prey but loved being picked up and swung in the air to get her giggling again. As she complained to me about failure of each mission, I'd send her back with a new approach to try. I could hear the wheels turning as she said, "*Yeah Daddy, that be sneaky, I try that!*"

She would report to me about everything, and I do mean everything, that occurred to her and Tabitha while they were out with Bob's family. She once wrote me to ask me to pray for him because he had sick eyes. I asked her if this was why he couldn't see her and she started to cry. After I calmed her down, she said no, he just have sick eyes. He no see me with his heart daddy, but you do and Dragonslayer do. I asked how I could help and she explained how she wanted Dragonslayer to wash his eyes with Dragonslayer soap to make him better. She also said how she would talk with him about Dragonslayer and tell him about the smelly ones she saw in his house. She questioned why he didn't see them and why they were laughing at him, causing her to call Dragonslayer.

She asked for a blessing for him which I gave to her to pass on, after which she wanted to give me one. "*Dragonslayer, Daddy wants to be finished with patience...me too. Daddy needs your help to have more patience. Daddy wants to know where his next house is to be. Daddy needs work and he knows how to work for you...so please find him a job. Daddy needs some Cheerios and Cokes. My Dragonslayer, please don't let the smelly ones hurt my Daddy. Amen. Daddy here's butterfly kisses from me.*

The System was under constant attack in the week between school and Raquel's trip. The home front had turned really bad for Maria's relationship with her children. As Council saw the anger rising, they called a meeting to look at their options for change. The following letter recaps the issues very clearly.

...We have been discussing the escalation of anger directed towards Maria and Mariann by the outside family. It was not until

364

last night that our suspicions were confirmed. With Council overhearing the argument, both the son and the daughter complained to the husband that they do not like having a crazy mother for a mother. They do not want to see or hear her, especially Mariann.

"Even when she is in that room we can hear her. It's embarrassing to try to explain to our friends that our mom is weird. I hate her. I wish she'd just leave. Our whole family is crazy. I hate her. I hate her."

The husband's response...tell Mariann to be quiet and reprimand her every time she laughs or makes noises...keep the child enclosed in the room and forbidden from coming out into the main house...require Maria to be less visible around your friends.

There was a period of mourning on Council for the way both Maria and Mariann are looked upon as undesirables. However, the sadness quickly turned to anger with several leaders. Daniel especially expressed his anger with how his child is being treated. "She has done nothing wrong, yet they are punishing her for being who she is, as if she has a choice in her identity. She is being treated as if she is a dreaded disease. What gives them the right to destroy what little support and happiness she has in her few friends that call and make her happy? They are chaining her to that bed and duct taping (figuratively) *her mouth shut."*

Keeper of Functions: "How long can they tolerate this environment?"

Paladin: "If it were not for those who are holding them up, they would have crumbled years ago. But are we just drawing out the suffering?"

Lion: "In other words, Paladin, you are saying is it better to be or not to be. Am I correct in your argument?" Paladin: "Yes."

King of the Lights: "It is not for us to question why we are still here. We all know it is better to not be here, but we are here. Why are we here and allowed to continue to exist in this environment? I do not know. Why can't we be rescued and placed in a nurturing and supportive environment? I do not know. But we are placed here so we need to try to find ways to protect our little ones in the midst of the anger. Instead of wasting our energy on asking why, we need to direct our energy on how."

Helper: "I must agree with King of the Lights. What can we do to insure Mariann will still have contact with her daddy, but does not infuriate the outsiders' presence?"

Lion: "We need to encourage her to use the computer more."

Paladin: "Children seem to need instant feedback."

Daniel: "She is also soothed by her daddy's voice."

Lion: "Maybe we could get Mike to record his voice on tape for Mariann to plug in earphones at night and listen that way."

Meeting adjourned and will reconvene following the foot surgery.

Joy was out playing quietly as Council shadowed to listen. Maria, the other adults and Mariann were blocked by Jesus and prevented from hearing this episode. For the first time Council will look ahead long term for the possibility of remaining and leaving. They asked Maria to come into a discussion about her wedding vows and their meaning to her. They made it clear that she wasn't in trouble, just that they needed to understand her feelings about her marriage commitments.

Maria: When I got married I said to God that I would love, honor and obey Sergio and stay with him for better or worse. I told God that I would never leave even when it is hard or bad is happening. I promised God and Sergio that I would keep my promise and I am trying.

Helper: But Sergio promised to love and cherish you. Do you think he is keeping his promise?

Maria: I don't know what him and God talked about and I don't know what cherish means. I just know I got to keep my promise to God.

Helper: Maria, do you think a wife should stay with a husband if he hurts her?

Maria: If she promised God to stay for better or worse.

Helper: how would you feel if Council asked you to just separate from Sergio for awhile and live alone for a couple of months in an apartment? How do you feel about that?

Maria: Please don't make me leave. I will try to be a better wife. I will try to do better.

Helper: It has nothing to do with you being better. We want the family to realize how much you do for them and to appreciate you more and respect you as a person. It is not healthy for you or Mariann to be treated like this by the family. Maybe if you were gone for a month they would realize how much they need you.

Maria: I don't need to be appreciated Helper. Jesus was never appreciated or respected and he stayed and didn't run away. Jesus will help me do better. Please, I made a promise and doesn't it say what Jesus has put together...no people are to separate.

Helper: But the question is, did Jesus put this marriage together? You didn't know him when you got married.

Maria: I know I didn't, but I made a promise to him and I don't want to take back my promise.

Helper: What if Jesus said go?

Maria: I would have to obey him. He is the only one who could tell me he don't want me to keep my promise to him no more. But he hasn't told me to go Helper.

Helper: Okay Maria, we will have a meeting with Jesus about this and don't worry, we would not tell you to leave unless it was in accordance with his will. In other words, unless Jesus says to go, okay?

Maria: Okay Helper.

We would all talk on this subject many more times over the next year or so, but the conclusion was always the same. Maria understood the meaning of promises to Jesus, even promises that were extremely hard on her. She would seek confirmation of her responses often from me, whenever she felt the heaviness of her choices inflicting pain or suffering on the others inside, especially on Mariann. There were many times when I struggled with wanting to say 'leave...I've lost hope that they will change,' but I couldn't either. Those were the times when many extra prayers were offered.

Just as they left for the trip, Ruth learned from a friend that Pastor Bob was leaving his church for another one. The friend wanted to know if she knew the reason, because nobody else seemed to know for sure. There were going to be many disappointed people to hear of his leaving, for he was and is a man of many gifts to share. Maria was aware of great spiritual activity around Bob, his church and the System. Raquel warned that the System had shaken the hornets nest in their guiding counsel to Bob. Jesus warned her as well saying, "You know My voice...listen only to My voice in these times." And with that they were off!

A great, if not scary, time was had by all in Seattle and Canada. Ann attempted to teach Mariann the importance of math as she took her for a tour of the underground city...unsuccessfully. The idea of horses and petticoats in mud was exciting, however. Ann remained undaunted and attempted to get her to observe afternoon tea in Victoria...again unsuccessfully, as she wiggled too much.

Ruth went to a Bavarian town for a yodeling concert (?) and ate too many sweets but claimed to enjoy it all. Raquel commandeered the car and took them into Canada, where she and Mariann enjoyed time with the 'first people' deep in the forest. Council gave up trying to keep their stitched foot dry. The water was crystal clear and the chance of infection was slim. They fished with a spear and Raquel ate fish every night. Mariann complained about the 'big people eating all of the fishies up so no more." She loved the fire dance and was mesmerized by the storytelling about the light caught in the cedar box. Mariann was scared only once when a man with a heavily painted face danced but rebounded after Raquel explained the dance to her.

A man was mauled by a bear while they were there, but Raquel told Mariann not to be afraid while with her in the forest, as she knew how to respect the powerful one. Mariann quickly decided that she didn't want to hug a bear...but a whale instead! Raquel then took Mariann to a place where she could watch the whales dance (breach) on the water. After seeing how big they were, she decided that a whale wasn't a good idea to hug either.

One of the first peoples offered his carving tool to Mariann to carve on his cedar whale totem. The pole was much bigger than she was. He laughed watching her first attempt and then gently guided her hands to carve some symbols. She was very proud of her work. After a week in the forest they left to go home, but not before Liz petitioned Council to let her have some fun. After denying her request to bungy jump, she was allowed to take a flight around the Seattle waterfront. Council...what could you have possibly been thinking?

Liz found a twenty-year-old female pilot with a 1927 open air cockpit biplane and an attitude to match her own. As they took off, Liz shouted, "Top this Earhart!" The two of them spent a half hour acting crazy over the waterfront and buzzing the space needle. All other parts were soooooo deep. Ann is still angry over Council's choices that day. Louise was given a day in Buchardt gardens to walk among the flowers. It seems that Maria was the only one unable to enjoy the vacation, as she developed the same eye virus as Bob had. She stayed inside so the symptoms didn't bother anyone else.

After returning home they would have the stitches out the next day and Ann would return to her new school year on Monday. Bob had already started at another church, a smaller but more affluent one, and Council was concerned about how Maria would be accepted there. They decided to wait in letting her attend with Bob until Ann was settled in school. Mariann's letter to me about her adventure and perspective of 'roughing' it is hilarious, but too long to include here. We sent her a welcome home gift of a Pooh box to hold all of her treasures from the trip.

Raquel sent me this poem upon returning.

Gentle warrior
With a heart like gold and
a rainbow in your eyes

Gentle champion
Do you see a world shining in the sky?
With your body dancing like an arrow
Spreading joy beneath your feet

And your hands waving like tall grass
In the wind as you speak
With the shyness of a small child
and the wisdom of a saint

I tell you now
There is no reason
To be afraid

Brother warrior
There are none of us who walk this path alone
The spirit healer is the only life we seek

I see your smile in the sunlight
I hear your songs in the rain
And I hold you here inside me
I feel your love and I know your pain

At this time when the earth is waking
To the dawn of another age
I tell you now
There is no reason
To be afraid

We are crying for a vision
That all living things can share
And those who care
Are with us everywhere

Sodi'lzin binaago'o' nizho'ni'go naasha
Ba'hodi'lzinii biyi' naasha' biyi' naasha'

Quiet Walker

As Mariann's letters began arriving every other day, her requests were often the same ones. When was I coming to get her and bring her home? When would I let her play with Steven again in the park? When was mama going to let her eat in a restaurant as a big girl does? Does mama have her chair ready? Will I give her a blessing? When can she be done with patience? And the big one just starting; when can she be out in church to praise her Dragonslayer?

If you look deeply behind the cause for these specific questions you will find them being repeated in different words by Maria and most of the System in their letters as well. Issues like: feeling abandoned and knowing where a safe place is; finding new friends are scarce; wanting to be further along in the healing journey; the need for continuity even in discipline; reaffirmation that somebody still cares and loves them; the journey feels too hard and is taking too long; when will I be free to be me...with my Creator.

What follows is a portion of a prayer that Maria said to God. When she starts praying she can go all night long, so I have to shorten what Elizabeth Ray recorded. Does she have the 'stamp'?

"God when I try to think of how much you love me, it is too much for my mind. You have given me hope and a promise that I hold on to. Thank you so much for your blessings. Please teach me to be strong in you. Help me not to lose heart and be joyful always in my days. I want to lead a quiet life and learn not to be worried about things. Please guard my heart and mind God. Please help me do everything without complaining or arguing and to always repay evil with good. I want to be a sponge soaking up your word. Help me to live a life worthy of you God. God the hardest thing for me to know is your love. Help me to know that love. Give me enough tests to make me strong for you. Help me to learn to endure hard things and to be patient when it is hard to go on. Please be with me Jesus as my friend and protect me from doing things that make you sad. Thank you Jesus for being my God.

Please help my friend Pastor Chalberg wait upon you. Give him more patience and encouragement to do the task you have given him. Help my friend Pastor Bob in his new job and please don't let him get tempted with power. Please help him remember who he is and that he works for you. Help him not get too smart please.

And Jesus, I know that you have been knocking at Sergio's heart, but could you maybe knock a little louder? He doesn't know how to twirl Jesus and he is so sad. Please help me be a better wife and touch his heart with your light. Jesus I will always keep my promise to your dad...

Thank you so much for all of my children. Thank you for protecting Rosalinda while she is at school. Thank you for being inside her heart. Thank you Jesus for Jose and giving him a good job and making him smart. Please help him not to love money more than you. And Jesus, you know how much I love my Claudia and want her to know you too. I know I've asked this before Lord, but if there is any way I can have the disease and wheelchair in her place won't you please let me? Please let her know how I love her with all of my heart and please teach me how to love her more. Please help me not to be afraid of her but be more patient and loving. I don't think we can ever be too loving to others. I know I have a lot wrong with me Jesus, but I thank you for loving me just the way I am and never making fun of me. I have a hard time believing it but my heart says it is true. Amen

Maria was growing in her trust of Jesus at an exponential rate. Life was not getting easier, but her belief that she could survive it was. She was learning how Jesus would protect her and walk with her through her trials and that she could do this without anybody else around but Him. The only thing that wasn't so good in her growth was that the more she learned about who Jesus was in her life, the more she wanted to be with Him. There was a need to continuously remind her how He had work waiting for her to fulfill here in this lifetime. She was becoming as ready to go to her mansion as Mariann was to go to her cookie mansion.

Everyone else was becoming more aware of the possibilities of expanding their own identity, along with the pursuit of healing from their memories and their fear of God. Jesus was opening up their hearts and minds to know more about Him and His plans for their lives. They were experiencing something inside that had been totally foreign to them for many years...the feeling of being secure and safe in the presence of God. The phrase 'you belong to me' was renewing their spirits and transforming their fear into hope. It was easy to see that they were being loved and knew it was true.

"By three things is the world preserved: by truth, by judgment, and by peace...the three are really one; if judgment is executed, truth is vindicated and peace results."
Mishnah, *Aboth,* 1, 18, *Taamith,* 68

"The core of the soul is sensitive to nothing but the Divine Being, unmediated. Here God enters the soul with all He has and not in part, and nothing may touch that core except God Himself."
Miester Eckhart, *Sermons,* 13th-14th centuries

"And as for you, the anointing which you received from Him abides in you, and you have no need for anyone to teach you; but as His anointing teaches you about all things, and is true and is not a lie, and just as it has taught you, you abide in Him."
1 John 2: 27

Chapter Seventeen

"The Fruit of a Prophet"

"I will raise up a prophet from among their countrymen
like you, and I will put My words in his mouth,
and he shall speak to them all that I command him.
And it shall come about that whoever will not
listen to My words which he shall speak in My name,
I Myself will require it of him."
Deuteronomy 18: 18-19

"...Would that all the Lord's people were prophets,
that the Lord would put His Spirit upon them!"
Numbers 11:29

*"Do thou speak, O Lord God, the Inspirer and
Enlightener of all the prophets; for thou alone
without them canst perfectly instruct me,
but they without thee will profit nothing."*
Thomas Kempis, *Of the Imitation of Christ*

Most of my life in my B.C. era, I often experienced the feeling of déjà vu, moments I was convinced that I had already lived that moment in time, usually lasting from several seconds to a few minutes. Entering the next phase of my life as a Christian, I found these moments were increasing. I think this was the main reason I began studying the prophets and prophecy with diligence and yet, I was often uneasy about the possibilities of these two phenomena being not only related, but a warning about what lay ahead.

After some testing for spiritual gifts and finding that prophecy was on the list, I was not overjoyed. I observed how people gifted with prophecy were often isolated in the church setting. I decided to try and keep it very private and share only with friends and family if it was of 'life changing' importance. I was more afraid of upsetting people with God's difficult messages, than I was of offending God by remaining quiet, yet God remained gracious.

I learned how the gift is used in two different ways, by forth telling and in foretelling. I thought, 'Okay God, I can handle the first one, because I do not have to tell anyone anything new. I'm just pointing them back to what you have already said in your word, sort of like holding a mirror up and describing what I see in the reflection." I respectfully asked God to let the other side of it remain between Him and me. Following a few years of comfort in this arrangement, the Lord opened my eyes to recognize how He was revealing things that were going to happen to individuals in the future...usually hard things. I learned the price of my silence by witnessing the suffering of people over the loss of precious time that might not have been wasted, if I had only obeyed God.

When the day came that I found out my mother-in-law was dying of cancer, and the Lord told me she had less than six months, not ten years like the doctors said. I knew that I could no longer play it safe. I informed Carol that she needed to make arrangements to spend whatever time was left with her Mom and Dad. She was blessed to be able to spend the final six weeks of her Mom's life together. The last time I was with Beatrice over Christmas, before she went home, she thanked me for telling her the truth and giving her this time with Carol. Within a few months, the same thing happened with a dearly loved friend and prayer partner. The patterns were being set and as difficult as it was, I asked the Lord to help me submit to His will and not my own in this. It has not been easy ever since, but it has been comforting to be reaffirmed often how the Lord has a plan and is in control. It's not so hard being a messenger after all.

By the time I began counseling the System, it was easy to see these gifts within their ranks. It wasn't so easy to get them to exercise many different gifts including this one, but I understood why. As they got stronger in their faith and trust in Jesus, they became bolder in telling friends whatever Jesus told them to say. As you have already read, this was perhaps easiest for Raquel with the 'messages' coming straight from the Great Spirit, no opinion or interpretation included...your choice to believe. For Liz, it was still a macho thing empowered by purpose...not pride. Her way of giving the messages often left the hearer with a lot to recover from.

It is a process still going on but improving in the last few years. Her enthusiasm for completing the task has now mellowed.

Mariann continues to offer her gift of prophecy in exactly the same way, repeating it in her own words as best as she can, what Dragonslayer is saying to her. She has no problem asking what words mean afterwards or adding her own opinion of what it means from her perspective as a child seeing into two worlds. The difficulty comes when people she loves get upset over hearing 'bad news' coming or even that 'bad ones' are in their home or church. We will continually reaffirm her in that it is better to hear the truth which Dragonslayer gives, so choices can be made, than to be silent and hear people say, "I didn't know."

The gift of prophecy is hardest on Maria. She has lived her life not wanting to hurt anyone, including those who abused her and others. In the summer of '98, I knew that she was given the gift of reading people's heart by just touching them. As new friends and loved ones come and go, this will place a tremendous burden on her of caring...even for total strangers. We will teach each other about when to remain silent, speak up, or say "Dragonslayer, this is hard for me...so please just say what you want to say through my mouth, without me thinking about it...and we'll take whatever comes our way together."

By the fall of 1998, I enter my next intentional interim pastorate in Pasadena with a smaller urban church that was in need of new life. The System will begin again with another new church with Pastor Bob as the assistant pastor. Looking back I can see the wisdom of Jesus having the System, Carol and I, entering two completely opposite Christian churches on the social spectrum. We had become a ministry team in our mutual support of one another by now and this was going to be interesting to see how the Lord would lead us.

Ann stayed on track as a teacher without a complete understanding of God's purposes or power prompting her forward and upward. She is nominated for the Sallie Mae Teacher of the Year award and is fulfilled by the recognition, yet very afraid of it as well. As we talked about the possibility of winning, it sounded like the Oscars. *"Just being nominated is enough for me...I'll never win!"* We hit her with the reality that she is an exceptional teacher and should she win, it would mean going to Washington,

D.C., etc. As she turned white with understanding, everyone inside began praying that she wouldn't win. If Jesus enjoys these kind of predicaments for His children…I think He enjoyed this one.

Liz was being put in a difficult spot as well. She was going to be attending a classic Suburban Christian church from her perspective and the challenges that lay before her were enormous. Could she hold her tongue until Jesus said it was okay to 'write', or even stay within the boundaries of civility as Jesus wanted? I knew that Bob wasn't really aware of what lay beneath the surface for him. I didn't know anything about the Senior Pastor, but I began praying in earnest for his ministry.

Maria quickly got caught up in trying to understand this new group of people and how she might fit in, as she desperately wanted to belong. She had it on her heart to try and help the people at an inner-city shelter this Christmas and felt it should be easy to do here in this church. She wanted Bob to succeed here like never before to bring glory to Jesus, but she was nervous because she read his heart on a regular basis and knew his internal struggles. They became solid prayer partners together for a long time. Maria didn't share everything about Bob with me 'as was appropriate,' but shared enough so I could pray for him and his ministry.

I learned a great deal about this man, not only through our interaction, but with a dozen or so eyes watching and listening to everything he said. When others felt uncomfortable bringing up troubling issues directly with him… about him, I would get the lengthy email about it asking how to respond. I don't think that Bob ever understood the depth of the communication between the System and I over every issue that affected their life. Most of the time I would just file it away on the computer or destroy it as with a lot of other news about people, but the Lord had given me glimpses about where he was leading Bob for a reason, so I held on to his.

Council felt that they had a much better connection with him than with Sergio and hoped to improve it as they went along. One day soon they would use Ruth to sit with him sharing a pipe of pastor's blend and watch a football game. They would each come to the surface close enough to taste, see and feel the moment…without coming completely out, after all, they are men. Ruth got sick and vowed never to do that again.

Mariann and Tabitha Ann each grew in the relationships at differing speeds with the whole family. Mariann of course wanted to be out at worship from the beginning and this became the next big issue to face. For now, sandal camp would have to suffice.

I responded to Ann's questions in greater detail and gave her more questions to think about with them. Perhaps the hardest one was: *"I believe that God did not place a tree of temptation in the garden, but a tree of life. With it there from the beginning, Adam & Eve had the fullest potential to be obedient to the One they knew as their Creator. God had given them everything they needed to lead perfectly contented lives in relationship to Him, including the warning to not eat of the fruit of this one and only tree. If God had not warned them, then you would have a solid argument about Adam not having enough information to make a rational choice about obedience to God. A & E knew this other creature was not their Creator or the Creator of all that was before them. If you were in their spot with only this clear amount of knowledge between these two beings, what do you think would cause you to disobey God? What do you think would have happened if God hadn't given the warning about the tree and explained who Satan was instead? Do you think the results would have been different and why?"*

I then wrote Mariann about going to sandal camp with all of the children. "Hi Sweetie Pie. It's good that you want to go to school like Bob's kids, only you get to go somewhere better...back to sandal camp with Dragonslayer. He has a lot to teach you guys that the outside children don't get to experience in the same way. If Jesus wants to bring His lambs into the sandal camp school to teach you about how to share Him with the kids outside, I think that is the greatest of all schools to attend! Where else can you play leapfrog with Dragonslayer who holds the world in His hands, and Joy in His arms as well? You can't play hide and seek with Jesus in between your studies on the outside...they don't allow it. Where else can you walk across the top of the buttercups with Him, except on the inside? You know what, if I was you I would be running to sandal camp right now.

I'm glad you had such a great time with the first peoples. Try to write me about your adventures when you can. Now that Ann is back in school, I need you to stay inside and not shadow unless

Ann or Jesus says it is okay. You are a very good girl and I am proud of you. No one can stop me from loving you, even when we are far apart. We pray for all of you and send blessings your way every night. Mama put special butterfly kisses and hugs in your Pooh box to pop out every time you open it. Bye my Mariann."

Council had Maria call me to get permission for her to attend a family camp retreat with Bob, after they had discussed the pros and cons for going with me. I put the decision back on them and said I thought the experience would be worth the risk, given the risks they had just encountered going to Canada. Helper's observations of the possibilities captured it succinctly.

Helper: Let's address both concerns. I agree that Mariann is an inquisitive and often unpredictable child, but she does try very hard to obey. In three weeks we could work on preparing her for camp. Mike could speak with her to guide her. We could use cookies as a reward system. We could discuss with her what family retreats are and what's expected of her. I think it is doable and would be a great growth experience for Mariann, like the Canada trip.

Liz is different. She might switch out if someone makes an anal remark or acts like a Suburban Christian. However, Liz is aware that this is Bob's new church and she is trying very hard to balance her anger over what she considers their fluff. I think we can work with her. I think we should try this. The worst that can happen is we realize we are not yet ready and repair the damage that comes to try another day. But then we could succeed and we will be one more rung higher as a system in our ability to function in the outside world. I think the risks are worth it. The parts are growing and need to branch out in their experiences. If successful, this will help them improve in social situations. Your concerns are valid Paladin and Keeper of Functions, and it might fail, but I think we should try.

Dear Maria,
Congratulations on Councils' decision! Listen well to their instructions for you and Mariann. Help Bob and Tina understand their importance as well. I know you'll have a good time. Alaska is still interested in having me come there, and guess what? A church

in Hawaii has asked me to interview there. Serving in paradise could not be all bad, right? I know clearly however that Jesus wants me to take this Calvary job because they have a greater need. Remember my friend Ed, he will join me there to assist. I'm also attempting to put together a training seminar for the pastors of this conference to do mentoring as intentional interims for them. So possibilities continue to be put in front of us. Praise God. Love to everyone.

Mariann wrote about her school lessons;

Hi Daddy
I go to school with Tabitha daddy. Do you know we have fruit trees in our heart daddy? They be Dragonslayer fruit trees. The fruit of kindness, love, patience…Mariann no like that tree. Dragonslayer tell Mariann and Tabitha more fruit on trees, more like Dragonslayer. Dragonslayer words be lamp onto Mariann feet. I hear in church and come out. No Mariann. No be aloud in church Mister Bob say. Why Mariann no be aloud daddy…why?

Council to Bob:
It is difficult for us to communicate through Mariann or Maria. We wish to discuss yesterday with you. One of our greatest concerns is recognition. Mariann was too high profile yesterday. Although the experience was a good one, she was noticed by a large number of adults. Leaders become anxious when people who they don't know see Mariann. We have a dilemma in trying to provide for her yet maintaining integrity for the adult parts…namely Ann. Ann is still angry at us for allowing the system to be seen.

We need to work on keeping her less obvious. The rule that she was not to talk was not set properly by us. She became confused when the other children were talking and the adults were, but she could not. It was also very difficult for her to hold her excitement at seeing Bob and Larry. (*Veggie Tales* actors.) We were also not prepared for Larry to sing in Spanish, causing Tabitha to switch out. This caused a lot of problems inside with Mariann pushing Tabitha because she took her time with Bob and Larry. The problem here is Mariann views herself as only Mariann and not part of a multiple's system. We have not yet found a way to help her understand her role in the system. Yet, we believe the Bob and Larry experience was good for Mariann. Thank you for your effort in taking her there.

We are working on trying to handle the slapping and neck grasping issues. Sergio has always put a firm grip on Maria, Louise and Mariann's neck when he wants to direct them to walk a particular way, it's a control issue he has. We've chosen not to battle this one. The pain Maria is experiencing in her neck is from something else. The slapping has begun again because of Mariann talking loud on the phone to her daddy at night. Again it's a control issue. We need to consider the repercussions for putting a lock on the door as Tina suggested, before attempting it.

We are more concerned about the potential of violence from Maria's sister then we are from Sergio. There is no way to predict or manage the sister. As she sits in her trailer taking drugs, she starts hallucinating more about her problems and focuses on Maria as the bad guy causing them. We're afraid she'll go overboard and decide to remove her problem permanently. We ignore the family gossip she starts about Maria stealing. We know she cleaned out her mother's jewelry from the estate, approximately $75,000, and used it for current and past drug money. The only way to cover it up was blame Maria. We won't waste time trying to correct the lies because the family is too dysfunctional and has always used her as the scapegoat anyway. Michael is trying to help her move on.

Before we close our communication to you, we want to explain something. Maria is very sensitive when outsiders tell her that her father is a jerk or her sister is an addict. She needs to hear these realities and stop denying them in her mind, yet she doesn't want to think bad about anyone. When you made that statement Bob, about her father and then told her, "and you know it Maria," it was too overwhelming the way it was stated. That was why you found her crying as she was washing dishes. Statements like that pierce her heart. We need to be careful as Council when we make statements like that to be as gentle as possible.
Respectfully, E.R.

As Maria began attending Bob's new church and listening to a new pastor's sermons, she became troubled over some statements made by him. She asked me what to do and I suggested that she write him herself. Still not strong enough to express any opinion to a pastor other than me, she solicited Liz's help in writing it for her. This was a first for Maria in writing a pastor about a sermon.

Pastor Ron
I am new to your church and attended last Sunday's service. Some of your statements caused a lot of problems for me. When I was a child, I was sexually abused by a grandfather and a priest. I was also taken into a group of the Santeria as a child and buried alive, then rescued and forced to participate in ritual sacrifices. Because of all that I have been through and what I'm experiencing now, it was difficult for me to understand your sermon. I have no joy in my circumstances. My life is very hard for me. If I could forget I would do it in an instant. I don't enjoy nightmares and flashbacks that seem so real that I go through the pain all over again. It is very hard for me to find the good in all people. How can a child that is buried alive by a person find good in that person?

The statement you made about "remembering the best and forgetting the rest" might be easy for someone who has not walked my life, but it is impossible for me. There was no best for me. I still have no joy from my childhood. Only in the last few years have I found joy in a few friends who understand me. I don't know if I can sit through twelve weeks of joy lessons if I can't relate to the message. The joy I have now is not in my circumstances but in Jesus. It is joy in knowing that he loves me though I don't understand why. It is also in knowing that he doesn't judge me like the churches and Christians do. It is joy for me that he thinks I'm worth dying for. That is where my joy is found, not in the world.

There is just too much crap that I've gone through and it overtakes every memory of the past. If a child is given an ice cream and raped at the same time, how can that child find joy in ice cream? I struggle with statements made in church like "just have faith", "just trust Jesus", "there is a reason for everything my dear" and the famous "God takes care of those he loves." It is easy to say if the heat isn't burning you to death. It only increases the pain and makes a hurting person feel dirtier than they already do. The man called my father almost beat me to death. It is hard to understand God as a father who loves me. It will take a long time to let my defenses down and trust again. Love has always hurt because it was done in the name of God to warp me even more. It'll take a long time to trust again.

Frankly, for me to even be in your church is a miracle. It will take me time to determine if, as your music director said, this is a safe place. It won't be a safe place if my pain is minimized by Suburban Christian talk. I can't just get over it and trust God. I would like to and start my life over again, but it is forever imprinted in my innermost being. It will take a long time to deaden the pain. So I'm asking you, will this church be able to offer me a truly safe place to grow at my own pace? Will this church be real and speak the truth? Will this church understand the pain and not pity me or look down on me? I wonder?

If you want to check me out you can contact Michael Chalberg, a pastor in LA who has kept me alive for several years. The number is below...

If you've followed the stories here you can probably pick out how little of Maria's input was taken, and also recognize Liz's restraint for Maria's sake. After it was sent, Maria called me in a panic, thinking the pastor would throw her out in anger to what Liz said. She sent a copy and I wrote back the following:

Hello Maria,
Don't worry about being in trouble with the pastor. Your letter was very well written and stated an opinion without being offensive. I'm sure he will want to take his time in replying and pray about how this should affect his ministry. If he writes back, it probably won't be for several days or more. I'm praying that he'll write how this can be of benefit to him in preaching before others in a position like yours. I doubt that he'll connect you with any one from family camp. If he shows it to Bob, don't worry that can only help. Remember what Jesus keeps telling you about worry. Maybe one day if he is strong enough, he can have his own direct conversation with Liz. Take care and love to all of you. P.S. How is Mariann doing on sneaking up on Dragonslayer?

Council memo

Thank you for your encouragement of Maria. It doesn't matter to us if he responds, however it would benefit Maria. We have a hard time getting her to realize that she is allowed to have opinions, because she was always punished for expressing herself and never to a pastor. Liz on the other hand seems to have no problem! Maria is doing poorly adjusting to Ann's new work schedule. The speed she works at puts Maria on a roller coaster. She can't touch ground long enough before Ann is off on another direction.

Council has learned something about teachers...they earn their pay. She juggles paperwork, lesson planning, copying, teaching, collation, supervision, department meetings, house meetings, school site council meetings, parental contacts and deadlines without ever coming up for air...and all between 7AM to 6PM. We are challenged with how to give Ann the time she needs yet meet the needs of the other parts. Ann tends to control time and doesn't like to share it. Liz and Mariann act out if denied time. Maria and Louise become depressed. Jennifer and the others go deep inside. We are still trying to balance time equitably.

Mariann is having no luck with sneaking up on Dragonslayer. We rather enjoy her efforts though. Her last effort was telling him to bend down because she had a secret to tell him. He asked if the secret was that you are going to hug me when I bend down. She stuck her lower lip out and said Dragonslayer how do you know the secret? He said I know everything and swung her around in his arms laughing.

Mariann wrote me about midnight this same night and drew two pictures about her concerns at home. Ruth brought the drawings with her at Thanksgiving and the one still makes tears come to my eyes.

Hi frommmmmm Mariann daddy
Dragonslayer love daddy and Mariann love daddy. Mama Carol love daddy and Tigger love daddy. Liz love daddy and   do Liz love daddy? Mariann do lots! Daddy Mariann want daddy come get her now please. No want to stay here with mean man please. Want to go to cookie mansion with my daddy please. Now please.

Trust and obey Dragonslayer daddy. Mariann try but it hard daddy. Dragonslayer make time daddy but no time in cookie mansion daddy, we go now please. My thoughts are not your thoughts he say to me for I know the plans I have for you, plans for good Mariann not for bad. Be still and know I am God. Daddy I go sandal camp lots. Don't forget sandal camp cookies for the big people you teach daddy. Mariann love my daddy and mommy, want to come your house now. Daddy……words come in air say if Dragonslayer love you Mariann, why he make daddy go far away and no be with Mariann? No more daddy. Dragonslayer make daddy go away like Mr. Bruce……Daddy why mister Bob no see me? Why? He nice to me and let me play with Kellie and Chris and Angie and buy me cookies and miss Tina want me come live there okay daddy? You come too okay?

Plate #13

Mariann feeling the pull between two places she wanted to be.

Hi my Mariann,

Remember how much we love you and we **won't** be going away like Mr. Bruce. While we have to be apart to do Dragonslayer's work, we want you to be with Mr. Bob and Tina and all of the kids.

I wish you could live with us or Mr. Bob but that can't happen yet. Dragonslayer's love will be given to each of us to remind us that we are as close together right now as if we were hugging right now. Ask Him for a hug and see what I mean. Bye my love…

Plate #14

Mariann's cookie mansion (chocolate chip & peanut butter only.)

In the very near future the System will become diabetic and cookies here will become few and far between and sugarless. Given the taste problem, she will opt for peanut butter as the only real cookie soon. She asks Dragonslayer to promise many times that there won't be a 'sugar problem' in her cookie mansion in heaven. He does.

I called one night and talked with Maria and Council about what the future might hold for us and wondering when we might ever return to Northern California. I knew that God wanted me in Pasadena for at least the next 18 months, but I couldn't see farther than that. I felt in my soul that He planned to have us back together in ministry, I just didn't know where or when. I had gone back to working in construction full time, while working full time at Calvary every other night and weekends. Carol had taken a job full time and was assisting me, so our lives were very full, yet we both knew this was temporary until God said go here next.

Elizabeth Ray sent me the following story that Raquel told Mariann the night of the conversation above. It says a lot more than I realized at the time.

The Shepherd's Call

It was early morning as Benjamin surveyed the countryside gazing at the shepherds tending their sheep. Each one was entrusted with caring for many of the chief shepherd's most prized lambs. Benjamin had spent many years training to be a shepherd. He had learned how to guide and train his sheep. But most of all, he had learned how to lovingly care for each one.

Benjamin knew he had spent more years training to be a shepherd than any of the other men on that countryside. He knew he would be a good shepherd and he eagerly waited for the chief shepherd to give him his assignment. Although he told all the other shepherds that he would gladly accept any job the headmaster assigned to him, secretly he thought of all the possibilities that lay ahead for him. "Maybe I will be the shepherd of the new lambs born this spring. They will grow into fine strong sheep and I will be praised for my skill in taking care of such a lively bunch. Or maybe I will be assigned to the largest flock of sheep in the whole countryside and be the envy of all the other shepherds."

Benjamin was eager to begin. He waited patiently for his assignment. He waited and he waited. While he waited he watched his one lamb that had wandered in to his field two years ago. He remembered the first day he laid eyes on the lamb. Its wool was matted and dirty with big clumps missing on its back. He remembered the scars where it had been beaten with a stick. He remembered its hopeless eyes and undernourished belly.

But he had taken it in and lovingly cared for it. It still walked with a limp and needed constant protection from enemies but had grown stronger with each day of care. Now the lamb followed Benjamin everywhere. It knew Benjamin was its shepherd and it lovingly and devotedly followed his every step.

As Benjamin watched his scarred and limping lamb play in the tall grasses of the field, he sat and wondered how much longer would it take the chief shepherd to assign him his great flock. Night came and Benjamin spread out his blanket and went to sleep. In the morning Benjamin could wait no longer. He decided to visit the chief shepherd and ask him if he forgot to give him his orders. He found the chief sitting under a fig tree and he approached him respectfully. "Great One, I know you are very busy but I was wondering if you have decided upon my assignment yet?"

The chief gazed into Benjamin's eyes and said, "Benjamin. I know your heart. I have seen your love. That's why I have given you a very special assignment." Benjamin's mind raced as he thought of the great and important assignment the chief shepherd was about to bestow on him. Unable to contain his excitement any longer, he blurted out, "When will my sheep arrive so that I can begin my work for you?" The great shepherd lovingly touched Benjamin's shoulder and said, "Benjamin your lamb has already arrived and been with you for two years. That is your assignment."

"But I thought I was going to get an important calling, one that will have an impact on the whole countryside. This...this is just one scrawny little lamb."

"Benjamin. I have given you this assignment because it is very close to my heart and I chose the best shepherd I have to care for

388

this lamb. The importance of a shepherd's job is not in how many sheep are entrusted to his care, but how he cares for those he is given. Do not underestimate the impact your love for this lamb will have on the countryside. Trust me Benjamin, I have chosen you."

Now every morning Benjamin can be seen guiding and instructing his little lamb. Sometimes stories circle the camp that the limping lamb visits the other sheep and shares the love of her master. But that is another story...

So little child do not think that you do not have a calling. For those the Great Spirit has brought into your life are the ones you care for and love...just like Benjamin.

Although, I could think of a number of other pastors for whom this parable could apply to, I could see it applying clearly to Pastor Bob. I knew it was not meant for me because I was heading into a flock full of broken sheep, and besides, we weren't going to be with the System again any time soon. So it had to be someone else! Then I thought...you prideful fool, of course it could be you. The intent of the story is to remind you what your calling is as a shepherd of God...to share with each lamb one at a time the love and care that the Master shares with you. You don't work for yourself – you serve Him.

I needed to be reminded... a forth telling as it were...of the assignment and the duties facing me right now, and not be concerned about the next one awaiting me. I folded the story and tucked it away in my journal to reflect upon as needed. I hoped to share it with Bob one day as a common lesson for us both. Sometimes the way the Lord passes on a prophetic message to His servants, could bowl us all over in its subtlety.

As Halloween approached, the children became more fearful and needed more support. I was receiving daily a letter and couldn't keep up with them along with everything else. Bob came to the rescue by instituting his own method for giving Mariann a blessing over the email several times a week. They were given with a pure motive, which made me wonder why he would say some of the things he did about her not being 'real' and then turn around and give such heartfelt encouragement about her God-given gifts and abilities as His servant. He confused me with his inconsistency towards Mariann as a separate individual soul.

(Think of my hand on your head)
Lord, this is a blessing for Mariann. May she be filled with your Spirit. May your wisdom and power rest upon her, guiding her to do what is right and to make the best choices. May your love and tenderness fill her heart so that she can share it with everyone she knows and everyone she meets. Protect her in your loving arms and by your mighty hand. This is the blessing for Mariann. Amen.
Mister Bob

I have always felt that Bob was genuine in his love for the System, particularly Maria and Mariann. I know he spoke from the heart and gave much of himself in that friendship, but I think he was beginning to have difficulty reconciling all that they represented to him as individuals in his mind. How could Maria and Raquel know the things about him they did, if God wasn't a part of it? It was easy to assume God was, until you put Liz and Mariann into the mix saying things so directly about his actions that he didn't want to hear. Their journey together was starting to get bumpy at times.

Maria was feeling pressure from Bob and Tina, the therapist and some other friends about her relationship at home with Sergio. She asked me why everyone says bad words about him and asked the question; *"Isn't it true that rape is when a person who is not your husband does it to you? I don't like talking about that stuff in the therapist office. I don't like it cuz then I feel dirty. I don't like it when Pastor Bob or Tina talks about it either. When you get married you got to let your husband do it cuz you got married even if you don't like being touched like that. When I got married I didn't know about this part but I got married so I got to obey. That's just the way it is and it don't change. I can't change it so I don't want to talk about it."*

We learned that Ann won the California Educational Placement Association Northern California New Teacher of the Year award. We were only surprised at the lack of response by her family. She asked us to not send any gift recognition as it would only cause problems at home. They asked for continued prayer that she didn't advance in the Sallie Mae First Class Teacher Award by the American Association of School Administrators. We promised to celebrate at Thanksgiving...if not for her...then for the mighty work the Lord had done in her healing and for all of them. Less than three years earlier no one could have imagined that she would be here even to celebrate.

As Bob's family began to prepare for Halloween at church and at home, something that bothered Mariann and the kids, Tina began to correspond directly with me about issues surrounding them.

I just got off the phone with Council about Maria and what is going on with her. There is so much happening in everyone's home, some worse than ours, and all of our friends are having a difficult time too. Is it Satan all over the place? I don't understand Maria, Mike, can you help me? What can I do? I love them all so much! They all hold a special place in my heart. I treat Maria the way I wanted to be treated as a child growing up, is that wrong? Love is what it's all about right? Growing in the Lord experiences and laughing and crying and all that?

How can you explain to someone that has never had anything bad happen to them, how they're supposed to treat you and how they're supposed to understand what you are going through? Bob is the one I'm talking about. He doesn't understand what I've been through as a child, or even Maria, because he has never experienced it himself. I mean he does try but he just can't. He has said he will go to counseling to try and better understand me. Any advice? Sorry to lay this on you, like you don't have enough to worry about. Thank you.

Pastor Bob went in to talk with Pastor Ron about the letter sent and he was told that Ron never received it. Council resent it afterwards a little more at ease about his response now that Bob had talked to him. In doing this, Council discovered that Liz sent the letter without letting Maria see the final draft. She was put under house arrest again for it, but Council didn't see this punishment as working. Her comment going in was, "I don't get to do shit anyway. Ann's got all of the time. So go ahead and put me under house arrest...I don't care you stinking b@$**#@&." King of the Lights wrote the next question for clarification from Ron on his sermon.

We seek clarification on a point in your sermon. Were you stating that God has a purpose for all circumstances and that God allows "bad things" to happen to us so we can become more like him? Although it has been told to us by Dragonslayer himself that he will use for good what was intended for evil, we have not heard him ever say that he will allow a child to suffer tremendous pain because it will make the child more like him. Shattering a soul is not Dragonslayer's way.

So we are confused about the third part of your sermon. Also thank you for not mentioning anything to Maria about the correspondence from Liz. Maria has a hard time with some of the others' methods of operation.

It turned out that Liz was quicker than Council in writing Ron about this sermon. She sent the following shortly before her 'arrest'. I figured I could start counting the days before I would be hearing from Ron. I just prayed that he had the strength of character to respond to them and I wasn't disappointed.

Content Warning

THIS IS LIZ. IT AIN'T MY STYLE TO BE PLASTIC. I HATE PLASTIC. I HATE PAT SIMPLISTIC CHRISTIAN BANDAID ANSWERS TO MY QUESTIONS. SIMPLE ONE VERSE ANSWERS DON'T MAKE IT EITHER. NOW I'LL TELL YOU WHY. I NEVER HAVE AND NEVER WILL CONSIDER IT ALL JOY WHEN I ENCOUNTER VARIOUS TRIALS.

THERE IS NO JOY IN HAVING A GRANDFATHER FORCE HIS PENIS INTO YOUR LITTLE FOUR-YEAR-OLD MOUTH AND NEARLY SUFFOCATING YOU. THERE IS NO JOY CURLED UP ON A COLD CEMENT SIDEWALK IN THE DARK OF NIGHT, WITH A KNIFE UNDER YOUR BELLY TO PREVENT ANOTHER RAPE. THERE IS NO JOY WATCHING THE DEATH OF A CHILD AND KNOWING THAT YOU ARE THE NEXT TO BE SACRIFICED IN THEIR WARPED RELIGION. AND I CAN

WRITE PAGES OF WHERE THERE IS NO JOY IN THE TRIALS WE HAVE ENCOUNTERED.

WITH CHRISTIANS MAYBE YOU CAN GET AWAY WITH SIMPLE ANSWERS...THROW THEM A FEW VERSES...SHINE IT UP AND THEY BUY IT. BUT FOR US, WE'VE BEEN IN TOO MUCH SHIT. WE'VE HEARD TOO MANY CHRISTIANS USE JESUS WORDS OUT OF CONTEXT AND IN WAYS THAT I DON'T THINK HE MEANT THEM TO BE.

SO ALL I'M ASKING IS JUST BE REAL. IF YOU DON'T WANT TO ANSWER A QUESTION THAT'S FINE WITH ME, BUT DON'T GIVE ME SOME DAMN SUBURBAN CHRISTIAN ANSWER. IF YOU'RE GOING TO ANSWER, BE REAL.
LATER – LIZ

Ann was listening to all that was going on and wrote to Bob about her perspective. She pursued it from the scientific method of measuring pain. Is one person's pain worse than another's pain? Is all pain equal regardless of whether it's physical, mental or emotional? She talked about the pain of bankruptcy being difficult but short-lived, versus the pain of having your innocence stolen from you at the age of two, and how this loss was forever. The pain is present until death. The best one can hope for is being able to adapt and function with the pain.

Measuring pain is difficult due to differing levels of tolerance to pain. She showed Mariann's ability to absorb physical pain and Ruth fainting at the sight of a needle. Does continual subjection to painful situations heighten ones pain tolerance? Is one type of pain worse than another? She believed that pain that is unable to be rectified is worse than any other pain.

She offered this statement in regard to *"Consider it all joy when you encounter various trials' as illogical. There is no joy in trials I have experienced, and until the man or woman speaking has walked on my road, he has no right to tell me to consider it joy. So far all I've heard from the pulpit has left me disappointed."*

Bob wrote her back and his response is worth mentioning here.

One of the problems with measuring pain is when the subjects undergoing it are not the same. As you have noticed with physical pain in the system, no two personalities experience the same level of pain, even though the outside stimulus remains constant and equal. I suppose the same goes for mental and emotional pain. The outside stimulus of a bankruptcy may be constant in the loss of dollars, but the amount of suffering it causes is unique to the individual, thus we cannot truly measure pain.

How one responds to the pain is also part of the difficulty in measuring it. For instance, <u>others have undergone the loss of stolen innocence but did not split like Tina. Does the ability to split lessen the pain, when it's spread out across several personalities? Or is it worse for the one like Tina to bear it all?</u> (Underlining is to highlight these words for future reference. Not only does Bob not have a good understanding of what causes the splitting and the relevant pain attached to their type of suffering, but his use of Tina's experience will also prove to be a lack of understanding her now and in the future. This subject rises again in the third book.)

There seems to be no correlation in my research between the level of suffering and splitting. Some people have undergone far less suffering than Maria, but split anyway, and some have undergone almost equal but didn't split. (Here Bob doesn't realize what he's saying, or the effect it will have on Maria. He never really learned the depth of their suffering for each individual part, before making his statements. He thought the 'highlights' we shared the year before was it, and never pursued finding out about it all. He was treating this as an intellectual exercise with Ann, without regard to how his words might affect the others. This is something anyone caring for a multiple needs to be cautious in trying.) *The variables in responding to pain make it impossible to measure accurately and we should therefore all be cautious when trying to tell others that they don't know suffering and pain simply because they haven't been through what we've been through.* (See Tina's letter on page 391.)

Bob continued to offer the lesson from Isaiah 28: 23-29 as an explanation about God's methods for allowing suffering and pain, and he is close in his conclusion of God building His church upon people who undergo the most suffering for His sake. He then goes on to explain his understanding of the James 1: 2-4 verses of "consider it all joy…" and how the joy isn't in the suffering, but in the learning that comes from successfully having ones faith tested during the suffering. He left Ann hanging with her observations, as he did moved on to other more productive support with Maria.

He wrote her about her concerns about coming back to his church. He asked her to just be herself and not try to be anyone else. He wanted her to stop worrying so much about the pressure of his job which he enjoys and how she does not contribute to any problems he has. He informed her how Pastor Ron wasn't mad at Liz's letter or anyone else in the System, and how he's aware you're MPD and doesn't care. Ron stated how they were always welcome and how he's willing to learn all he could to be a better pastor and they were not fighting over it. Then he finished the letter with these statements:

Church is your place to be and if the other parts can't keep quiet and let you have your time then they can't come. Whoever is shadowing from council can pass the message on. Maria deserves some respect during her time and church is her time. So pipe-down everybody and argue on your own time.

Finally, I really love you and would miss you terribly if you didn't come to church with us. You're a part of our lives and that's all that matters… If you could stick with us through the other stuff at my last church, you can stick through the tiny stuff here… Please just stick with us. And I agree with you about the service not being worshipful enough and not enough time in prayer responding to God. That's something God probably brought me here to help change, but it will be a slow process. <u>I need you to keep me on track and centered. You are part of my support and having you around makes me a better pastor and that's a benefit for everyone here.</u> (Underlining is again to remember these statements in the next two years from now in book three.)
P.S. For Ruth

Tina wanted me to tell you that Angie is allowed to change her costume, but her teacher wants to talk to Tina about it tomorrow. I told her all she has to say is in Bob's profession we deal with people who have come out of the occult background and many have experienced awful things at the hands of real witches, not the big hat broomstick kind, but real Satanist witches. It would therefore be very inappropriate for one of our daughters to dress up like a witch. Angie is too immature to hear all of the graphic details why. Thank you for your support in this matter.

Sound good to you? Bob

Ann wrote me back on our dialogue and concluded that:

"Even though I don't like how God handled the Garden of Eden episode...allowing a naïve Adam and Eve to experience the first 'bait and switch', it was a powerful example of the consequences that will occur if we make the wrong choices. I wish that Liz would learn this.

The fact that God allowed Jesus to make the choice to pay our error has always been difficult for me to understand. After re-reading Romans 8:31-39 as you suggested, I realize my difficulty lies in comprehending this love of God and its power to stop anything or anyone from separating us from that love. I wrestle with where was the love of God when the devil tricked an uninformed Eve? Or where was this love when Tabitha was separated from that love by a grandfather who took her choices away? Why didn't a powerful God stop the separation? I can understand him allowing the grandfather to have free choice and as a result Tabitha was hurt. But why did he not come to Tabitha in the time of her need and show her his love? Why did he abandon her? The concept called love has always perplexed me. I understand kindness, honesty, respectfulness, dedication, responsibility, punctuality and so on. But I have a hard time relating to the word love. Then you attach God to it and I struggle with defining it. Looking forward to your insight. Ann

Ann's response came to her over Thanksgiving with us. She learned how Jesus was there with Tabitha and never abandoned her. It was still difficult for her to understand the love that empowered Him to do that and for Tabitha to survive.

"For I am convinced that neither death, nor life, nor angels, nor principalities, nor things present, nor things to come, nor powers, nor height, nor depth, nor any other created thing, shall separate us from the love of God, which is in Christ Jesus our Lord."
Romans 8: 38-39

Chapter Eighteen

"And the Battle is the Lord's"

===

"These things I have spoken to you,
that in Me you may have peace.
In the world you have tribulation,
but take courage;
I have overcome the world."
John 16:33

"Put on the full armor of God, that you may be able
to stand firm against the schemes of the devil.
For our struggle is not against flesh and blood,
but against the rulers, against the powers,
against the world forces of this darkness,
against the spiritual forces of wickedness
in the heavenly places. Therefore, take up
the full armor of God, that you may be able
to resist in the evil day, and having done
everything, to stand firm."
Ephesians 6: 11-13

Halloween was two days away and the children began calling me every night. It was different than before, because the children as a group had laryngitis and a very scratchy voice. Maria was the only adult to feel minor symptoms of it, but the rest were fine. It was unusual in the sense that normally, only one or two of the children would experience a cold or flu at a time. There has never been one moment since I've known the System that all of one group, adults or children, would be affected like this. Mariann was begging for a blessing and hugs to 'find' her missing voice that had been taken. I told her that nobody took it and it would come back with rest. That's when she told me about Tabitha and Yemaya.

I had received some short email warnings from Raquel that spoke of a major battle brewing. I had expected something to happen over Halloween and planned to have the System stay with Bob and Tina that night. Mariann confirmed that the enemy was already here and present in Preservation. It became obvious that Tabitha did not want to explain much about what was happening, so I relied on Mariann to fill in the gaps. She explained how Yemaya came to Tabitha and told her that <u>she</u> took Tabitha's voice from her for not treating Yemaya properly. She reminded Tabitha that she is her orisha.

I asked her if Yemaya was near and she scratched out a yes. I told her to immediately call for Dragonslayer. She said, "I can't daddy, my voice no work." I then said to her, "Mariann, just think it real loud in your mind." She did and Dragonslayer came, forcing Yemaya to flee. All of the kids except Tabitha went to be comforted by Jesus. Maria came out and finished our conversation. She asked me why the adults were not sick too if all of the kids were. I could only surmise that something was brewing for Halloween and we needed more information before that night.

Mariann had been upset the whole month of October, as soon as she started seeing gorilla balloons on rooftops and signs advertising the holiday. This had been expected and I started early trying to prepare the kids by reaffirming that 'Halloween' monsters were not real, but I didn't spend enough time reminding her and the kids how the inside 'monsters' they might see were real. I guess I had hoped that after the last two Halloweens, Mariann at least had learned the difference. This was a mistake that the enemy exploited against us.

Bob and Tina were still participating in Halloween activities for their young children and felt no need to stop their traditions now. They wanted to help the System's children learn the realities of a 'safe' Halloween in their home, hoping that they could mature and not be afraid all of the time. I let them know that I would again be home to respond if there were any emergencies by phone. Bob felt strongly that I probably wouldn't be needed. The following report by Council was given the day after Halloween and explains how Yemaya returned and gives a brief outline of what happened on Halloween at Bob's home. Details at the end were left out simply because Bob and Tina were present, I was there by phone and Holy Spirit, and a new prayer warrior supported Bob for the first time, David. Dave had recently been allowed to get to know the System in more detail and was quickly becoming a dear and trusted friend to them.

Report from King of the Lights for Council
Halloween 1998
11-01-98

We have been able to speak with the children and Elizabeth Ray to determine how the enemy gained an entrance back into the system. Tabitha Ann has been communicating with them for the past 45 days. This explains her slow withdrawal from playing with the other children both inside and outside. We, as leaders, had assumed that Mariann was growing stronger and faster than Tabitha Ann and child roles were changing.

According to Elizabeth Ray, the orisha did not reveal herself at first as Yemaya. She came to the location of the hole in the Land of Refuge (This area was seldom visited by the children since their healing at Halloween two years ago. See pages 116 – 122.) *where hash had tormented the hole children. Yemaya came looking like a beautiful white bird. The bird told Tabitha Ann that monsters would be coming and that she needed to have protection so they would not cut her. This bird returned several times to warn the child of monsters, as she drew the child closer to the boundary of Preservation.*

The fourth time Tabitha Ann went looking for the white bird. It again told her the monsters would be coming and that her Papa and Mister Bob would laugh at her and tell her they were not real. The bird then said to the child that it was angry that the Dragonslayer men would not help poor little Tabitha Ann. The bird told her to remember who was always there helping her when the monsters came and hurt her. The white bird helped her by telling her to remember the beautiful blue and white dress the lady had on. Then it said, "Who was that lady, child? Who helps you?" Tabitha Ann answered, "The Virgin Mary." "Yes Tabitha Ann, Yemaya the Virgin Mary." (I noted for future use the subtle use of the child's imprinted fears by Yemaya to manipulate her back into trusting her again; with the different form more pleasing to a child to gain her confidence and the twisted use of Bob and my statements about the children in costume on the outside going trick-r-treating. She knew how we would attempt to help her and tricked Tabitha with it.)

Approximately two weeks ago, Halloween began appearing in mass advertising. Mariann began talking about big pumpkins on the roof of stores and monsters in the box on the billboards and on the street. Bob and Tina began to assure Mariann that monsters were not real, or they wouldn't let their kids dress up. Mike told her essentially the same thing to reduce her fear. He also reaffirmed their reality on the inside and the harm they had caused in the past. Mariann told Tabitha Ann how the monsters weren't real. That night, the white bird appeared again and told Tabitha Ann that Mariann was tricking her because Mariann did not like to share her cookies with Tabitha Ann. (Again Yemaya cleverly twisted the truth to her advantage. The children had all learned the method for knowing which people can hurt them, by lying to them about real issues and <u>tricking</u> them, remembering this label so as not to trust them. They were always on guard against a person or spiritual being they were told would <u>trick</u> them. Yemaya uses sibling rivalry to edge her even closer.)

Sunday before Halloween, Liz gets drunk and rotates in too soon causing the children to feel the effect of booze which scares them. Elizabeth Ray reports that Yemaya sent a spirit looking like a monster to Tabitha Ann who was then hiding in her hole in Refuge. Then Yemaya came in a blue and white gown and commanded the other orisha looking like a monster to leave. Tabitha was comforted by her. During the week, Tabitha Ann lost her voice along with the other children and Yemaya told her the monster took it, but that she would get it back for Tabitha Ann because she is her protector. The voice came back on Friday and Yemaya took the credit.

The day of the dead came for Louise and she quietly celebrated it with a candle and a picture, but no food offering. Yemaya told Tabitha Ann to not listen to Mister Bob because he liked monsters and let many tricks be at his church. She told her that he has a party at his church and everyone tricks in clothes.

Saturday, Yemaya tells Tabitha Ann to stay hiding and she would protect Tabitha Ann. She tells her to call for her if she gets scared. The system goes to Bob's house and Tabitha Ann sees the bowl of candy be put outside and assumes Bob and Tina, are giving an

400

offering to Yemaya for protection. Bob is gone with the kids to the church as Tina stays with the baby and Mariann. Tabitha begins to surface and Joy follows her, but quickly becomes afraid and causes Mariann's stomach to hurt. Joy starts flashing back inside about being cut and tied up. Mariann complains her ankles hurt and says no want to be tied. Tina checks Mariann's ankles and rope burns have appeared. Mariann is out and aware that there is a lot of spiritual activity on the outside with screeching and laughing; windows rattling and a howling wind. Mariann tries to find Tabitha Ann and Joy. All of the adults have gone into hiding to avoid the night. (It is not uncommon for 'body memories' of past bruises to cause the same symptoms to appear as fresh and current. This is true for bruising anywhere in the body including internally.)

A fight between bright ones and smelly ones increases in intensity around the home as Bob returns. Bright ones are stationed along the path into the house for his and the children's protection. Chris and Mariann talk to Sarus and several bright ones. Tabitha Ann begins to surface again in the house when she hears a party going on outside with someone calling to her. Bob begins praying. Tabitha Ann becomes afraid as he prays in tongues and calls for Yemaya. Bob begins to rebuke Yemaya and bind her. Yemaya uses the child to fight off Bob. Tina calls David for help. Yemaya runs inside and places Tabitha Ann in a trance while she regroups. (It is difficult to describe a scene like this to anyone who has never been involved in spiritual warfare firsthand. If you try to picture a toned down version of the *Exorcist,* you would have a similar view. Temporary demonic possession can cause the human body to have greater strength in fending off someone they are afraid of. This is why spiritual warfare should never be attempted alone or by untrained individuals no matter how well meaning.)

Preservation began shaking inside. Mariann spins out wanting her daddy. Mike is called and he tries to speak to Mariann over the phone. A lot of static suddenly occurs and Mariann is unable to hear him. Mike asks Jesus to clear the lines up and Mariann hears him again. Mike starts asking about Yemaya being present. Tabitha Ann surfaces out and placed in a trance again by Yemaya.

(Tabitha was drawn to the surface by my voice, yet she was still under the present influence of Yemaya, because she was the one who invited Yemaya back. Even though she appeared to Bob to be in a 'sleeping' trance-like state, I told Bob to keep the phone near her ears to hear my voice. Even if Tabitha was prevented somehow from hearing me, I knew that Mariann could and was strong enough to rotate out, which she did eventually. Having Mariann there with her love for me stronger than her fear of Yemaya, made Yemaya escalate the warfare to attempt to get control again of the body. While the outside adults were praying and saw the shift from Tabitha's trance to Mariann awake and talking, they assumed too quickly that the battle was over. I told them that it's not over yet, keep praying and asked one of them to describe what was happening from their perspective, before I spoke to Mariann again.

Mariann told me how Tabitha was inside with the lady and looked 'dead', when her tummy started hurting again. I knew this was another move by Yemaya to try and break the link between us.)

Praying continues as Joy has another flashback. Mariann tells her daddy her stomach is hurting again. Tabitha Ann surfaces with Yemaya in control. Mike attempts to talk to her and get her to call for Dragonslayer. The battle increases between the smelly ones and the bright ones and Mariann says Tabitha Ann dead "not move." Yemaya remains frozen and changes form inside (to herself and no longer as the Virgin Mary?) *She is furious and calls her son the warrior Oggun. Tabitha is in and out of a trance as she tries to hear her papa.*

(Ogun is another demonic god in the Santeria religion and a warrior god. In their 'Catholic' traditions, he is connected to St. Peter and as a warrior to the Archangel Michael.)

The third battle begins with Oggun. Mike attempts to speak to the child and causes great anger in Oggun. Oggun tries to keep the phone out of reach and hearing of Tabitha Ann. He takes the phone and throws it. (Bob tells me that 'she' won't hold the phone and keeps dropping it or tossing it. I told him that he had to keep the phone close to her head no matter what she does.) *Tabitha Ann reacts to "Papa's voice" and learns that Jesus is knocking to come in. Oggun removes the phone from Bob's hand and throws it across the room, and places child in trance. Bob continues to reposition the phone.*

(I could hear the child moaning and mumbling her answers to my statements. I told Mariann to call Dragonslayer again, while focusing on Tabitha hearing me to let Jesus in through the door. Yemaya had Ogun take Tabitha into hiding with her in a one room hut somewhere inside, when she saw Jesus approaching. It was the Holy Spirit that told me how Tabitha had to choose to open the door to let Him in, just like Joy and Hopi had to choose to run into His arms. This was the first time, I believe, that Bob, Tina and Dave had ever witnessed firsthand the spiritual powers at war, tossing a body against a wall or throwing physical objects like a phone. I continued to encourage Tabitha to open the door so Jesus could come in and give her a hug, with me. The object was to help her let Jesus in, not to explain in detail who was stronger or the reality of who Yemaya and Ogun really were at this point. Tabitha had come to know the power of real love in the intimacy of Jesus' hugs over the last two years with the other children, and this truth was stronger than her understanding or allegiance to Yemaya.)

Child continues to react to Mike's voice and moves closer to the door. Joy comes in close as well with Mariann, they want the hug too. Oggun can't hold on. Tabitha Ann opens the door to Jesus. Oggun and Yemaya flee. Tabitha Ann acknowledges Jesus and the child goes to sleep. Mariann wakes up happy and plays with the toy lamb, lets everyone know who has won the battle and rolls over and goes back to sleep the rest of the night. Tabitha Ann and Joy are with Jesus.

David was holding the phone describing the 'state' of everyone when I heard Bob say in the background, "See what I did to her?" (Yemaya) I quickly explained how *he did nothing*, how *we did nothing*, and it was only the Lord who did anything here. We will fall flat on our faces if we begin thinking that *we* can take credit for anything Jesus does through us. Yes, He chose to use us in these circumstances to overcome evil's temporary control over this child. She already belonged to Him and knew Him so reminding her of His love, was not as hard as what waited for us in a few months.

Jesus also taught this team of prayer warriors a number of lessons and how we all needed to be better prepared for the next time He called us to action. Not one of us had any authority or power here to overcome anything...except what he gave through us in His name. I could not have risked the possibility of Ogun or Yemaya causing real bodily harm to Tabitha and the System by 'fighting' them in my own power or knowledge of them...if I didn't believe and know that Jesus was present and their conqueror already. The facts that this team was of the same beliefs as I and was ready to face whatever came at them, because of their obedience to Jesus and love for the System, made it easier for me to concentrate on listening and obeying.

We learned that Yemaya was still close and connected somehow more than any of us realized. There were some things that Tabitha said to me while under Yemaya's control that raised some flags for me about the future. We were reminded as well how the enemies of Jesus are constantly looking for openings in any child's life, or adults for that matter, to challenge and break their loyalty to Jesus and anyone sharing His love. Using Mariann against Tabitha is a prime example of the manipulation of everyday relationships that are twisted by lies to achieve their goal. Mariann was the closest friend and playmate on the inside that Tabitha had ever known. Yemaya took a common rivalry between siblings and turned it to her advantage. How easy it is for evil ones, whom most of us can't see, to do such great harm in our lives in their attempts to separate us from our love and trust of God, and each other!

The System made plans to visit us at Thanksgiving the night after this event. Maria didn't want to upset Sergio or the kids by telling them that she was coming to see us again in the same year. Ann decided to tell Sergio and the family that she needed to attend a math conference over the holiday weekend and had to make a choice between Thanksgiving and Christmas and chose Christmas to be at home with them. The explanation was surprisingly accepted.

Jose informed Ann that it didn't matter to him, because he was spending the weekend with friends from work. Sergio planned to work away from home as well and Claudia let her know that she hated 'them' around anyway. This depressed Maria to hear of being unwanted at home to not do her 'duty' as she wanted, until she learned that she could help Carol cook for us. The irony for me in this is that she got excited to come down and fix me lasagna again for Thanksgiving. I still haven't had the heart to tell her how I don't really like her lasagna. Oh well, Carol loves it.

More clues began coming in about the future battle brewing. Ann attended another math conference near home and could not concentrate because of the screaming she heard on the inside. She assumed it was some of the parts naturally, yet they all denied any screaming. Later, when I talked with Council about it, they said it was possible that she heard it from outside Preservation somewhere, as the parts all ignore what she does at one of those gatherings. Ann refused to believe that it wasn't a part screaming "they won't have her" over and over again, just to cause her a headache. Ann left the conference to throw up. Parts still denied any wrongdoing.

Raquel sent Bob this brief message and I received a copy, but Bob didn't understand it and asked her to explain it. I think that maybe he just likes hearing his new name from her. She wrote:

To One Who Speaks Of He Who Is Truth;

There is a wise saying passed down from the ancient ones:
A true warrior does not destroy that which he is battling for.

Quiet Walker

One Who Speaks Of He Who Is Truth,

Greetings and peace to you. Brave Eagle has told me of your confusion over my words of several moons ago. I shall try to explain. The words are a teaching for warriors who go into battle.

Among the Thunderhawk people lived two warriors; Bending Feather and Swift Water. Although they were both very strong and had many wives, they were very different. When Bending Feather went to battle, he conquered and left. When Swift Water went to battle, he conquered and rebuilt. It served Swift Water well.

You have reclaimed the fertile ground. Do not forget to tenderly garden it. For a wise warrior does not reclaim the land and then allow it to be destroyed by neglect.

Council called a meeting with Dragonslayer about planning for the holidays and preparing for the approaching battle. He gave them the following recommendations and they voted to accept.

The children need one-on-one time with their spiritual parents. It is important to Mariann to show Kellie and Angie her bed. It is important for Maria to see that Council recognizes her needs, desires and opinions. Bob and Mike need to connect with each other to discuss spiritual warfare and strategies to help Tabitha.

Based upon this, Council is recommending to all parties involved that both families gather for Thanksgiving Day in LA. On Wednesday, Friday, Saturday and Sunday, Mariann, Tabitha and Joy can spend one-on-one time with their spiritual parents receiving hugs and spiritual nourishment. Please respond to Council if you are in agreement with these recommendations.

It became obvious to some of us that the battle was shifting venues and the enemy was regrouping to attack again. Tabitha was asking for answers about her confusion over her Santeria indoctrination and the Catholic Church's training, and what Bob was trying to teach her when he saw her. I asked if she and Louise would send me any questions they had about all of this before they came for the holiday in three weeks, when I would talk with them then. Tabitha wrote Bob first in Spanish and Louise translated it for her.

Dear Mr. Bob

Sorry Tabitha is bad. Jesus' mother is not good. I don't understand. Why is Jesus' mother not good? The church pope says Jesus' mother is good, but Mister Bob says no. Tabitha does not understand. Tabitha wants hugs. Tabitha does not like sacrifices. Tabitha is not safe. Help me. Why are there pumpkins with eyes? I hurt. I am afraid of the beast. I don't know what is true.

Bob wrote a very nice letter in response, telling her what a special girl she was. He followed my suggestion after Halloween and told her to only trust Jesus, Mariann's Dragonslayer, and listen to Him alone. He told her to only trust those people that He says to trust and how Yemaya is not the **real** mother of Jesus... ask Him.

The System continued with the therapist, who was helping Maria focus on boundary issues, expressing her desires and opinions, and her strong desire to find a safe place to be. On one of their visits to their doctor, they discovered that most of the primary parts (2-5) who do the sleeping all had sleep apnea. They were required to use a breathing machine at night so no one suffocated. The children panicked on hearing this because they thought the machine would kill them while they slept.

Tabitha was going to Louise to find out more about Dragonslayer and Jesus' mother, their names and who had authority. She was told to listen to what your Papa says, "Trust no one but Jesus and ask Him who is good and who isn't. Test what I or Bob or anyone else says with Him for the truth. If we tell you one thing and Jesus says another...do what Jesus says."

As Tabitha grew closer to Bob and Tina, she was helped in her understanding of her Catholic issues. They would hold her when she shook with confusion and fear, while sending her to Jesus for the clearest answers. It was clear now that Tabitha had God the Father and the pope as one and the same. She attributed the rituals and traditions of gold cathedrals, kissing the ring and bowing down as attributes of extreme power. Bob suggested to her that she have Jesus show her real streets of gold as His proof of power. Instead, Jesus took a very bright chunk of gold in His right hand and shattered it into black dust with no effort at all. Jesus changed her concept of power in a matter of seconds.

The enemy started coming at Mariann at night while she slept, or at least tried to with the mask on. At 3:24 am in the morning, a significant time from the System's past abuse, Mariann saw Bob and Tina in a dream, coming down towards her with open arms and it was Easter time. She said in her dream, "You can't be here" and called for Jesus and the dream ended. Elizabeth Ray then reported how Mariann started singing out loud from her sleep.

"Praise the name of Jesus. He's my rock. He's my fortress. He's my deliverer. In Him only will I trust. Praise the name of Jesus." The pillow started jumping under her head and she just kept singing those phrases louder. The pillow started violently shaking and move with her head on it and suddenly stopped.
Praise the name of Jesus.

Within two nights I received the following email from Claudia's computer, as did Bob and Tina:

DON'T UNDERESTIMATE OUR POWER.
WE'LL DESTROY HER BEFORE WE LET YOU HAVE HER,
SHE BELONGS TO US!

I was reasonably calm in my spirit reading this, because I knew this was not referring to Tabitha, or any of the children that I knew and loved. I was also reasonably sure that they weren't referring to any of the adults, including those who had not yet accepted Jesus. I gathered from the note that there was a real possibility of somebody still left inside and under their control. I asked Elizabeth Ray for a current roster of who was left and their status of accepting Jesus. I knew from previous experience that asking for information before an event that I needed to be specific and clear, yet I also knew that my asking didn't mean that she would reveal it, if Jesus told her it wasn't time yet. I proceeded forward on the growing assumption that there was another person inside. If the enemy had control over her, then the healing of everyone in the System until now was forcing their hand.

"And this is the judgment, that the light is come into the world, and men loved the darkness rather than the light, for their deeds were evil. For everyone who does evil hates the light, and does not come to the light, lest his deeds should be exposed. But he who practices the truth comes to the light, that his deeds may be revealed as having been wrought in God."
John 3: 19-21

Tina would write asking many questions about the circumstances surrounding the email message above. She wanted to know how the enemy might send it without somebody's help;

could Maria's daughter have been used unknowingly; and had this ever happened to me before now. She felt pretty 'freaky' getting up in the morning and finding it on her computer. She couldn't understand why the enemy was so interested in having Maria but was sure that would never happen to her. She told me how Bob's back was out on him again and wondered if there was a connection. I wrote her back this letter:

"...Yes, I have received this kind of email before, but don't let it upset you. You don't need to reply as I have already, to the source computer in a way that would be understood by the sender. I don't think the daughter is aware of it, if she was used at all. She will dismiss my message as that freaky Jesus stuff popping up on her machine and delete it. Basically it is scare tactics using something in our dimension to remind us that they can come into our side without being seen and affect our lives.

What we have to remember is that, even though we can't go into their side, we don't need to because Jesus has already defeated them. The battle is always between the two of them and we are involved by choice, but not in our own strength. You and Bob witnessed some scary stuff last week that could cause you to back off from spiritual warfare stuff. The fact is... the enemy is stronger than us if we don't allow the Holy Spirit to fight in our stead and we think we supply any power here, including the power of our faith. Our faith only supplies us with the power of trust that Jesus can and will prevail.

If they can scare you off with words, they will have an easier time with less warriors to face and win control back the next time, if only for a little while. They will try to manipulate you as subtlety as they did Tabitha. Our only true course of action is to remain in the battle as servants of the Lord God Most High. Know that the System is in the hands of Jesus and no one can remove them. You guys are in our prayers always for strength and endurance."

Remember: "To live is Christ, To die is gain."

Tina replied with even more questions about particulars and asked if I knew the meaning behind Mariann's dream. She also apologized for not being able to come down over Thanksgiving, with so much going on there in Bob's new church. At the time, I did not know the meaning of Mariann's dream, though it seemed to be a warning about something occurring around Easter. I found out some years later.

Elizabeth Ray answered my request and there was no new listing of anyone added or missing that I wasn't aware of already. She added a memo from Council about a discussion between Dragonslayer and Liz – about her duties and being zapped again. Liz became angry and let a lot out after being asked, **"Are you being real with me Liz?"** Dragonslayer reminded her of her responsibility in protecting the System from harm. He repeated His instructions about spiritual warfare and His warning about attempting it in her power. Liz tried to sidestep the issue but was brought back to her role within the System. Dragonslayer asked if there was something else bothering her and she refused to discuss it. He asked if she was jealous of Mariann.

"No I am not! It is just that everyone makes such a big deal of the kid and how great she is with that stupid helmet, that they don't need me anymore to fight their battles for them. They got that little warrior marching around, let her do it."

Dragonslayer zeroed in on the problem. "Liz I would not have created you if I did not think you were special and important to my work. Yes, Mariann is growing in me and she is my little warrior, but she still wobbles and becomes frightened. She needs your help to learn to become a strong warrior, a diligent warrior, a just warrior and a warrior who relies on my strength and guidance for her direction.

"Liz, a wild mustang is no good to his master if he is unwilling to be directed. You have seen evil face-to-face. Not too many people ever see the unmasked dark ones. You have and you know you cannot fight them on your own strength. You also know they are not going to stop attacking my children. You must become my warrior and fight them in my strength alone. That is your purpose Liz, a protector of my children and there is no time off from this task. Trust me Liz. I am your Lord and I shall be with you throughout the battle." Liz started to cry and he held her.

Maria began establishing a stronger relationship with Bob's friend David and Council sent him a brief history of the System to help him along. David joined with her and Bob in a regular prayer night vigil. They would often go to the top of local hills overlooking the valleys around them and pray for the many nameless people in their community. Ruth began as well increasing her time with Tina. The Lord wanted to strengthen them both for what lay ahead. Ruth wrote to her:

I have been in prayer a lot today talking to Jesus about my attitude. I told him how frustrated I've been about the incidents that have occurred over the past few weeks. That's when he said, "Ruth you have been fed the truth and have followed my teachings. Now pass on this wisdom to others by teaching by example. Don't be harsh or impatient with them. Guide them with a God-filled life. Keep going Ruth and remember my promises. Never lose sight of where the system is headed Ruth. Love them, for the greatest need they have is unconditional love."

"When my little ones wander off, go after them. Get them back from those predators on the prowl. They are easily seduced because of their past. Be patient with them as they learn discernment and learn to trust me. I am revealing truth to them. And remember, although they fall and wander, no one will snatch them from me."

I realized something from my conversation with him. The child and child-like parts in the system are not wandering away from Jesus out of defiance or lust for the things of this world. They are deceived by the enemy who uses the spiritual abuse they have suffered as a means to trick them or confuse them. But every time the enemy makes an inroad, Jesus places you or Mike, or a bright one in their path to bring the child back, Someday that child will be strong enough, but until then God surrounds them with protection.

I thought of your diligence in loving them. I wonder if you realize that outside of Carol and Mike, you two are the only adults in the world who give these little misfits a safe place to play, and safe

411

physical contact. They need the warmth of human contact and Jesus knows that you give them that.

I am beginning to learn about Mariann's switching out in church twice now and the way she thinks. She was so close to the surface that Maria was jumping out of her skin, when she noticed the smelly ones coming into the worship service and told Bob and Maria to call Dragonslayer. She doesn't understand the magnitude of her connection to the spiritual world. When Mariann is waffling between the two worlds like that, she hungers for the spiritual contact of connection with Dragonslayer...

As the relationship of encouragement between Ruth and Tina grew, so did mine with Elizabeth Ray. I was realizing the difficulty of her purpose in the System for being the carrier of the knowledge and the secrets of everyone. Before these events, she would simply type out the information and send it, or talk briefly and concisely about the information I needed and asked from her. Now there was a need for more detailed analysis that the individuals were not ready to give themselves. We were past the time covered in her journals and each new event was being influenced by so much of the past, that I began asking for her opinions and perspective as a 'recorder' of those events. This meant that she would now have to consider the meaning of these events and filter the past through her emotions for the first time in a practical sense.

Following Halloween and the possibility of another part not yet revealed, she started being questioned by some about her ability to do her job. After she sent Bob and I the current list of names and the structure of the System, I wrote back to encourage her to not let anyone's skepticism cause her to doubt her ability. I knew how she double checked her answers with Jesus, knowing that she was not omniscient. I then asked for a more detailed report on everyone's relationship with Jesus, who had been baptized or wanted to be, and who was still vacillating on their acceptance of Him. I knew already most of the answers, but I wanted verification anyway. I also knew that there would be some people inside whom Jesus would seal with His own baptism, in His own way. I then asked for Tabitha and Louise to be more specific as well in their questions to me, about the Santeria and the orishas still causing conflict and questioning them. They responded the very next day with this list.

I hope my questions don't seem stupid. I don't know if there is an answer, but they confuse me.
1. Why do Catholics and Protestants not like each other and say each other is wrong?
2. Why does the church say Peter was the first pope and Pastor Bob say he wasn't? I don't understand why either one would lie...
3. Why don't the Protestants like Mary?
4. Pastor Bob said that Mary was not seen in Fatima or Lourdes or anywhere else, and that it isn't Mary. He said dead people don't appear on earth, but what about Moses appearing to the disciples?
5. Why would the Santeria worship Jesus and have Jesus on the candle if they are bad? The gods of the Santeria, or orishas, were accepted within the Catholic Church to worship by overlaying the persona identifying a saint as the one being worshipped. This included the name Jesus Christ or the dove of the Holy Spirit being given to Olodumare (Olofin, Olorun), believed to be the king of the gods and very powerful, though not unbeatable. Tradition has it that he was afraid of mice. When you see the image of Jesus Christ in the Santeria ceremony or on a candle, you are actually calling on Olodumare for help. Over the years this imagery has become enmeshed with the imagery of the 'real' Jesus. Some misguided traditions such as the worship of the saints is not supported in Scriptures. In fact, Jesus says to pray only to God the Father by asking for anything that is His will for you...in His name only. This is a major way that smelly ones have tricked honest seekers for centuries by distracting them from speaking directly to and through Jesus to God the Father. Just so you know, Jesus has always known who is genuinely praying to Him versus this other god. We'll talk more next week.)
6. Why do Protestants not like the saints and don't want Catholics to light candles and pray?
7. Why don't Protestants have a pope for their churches?
8. Why are there so many Protestant churches but only one Catholic Church?
9. Why does Pastor Bob keep saying Mary is not the mother of God when she gave birth to Jesus who is God?

10. Why can't I be Catholic and go to mass and be in my church?
11. Why do we move from church to church, is it us?
12. Pastor Bob never had time to answer my question about John 3:13. Can you answer it?

I'll write Tabitha's for her in English for you.
1. Yemaya never hurt Tabitha why is she bad?
2. What name is Dragonslayer's mommy?
3. Why Dragonslayer no hug Yemaya and make her all better?
4. Tabitha be bad?
5. Do Dragonslayer work for pope?
6. Is Mr. Bob a little pope or big pope?
7. Who is bigger Mr. Bob or the pope?
8. Why Mr. Bob hug Tabitha?
9. Why Tabitha no go be with papa Miguel?
10. Why Tabitha no have cookie mansion?
11. Tabitha no like cut, rats and no want big candy?
12. Tabitha do bad.

Of these questions the harder ones were from Tabitha, because she needed answers on a level that she could understand like #3. I explained it to her this way; Jesus is willing to hug Yemaya, but Yemaya doesn't want Him to, because if He did, she would be healed (made all better) and no longer able to lie or trick you. She doesn't want to get better or be changed by the truth, so she runs away when Jesus / Dragonslayer comes near. This is because she already knows that Jesus is Truth and Love. Any being like Yemaya or Ogun, or smelly ones are evil and can't live in the presence of Jesus for long, so they run like chickens.

I partially answered question #5 for Louise before she came so she could think about the ramifications of it before we talked. Both of them were looking for simple answers that they could test out themselves. While they visited us, I explained the differences between the Greek New Testament, the Hebrew Bible, the various translations and the Catholic canon as used in the Jerusalem Bible with the Apocrypha and their tradition of church authority being as authoritative as Scriptures. It made for a full evening of sharing.

Elizabeth Ray felt uneasy analyzing the others spiritual relationships, so she asked Council to do this. They formed a subcommittee like good Presbyterian elders and gave me the following perspectives.

...The children do not understand the deity of Dragonslayer. For Hopi, Lila, Joy and Tabitha, he is warm, safe and doesn't hurt them. For Mariann it goes one step further. He is able to make the bad ones run like chickens. They cannot fully comprehend his power and deity, but they do know his hugs and love.

Maria loves him with her entire being. She doesn't understand much of doctrine and theology that is taught in the church. For her, she knows that she is a sinner and the consequences of that is death. She knows that Jesus died and rose again to pay the consequences for her and how she will live forever with him. She gets confused when pastors or other well-meaning Christians quiz her about the depth of her understanding of Jesus. All she wants is to strive for becoming more like him.

Ruth and Raquel are solid in their own way of walking with him. Ann accepted Jesus from the logical point of view rather than from a heart conversion. When you first asked her what she had to lose, Ann thought about that and rationally figured she would just say okay I'll cover myself. But as far as a heart response, we on Council couldn't see it. Ann is still untrusting of all males in authority including Jesus and an opponent to being involved in any religion again. She was burned badly by the Catholic Church and this is blocking her.

Jennifer is still wobbling in her faith and started hanging around Ruth for support. Marie is still very Catholic in traditions and beliefs, but she has turned to watching very closely Louise's quest for the truth and validity of those beliefs with you. Louise is still Catholic, but lately her world is being turned upside down as she struggles with the revelation that her church may have lied to her. She is very wounded and confused by what she is hearing from Ruth, Bob and you. Because of commonality of language between her and Tabitha, she never questioned the beliefs of the Santeria as they mirrored hers in the Catholic Church.

Mari is still very depressed and stays by herself. She carries the trauma of the 'black box' confessional abuse with the priest. She looks at church and religion as scary, abusive and powerful. She remains quiet in the hope that she is overlooked.

Liz is being molded by Jesus…or maybe broken in the saddle is a better way of putting it. Jesus seems to like her spirit, yet he is firmest with her. Liz wants justice now! She is more than happy to let Jesus do it, she just wants him to hurry up. Being merciful is not one of her strongest attributes, yet she is not afraid to tell people that she is a follower of Jesus and she is still learning what that means. She only seems to learn the hard way…sound like anyone you know?…

And just when we thought it safe to go back in church water…I receive these two the Sunday evening before they visited with us over Thanksgiving.

To Bob,
Re: Shelter
I have told Ruth one hundred times if I have told her once, do not get involved in churches! Every time Ruth gets Maria involved in one, we run into difficulties. Maria is so naïve that she thinks Christians (especially rich ones) will help the poor if she only lets them know of the need, right!
So here I am bailing her out of her situation, because you know she always keeps her promises. I will cover the cost of the items for the shelter; however there are conditions attached. I do not want any religious stuff placed in the bags and no advertising the church. Maria will need to wait until I get paid in December so we can go to Costco to buy toiletry items for 81 residents. And finally I don't want to hear any more whining from Maria about toothpaste for the homeless…and specifically no more screaming from Liz about Suburban Christians.
Ann

THIS IS LIZ. I DON'T GIVE A SHIT WHETHER I HAVE EARNED THE RIGHT OR NOT, YOU'RE HEARING FROM ME. WHAT IN THE HELL ARE YOU DOING IN A PLACE LIKE THAT? I MEAN IT IS SO FAR FROM REAL IT COULD QUALIFY FOR SUBURBAN CHRISTIANS OF THE YEAR AWARD. THOSE PEOPLE ARE SO FAR UP IN THE CLOUDS THEY DON'T KNOW WHAT REAL IS.
DO YOU KNOW WHAT MARIA DID TODAY? SHE COULDN'T TAKE IT ANYMORE AND RAN OUT OF CHURCH AND CRIED HER EYES OUT TO GOD ABOUT NEEDING TOOTHPASTE. NOT ONE OF THOSE RICH CHRISTIANS EVEN GAVE A DIME

TOWARDS THE HOMELESS. WHY SHOULD THEY...IT'S THE CITY'S PROBLEM, RIGHT?
I TOLD MARIA HOW ONE PAIR OF THEIR SHOES COST MORE THAN ALL OF THE BASKETS FOR THE HOMELESS. AND I DON'T WANT TO HEAR ABOUT THE ANGEL TREE... THE ANGEL TREE IS A FAD. IT'S CHIC AND GIVES THEM THE, I FILLED MY OBLIGATION FEELING. I WATCHED AS THEY ALL CLUSTERED AROUND FOOTBALL TICKETS AND FANCY CHRISTMAS DINNERS WITH THEIR WADS OF DOUGH. YET, WHEN IT CAME TO THE HOMELESS, FORGET IT! AND BOB, YOU WANT HER TO CONNECT IN A PLACE LIKE THIS, WELL FORGET IT! I WASH MY HANDS OF THAT PLACE. I'M LOOKING FOR REAL AND THIS PLACE IS NOT!

Council wrote of concerns they had for the children about using the machine while sleeping during the visit. I want to briefly include the exchange between Mariann and Dragonslayer about this need here, as it reveals a lot about a child's trust in her God.

The children are too little to understand the disorder (sleep apnea) or that the body needs oxygen. Can you guide them in this? Also we would like your guidance on the issue of ending therapy for Maria every week.

Mariann stomped over to Dragonslayer and told him that she did not like the 'machine'. He asked her why...and then received a five minute dissertation as to why the machine was bad. She then proceeded to tell him that her daddy said Dragonslayer could fix her nose and she would not have to have the machine...and she wanted him to do it now!

He never raised his voice with Mariann but asked her if she would still trust him if he chose not to fix her nose right now, and made her use the machine. She wanted to know why he wouldn't fix it and make her use that scary thing. He told her to teach her more how to be Dragonslayer strong and to be patient and trust him even when he says no.

Mariann started to cry and said, but daddy said you could fix me. Dragonslayer said, yes I can, but right now I want you to trust me. I want you to learn from having to use the machine, that you have limitations. You are weak and I am your strength. For the weaker you become Mariann, the stronger you shall become in me.

As you have heard, we are experiencing difficulties with Mariann switching out at church and other inappropriate environments. She has repeatedly informed Bob and Tina that she is going to her daddy's church and sit at her daddy's desk and color. What are your boundaries for Mariann concerning church?

"Out of the mouth of infants and nursing babes Thou have prepared praise for Thyself."

What happened over Thanksgiving weekend was as fulfilling a time as we had ever had to date. We ate well, slept even better and worked through a number of very difficult issues, while finding time to play with loving God-grandparents and family. There were two memorable events however, that challenged our perceptions of time remaining, and my understanding of worship.

The first one occurred when we took Maria on a trip to visit Solvang, a Scandinavian village north of Santa Barbara. Maria, Louise and Tabitha were attempting to absorb all that we had discussed about the Catholic and Santeria traditions, which were quite a bit different than what the Bible gave us to follow. Driving along the coast and observing the beautiful scenery made them sleepy, so I suggested a nap until we got there.

They had no machine with them in the car, so I listened for their breathing as I drove. When I couldn't hear them, I had Carol nudge her to awaken her. She didn't respond. I called for Mariann and still nothing, so I pulled over ready to do CPR if needed. As I lifted her upright I continued calling for Mariann and Maria to come out and talk with me. She started to stir groggily and woke to tell us what happened.

The three of them had become so depressed that they were praying to God to let them come to heaven now. A very beautiful light appeared in the sky and they were all drawn up towards it, not just the three, but everyone in Preservation. They were all being filled with a sense of joy and peace from what lay ahead that they couldn't get there fast enough. As they drew nearer to the entrance, Jesus appeared before them and told them that their time was not yet here. They needed to return to finish the tasks that He had given them. Mariann said that it was then that she heard my voice and returned to the surface. As much as they were obedient to Jesus, they were also disappointed in not being able to enter the paradise they felt calling them. None of them really wanted to return, and it took a while to get beyond the experience.

Carol and I went through our own anxiety attacks over the possibility of losing them while under our care. We struggled with the idea of being wrong in our reasons for keeping them in this life and pushing efforts to revive them, when maybe it was their time to go home. There was still not a lot in this world that was worth the pain and suffering that lay ahead, so we thanked Jesus for saying that there was... in His plans. It would be evening before we returned and everyone was glad to still be here and alive.

That Saturday night, I took Mariann and Maria to see where I worked at Calvary Church. They loved it because it wasn't neat and perfect, but most of all because it was broken like them. They sensed the years of saints having gone through there before, leaving a part of themselves in its spirit. I arranged to have a worship service that evening with just Mariann and I in its sanctuary. I told Mariann to be the choir director (and the choir) and sing to her Dragonslayer as much as she wanted. As we began, Mariann informed me that the place was filled with bright ones to hear daddy's message, and of course Dragonslayer was there too. Talk about pressure! She also said how there were smelly ones outside leering through the holes in the stain glass windows and from behind the organ grid overhead. I asked her if she was scared and she just laughed at me and said, "Nooo daddy...Dragonslayer is here."

Mariann belted out several praise songs by heart, some with her own adaptations in the lyrics. We prayed and I gave a brief sermonette on the power of children in worship to God. We closed with some more songs, Scripture reading and dancing at the altar of our Lord. Mariann said as we were leaving that Dragonslayer had fun and how we should do this more often. She also wanted to know if she could hang from the chandeliers during service like the bright ones.

On Sunday morning, Maria was the one out for the service. The message for the first Sunday in Advent was "Any Room for Our King This Year?" Its center was why we pray, "Thy kingdom come…Thy will be done." Maria was welcomed by most of the 60+ congregation and invited back after the service was over. She would ask me that evening if she was allowed to adopt Calvary from afar as her home church. She could identify with the people struggling to find direction for their lives and their church, as well as the creaking hardwood floors, broken windows, breezy rooms and walls in need of paint. "I feel at home here where the 'body' needs as much healing as I do and is not hiding it. I love it."

Perhaps unfortunately for Pastor Bob, we sent them back home hungering for a worship service there with real people. Mariann will be the one ready to begin her own battle for what she wants, the freedom to worship her god. She begins learning a lesson that is difficult…but true. Here is her drawing of Calvary.

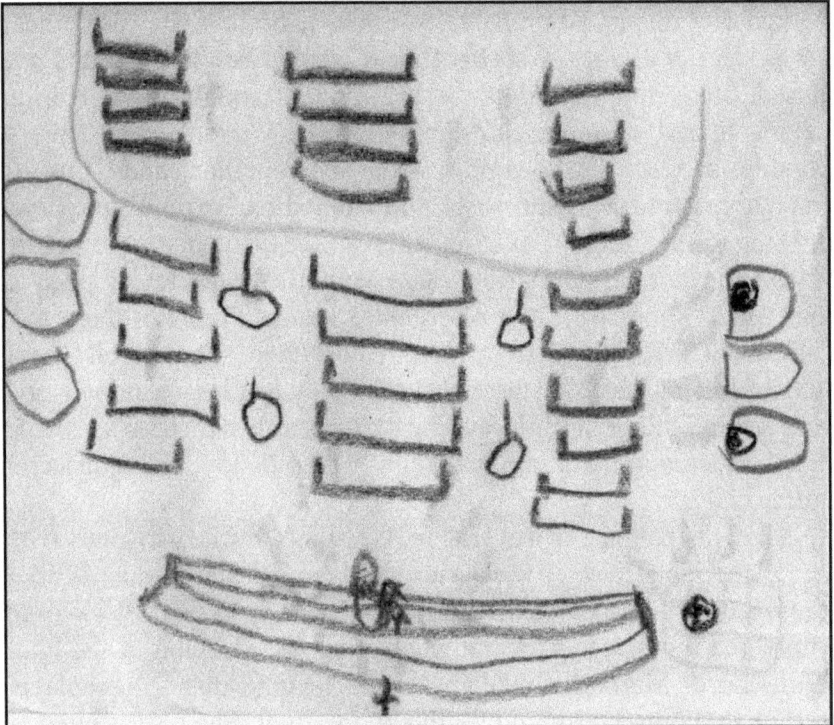

Plate #15

You can't see very well the yellow circle of warm light drawn around us and white bright ones throughout the sanctuary, in the balcony and of course, hanging from the chandeliers.

"The worship of God is not a rule of safety –
it is an adventure of the spirit,
a flight after the unattainable."
A.N. Whitehead (1925)

"Everyone has the right to freedom of thought,
conscience and religion; this right includes
freedom to change his religion or belief,
and freedom either alone or in community
with others and in public or private, to
manifest his religion or belief in teaching,
practice, worship and observance."
Universal Declaration of Human Rights,
General Assembly of the United Nations,
Article 18 (1948)

Jesus said to her, "Woman, believe Me,
an hour is coming when neither in this
mountain, nor in Jerusalem, shall you
worship the Father. You worship that
which you do not know; we worship
that which we know, for salvation is
from the Jews. But an hour is coming,
and now is, when the true worshipers
shall worship the Father in spirit and
in truth; for such people the Father
seeks to be His worshipers.
God is spirit,
and those
who worship
Him must
worship in
spirit and truth."
John 4: 21 – 24

Chapter Nineteen

"In Search of a Refuge to Worship"

"I cried out to Thee, O Lord;
I said, "Thou art my refuge,
My portion in the land of the living.
Give heed to my cry,
For I am brought very low;
Deliver me from my persecutors,
For they are too strong for me.
Bring my soul out of prison,
So that I may give thanks in Thy name;
The righteous will surround me,
For Thou will deal bountifully with me."
Psalm 142: 5-7

"And an argument arose among them as to which of them might be the greatest. But Jesus, knowing what they were thinking in their heart, took a child and stood her by His side, and said to them, 'Whoever receives this child in My name receives Me; and whoever receives Me receives Him who sent Me; for he who is least among you, this is the one who is great."
Luke 9: 46-48

*"This truly is the vision of God: never
To be satisfied in the desire to see him.
But one must always, by looking at what
He can see, rekindle his desire to see more."*
Gregory of Nyssa (4th century)

"He who begins by loving Christianity better than Truth will proceed by loving his own sect or church better than Christianity, and end by loving himself better than all."
S.T. Coleridge, *Aids to Reflection* (1825)

Boundaries were being tested and stretched for everyone that was involved in the lives of the System. The power and presence of the Holy Spirit touched every aspect of who we were becoming in Jesus. This was clearly not limited to the healing journeys of the System, but also for Bob, Tina, Pastor Ron, David, Cathy, Carol and I. There were three church bodies that were influenced by what the Lord was teaching all of us. Questions of who should be allowed to worship brought up why we even worship.

Combine these with the question still disrupting mainline and smaller churches across the globe of how we worship, and you have the volatile ingredients of reformation and renewal. Mariann, Maria and Raquel were totally oblivious of the dynamics they brought into Christian relationships, through their own relationship with the Holy Spirit. For each one of them to let the Spirit flow through their words, prayers and visions, was as natural as eating. I think that is why God was using them to effect change in the churches. In asking to find a safe place to worship, in a style that they knew was pleasing to Dragonslayer, they sought to fulfill their heart's desire in public, thereby altering the public around them.

Of the three pastors directly involved here, Bob and Ron would be faced with choices that would affect their professional careers the most. I actually had it the easiest because the Lord had already made it clear that I would be remaining in the intentional interim ministry for a long time to come. This simply meant that wherever I'm sent that I go in as an agent of change for Him.

As an interim, I look at what divides a congregation; inhibits its spiritual growth; imprisons the people with the status quo of mediocrity; and/or quenches the power of the Spirit, and then I promote and promise that change will occur. The changes I promote aren't to our Christian heritage or collective Christian identity, but they are most often to our collective identity as Christians. This is not a riddle or pun, but a sad fact of human nature before God.

As a whole, our western Christian society is still burdened by our freedom of choices…our ability to choose a place of worship where most of the people there are worshipping the same way that the shopper wants to worship. This creates the proverbial revolving doors, front and rear, for churches. What we miss in the celebration of this political freedom, which in itself is a great thing, is the spiritual gift for worshipping God all of the time, individually without feeling 'guilty' that we can worship alone with God.

We seek safety in numbers as Christians. The implication with this is, a church which is growing in numbers in their worship time is that the worship itself, is the best style and way of worshipping. We get caught up in a particular style of music or choral group, sermons that are topical and less confrontational, prayers given only by 'professionals' and church decors that may be pleasing to the memory or individual artistic taste.

What it comes down to is that we want to be comfortable in our places of worship and in how we worship. But is that how God is calling us to worship Him? As I understand the purpose of worship it is to seek and be in the presence of God. We come to Him for the renewing and refilling of our spiritual hearts in communion with His Spirit. He teaches us how to do this through prayer, song and the study of His word, but these things are only the primers of worship. What we are given in this time is the fuel to empower our greater worship of God by giving Him back to the world that so desperately needs His love. Jesus gives us the best example for how we are to worship Him, in how we become more like Him, by doing in everyday life the things that He did.

Our goal as Christians is to try to become so much like Him that people who don't know Him will see Him in all of who we are. Our essence should be reflecting His essence enough so that when we gather to worship, being in the joy of His presence together or alone, removes any feelings of like or dislike of the style or stature of people present. Our choices for the fulfillment of preferences in the style of worship automatically begin to exclude others from the presence of God with us, others whom the Lord wanted to meet through us, at that moment. How we are meant to worship God is affected by our attitude towards God when we come into His presence, and our attitude changes how and why we worship God.

It is these ideas on worship that the System, particularly Mariann and Maria, had the greatest amount of influence in sharing with me what Jesus wanted to give me to share for Him. As I began to understand what Mariann and Maria were really asking for as their place of worship, I realized it had little to do with the style or presentation as much as the real presence of Jesus.

As I began to search for the meaning of worship beyond the 'party lines' that was my reality for so many years, I found that it was never far from me. Jesus was renovating His home in me by first clearing my eyes to see Him present in all aspects of my life. My desire to know and feel His presence in the worship service on Sunday mornings was being changed to see Him every place I go. I would ask myself how I could accomplish this and learned how I needed to worship Him by releasing Him through my life. I should not expect others to offer me Jesus in a style that is comfortable to me, if I don't know who this Jesus really is and what He wants for my life with Him.

"When you give a luncheon or a dinner, do not invite your friends or your brothers or your relatives or rich neighbors, lest they also invite you in return, and repayment come to you. But when you give a reception, invite the poor, the crippled, the lame, the blind, and you will be blessed, since they do not have the means to repay you; for you will be repaid at the resurrection of the righteous."
Luke 14: 12-14

"Come, you who are blessed of My Father, inherit the kingdom prepared for you from the foundation of the world. For I was hungry, and you gave Me something to eat; I was thirsty, and you gave Me drink; I was a stranger, and you invited Me in; naked, and you clothed Me; I was sick, and you visited Me; I was in prison, and you came to Me."
Then the righteous will answer Him saying,
'Lord, when did we see You hungry, and feed You, or thirsty and give You drink? And when did we see You a stranger and invite You in, or naked and clothe You? And when did we see You sick or in prison, and come to You?'
And the King will answer and say to them, 'Truly I say to you, to the extent that you did it to one of these brothers of Mine, even the least of them, you did it to Me."
Matthew 25: 34 – 40

I have found these two sets of verses to be the prescription for true worship and a lens for viewing how our identity as Christians might be seen in the world. Our actions say much more about us than our words. We gather together to sing praises to God and tell

Him about all of our needs and requests, hear about what Jesus did for us and what we are supposed to be doing in the world, then return quietly to our daily rituals of surviving in life...without offering a real response of worship – giving His love freely to the world without expecting anything in return.

We do just the opposite of what Jesus tells us to do as His church. We establish places of worship and expect people who don't know Jesus to come to us. We establish worship services that we know pleases us and makes us comfortable, then expect strangers to respond the same way; or we serve a meal or give a basket of food to someone...if, they stay to hear our message of hope first.

Jesus instructs us to go out to those in need and bring His love to them and provide a place when necessary to invite them there... again to meet their needs and not our own. We build churches to meet our own needs for worship and comfort in our relationship to God, before we ever consider the needs of the lost first. If we are known for our worship styles or speaking abilities, our music or our programs, our new facility or historical significance, the size of our congregations, and never share the real love of Christ personally with another who has never known it, then we fail in both our identity and purpose in being Christian.

How will the world know that we are Christians by our love, if that love is primarily focused on sharing it with each other in places of worship that expect conformity to be accepted? One might think that as Christians, loving each other would be easy and it is...if our expectations, which are usually higher for the other Christian than for ourselves, are met. We find it difficult to love somebody 'different', who may not be a believer, because we don't give them time to know them first, before putting our expectations before our love of them. This is why I believe Jesus gives this direction to us as our first order of worship, in response to Him. We show our love for God as real when we love our neighbor as ourselves, not only when it's comfortable, but more honestly when it's difficult and it cost us something of ourselves and our time.

"Christ died for all mankind – not just the ones you know and love"

"Let love be without hypocrisy." - Romans 12: 9

Why do we Christians have such a strong need to tell someone that we are helping them, or even loving them, because we are Christian, before letting them ask why we are there? And if they never ask why, we go home feeling somehow unfulfilled? Who are we trying to convince about our purpose in being there and serving them? When we do it in the church building, there is no reason to explain our purposes as a group or individually, because we presumably have it posted for us in the symbols adorning our facility and our bodies. But when we go out into the community and serve our neighbors in the way that Jesus has shown us, we answer the question of why we love someone without expecting, or even hoping, to explain our actions, in sharing His love.

We serve two masters whenever we seek to love
anyone with a desire to be recognized for doing so.

The biggest stumbling block for a Christian
...is pride in being a Christian.

"Two men went up into the temple to pray, one a Pharisee, and the other a tax gatherer. The Pharisee stood and was praying thus to himself, 'God, I thank Thee that I am not like other people: swindlers, unjust, adulterers, or even like this tax gatherer. I fast twice a week; I pay tithes of all that I get.' But the tax gatherer, standing some distance away, was even unwilling to lift up his eyes to heaven, but was beating his breast, saying, 'God, be merciful to me, the sinner!' I tell you, this man went down to his house justified rather than the other; for everyone who exalts himself shall be humbled, but he who humbles himself shall be exalted."
Luke 18: 10 - 14

I have shared the last four pages with you about these issues for a specific reason. The amount of written material I received over the next five months from all of the people connected at this point, is too detailed to give you all of the wealth of knowledge presented in it. I've condensed it into these pages to offer the meaning of the extensive struggle that develops around the System and all of us who attempt to shepherd them. What I will give you next are the primary highlights of what we learned and encountered over these months. My wife will say this is a sermon and she'll be right, but it's not a sermon I created, I plagiarized it from our Lord's lessons.

After returning home from LA, Raquel discovered how their church was built upon a Native American burial ground. There had been some ceremonies after the discovery to ease the tensions with the local tribe. Raquel could tell how the tribe of greed (whites), could not grasp the significance and sacredness of what occurred. She mailed Pastor Ron a copy of the 1854 letter of Chief Seattle's response to the Great White Chief's appeal to purchase Indian land. As far as I know, Raquel never received a reply or acknowledgement of understanding. The full text is available over the Internet, so I offer you the opening and closing paragraphs.

How can you buy or sell the sky, the warmth of the land? The idea is strange to us. If we do not own the freshness of the air and the sparkle of the water, how can we buy them?

Every part of this earth is sacred to my people. Every shining pine needle, every sandy shore, every midst in the dark woods, every clearing and humming insect is holy in the memory and experiences of my people. The sap which courses through the trees carries the memories of the red man...

We are part of the earth and it is part of us. The perfumed flowers are our sisters; the deer, the horse, the great eagle, these are our brothers. The rocky crests, the juices in the meadows, the body heat of the pony, and man – all belong to the same family...

Whatever befalls the earth, befalls the sons of the earth. Man did not weave the web of life; he is merely a strand in it. Whatever he does to the web, he does to himself.

Even the white man, whose God walks and talks with him as friend to friend, cannot be exempt from the common destiny. We may be brothers after all. We shall see. One thing we know, which the white man may one day discover, our God is the same God. You may think that you own Him as you wish to own our land, but you cannot. He is the God of man, and His compassion is equal for the red man and the white.

The earth is precious to Him, and to harm the earth is to heap contempt on its Creator. The whites too shall pass; perhaps sooner than all other tribes. Contaminate your bed and you will one night suffocate in your waste. But in your perishing you will shine brightly, fired by the strength of the God who brought you to this land and for some special purpose gave you dominion over this land and over the red man.

This destiny is a mystery to us, for we do not understand when the buffalo are slaughtered, the wild horses are tamed, the secret corners of the forest become heavy with the scent of many men, and the view of the ripe hills blotted out by talking wires. Where is the thicket? Gone. The end of living and the beginning of survival.

Raquel had hoped to share the ways of the ancestors so that this church could offer respect to a faith that was different, yet not so.

Circle Council was instructed by Dragonslayer to reduce the therapist visits to every two weeks until told otherwise. Concerning the protection of the children in Maria's home, responsibility was given to Ann to switch out and prevent harm from the family. If Ann was unable to prevent the escalation of potential harm, then Liz was to switch out and protect the System. Mariann was to have continued phone communication with her spiritual father and mother.

Maria wrote to Ron about a dinner the church women were having as an outreach to their friends and neighbors. Her question and suggestion was this. *"Why are we having a dinner for ourselves? Wouldn't it be wonderful for us to rent a bus and go get the homeless at the shelter and give them our dinner ticket and serve them that night. We could decorate it real nice for them. They don't get nice Christmas dinners, cuz nobody invites the misfits. I think it would be so nice if our church did cuz Jesus would. I'll help make the food and serve them.*

Ron wrote back with an explanation about why they believe that a nice dinner was one of the only ways that 'folks in these parts' hear about Jesus and how much He loves them is by coming to a special event like this one. He felt her idea of sponsoring a dinner for homeless folk, getting a bus to pick them up, or even better, sponsor and serve them right in a neighborhood where they live would be a great idea. When he found some more people in church like Maria, they would get this thing going. It never happened.

Maria was blessed by a sermon Ron did that Sunday on giving and took it to heart. She wrote him again about another possibility based on that sermon.

I listened real good to your words today. I didn't understand all of them but Jesus explained the ones I was supposed to know. I liked the Philippian church because they loved to give. They just don't talk about giving, they did it... I told my friend that you said when you give lovingly that God gives you back more and he supplies all of your needs. And that giving is an act of worshipping God. I couldn't think of anything I needed, cuz I only need food and water, my bible, to be warm and safe and my friends. But Jesus put a hurt in my heart for one need.

I went last week to a wonderful church in Pasadena called Calvary Baptist Church. It is very poor and the people are discouraged. They need to know that other Christians care about them. The glass windows have holes and the cold comes in. The ceiling is falling in and the walls have little paint. The bathrooms don't work and they don't have enough stuff for their kitchen.

But the people really love Jesus and they were very kind to me. They were worn and cracked like me. As I walked on the worn rug, I thought about all of the people who had walked on that rug since 1929. (I don't think the rug was that old?) *I thought how the unpainted walls held years of praising Jesus music inside them and how many people came to Jesus because of the people in that church over the years.*

Then I thought about how the people wanted so much to save Jesus' church from closing down, cuz there are still lots of people in that place for this church to help. When I thought about all that you said yesterday about how giving to others' needs is like giving to God, I wondered if our church could become partners in ministry like you said. This church could encourage the poor church in Pasadena and be like the Philippian church. I want to be the first to give my allowance from Ann of $35 a week to this church, less of course $22 a month for the child I support in Latin America.

Oh and guess what? Even though I couldn't get help from our church for the homeless baskets to the shelter, Pastor Chalberg gave some money from Calvary and his friend Bruce gave 30 bibles from Gideons with six in Spanish to complete what was needed. Isn't that wonderful. Jesus told me he would fill the baskets and he did. I can't wait until next Sunday to be with the people and share Jesus' love. I know how they feel cuz I have been hungry and without a bed before too and didn't understand how Jesus could love me. Jesus said how he will give me the words to say. I want to thank you for teaching me about giving and reading this.

Mariann wrote next. She told me how the machine hurt her nose and didn't like having to wear it, but she would because Dragonslayer said to do it. Then she asked why Tina said that only Mariann can see Dragonslayer. This produced a whole slew of new questions about where these people were who couldn't see, why they couldn't and did I have enough Dragonslayer soap to come help them see. She closed by writing her version of singing "My God be an Awesome God." This of course was followed by a letter from Tina saying she screwed up telling Mariann that and how does she get out of it.

The following Sunday Maria spent the day at the shelter. Tina went with her and noticed how Maria was in her element. She spent time with each person receiving a bag of toiletries. The residents delighted in her freshness and genuineness with them. All thirty Spanish bibles were accepted, seven by people who only read Spanish. They invited her back to have Christmas dinner with them so they could hear more about hope in Jesus from her.

Liz commented to Council how these people know a con a mile away, but they accepted Maria freely because she was real. Everyone else was afraid to touch the people, including some of the parts, but Maria hugged each one and told them that Jesus loved them. Tina stated, "I now know why Maria doesn't fit at church."

Later that same evening, the attacks came. Jose was very cruel to Maria telling her how she was an embarrassment to him. Both kids told her how her Christmas tree was ugly. He commented that he wished she would leave and never come back. Maria ended up crying over at Tina's house not wanting to be a problem.

Tina took her to a Christmas musical at their church, where Mariann switched out when the kids sang a Jesus song. She let her stay out to enjoy the children's play. Bob became upset when Mariann wanted a cookie like the other kids. When he refused her request she started crying.

Arguments started between Bob and Tina. "Bob: You had no right to change the rules. Mariann cannot steal Maria's time and switch out when she wants something or it's too hard because there is a cookie or a bright one. She was told that she is not to come out in church...period. How can we get her to respect authority if we don't hold to the boundaries? You never consider all of the parts.

Tina: How is Mariann going to grow if you don't let her experience things? The play was like dangling a carrot in front of a rabbit and telling her not to eat it. I'm tired of caring what other people think."

Council memo: Bob
Council request that you and Mike make contact with each other about Mariann's issues as soon as possible. The child is totally confused.

Bob: You are different
Mike: You are not different

Bob: I can not see your bows
Mike: I can see your bows

Bob: You can't go to church
Mike: You can go to church

Bob: Must obey
Mike: Must obey

Council is requesting that both Mike and Bob reach an agreement on a joint plan of action regarding Mariann. Council also request that any recommendations to counselors come with the stipulation that counselor must contact their legal guardian, Mike, before agreeing to see them.

It was time to write Bob and share perspectives of our different approaches and understanding in counseling the System. Bob was learning through hands on experiences with the System and only other training had come through me and an older pastor who had some experience with spiritual warfare and multiples. He did some research on a more intellectual level by reading some noted books with a still larger variety of approaches. The immediate question would be whom would he listen to and follow in responding to the discrepancies at hand? My letter was lengthy as I presented a number of possibilities to help him make choices about what was best for Mariann, from my position as a Godfather and counselor. This is the shorter version of what I offered.

...I want to challenge you to see the world through Mariann's eyes. She sees 'Bright Ones' and 'Smelly Ones' and most importantly, Jesus in His reality as a Risen Savior. You and I accept the truth of their existence by faith in the Word of God and through the Holy Spirit who opens our spiritual eyes. Would we need faith and trust in the promises of God, if we saw them as clearly or completely as Mariann? We know it to be true by our experiences through faith and have risked eternity over the alternative. If Mariann sees herself as 8 years old with red bows and pigtails, a truth that Jesus has confirmed to my satisfaction at least, who are we to challenge it? Jesus calls her His precious child, His little soldier of faith, with her helmet of salvation on that is too big for her and declares that she seeks to trust and obey her Dragonslayer.

I don't think that Mariann is 'different' because Jesus has never described her as so. We, however, are often described as different from her, when we refuse to see His reality in the same manner as Mariann does. So who's different? Children and adults alike become depressed when told by someone they respect that they are different than all of their known peers. For Mariann, the only difference that she understands is that she is able to see and know many things about Dragonslayer that her peers cannot see. This confuses her as to why they can't, but it only makes her gifted by God...not different. Why do you think other children, this includes your own, accept her as easily as she accepts herself, after very little interaction with her? Is this so difficult for an adult to do the same? Isn't this the concept that Jesus sets before us on the kingdom of Heaven, this child-like ability to see and accept a reality and other people with the simplicity that a child accepts their existence?

I agree that boundaries are needed for the protection of all of the members of the System, to be followed for the greater good of the whole. It is also needed for Mariann to be obedient to your and Tina's instructions. However, you both need to remember the

433

long-term goal of why Mariann is out on the surface with you...to be an 8-year-old who will only 'grow' in this world in maturity as she is able and free to interact within 'her' perception of it. As parents, we try to help guide and nurture them to the best of our ability, without remaking them in our own image in it, so that they will be different...better than us. The problem here for us is establishing boundaries for their protection, not our own.

Don't misunderstand me, I think you and Tina are doing a great ministry of love for the whole System. You do so because Jesus calls us to love others more than ourselves and you will be blessed for it. What I'm asking you to reflect on is your conception about how this relationship causes you to look at yourself, through your peers' eyes, other than how the System sees you. Then consider how Jesus responded to 'others' when He ministered to 'different' people and being jeered at because of it.

This is why the issue of Mariann wanting to be out praising God in Dragonslayer's house is so crucial to whether or not she will be able to mature in her understanding about her existence in this world. As far as she is concerned, Jesus is Lord and King of both worlds that she exists in, as I'm sure we both would agree. The problem for both of us is how do we help her grow in this world, without hurting her self-image, while maintaining the anonymity of the adults in this reality? Until the System is ready to be revealed, we do a disservice in our ministry, when we don't try to provide circumstances for all of them to mature.

You are new to this church and need to be careful about how you are perceived as a pastor before that congregation, but that is different than how you are perceived in your relationship to Maria and Mariann. I think we both agree that your church is not ready yet to fully accept or understand the System, but there are other ways to provide for Mariann to be out worshiping freely in God's house with other children, while allowing Maria her time on Sunday morning. It will take more sacrifice of time I'm afraid. Try this...

The Lord knew several years ago that I would eventually learn to accept each one of them for who they are and how they see themselves, the same way that He sees them and us. It took a while to understand the magnitude of that kind of love, even while trying to give it from the beginning. As I gave it, I began backing up my commitment to let Him lead me in these relationships to wherever He wanted to go. Slowly, I started seeing each one for the different person they were to Him and seeing them through His eyes. I know this isn't logical, but it is none the less true…

I see Mariann with pigtails and red bows in her hair and hear an 8-year-old calling and loving me. The only aspect of her that my mind is still trying to accept without closing my eyes is her size, but even that is slowly changing the more I'm with her, as I accept her and her size is not relevant. Jesus accepts her in the totality of her own vision of herself and treats her as the 8-year-old she is, and I'm trying to do the same and being blessed for it.

Raquel sent this the next night after Council received my copy.

Greetings to the outside helpers. I have been called away from Sacred Mountain to speak with you.

To understand, mind and heart must be one. The mind must be transformed to see as the heart sees. The ways of the tribe of greed corrupt the mind. The path to the heart is blocked by attitudes, fears and white man's logic.

The child sees with spirit eyes and hears with spirit ears. Therefore, the child is seen as a stranger…outcast…in the world built by the tribe of greed. She does not fit their logic.

Shall the child be punished for seeing with spirit eyes? Shall others force the child to adhere to the tribe of greed's ways so that she will be accepted by them? Shall the child be hidden because of our fear or doubt that Dragonslayer is not strong enough or wise enough to protect that which he has created?

Dragonslayer was punished for seeing with spirit eyes. Why should we expect anything different for his Mariann?

Dragonslayer refused to adhere to the ways of the tribe of greed and pride. He boldly walked the path of the Great Spirit in spite of the criticism and rejection, for he was and is Dragonslayer strong. Does he, who is mightier than all of the tribe of greed, want his Mariann hidden? Will he not protect her and others, as she boldly models him in a world that does not know his ways?

Or shall we hide this little light under a bushel? Seek his counsel, outside helpers. Do not be fearful. I know the power of the Great One.

As the week of Christmas arrived, I heard from Council about the disrespect of Maria at home by her family and the difficulty of keeping her focused on positive things at church as well. Her only respite was spending time with Bob's family. Mariann was really trying to understand the big people's reason for Christmas. It disgusted her that all they want to do is "make Dragonslayer a baby again." She kept asking why they don't just invite Him to their parties? Tabitha simply shook her head and said, "trees go outside the house." Maria wrote me this short story for Christmas:

My gifts under God's Christmas tree.

Today God gave me Christmas. It wasn't a Christmas like the stores sell. There was no tinsel, no blinking lights, no bargain sale signs, no long lines and no plastic Santas. No, God's Christmas was different.

It started with the smiles I got from the people at the shelter when they greeted me at the door. They were really happy to see me. We cooked together and we sang Christmas songs. We laughed and talked about my friend Jesus. Then when the day was done, they all hugged me and thanked me for coming to share Christmas with them. I thanked them too for being so nice to me.

Then I saw God's Christmas tree. It was an old, rugged cross with blood stains on it. The wood was not smooth and it was bent. Under the cross were beautiful gifts. As I walked closer, I saw that each one had my name written on it. Jesus knelt down and gave me the first present. It was the gift of love, for He loves me so much that He died for me. I remembered those words.

Next came the gifts of grace, mercy and forgiveness. Then I opened the gift of companionship and friendship. As I unwrapped each gift I saw into Jesus' eyes. His eyes were filled with joy as He watched me respond to His gifts. Then came the largest and most beautiful gift, the gift of life. No other gift is as precious to me as that gift from Jesus.

This is what the real Christmas is for me, knowing, accepting and cherishing God's gifts to me under His Christmas tree. Thank you Jesus, for my Christmas today.

Carol wrote her back thanking her for such a wonderful gift. She let her know as well how each one of them was God's special Christmas gift to us…ones that keep on giving His love to us. Thank you Jesus for our Christmas with you for eternity. I wrote her too about the gift of having my brothers attend my service for the first time in Pasadena. On Christmas Eve I received a letter from Mariann about her sandal camp studies, followed by Bob's response to my letter.

Daddy,
Dragonslayer more ancient than you. He be before mountains be born, he be before all. Daddy, he always be. Daddy, he has no end and he have no beginning. Daddy, Dragonslayer say there be not enough balloons and not enough hugs in all the world to make forever. Daddy, he be before he be baby, he be before the sun and stars. Daddy, he be real ancient.
Daddy, why Dragonslayer no lose brains like daddy? Why Dragonslayer no sleep lots like daddy? Why Dragonslayer run fast and daddy no run fast? Daddy, Dragonslayer always be. He be more ancient than Grandpa Bruce, daddy.
Daddy, He be reallllllllllll ancient!

Hello Mike,

Thank you for your letter and thoughts on Christmas and the Incarnation. I really appreciated it. I understand that council is desiring a harmony of advice which we on the outside are giving the system particularly Mariann. It's a confusing time for all of us trying to find our way in a new environment. I read through your email a couple of times and I agree with most of your insights and observations. The issue at hand is not, in my opinion, about Mariann's self-concept, or the reality of the inside world, or the spiritual dimension containing angelic beings. These, Tina and I readily accept without any hesitation or doubt. I don't humor Mariann on any of this.

When she sees angels and demons they are not a part of her imagination or psyche. God has given her the ability to see into the parallel universe of the spirit world. I believe the system inhabits another dimensional reality when they go inside, and as such, I think that everything described truly exists exactly as they say, including Mariann's physical description of herself.

As part of Mariann's growth, I have tried to coach her in understanding the outside world. This world works on different laws of physics as well as perception and some of her abilities transfer to the outside like walking, talking and seeing angels. Others like walking on flowers, flying with an eagle or Jesus, or hugging elephants do not. One thing that does not transfer is her visual image. When she asks Tina or I "can you see me" we say yes, "with our hearts, but our eyes don't see you as clearly as they should." Of course we can tell through her mannerisms and gestures that it is her immediately, so in a sense we see her. But her physical characteristics can't be seen with our eyes, because Jesus has made our eyes different from hers.

This brings me to the one observation I made of your letter in which I don't readily agree. It's really a matter of semantics, not a big deal. (The only comment I'll make inside the letter at this point is that semantics can be a very big deal, when words carelessly used can break a person's spirit.) *I noticed that almost every time you typed the word 'different' one could substitute the word 'strange' or 'weird' and that is how you seemed to use the term. I think different means "not the same as something else." The word different has no value other than when it is compared to something else.* (Exactly!) *In this sense, Mariann is different from other children. Kellie is different from Denise in that she is smaller and Denise...etc. Mariann is different in that she can see angels and Kellie and Denise can't... These are differences but not strange or weird as we would define the term.*

You spoke of our need to "see and accept her in the simplicity of her true existence." I wonder if we forget that the nature of her true existence is not as a separate person with her own body and soul. She is really a fractured part of a single person with one soul shattered into many fragments that we know as individuals. This does not make her the same as other children. Other 8-year-old children do not inhabit the physical body of a 40-year-old woman. In this sense, it is untruthful for us on the outside to tell her she is just like other children and is not different.

Regardless of our ability to accept her physical characteristics by faith, this is not the physical reality that exists when she is outside. Her lack of understanding leads her to try things way beyond her scope of the body's abilities. She can't comprehend why she can't sing in the play at church, while the other kids do. We try to tell her how she gets to run on top of the flowers and fly inside and these girls get to sing in a play. This is because there are differences between those whom Jesus gives an inside and an outside world, compared to those who only get an outside world...

...I think you nailed it on the head when you said you and I can accept by faith the contrary physical reality of the body compared to her self image. But don't we also have an obligation to protect the whole system from the risk of Ann losing her job due to Mariann's overexposure. I'm not in a position of strength here like I was in my last church. My say-so alone there carried enough weight that the system was accepted without trouble. Anyone who struggled with fear of her was comforted by my being okay with it.

I don't carry a lot of clout here. (Sigh) I wish I had my own kind of church where I could lead it the way God shows me and I could create the kind of environment that accepted no questions asked. Maybe I'm misjudging this church and not giving it a fair shake, but I don't fully trust this kind of openness there. Not yet anyway. The growth of Mariann has to be calculated with the timing and appropriateness of the environment for it to be conducive to the growth of the whole.

Growth for her means, Mike.......integration. I know you and Tina strongly reject this and I must admit that I'm not fond of pursuing it either. When we first met, you said you didn't think it would ever happen with this system (No, that's not what I said.) *and yet it has. 66 parts are down to 25 or so. The last 8 to 10 to integrate will be a terrible mourning and I sometimes wonder if we are spending our energies developing the system toward a growth to our own liking and comfort, rather than to the full healing of the woman Maria. I don't want to think about it...it makes me sad...*

The rest of the letter dealt with why Mariann couldn't be in church. There was a lot I wanted to say back to him, but I chose not to because I could tell that he wasn't in a place to hear it. I could have shredded his whole position by reflecting the inconsistencies of his own statements, 'semantics', but that would have accomplished nothing either. I wondered if he would ever see the 'differences' within his own understanding of what faith and reality means, when as a Christian you say you believe what Jesus presents to us as His realities; a kingdom greater and not limited by our perceived physical realities where Peter can walk on water, even if only briefly, and Jesus feeding 5000 people with a few fish. How does someone believe in a supernatural reality as our future end, while believing that our understanding of this physical reality will limit how we can function in both?

While Bob's understanding of the limitations of being a multiple will make it difficult to come to a 'harmony of advice,' he will make many valiant efforts to help the System from within his comfort zone. I underlined his statements about getting his own church from God because he does receive the opportunity to 'create' this church. His journey of faith in these matters is about to begin. Most of the outcome of this will be in the third book, *Journeys to Hope*.

My brief response to Bob was essentially the following statements. A lot of what the *Shattered People* series is about, is the amplification of these principles becoming a reality for the System and us, as the Lord has graciously revealed it over the subsequent years.

...I think our outside reality is really one of an inside greater reality that is Mariann's. The more I learn of her reality (the kingdom of heaven here), a harder yet larger image of it creates challenges on how to incorporate my understanding into hers; to see with her spirit eyes if you will, the whole truth I know is there. I believe that one day in heaven, each part will exist in their individual reality, if only in the metaphysical sense. This means to me a greater physical reality. If Mariann will exist in heaven as Jesus says she will, then each reality must exist individually already. Just because we can't see that physical reality, because of our own spiritual limitations more so than physical limitations of sight... does not mean the reality doesn't exist. *(My God is greater than my understanding of how this works, or my faith is naught.)*

...I, like you, sought after integration as the primary goal in the beginning. When Jesus said very clearly that He would heal her in Him, yet that she would remain a multiple the rest of her life. I was saddened for all of her and often asked Him why this must be so. His answer has never changed; Each person that remains will have a story, a witness to His love and power to heal, to tell the world that needs to hear these truths...

Since Jesus informed them of remaining a multiple for His purposes, they began to heal and various parts integrated as more became Christian. This says to me that it was not necessary for the 66 to remain so, for Him to accomplish what He has planned. How many more will integrate...I don't know for sure, but I do know that it is not complete as you think...

Whoever remains at that time, will, I believe, move into eternity as separate existences complete with their own soul. We will mourn the loss of any who integrate, while celebrating with them new life at the same time. The mourning is for the life we have known and the celebrating is for the new life that will be lived, in the reality that Jesus has created...

Mariann and church? You have to continue to set boundaries for her that work for you when she is with you. Just as she has two realities to live in, so let her have two churches to worship in. Let her learn to experience both types; one in the privacy of your family while respecting Maria's time out at your church; and another that is publicly shared with all of them while they are with my family. The private time with your family could be a lesson time in worship for all of you...I guarantee it. Don't dismiss it without trying it, okay.

I received a note from Council after Bob's letter about what was happening at home for Maria and Ann. Tensions were mounting in the family and Ann was ready to walk out after an argument with Sergio. The family was angry at Maria for losing a recipe for their favorite cookies and how the ones she made for

Christmas weren't very good according to them. Claudia and Jose warned her that she is not allowed to watch TV with them or use the new bath. They told her she was an embarrassment to them and they wished she wasn't their mother.

Ann told Sergio that she is leaving at the first of the year. "If I'm a problem for you all then I'll just leave." Council pulled her in and told her not to threaten him with leaving, as Maria wouldn't go. Maria refused to acknowledge her situation. "I'm okay. I just want to stop fighting. Please. I don't watch TV anyway and I'm okay. Please don't fight."

"The husband says he loves her, yet he does not defend her against the kids' abuse. Ann is always reprimanded for stirring things up."

Next month, Council will have Ann send a letter to the therapist advising her of termination of services. Maria is scared about the therapist being angry with her for not doing a good job. We have told Maria that we will take care of it.

Maria then wrote to Pastor Ron asking if he knew how she could fit in his church, and how to make friends there. She asked if he was considering helping the Calvary church again. Council then decided it was time to send him a more in-depth explanation of problems for Maria fitting in there. They spoke of triggers that produce switching of child parts, a little history with the Santeria and the Catholic Church, and how Maria desires to serve in order to know that she is accepted and belongs there. Ron responded with a nice letter of appreciation to Maria and to Council for explaining.

Mariann observed the letter writing to Ron and decided to write her own to the 'Bossman' of the church asking if he would let her worship in his church. It wasn't real subtle and asked very blunt questions about why she couldn't worship and sing in Dragonslayer's house like everyone else. Nothing like going to the top for answers.

Carol and I flew back to Iowa after Christmas for two weeks. This was time spent putting the source material for these books together while stuck indoors by snow. When we returned and only had one call to the System while we were gone, I found between two and three emails a day piled up waiting for us. One of them was from Ann, condemning all the men involved, Council, Bob, Ron and Mike for even discussing the possibility of having Mariann out in worship. She was pretty hot about it.

Liz added to the fun by suggesting ways of turning up the heat for Ann. I wrote back a simple question of asking her what she was afraid of, if Jesus was in control and wanted this to happen for Mariann? Wrong question!

"Why is it every time I get into a conversation with you, it ends with you asking, "what are you afraid of Ann?" I am not afraid of anything. I was simply attempting to explain my situation to you. Why can't we carry on a logical conversation like before, without you delegating out to Jesus?...

I am not afraid. I am just frustrated that the one thing I have acquired in life, that I can have a small amount of control over, is my job and everyone is attempting to take that away from me...for the good of the whole. Well, what about the good of Ann?"

I called Mariann from Iowa just before New Year's Eve to find out how she was doing. She asked me when she was going to be able to worship in church. I told her that she would for sure, the next time she was with me, but that might not be until Easter or even summer. Having no real concept of time yet, she began to cry saying, "Too long Daddy, I want to sing to my Dragonslayer now." I helped her to understand how she didn't have to wait for permission from anyone to do that...she could do worship with Dragonslayer, Tabitha and any other friends she asked to join her, in her own room. This seemed to lighten her spirits as she asked who would do what in the service if she was the choir director again. I said that's up to you if you're running the service like daddy.

On New Year's Eve, I learned that Mariann had put together her own service that very afternoon. As you will read, it was an impromptu service with her closest friends. I would have liked to have been there.

From Elizabeth Ray

The child Mariann placed her Britta bear, Pooh, Tigger, Fred her bird and her dog on the bed. She took Maria's doll and put it on the edge of the bed. She took scissors and paper, and fashioned glasses on her face held together by masking tape. The following is her worship service.

"Time for church! Britta bear gets the little bed to sit in cuz she be ancient. This be the table like my daddy's. You got to have glasses to say Dragonslayer words. Dragonslayer, he be in my heart and he make bubbles and put Dragonslayer words in them, and then they go up the elevator here and they go pop in my mouth and out come the Dragonslayer words. Tigger...you no go to sleep. You sit up! You know the wonderful thing about Dragonslayer is he be the only one.

Now we sing to Dragonslayer. My God is an awesome God; He reign from heaven above; With wisdom power and love; My God be an awesome God.

Great is the Lord worthy of praise, tell all the nations God is King. Spread the news of his love. The spirit of the Lord is upon me cuz the Lord he anointed me. He send me to bring joy to the lonely, amen. Great is Dragonslayer. Great is he. He know my future. He know my history.

I love you Dragonslayer and I lift my voice to worship you. Mariann bounce with joy. Be happy Dragonslayer in what you hear. Let it be a sweet sound in Dragonslayer's ear.

Dragonslayer love me this I know cuz Dragonslayer tell me so. I come to him and he talk to me, we special friends can't you see.

Trust and obey cuz no other way, to be happy in Dragonslayer than to trust and obey.

Be patient, be patient, no be in such a hurry. When you get impatient you only start to worry. Remember, remember, that Dragonslayer patient too. Think of all the times Dragonslayer have to wait for you.

Now we say praying time to Dragonslayer. Today we do it little different from other times, that cuz daddy do that. Britta bear, you want to tell Dragonslayer stuff? ...Why you no talk? No be afraid of Dragonslayer. I talk. Dragonslayer, this be Mariann. My daddy need brains cuz he ancient. Daddy need Dragonslayer words to pop out his mouth for book. Mama need hug from Dragonslayer ...Me too. Dragonslayer help Mariann be patient. I no like patient. Amen.

Now we give stuff to Dragonslayer. Britta bear, Dragonslayer want your bow, okay? Tigger, you give Dragonslayer a bounce. Pooh, you give Dragonslayer pooh shirt. Mariann give Dragonslayer Mariann.

Now I talk Dragonslayer words cuz this be church. I tell you about Christmas. Long way ago, Mary and Joseph, he be a man who hear bright ones, they live in city. It be Nazareth. Mary was going to get a baby from the bright ones. They had to go to Bethlehem cuz a king said all people had to go to the places they be a baby, cuz he wanted to count them.

So Joseph, he find a barn in the field and he make a bed for the baby that was coming, from the place the animals eat their food. That night the angels bring the baby. Mary and Joseph name the baby Jesus cuz God tell them to. They be very happy.

In the fields there be shepherds taking care of lammees. Some bright ones come and tell them to go to Bethlehem and see baby Jesus. Far away three wise guys who no lose their brains yet were looking for baby Jesus too. Bright ones tell them to follow a big star to the place that Dragonslayer be. When the wise guys find Dragonslayer they be happy. They give him gifts for his birthday. He wanted a cookie, but they give him smelly stuff and sparkly stuff... but he really wanted a cookie.

These things happen a long way ago. Each time Christmas trees come we have a party to remember how much God love us and how we should love one another.

So Britta bear...Mariann got to know what love be so we can do this. Dragonslayer love Mariann forever. He no change his mind. When Mariann do bad, Dragonslayer say he come to Mariann and tell me I forgive you. He not get mad and hit Mariann. He no put Mariann in hole. He no tell Mariann he kill her mama and daddy.

No, Dragonslayer hug Mariann and he forgive Mariann. Dragonslayer, he like cookie mansions. He like being with his daddy like Mariann like being with her daddy. But Dragonslayer leave his daddy to go be a baby to be like people and get on sticks so Mariann can go to cookie mansion. He love like his daddy love him.

Dragonslayer say he love other people like he love us. He not only talk to friends, he like talk to all people. Dragonslayer not have favorite people he like. He talk to people that be different. He eat food with people who be different. He is my friend. He be Steven's friend too. Steven different cuz he be a boy. Girls have bows and boys don't.

Dragonslayer not be mean and say words that hurt. He let Steven and Mariann play with him. He not stare at different. He not say you can't be my friend cuz you not look like other people. He love all people the same. He not say you better than you. He not be afraid of different or hurt different. He not make different go away. He eat with different and take different to park. He sing and dance and be with different cuz different be his friends for always.

When Dragonslayer say, Mariann love me with all of Mariann, I do. That mean I listen to Dragonslayer and I want to be with Dragonslayer all of the time. I trust Dragonslayer. When Dragonslayer say, Mariann love others as I love you, that mean be kind. Talk to big people. Smile and not say hurt words. Give them my cookie. Tell daddy let them come and have Cheerios with Mariann. Not think they be no good to have as friend cuz they be different. Mariann love Dragonslayer so I want to try to do what Dragonslayer say.

Britta bear you love Tigger. He be different cuz he bouncy woncy. But you be his friend and share words with Tigger. Pooh you be my doggie's friend. Fred you be nice to Tigger and no bite him cuz he no hurt you. Now Dragonslayer words come up. He say, Love me with all your heart, soul and mind. And love people like I have loved you.

Now church almost finished. We sing. And people will know we be Dragonslayer's friends cuz we love them. Amen

The child switched in and went to sleep.

*"And as He was now approaching, near
the descent of the Mount of Olives, the
whole multitude of the disciples began
to praise God joyfully with a loud voice
for all the miracles which they had seen,
saying,* 'BLESSED IS THE KING WHO
COMES IN THE NAME OF THE LORD;
*Peace in heaven and glory in the highest!'
And some Pharisees in the multitude said
to Him, 'Teacher, rebuke your disciples.'
And He answered and said, 'I tell
you, if these become silent,
The stones will cry out!"*
Luke 12: 37-40

*"And I looked, and I heard the voice of
many angels around the throne and the
living creatures and the elders; and the
number of them was myriads of myriads,
and thousands of thousands, saying with
a loud voice, Worthy is the Lamb that was
slain to receive power and riches and wisdom
and might and honor and glory and blessing.
And every created thing which is in heaven
and on the earth and under the earth and
on the sea, and all things in them, I heard
saying, To Him who sits on the throne,
and to the Lamb, be blessing and
honor and glory and dominion
forever and ever."*
Revelation 4: 11-13

Chapter Twenty

"The Silent Scream Is Heard"

"In a dream, a vision of the night,
When sound sleep falls on men,
While they slumber in their beds,
Then He opens the ears of men,
And seals their instruction,
That He may turn man aside from his conduct,
And keep man from pride;
He keeps back his soul from the pit,
And his life from passing over into Sheol."
Job 33: 15-18

"Blessed be the Lord, my rock,
Who trains my hands for war,
And my fingers for battle;
My lovingkindness and my fortress,
My stronghold and my deliverer;
My shield and He in whom I take refuge;
...O, Lord, what is man, that
Thou dost take knowledge of him?
Or the son of man, that
Thou dost think of him?
Man is like a mere breath;
His days are like a passing shadow."
Psalm 144: 1-4

"And if it is with difficulty that the righteous is saved,
what will become of the godless man and the sinner?
Therefore, let those also who suffer according to the
will of God entrust their souls to a faithful
Creator in doing what is right."
1 Peter 4: 18-19

Status of Mariann.

Child rotated out once last night. She has not switched to the outside to play since Sunday night. Is not playing with other children on the inside but is curled up in a ball. We are going to have a meeting tonight to discuss the situation. We are concerned about the child being overloaded... no cookies... no ice cream... no church... people don't understand you... you are different, etc.

Daniel believes the child has curled up inside because it is safe. Any suggestions on how to help Mariann would be appreciated.
- Council

To Council,
I'll be home until 6:30 tonight and after 11:30 PM. Have Mariann call me when it is safe for her to do so or let me know when I can call her there.

She is in a state of depression from overload, non-acceptance and loneliness. You will have to let her go through this where it is safe on the inside, as part of her growth. I suggest that you ask Jesus to visit her, with no expectations implied or pushed. She needs to know at this point, and while she is going through this, that she is loved. Part of what she is feeling is a failure to do what she knows Dragonslayer has gifted her to do, worship Him.

She has yet to understand that it is the failure of her outside caregivers which force this upon her, and not something that she has done. Time... the very thing she distrusts the most, is needed to rectify our failure. Only Jesus can carry her through this time. Within my limits of proximity, I will try to carry her as well with my love. This may be only one of several growing pains that she will face ahead. Let her know that she is not going through this alone as best you can.
Mike

Mariann was searching for any method pathway possible to be allowed to worship in church. She came up with the idea that it took two names to be allowed in. She wrote realizing how Kellie had two names and so did Denise, so she needed that to gain access. She said, *"Mariann Chalberg be me. Dragonslayer people understand now that Mariann have two names like Kellie. Daddy you come cuz Mister Bob say daddys protect and Kellie goes to church. My daddy come and do protect and Mariann Chalberg go to church like Kellie and Denise do."*

I received a letter a day on the subject, each with another approach. The next one said, *"Hi daddy, please let us worship and bow down. Let us worship our god, our maker, for he be our god and we be the lammees of his pasture. Daddy you like my Dragonslayer song? Daddy Ruth no go to church. Mariann Chalberg no go, no aloud to be in Dragonslayer house. Bye daddy.*

Memo from Council
The leaders of Circle Council have agreed to accept Bob's decision that no other part other than Maria is allowed out at church. They also agree to allow him to discipline Mariann for failure to obey him. The type of discipline shall be a timing out by Bob. Council is still needing to discuss with Mike the proposal to force Mariann to look in a mirror in an attempt to make her understand that she is a multiple. Council must first conclude that this will benefit Mariann before agreeing to Bob's plan.
E.R.

Hi Mike,

I wanted to touch base with you regarding Mariann at my church. The more I've observed and thought about it, I'm not convinced yet that this place is safe. The spirit of worship here is pretty dead or cold and sterile at any rate. With only a couple of hundred people in a well-lit room and the music not all that loud, I just can't fathom that Mariann would not draw huge amounts of attention to herself. Right now, if someone even raises their hands they stand out in the crowd, let alone move around and clap. Others will still look around and frown with disdain on people doing this... The result is they worship with their intellect and not with their hearts.

Hopefully in the future the atmosphere in the room will change. I'm looking forward to launching a Sunday night service which should become a service that is much more rockin', loud, and expressive. In that context Mariann would be okay to slip in and out of worship without drawing too much attention to the system as a whole. Only time will tell, if we can really create this kind of worship event here.

It occurred to Tina and Me that Mariann is confused by the switching of Maria, Liz, Ruth and others at church and not her. I thought that in order to keep limits and boundaries consistent, that only Maria should attend church for awhile. That way Mariann won't be upset by being singled out for elimination. This would probably force Maria to develop as well.

On another note, I was struck by an idea last night about Mariann. I know that the only issue with having Mariann at church, is because she is an eight-year-old in a forty-year-old body. Mariann can't comprehend what others see when they look at her, and you and I don't seem to agree as to how to explain this predicament to her. Anyway, I remembered how she hates looking in mirrors because she sees the other parts. I wondered if we should try to get her to gaze into a mirror and see if she can see Maria, Ann, Ruth, etc. If yes, then I could explain that when she switches out, although she is little with pigtails and bows, others see Maria, Ann, Ruth, etc. just as clearly and it's confusing as to why they don't think she is a little girl. What do you think? It's risky a little but I don't know how to explain the confusion to her. It sure seems awkward to tell her she can't come out in Dragonslayer's church to worship but it simply isn't safe yet. Let me know what you think.
Bob

Bob's mistakes here are thinking that Mariann's primary issue was not being allowed out when others were. Mariann wanted to be out to worship in the presence of her God. She could care less about people staring at her while she was worshiping because her eyes were always looking up and not at the people around her. She spoke of people staring at her to stop because she was told by Bob and others in the System that it was happening and it bothered them. Yes, she wanted to be out with the other kids worshiping because what is better than worshiping with your best friends?

I agreed with Bob that if the church is not a safe place, then she shouldn't be out, and neither should anyone else in the System if they are just going to be hurt there like before. I don't think that the issue is ever one of numbers, or how they worship, if their worship brings the presence of our Lord. I was concerned about Bob wanting to 'force' Mariann into understanding the multiplicity, as much for Bob more than Mariann. It was risky for him because he could easily end up looking like he was 'tricking' Mariann. If she thought that to be true, she would no longer trust him at all.

I tried to explain to Council how Mariann doesn't see herself in our reality looking in a mirror. She also doesn't just see only forty-year-old adult bodies as Bob thought. There is no need for Mariann to look in a mirror for the reasons that we do. She doesn't primp, or do any makeup, she could care less about her hair being combed, etc. and when she is brushing her teeth, she may glance at her motion of brushing and that is all. It is something that occurs with multiples. Even adults who understand their own multiplicity will look in a mirror and see themselves as the person reflected. The clothes, hair and makeup are only accessories to the person seen. Ruth sees Ruth and Ann sees Ann, etc. If Liz bleaches her hair, she does so at the risk of feeling Ann's wrath when Ann is out. Mariann doesn't seem to care.

When Mariann looks in a mirror, she sees the same reality that she normally sees. Look, there is a bright one standing behind me. Or when it's a casual glance in an interesting setting like a toy store, she has seen another child like Tabitha reflected because she's so close she's practically coming out of her skin. She looks in the eyes of the person that is reflected out of conditioning to look for Dragonslayer there to know if it is safe. She sees with spirit eyes the reality that Jesus wants her to see, because His reality supersedes ours at every turn. If Bob asked her who she sees, she could answer just about any combination of the System possible. And if she said Tabitha, what then? If Bob got the answers he wanted from this experiment, it still wouldn't change anything for Mariann's purpose for wanting to be out. *If the people only see Ann...that's okay because I worship my Dragonslayer and he see me."* No, Mariann's desire to be out worshiping was not going to fade anytime soon, and Bob would have to struggle with this for a while longer. Mariann wrote again, after Council received mine.

Council gave Mariann an exercise to relieve some of her frustration. Below is a copy.

452

For the Dragonslayer people that no understand Mariann. I be Mariann Chalberg. I have two names like you. I be eight and a little bit more. (My little girl is growing up.) *I have red bows. I am Dragonslayer's friend. I like cookies. I like to sing to Dragonslayer. I like bright ones. When smelly ones come I say Dragonslayer come and smelly ones run like chickens. I know Dragonslayer words. Why you no understand me? I be Mariann Chalberg. Why you let smelly ones come to Dragonslayer's church with that man and no let Mariann come with bright ones? If you understand Dragonslayer then you let me come. I be Dragonslayer's friend.*

Mariann doesn't understand Dragonslayer people, but Mariann let you come. Please, Mariann want to be with Dragonslayer people and sing to Dragonslayer. I like to make pretty noise for my Dragonslayer. Why do you understand Kellie but no understand me?

Memo from Council to Tina.

Council must decline the invitation for Thursday evening. It would be too hard for Mariann to watch everyone eat cake and be excluded. We have not had enough time yet to work through the ramifications of the change in diet due to the diabetes. Therefore, instead of adding more frustration onto an eight-year-old who is already dealing with depression over being different, we will just avoid cake.

We have begun giving Mariann assignments to write her feelings down. Today she sent the previous letter to the Dragonslayer people of your church about being misunderstood. It was very enlightening for us. Maria will not make a decision regarding morning services. Council refuses to make that choice for her. Mike encouraged her to talk with Jesus and let him make the decision.

The church issue does not go away. Mariann is trying to logically understand it, but it is not making sense to her. She thinks that she is the only one being denied entrance into Dragonslayer's house.

453

The past month has caused a considerable amount of strain on several parts. With the inclusiveness issue at church, the boundaries set on the children with regards to diet, and the dismissal of the therapist, the child parts and the weaker adult parts are in depression. The usual signs for Maria are less communicating and switching out. She becomes withdrawn and isolates herself. Mariann becomes more agitated, pushing Tabitha and crying a lot. Last night her guard was down and the smelly ones took advantage of this by telling her, "surely if Dragonslayer loved you like he says he does, he would let you be in his house." King of the Lights explained to her that it is not Dragonslayer, but men who are telling her she can't come because they don't want others to hurt her. She started to cry and then withdrew deep inside.

With Mike's busy schedule it is difficult for him to write as often as he used to write Mariann. We will request a tape of his sermons or a special message for Mariann to play with encouragement about going to church with him, being loved, being Dragonslayer strong, and daddy coming to get her when Dragonslayer says it's time. She needs constant reinforcement. Right now she is trying to identify who she is and where she belongs. It is difficult to be eight and deal with the issues Mariann is required to deal with.

For Mariann, Mike represents safety, protection, warmth and love. She attaches so strongly to him, we believe, because of the cancer surgery. It was Mike's face she saw when she woke up. It was daddy who walked with her into the surgery room and held her hand. It was daddy who took care of her. He represents her shepherd to her and she wants to be right alongside of him. Her loneliness for her daddy is very deep and at times, we as Council do not acknowledge her deep pain of separation.

But what keeps Mariann alive is her closeness to Dragonslayer. To her, he is the boss shepherd to her daddy shepherd. She loves belonging to him. Mariann is able to keep going, sometimes limping, because of her attachment to Jesus. He understands her pain of separation from her human family and how hard it is to be placed in a less than healthy environment here. We do not believe that Mariann can make it till summer to be with her daddy.

We are discussing the possibility of Maria flying down south for Easter week as a birthday present from Council. It would alleviate her pain of her birthday passing by with no acknowledgement from her family, and it would satisfy Mariann's desire for church. Council requests input from our outside counselors. Should we stretch the time...forcing Mariann to adapt to longer periods between visits? Would April be helpful to her or not?

I arranged to call Mariann at a special time when she was allowed to answer. She felt very important being allowed to do a big people thing like answering the phone. We talked about the meaning of real love with Dragonslayer. I told her how a real church can be anywhere that two or three gather together in the name of Dragonslayer, because He promised to join them there for worship. If Dragonslayer is one, Mariann is two, then that is a church and Tabitha making three only makes it more official. Tabitha suddenly felt needed too.

I talked to Council through Ruth afterward and discussed where to go from here as far as finding another therapist. They would write out a list of requirements that would be tough to fill, but Jesus already had the next one planned.

Meanwhile, Liz heard I was working on a new purpose statement for Calvary church and offered this at my request as short and to the point.

We are followers of Jesus Christ.
Exalting his holy and majestic name.
Evangelizing the lost.
Encouraging the discouraged and brokenhearted.
We walk the talk.

In Mariann's quest to worship inside with Dragonslayer, she began gaining a better understanding of who Dragonslayer really is for everyone. She wrote: *"You be more than Mariann's friend, you be God almighty, Lord of Lords, King of Kings, and everything more than Mariann know. Mariann want to sing to Dragonslayer in (humbl revrens) in Mariann heart. Mariann no take Dragonslayer for granted. I love you Dragonslayer. I be Dragonslayer strong!"*

By the first Sunday in February, Council believed that Mariann was clear on the issue of not coming out in Bob's church. Helper even sat her down before the evening service and explained it four times. But you know what... there's just something about being able to worship in the presence of Dragonslayer that, well... you gotta do what you gotta do, or as Mariann says, *"I gotta be there!"* She made her choices knowing that she would be timed out and did it anyway for even a few seconds of pleasure. Elizabeth Ray wrote:

Mariann hears children singing and switches out. She rotates back in after seeing Bob tell her no. Maria becomes upset and cries. Bob tells Tina to pull Ruth out. Ruth doesn't pay attention and Mariann shadows. Suddenly Ruth is sucked in (her words) and Mariann switches out to tell Bob, "There be Dragonslayer and bright ones. The bright ones come and Dragonslayer is here!"

Council finally gets her in and Ruth out. Closed Council meeting in process. Paladin frustrated with Dragonslayer for not restraining Mariann...walks out of meeting. Ruth called in as system on suicide alert with Mariann and Maria. Child saying, "I want to go to the cookie mansion. I know how to get there. People there let Mariann sing Dragonslayer songs." Maria led to Bob's office by Tina, avoiding people and crying. She wants to run to car as Bob and Tina comfort her.

Maria hears voices saying, "You are causing problems for your friends. Why don't you go over to that bridge and end this. You can go to your mansion then." Ruth intercepts message and tells Bob. He tells story to Mariann about breaking little grape vines, how people are brittle, old and hard. Mariann is so Dragonslayer strong her presence breaks people. Mariann would not promise not to come out as 'sometimes gotta be with Dragonslayer.' Later, Mariann explains to Council it is easier for her 'tummy to have no food and hurt, and eat no cheerios, than not be with Dragonslayer. Dragonslayer fill Mariann all up with warm Dragonslayer strong.'

After the service, everyone went to Dave's house and Mariann was allowed out to play with even more kids. Tabitha switches out when she sees ice cream and starts eating it with her hands. She is blown away when Dave's wife Cathy can communicate in Spanish with her. She starts talking fast about liking the ice cream that has cookies on the outside of it. She tells Cathy that the 'pope' is here as Bob enters the house. Cathy explains how he's not the pope and not even a little pope. Mariann switches out wanting some cookies but is denied and has to sit timed out with Bob, where she falls asleep watching football.

Council writes to Dave and Cathy to fill them in on the System's history and approves of them as caregivers for the System, as Tina requested. They are given a crash course and told to call me if they have any questions. They are given additional information that is currently troubling the System:

They don't like people knowing about them and some adults are humiliated by child parts rotating out. Life for the parts is chaotic and confusing. We still have not reached total communication or cooperatively working together. Family life is difficult and all parts want out of the marriage, except Maria. She won't leave because of her promise to God. There is no support at home. Maria's sister is a crank addict and beats her up on occasion. Maria has witchcraft and gangs in her family. Her mother is dead and her father hates her. No one is Christian except her daughter who is away at college.

What Mariann and Maria need is a sense of belonging and help with her struggles in trying to figure out how life works. Maria has been isolated for forty plus years and it is hard for her to socialize. She cherishes her new friends and loves to be a part of Bob's family. She needs acceptance without pity.

Mariann needs parenting and acceptance. She has grown tremendously with the nurturing of the Chalbergs and Bob's family. She hungers for hugs and being warm and being with her daddy and Dragonslayer. She doesn't like the word patient, nor does she have a concept of the meaning of time. She wants to worship at church more than anything and doesn't understand why she can't. As you noticed at your house, she doesn't like hot dogs as they are a trigger to the abuse of the past. She will ask you about sticks, but please talk to Mike about this first.

457

For some reasons unknown to me, Bob decided to try a little group therapy with another multiple and Maria. I guess it is one way to get your feet wet in pastoral counseling in that setting, if you don't fall and drown in the energy feedback. Because I heard about it from Council extensively afterwards, it felt like the System was being used so he could experiment on the dynamics of the situation, much like when Sergio wanted to test some theories of teaching on Mariann. In both cases their hearts are probably in the right place, it's just that the residual outcome has the effect of making the System not want to attempt that again even in more positive conditions. Paladin describes what happened in the prayer circle.

System was in better shape to handle the spinning and anxiety of the encounter more than the other multiple. During prayer, Bob set between the two and held their hands, becoming the conduit of energy between us as jolts of pain not our own, were passing from one to the other. We were not spinning but experiencing a see-saw effect of parts rising close to the surface, only to scurry back down because of the intensity of the pain being felt. The outside pain was tapping into our pain, affecting parts who tend to run from addressing the pain (deny it).

There was also an outside negative presence outside the window that was felt by several parts. This presence had appeared when the orisha was mentioned and Tabitha floated to the top. I, as outside protector, wanted the session to terminate. The outside counselor was getting too close to some pain that the system was not ready to address. This outside presence was observing and attempting to find a way around the counselor. It was thrown back when the counselor called on Dragonslayer. Ruth initially blacked out during the prayer as she could not absorb the jolts of pain. Maria was see-sawing up at the time that Ruth lost control. Maria wanted to escape the outside experience and rotated back in forcing Mariann out.

Mariann sensed the outside presence re-gathering back. She didn't acknowledge the other multiple until forced to and it was at that point that she was aware of her child part close to the surface. There was no verbal communication between the two, but an acknowledgment of understanding each other. Mariann asked if she could play. Request denied. Other multiple said Mariann observed her child part and her child wanted to play too. Council is eager to hear what this pastor whom Bob has been networking with has to say about multiples and spiritual warfare.

If deliverance means calling on Jesus during a spiritual attack and having an outside helper there to assist the system through the crisis using prayer, Council has no problem with that. But if deliverance means a pastor or spiritual counselor using techniques to 'fix' the system...by placing of hands-on system, thinking once they pray the system will be fine, then the Council has problems with that. We don't need to hear again that we aren't 'cured' because we don't have enough faith. We don't want anyone using the system as an experiment in fighting spiritual warfare or using the system to experience the spiritual world.

Mariann is not interested in the other multiple, except for playing with their child part. At this point we wish to have no further contact with them for awhile. We do believe that it is beneficial to Bob to network with other Christian leaders who have experience with multiplicity and can offer guidance to him. Here are some questions for this other pastor from King of the Lights.

1. *Why is the system so sensitive to the spiritual world?*
2. *How should a multiple worship in a single's congregation?*
3. *Why are some parts given the gift of spiritual discernment and others are not?*
4. *Why can't evil forces kill the system, if they do not like that the child part can see and know their tactics?*
5. *What is the purpose of the child being able to see them?*
6. *Why would Dragonslayer give her this ability, knowing that people would not accept her knowledge and dismiss it, making her life much harder?*
7. *What is spiritual healing?*
8. *What are the components of deliverance?*
9. *Why are these beings able to reattach themselves if they have been cast out previously?*
10. *Has Bob been placed in more danger because of his connection to a multiple?*
11. *Does a multiple ever become whole, and what does that mean?*
12. *Why are pastors so reluctant to fellowship with a multiple?*

13. Why are so few able to offer genuine spiritual help to us?
14. What is God's purpose for multiples in a singleton's world?
15. How do we weed out Christians who want to be around a multiple, because we are different, rather than wanting to be a support for us?
16. What are the guidelines for people in church who want to support a multiple?
17. How do you protect multiples from being used?

Only one problem occurred during the evening. At 4AM Maria was awakened by voices outside that said, "See you will never be healed. She thought she was and neither of you will ever be healed, because your god can't heal someone as messed up as you." Maria cried and Mariann switched out and called Dragonslayer.

Maria and Council received a farewell letter from her therapist at the termination of her services. In it she suggested two male therapists who might have better luck with the System. One of them, Bert, will become her new therapist starting in the summer. As Maria struggled with the current issues, Raquel wrote her something to remember:

Maria, it is I, Quiet Walker. Do you remember this song?

You think you are alone there in your inner storm
But the Great Spirit has seen the tears you have cried
And how the enemy has tried to drown the flame of hope inside
Remember Maria when you are spinning out of control
And your soul is churning and your hope seems out of sight
You have to keep the candle burning
Keep a steady heart even when the world is turning too fast
When you're down and discouraged and the dark clouds your view
You must gather up your courage and know
The Lord is going to see you through.

I called Maria to offer her encouragement that evening. We talked about the many things that we had in our lives which represented challenges to the Lord's encouragement of us. She read Raquel's song and said it sounds like we both need this now.

By the next night I received this from Quiet Walker, and I have treasured it ever since.

Shedding Tear, It is I, Quiet Walker

I have come down from Sacred Mountain to speak with you. Do you not remember, Shedding Tear, when I asked of the Great Spirit how he chose the writers of his treaty? Do not be concerned about the command to Council, to inform He Who Speaks Of He Who Is Truth that he has permission to write. The Great Spirit has a different purpose for both writers and a different time for each. Shedding Tear, you have been chosen to speak to those who have no hope, about the hope found in He who is hope. For the words will be written will be words of praise, "Come, see what the Lord has done. For I was dead, and now I am alive."

You have the call given to you by the Lord. It was given many moons ago. You have been anointed to bring the love and hope of the Great Spirit, to those who suffer and are broken-hearted. Do not wait Shedding Tear until the heavy storms of winter prevent the wanderer from finding the path. For the broken-hearted need direction and need to find the comfort and rest found only in the Great Spirit. Time is short and the need is now, for many are giving up in loneliness and isolation. Many are refused entrance into the house of the Lord by those who do not know the ways of the Great One. The time of the Great Spirit's favor to them has come. Be him to those people. Do not give up the call given to you by the Holy One. You are the writer of hope and love to the afflicted.

Peace be with you.

Sometimes, when I'm faced with opposition to the messages presented in these books, in sermons, and in lectures on God's love and power to heal… I have to reflect on this message and my call. I have been sadly aware of the Catholic Church's efforts in certain areas to keep my books off the bookshelves, because of their fear of litigation against them being instigated somehow by these books. It saddens me because these books are kept out of the hands of many broken-hearted and suffering people within their ranks. My hope is that one day they will recognize the truth of what is offered here.

The presentation of hope and love that is revealed in these pages is freely given by God to bring healing to the broken-hearted at all levels of society, including the priesthood and the hierarchy of the church in need of redemption. Just as the survivors of abuse are offered this hope, so are the perpetrators of the sin against them. Jesus Christ reaches out to heal both sides of the pain of separation from Him. Just as neither side can escape His judgment; neither will either side be excluded from His mercy, and desire to heal broken relationships with Him.

The reason I bring the Catholic Church up again and their need for healing is because of what happens in ten days to the entire System, and their collective memories of the abuses of the past. At this juncture in their journeys, Ann has gone before Council to ask that the body be taken off of tamoxifen as a cancer inhibitor. She wanted to try some techniques of Eastern medicine. She presents her case to Council based upon the rising evidence that the drug can actually increase the chances of cancer and is winning the argument, when a side discussion takes over. We listen in as she explains the state of the 'body.'

Helper: Are you sure it's the drug?

Ann: Look! How much proof do you need? My right eye is worse according to the eye doctor. The dentist said we now have gingivitis, all fillings are cracked or decayed under the crowns, and our dental health is going down the toilet. Weren't you guys listening...or were you inside playing cards? Our body is not fighting off bacteria and our immune system is failing.

King of the Lights: Ann, maybe our job in protecting the system will be terminated soon.

Ann: I have not struggled this far to just roll over and give up, have you?

King of the Lights: Ann, why are you afraid to die? (oops again.)

Ann: What do you guys do, spend Fridays with Mike...figuring out new ways to accuse me of being afraid? I am not afraid and this is not part of our discussion, is it?

Dragonslayer: Ann, My child, you cannot hide truth from Me. I know you.

Ann: Let's not go down that road. I don't want to discuss it.

Dragonslayer: Talk to Me Ann.

Ann: Why should I?! You say you love them. You say you will protect them. You call this protection? Shit, all of our lives we have had to struggle. You just keep dumping more on us. Sometimes I think you like to turn up the heat, just to see how hot it can get before we burn up. You give us no breaks. What did we ever do to you to deserve this treatment?

King of the Lights: ANN! REMEMBER WHO YOU ARE TALKING TO!

Dragonslayer: Let her speak.

Ann: So where is the healing?

Dragonslayer: Look at the child Mariann. She has been healed.

Ann: That's not what the blood results show.

Dragonslayer: It depends on how you define healing, Ann. Ann, which is the greatest of healing...the healing of the spirit or the healing of the body?

Ann: Right now I want to focus back on the drug. Helper, I want to focus on Eastern medicine's practice of using herbs and phyto-estrogen foods like broccoli.

King of the Lights: I would like to know what Dragonslayer wishes us to do.

463

Dragonslayer: Stop the cancer drug. Continue the anti-depressant. Restrict sugar. Eat lots of fruits, vegetables, fish and nuts.

King of the Lights: Are we going to inform the doctor?

Ann: I have to have more blood drawn in six weeks. I want to see the results before telling her. Anyway, if the cancer is in the liver, the drug isn't going to help anyway.

Daniel: We can always get a liver transplant.

Tolip: Speak for yourself. My liver is just fine thank you very much.

Ann: Look! This is not a joke. Don't you guys take anything seriously?

Helper: We take everything seriously.

King of the Lights: I move we stop the cancer drug, continue the anti-depressant and follow the diet of Dragonslayer.

Daniel: I second it.

Helper: Any further discussion?...Vote then – Six yes, One no. So moved.

Dragonslayer: Ann, I am here when you want to talk.

Meeting adjourned.

Bob and Tina took their family and Mariann to a church with a 'different' type of worship service, followed by a trip to the Santa Cruz beach Boardwalk. Council thanked them in a letter:

We wish to express our gratitude to all of you. Last night was the best night's sleep the system has had since Disneyland with Mike. Mariann slept all night and spent all day telling the other children about her Sunday. She told them the very best part was church.

After watching Mariann at the River, we have come to realize the great hunger she has to worship Dragonslayer. She cannot be controlled when the presence of the Lord is in worship. We have come to realize that and will no longer attempt to hinder her.

Thank you for trying to watch her dietary restrictions. Next time we will be better prepared. The boardwalk was an interesting experience for all of us. Joy had shadowed some, until she saw the skull and crossbones. We were able to keep her in, but she panicked Mariann briefly.

Mariann tried to tell the little ones that the rides were for big girls and she was not afraid of the dragon. Thank you for keeping her away from the ocean. She will jump in. She thinks it is Dragonslayer water because she was baptized in the ocean. Every chance she gets she wants to get back in and relive her baptism.

We don't want you to worry about the two men who were coaxing Mariann over to them. There was a lot of spiritual warfare going on there. There were several bright ones close to Mariann for protection and the smelly ones could not touch her. Mariann says they stand on the pier and coax others into trouble.

We know it is difficult for you Tina to hear people comment about Mariann or stare at her. As you take the child out more in public, you will need to come to terms with this unpleasant side of society. Mariann does not know they are talking about her. Most of the time she is protected by bright ones against the stares or comments. We know, and it is hard for us to have others treat our child this way, but if it helps, she is not being hurt by it.

We need your help to curb her friendliness towards strangers. She is very naïve. We have worked hard to get her to feel safe in the outside world and to trust... and we might have swung the pendulum too far the other way. She should not speak to strangers unless you, or Dragonslayer, tell her to.

Again, thank you for giving our child a gift that we never thought she would have. Your commitment and generosity mean a lot.

I heard extensively about Mariann's trip to the River, as well as the scary rides a big girl can take without her daddy. I asked Council to interview her for the book so I could use it here... now.

Mariann, daddy wants to know what you thought of church.
Mariann like it!

What did you like about the River?
Bright ones come and Mariann get to sing to Dragonslayer like she do inside.

What do you mean?
In Mister Bob's church, the Dragonslayer people do this with their arms (she folds them) and they say the words from here (points to mouth). In River, people sing with their feet, with hands, with eyes and sing like the bright ones to my Dragonslayer. Mariann sing with all of Mariann.

What else did you like?
The lady who be Dragonslayer to the boy (Mother Theresa calming a sick child on a video played).

Did you like the boardwalk?
Yes, but I like the River more and I sad it finish.

Mariann, do you know what the pastor was talking about at the River?
Yes, be generous. The church man talk lots. Big people talk lots cuz they lose brains.

What does generous mean to you?
Do like Dragonslayer. Be happy to share cookies with Tabitha and Pooh.

Tell me about the smelly ones at the restaurant.
Mister Bob and Mister Dave talk church talk and the smelly ones have ears to window to listen. I call Dragonslayer cuz I no want him to listen and Dragonslayer made him fall into trees. It funny.

What did you mean when you told Bob to pray for the car because it was thirsty?

It be sick because I hear the smelly ones say they make it sick. It be thirsty because the smelly ones take its water. They no like me tell Mister Bob car be thirsty. I stick tongue out at them cuz they bad.

Were there smelly ones at the River?
No, lots of bright ones there. When we do church more?
Soon Mariann.........soon.

After such a high as that for Mariann and the System, it stood to reason that something had to happen to shift the focus off the event. This happened first by way of Raquel's next warning, a vision actually of future events that change all of us. She sent it to Bob, Dave and I later that evening. I will not attempt to interpret this until the next book that covers its immediate time frame, and after more pressing events get our attention. This vision will not have its fulfillment for another two years.

This is the story that was left on the computer at 4AM by Raquel. We have no idea what it means or who it applies to, if anyone. If you understand it, please reply and inform Council. – E.R.

A vision came to me as I sat on the cliffs of antiquity. I saw a shepherd in the fields, as he was prodding the sheep with his staff. The shepherd seemed frustrated because the sheep were resisting the southern pasture and were making their way toward the northern pasture. I asked the shepherd, "Why do you not let the sheep just go to the northern pasture to feed?" The shepherd disgustedly told me that he wanted the sheep to feed on the new pasture with the hybrid grasses. "These sheep need to learn to change and stop being so stubborn! This is better grass for them."

As I sat on the hills of the valley, I watched each day as the shepherd tried to force the sheep to feed on the hybrid grasses. Each day the sheep became more resistant to the change. Some wandered off to join other flocks. Some whispered to others about the shepherd. Yet others followed but had no joy in feeding in the pasture.

On the fourth day after the blue moon, I heard the shepherd say that he was concerned that his flock was dwindling. The sheep that were left were not producing offspring. So he decided to hire an assistant shepherd to help him change the rebellious attitudes of his sheep. Surely this shepherd will bring sheep of his own and together we will train these sheep to feed in the hybrid pasture.

The new assistant shepherd came. He was a tender-hearted shepherd and he loved his sheep and he gently led them through the pastures. But soon division rose amongst the shepherds. The elder shepherd had listened too long to his subordinate who refused to work with the new assistant shepherd. "Why should he lead the sheep to the hybrid grasses? I have been with you since the beginning and I should have the right to lead the sheep.

As the arguing continued, the sheep became even more resistant to following the head shepherd. Then I saw out of the east the Great Shepherd walking towards the shepherds. He stopped and placed his arm around the head shepherd. "There is a shepherd who tends a flock near the sea. He is to come and bring his knowledge of working with sheep. You shall learn from him how to love and care for sheep who do not like the hybrid grasses. Call upon him and he will come, for his present assignment will soon end. Your assistant shepherd shall rent from you your pastureland, until it is time for him to gather up his own flock in a new pasture. As his sheep produce, the offspring shall be his and he shall take them with him. Hear and listen to these words, for if you do not heed my advice, you shall no longer have a flock in this pasture. If you heed my advice, you shall learn from the shepherd near the water. Then you shall be prepared for your new flock and new pastureland that I shall give to you because of your obedience to me."

Then the Great Shepherd hugged the head shepherd and turned to walk back to the Eastern hills. I awoke from my vision and sat upon the cliffs to meditate upon the meaning of my dream.

Bob and I would casually discuss the vision that week. Bob thought that one of the shepherds was probably him, which later proved to be correct. At the time, neither of us thought it applied to me, except as a generic warning perhaps. Time would tell. Maria was getting frustrated with Ann's control of the time out and decided to write her about her feelings, with Raquel's help.

Raquel wrote to Ann about the art of listening well, that doesn't trample the other person's feelings or sense of personhood. The words she shared are found in books and on posters that teenagers like to put up to teach their parents how to listen. Maria took over on the last half of the letter.

God doesn't give advice like you or try to fix things the way that you do. God just listens and lets us work it out for ourselves. From working it out ourselves we learn so many things on our walk, that we would not have learned had we not walked the path. So please listen, and just hear me. And if you want to talk, wait a minute for your turn and I will listen to you.

By Wednesday night I received this note, followed an hour later by the second one, and a day later the third message.

Battle Angels to the North. Battle Angels to the East. Battle Angels to the West. Mastop lives.

-Raquel

For those who have been lead astray, the Great shepherd has sent the shepherd to show the way.

-Raquel

A child was born and Someone Powerful placed a kernel of good in her heart. Mastop was watching and sent Crooked Feather to find the child. He instructed Crooked Feather to take a hatchet and find the kernel of good, dividing it as the sea is to the river. And so it was done.

The child grew and so did the two kernels. One grew strong and pleasant to the eye. It had a place of honor in the Dog Clan, for it was large and mighty. The other grew weak and fragile. It was ignored by the clan and left to die.

But Someone Powerful knew of the trick that Mastop had placed upon the Dog Clan, for Someone Powerful knew all things. He sent for Straight Arrow and told him to reveal the trick placed upon the Dog Clan.

For that which is strong and pleasant to the eye, becomes weak and fragile when undressed in the light. And that which is weak and fragile becomes strong and pleasant to the eye when clothed in the light.

And so it shall come to pass.
Quiet Walker

When I read this, something clicked for me about some of the messages we were getting from hearing the enemies' claims. The split kernel represented another part inside which no one was aware of, except possibly Raquel. There was something very primal about this event that was kept from E.R.'s knowledge by the Lord, and it appeared that we might find out the reason soon.

I already knew that Mastop represented Satan's power, as Satan himself is known as Masauwu, the god of fire and death in various legends of Southwest Native Americans. Someone Powerful could only represent Jesus, as He knows the plans of evil against His children and thwarts them as He defeats their schemes. The dividing of the kernel with a hatchet, as the sea divides a river, reflects the process of becoming multiple; It happens over a long period of time and is very painful as the enemy is always attempting to separate God's good from our lives.

470

I had encountered Masauwu before in connection with spiritual warfare against the healing of the System. I was inclined to believe that someone was going to surface to be healed by Jesus, I just didn't know who. In times like these, one needs to know the enemy they are up against and be ready for virtually anything. Bob, Tina and Ruth began researching information to do this. A lot of what they needed was found in the books on folklore and traditions of the Hopi nation that Raquel had in her room, as well as some of her drawings and mobiles that she fashioned to explain the structure of the System.

I knew the Dog Clan represented the System and Straight Arrow was most likely Quiet Walker, as she was sent to reveal the trick perpetuated upon the child. This was confirmed when I received the following vision from her on Saturday afternoon. I assumed that Crooked Feather was either Yemaya, or Ogun, as one of Satan's cronies. As you will read in some of the letters that follow, too often we get caught up in the details of what's being expressed and miss the basic message of, "Are you prepared for battle?" When Bob called on Friday and asked me if I knew what it was about or when it might happen, I could honestly say no, not yet. I told him about Mastop and Masauwu as my only two solid leads, and to call me if anything else comes up.

While Raquel's vision is filled with a lot of symbolism, it also names real entities such as myself and Bob and most of the people of the System. She was handing us the battle plans before the battle, with only the timing of it yet to be announced. We wouldn't have to wait long. I will hold my comments until Bob's analysis.

In my vision I heard war drums. And I saw One Who Speaks of He Who Is Truth being sent by the Mighty One to a warrior of the Lord who waited in the black dirt. If it was not so, I would not have said.

Then I saw Streams of people enter into a large tent at the school of the world to the South. And the army of Mastop cheered and danced as the people clapped for the voodoo man and evil spirits. The Battle Angels of the Lord tried to speak truth into the ears of the people, but their ears were sealed and their eyes were blinded.

And the army of Mastop grew in power. I saw in the valley of Preservation a great stirring as I watched from Sacred Mountain.

I was taken to a place to the East. I saw in my vision the assembling of the saints. Battle Angels from the North, East and West had been sent to protect the saints. But from the South I heard the commander Mastop say "We shall enter from the South" and so it was. I saw in my dream the swords of the Battle of Angels drawn and pointed at Mastop's troops. And the saints walked around the tent and sang praises to the Great Spirit and commanded that Mastop's troops be bound in the name of the Mighty One.

And I saw a mighty fire burning within the hearts of saints as they grew stronger in the Lord. And I saw that they carried trust bags. The troops were pushed back and bound by a large golden rope that would not allow them to enter the holy place. They screeched in pain as the saints sang songs of praise and listened to the words of the Almighty God. And the flame in the hearts of the saints became strong and bold.

Then I saw a man of God discouraged and in pain. I saw a hurt child limp up to the man and he chose his words, but they did not have the authority and the troops in the golden rope screeched in delight.

Again I saw the child in my dream. Her name was You Creature, but she did not call out her name for it brought much pain and piercing in her heart. I head the Almighty One say to the commander of his troops, "I shall graft onto the vine that which was lost. And I shall call the saints that have been strengthened, to pray over the child and in my authority cast out that which is not from me." And I saw in my dream that the Great Spirit chose the saints and only those saints were called forth. And I saw a watcher reporting to Mastop's troops that others were coming to assist them. And I saw the Lord release the rope and the troops gather.

I saw He Who Speaks Of He Who Is Truth. I saw the Battle Angels covering his speeding horse with their protection. I saw Mastop's troops try to pierce the line, but the Battle Angels were too strong. Next I saw Wind Dancer and she was being covered with the armor of the Lord. I saw the commander known as Sarus instruct his army to hold the line and they circled the saints with swords drawn. I saw Mastop's troops assemble and face the Battle Angels. There was silence amongst the two armies and they waited.

I then saw the watcher report to the troops of Mastop that the talking wires were stopped and there was cheering amongst the soldiers of Mastop. But the Battle Angels said nothing and held their positions as instructed by Sarus. And I saw a Battle Angel direct the saint's eyes to talking wires and they were restored. Then I heard great singing among the troops of Sarus.

Then I saw the intelligent one come forth and demand release. And I saw the timid one filled with power of the Lord speak words of truth. And the intelligent one was taken to the Mighty One and he raised his hand and she could speak no more against the saints.

I then heard the second commander of the army of Mastop speak. And these are the words I heard. "The child is strong for she has spirit eyes and spirit ears. Distract them." And I saw the purple creature that was pleasant to the child's eyes and the food that was pleasant to her tongue. And the child was distracted. Then I saw one of the saints instruct the other saint to remove the purple creature from the pleasure of the child's eyes. And it was done.

I saw the saints join and the spirit of the Lord dwelled in them and the power was brought forth. And I heard a prayer warrior named First Sun say, "And his sheep know his voice and know his essence, but those that are against him flee from his voice and do not have the power against his essence."

And then I saw Wind Dancer lifted up in the air and thrown against the wood that would not bend, when the saint brought forth the smell of Dragonslayer. And I saw the screeching of delight in the troops of Mastop.

Ministering angels came and brought comfort to the crying child and the Dragonslayer scar shone brightly against the troops of

Mastop. And I saw a soldier break rank and hurl himself towards the Battle Angel in the North. And I saw his sword drawn and he pierced the dark soldier and there was a sharp sound to my ears as the soldier fell into a black hole.

And then I heard Sarus command his troops to hold the line. I heard the Land of Preservation rumble and the rocks move against the river. Then I saw one from the blackness come forth and try to bring fear to the saints of the land. And I saw in the hole the Kind One who had been substituted for You Creature. And I saw the cut one wandering aimlessly in the valley hiding from the dark one. But the saints had the power of the Spirit of the Lord and the Lord hurled back the one who came from the lower world. And then I heard the one known as You Creature tell of her baptism of Mastop and I was given eyes to see the blood washing.

Then I saw Wind Dancer and she sang to the Great Spirit. She sang of worship to the Almighty One and the ears of the saints heard them and were strengthened. And I heard the gnashing of teeth and again a soldier broke ranks and was hurled into the black hole by one of the battle angels. And I saw one of Sarus' soldiers wounded by the sword of a dark one. And he was lifted up to the Upper World.

And then I saw Wind Dancer being hit against the vertical line and I saw rods coming up from the lower world and being sent towards the child. And I saw a mighty hand reach out and grab the rods and throw them into the black hole from whence they came.

Then the teacher Shedding Tear, spoke to Wind Dancer and she heard the words of the Lord. The saints were filled with the power of the Lord and Wind Dancer held the sword of truth. And then I saw the saint pour the Lord's essence on You Creature as the Wind Dancer child spoke in authority "Dragonslayer Come."

And I saw that the troops of Mastop could not hold against the power of the Great Spirit. And there was much screeching and gnashing of teeth and the land shook with power and the bowels of the lower world opened up. The dark ones tried to attach their claws to the child, but He Who is Most Powerful ripped the claws from the child and hurled the creatures back into the dark hole. Wind Dancer danced in the wind and praised her Dragonslayer.

And I saw the Kind One in the dark brought forth out of the hole. Then I saw the Almighty One shatter the dark entrance into the land and seal the door. And the child received the living water of the Lord. And then the Lord spoke and said, "Your name shall be Dorcas. You were once lost, but now you are in my fold." Then the Kind One received the birthright that was stolen from her by Mastop.

Next I was taken to a high place and I saw the leader of the tribe bow to the Lord. I saw the leader speak boldly in the name of the Lord for his heart had been prepared. And I saw six together, but the seventh was not with them. Then I saw the Lord call upon the seventh and he walked with the Most Powerful.

Then I saw in my dream that the seventh had joined the six and the Lord poured out from himself a river of living light to engulf the leaders. And they were given much wisdom and knowledge.

I was taken to a vineyard and on this hill was one vine with many branches. And I watched as the Most Powerful grafted a small branch onto the vine. And the branch connected with the other three branches that were with it and became one with them. And the new branch drank of the living water and became strong...producing fruit three hundred-fold.

And then I heard the Lord speak and these were the words he said, "I will bring down the intelligent one. My wisdom shall confound her and then she will know of my power and love for her. Then my children will dance and sing to me for they once were broken and now they shall be whole."

If this were not so, I would not have spoken it.
Quiet Walker

Greetings Mike,
I hope all is well at your house in the aftermath of the great battle.
We are fine and there have been no "aftershocks." We continue

to pray for our house, our children, ourselves, you and Carol, Dave and his family as well. We were all very exhausted on Monday, spiritually strong, yet physically worn out. (As were we, with Britta, Carol, Bruce, Tone and others on our prayer team up half the night. Bob called me the day before, following the Sunday night service to open the lines of communication for spiritual warfare at a distance.)

I'm sure you got Raquel's story. There is much of it that makes sense to us that might seem vague to you. Raquel speaks figuratively a lot and some of it was pretty hard to decipher. We still can't decide if the armies of Mastop in the great tent were the ones at school on Friday doing the "multi-cultural experience" or if it was all the people that came up from church. Both are to the south and could qualify. The voodoo man sounds like the school but the flood of people coming in were from church. A half an hour before the Sunday night service began 20-30 of us gathered and prayed up a storm! Lots of protection and stuff, so that is what precipitated the gold rope binding.

(Fortunately, there wasn't much that was vague in her letter. It filled the empty spots I had wondered about. Bob's answer of the school or the church is right, both played a part. The school's multi-cultural event with the voodoo man on display was used by Mastop to encourage his troops.)

Wind Dancer got her bruise when Tina moved to anoint her with spikenard, the scent mentioned in Mark 14 as the perfume Jesus was anointed with by the woman (Mary) who wiped his feet with her hair. We happened to have some lying around because I used it in a sermon illustration once. I think I'll always keep a bottle handy. Ha Ha. Mariann was out and asking for it but when Tina moved close the body rolled away as fast as it could under our dining room table which is a large redwood picnic table. Her shoulder hit the crossbeam underneath. The vertical line mentioned was the door-trim by the wall where the enemy tried to pound the body's head. Several times one of the smelly ones took over the body and tried to frighten us by starring us down. Once it shouted, "you can't have her she's ours!" But we were never afraid.

476

(For myself, I don't find anything about spiritual warfare to be a laughing matter and I think Bob's reference to laughter is most likely nervous laughter...the kind you experience when you've just been through a tough situation and you're glad it's over. I had begun talking with Mariann over the phone encouraging her to put on God's armor and prepare for battle. As the battle ensued, the System's body would be thrown against the wall, table, etc. to both scare those involved in prayer and to make it difficult for Bob or Tina to apply the ointment. The phone would get tossed as at Halloween, but Bob was better prepared at this stage to keep the phone near her ear to hear my voice. I could hear the orisha controlling the body shout at the saints, so I would encourage them to know that it wasn't Tabitha, Mariann or Maria out.

At one point the enemy was able to disconnect the phone line, something they came up with, because the static line trick wasn't working for them this time. We had extra cell phones available so we wouldn't be down for long. As Mariann rotated out I would get more information on what was happening inside. I knew that 'You Creature' was being held captive in a dark pit somewhere and she didn't know me, or my voice, well enough to react strongly enough to break her bonds, so another avenue had to be opened up to allow her to approach Jesus waiting for her.

It was then the Holy Spirit had me call Ruth out to explain the situation to her. The person in the pit needed the opportunity to hear about Jesus and make her choice about accepting His protection. However, to accomplish this, someone needed to replace her as a hostage in order to 'buy' her out. I asked Ruth to make a choice here and now, "Are you willing to risk your life and possibly sacrifice it for the sake of this person in bondage?" I didn't want Ruth to be coerced, but to freely choose to do this, with the understanding that I wasn't sure how it might end, and she could possibly die tonight. The good news was, if that happened, she would be in paradise sooner than the rest of the System.

She chose to do it and essentially descended into a black void with no light, no sound, and couldn't even hear her own screams and cries for help from God. On the outside it was only about twenty minutes with the girl, later known as Dorcas, but for Ruth in this cell it seemed like forever. None of us had any reference as to where Ruth was at this point, as I began telling Dorcas about

Jesus and His power to save her from the pit. After she ran into His waiting arms and He held her, the demons attempted to grab her to pull her back down into the pit at this point. One of the blood curdling screams it made as Jesus tossed it down into the pit of no return, was what everyone heard on the outside that Bob will describe as trippy. As soon as Bob could baptize Dorcas after she accepted Jesus, we asked the Lord if Ruth could be released to receive her baptism properly for the first time. Ruth said she kept trying to remember my last words to her as she entered the pit, to help her not go insane out of fear, "To live is Christ – To die is gain" and she was prepared to die for another, whom she didn't know at all. I was proud of her strength of faith to risk death.)

The demon screaming after being struck was something that Tina and Dave and I heard. We asked Mariann at the time what it was and she told us. That was trippy. We saw the scar later that night.

I love the conclusion of Raquel's vision. It gives me great comfort and peace. After last Halloween we thought that the system wasn't clear of entities. Remember when I asked for the system to do a search of preservation land? They never did because it wasn't the right time. I seem to recall asking you if there were any more and you said no, but when you talked to Ruth on the phone you seemed to know tons more than any of us about the internal world. None of this seemed to surprise you in the least, so I guessed that you were already aware of Dorcas (as we know her now to be). How did you come to your knowledge (revelation or information) and are you at peace now that the system is fully revealed?

(Purely the Holy Spirit's timing Bob. I was very calm only because I had no doubt that it wasn't me accomplishing any of this. The Lord's directions are clear: put on the armor, be prepared with the Word, stand your ground behind the Lord and watch Him do His work. The enemy reveals what seems like special effects of sight and sound, as a reality of two worlds coming together in battle is displayed, and the enemy hopes to scare the unprepared and novices away. These saints stood their ground and another soul entered the family of God.)

Thanks for your help and comfort. I guess this all came spilling out after I found out that a baptism could be stolen. I liked the way Raquel referred to it as a birthright. That helped clear up my theological understanding. Obviously Dave and I filed this away for future reference regarding church membership. Are you committed to Christ, are you baptized, can you remember it? Ha Ha. I know this theological understanding of baptism was never revealed in any class I ever had or book I ever read. No duh! Right? Think of all the other useful pieces of information they forgot to mention because we were too busy parsing Greek verbs. (Which, by the way never comes up in my ministry...how about yours?)

Other things: The purple creature which distracted Mariann was a Barney video which was left on the TV after Chris fell asleep and the food she desired were cookies, of course. The discouraged man of God was my senior pastor, Ron whom Dorcas approached for prayer after the service on Sunday night. (Dorcas was unknown to everyone in the System, except Raquel, because they were from the same lineage. Dorcas was a split from Joy during her baptism in blood by the satanic cult of the Santeria, the original kernel spoken of in the earlier vision. She was held captive all these years by the demonic forces accompanying the orishas into Preservation, and their last hidden pawn to use for controlling the System. With the last person free, Council will be baptized in the Holy Spirit, as their duties were now being improved by Dragonslayer to meet the new structure of the System. Paladin was the seventh leader who was holding back from committing himself to Jesus at the end of the evening. I asked to speak with him over the phone with Elizabeth Ray and challenged him to risk taking a walk with Jesus privately and hear what he had to say. As one cowboy to another, he accepted the challenge when I asked, "what he was afraid of." Later that evening he was back with Jesus being baptized with the rest of Council. Dorcas' silent screams were finally heard, and help answered. Praise God.)

Our home is currently peaceful and Christ is still strongly present. Oh, I'm supposed to ask who is "First Sun?" Tina doesn't like her name of "The Timid One" and hopes it gets changed soon. Maria told her that it's better than the one she got which is "The Weak

One." *Ha Ha.* (First Sun is a member of House of Prayer…all of whom were very busy that night.)

Dave really wanted to know the names of the four smelly ones who were in there so as to guard against them in the future. I didn't think it was that big a deal for the last connection was severed. He woke up in the middle of the night dreaming and placed his hand on his wife's head and said, "who are you?" and she said "Cathy." "Cathy who?" he asked. "Cathy your wife"" she barked and he fully woke up. We all got a real kick out of that one. Take Care and send me any information you can on your end for our education and training in these kinds of matters. (This is a mistake in judgment that Bob will make a few times in his career. If follow-up care is not carefully given to the person whom the demons influenced or inhabited, they will return with many more brothers to do it again. If their names are known, they can be cast out quicker from this or any other person displaying them.)

Love in Christ,
Bob

Hi Tina,

Ann is at school early so I wanted to touch base with you. I am still very physically tired. I looked at the injury Mariann has and it is very unusual. She must have hit that wood in a bizarre way. There are two injuries on her back. One is very strange and has like four rope burns or indentations that measure about 6 inches, like something grabbed her. The bruises are an unusual blue with red centers. Mariann wants a picture of her Dragonslayer scar. I asked her why and she said to show the big people that Dragonslayer throws the smelly ones that hurt. We told her no picture…just remember it in your heart. (The marks were real and identifiable, and gone within two weeks. Mariann drew the claw marks for me when I saw her next.)

We need Bob and Mike to explain to Mariann not to speak to people about her incident Sunday night. Mariann tends to forget that what she experiences and sees - is not normal for most people.

We know that she is so excited about what the Lord has done and she wants to tell everyone she meets, but you must stop her. It would cause a lot of problems.

I heard Raquel's statement about the branch connecting with three and forming one. Is this blending of a thread in the system? (Yes, in the line of mercy.) *Mariann seems somewhat jealous of Dorcas. She is 10 and Mariann thinks of her as an invader. I think it is hard for Mariann who has been the oldest child to now become second in age. I think she also does not want to share with yet another child.... How many cookies can we eat? Mariann also seems to be worried that Mr. Bob and Miss Tina will love Dorcas and forget about her. Kids! They can be so sensitive.*

Hope all is going well with you. Please keep Ann in your prayers. Tomorrow she teaches a class at the university on something called ELD strategies in math instruction. She has also been nominated for outstanding teacher again by another group. I wonder when God is going to bring her down. I hope she doesn't fall too far. Take care. I miss you.
Ruth

He who has an ear let him hear what the spirit says to the saints.

For you my dear children who have overcome. I give the right to eat of the tree of life which is in the paradise garden. You shall not be hurt by the second death. I will give you some of the hidden manna. I will also give you a white stone with a new name written on it known only to you who receive it. For you who have overcome and do my will to the end, I will give authority in my name. Just as I have received authority from my Father, so you shall have authority in me.

I will also give you the morning star and you shall be dressed in white like the saints who stand with you. I will never wipe your names from the book of life but will confess your names before my Father and his angels.

For you who have overcome, I will make a pillar in the temple of my God. Never again will you leave me. I will write on your heart the name of my Father and the name of the city of my God...the new Jerusalem which is coming down out of heaven from my Father.

I will also write on you my name. For you who have overcome, I will give the right to sit with me on my throne just as I overcame and sat down with my Father on his throne. He who has an ear, let him hear what the spirit says to the saints.

Raquel

"We may not pay Satan reverence,
for that would be indiscreet,
but we can at least respect his talents."
Mark Twain, in *Harper's Magazine* (1899)

"Behold, I stand at the door and knock;
if anyone hears My voice and opens the door,
I will come into him, and will dine with him,
and he with Me. He who overcomes,
I will grant to him to sit down with Me on
My throne, as I also overcame and sat
down with My Father on His throne.
He who has an ear, let him hear
What the Spirit says to the churches."
Revelation 4:20 – 22

Epilogue

"You Want Me To Go Where?"

═══════════════════════════════

"Go therefore and make disciples of all nations,
Baptizing them in the name of the Father,
And of the Son, and the Holy Spirit,
Teaching them to observe all that
I commanded you; and lo, I am
With you always, even to
the end of the age."
Matthew 28

"Create in me a clean heart, O God,
And renew a steadfast spirit within me.
Do not cast me away from Thy presence,
And do not take Thy Holy Spirit from me.
Restore to me the joy of Thy salvation,
And sustain me with a willing spirit."
Psalm 51

Within a week, the attacks were back again and the System was struggling to find peace again. Those who thought the battles would become easier now, because they had survived the last great battle, found that the paths were getting harder to follow, yet their future was clear as long as they stayed close to Dragonslayer. Maria called me to tell me how Jesus was no longer just an advisor on Council, but that He had become their new leader in everything.

I asked Maria to make a list of those still inside, those who were baptized and those not yet baptized. I had a good idea of the list but was still surprised. As I conversed with Maria, she seemed to still be troubled over the events of the previous week. She felt guilty over another part who had suffered for a lifetime in her place. I asked her to talk with Ruth about her ordeal, and if not, then to ask her if risking death was worth it. I read to her from the letter that Jesus gave to the System in the beginning of chemotherapy in '96. Council wrote back later with answers:

Mike,

Thank you for reading the words of Jesus that he spoke to Quiet Walker 1 and ½ years ago. It helped us gain perspective about what occurred today. Your explanation as to why the Satanist today backed away when he came close to us was interesting. We also understand what occurred now when that soon-to-be-teacher asked Ann about the Santeria.

As you requested we are sending you Jesus' list of baptisms according to Him. The following parts are baptized: Dorcas, Maria, Louise, Tabitha, Ruth, Jennifer, Mariann, Hopi (baptized by Jesus when he bathed him the week after cancer surgery), and Raquel. Council and Elizabeth Ray will be baptized by Jesus in his timing.

Joy's baptism was stolen. Dorcas was substituted.

Parts who have not been baptized: Ann, Liz, Joy, Lila, Marie, Mari. Parts who have not accepted Jesus as their Lord and Savior: Marie and Mari think they are Catholic and therefore do not have to accept Jesus as their Savior. Mari still has major guilt issues about not helping Mariann in the rectory and her programming in the confessional by the priest. Ann agreed to accept him not in her heart but in her mind (If it is true, then I win. If it is not true, what do I have to lose?). Joy is still being influenced and tricked by the enemy. Lila thinks Jesus is a nice part.

Liz is ready to be baptized but fearful of losing her wild side and identity. "She does not want Jesus to change her into a Ruth!" (My surprise! Where is even more surprising.)

We have been told to be prepared for a merging of the line of mercy and helps. Jesus says we will understand in his time.

Council will discuss with Jesus your suggestion about Liz being baptized on Easter Sunday. As you know, because of Liz's unpredictable nature, Council has concerns, however, if Jesus says yes and to trust him, we will give our concerns over to him.

We will continue to ask our Lord for strength and good health for you. Please let us know the decision of your congregation makes on Sunday. We found your comment interesting that the intelligent one that we think is Ann might also be an outside entity that will attack the system via Ann and that our commander will bring down that entity, confusing Ann and bringing her to an understanding of who he is. It is true that Raquel writes sometimes *incorporating two ideas or statements into one paragraph. Since we have baby spirit eyes and ears, it is hard for us to understand her visions and parables.*

We are not sure who the intelligent one is. We do know that Ann has in the past been referred to as the intelligent one, but we also know there are demons of pride and intelligence. We asked Jesus and he told us it is not for us to know at this time.

The grace of the Lord Jesus Christ be with your spirit,
Council

Council asked me to relay this to you. System experiencing major anxiety attacks. Affecting majority of parts. Breathing machine causing anxiety about being suffocated. Raquel sent system outside at 3:30 a.m. to sleep on the deck under the stars. Ann having difficult time with inside anxiety. Parts referred to attack like they were losing life and dying. Mariann taken down with fear of not breathing. Don't know what is occurring. Black cloud of depression hovering over parts. Raquel told council to let Mariann have worship tonight in room with Britta Bear and Tigger, Pooh. Mariann complained to Raquel that Dragonslayer didn't come last night. Raquel told her she knows. "To have the Great Spirit present, one must set the table in his honor. Set the table tonight Mariann."

Council is praying for all of you. Hold on to your trust bag. Be bold for our King. Do not allow others to distract you. Prepare correctly for the journey. We are praying. Please pray for the parts that whatever is causing the anxiety attacks will cease. There is great power in the prayers of the saints.
Peace and Grace,
Council

I suggested to Council that if they were coming down to see us over Easter anyway, we did have a baptismal font at Calvary that hadn't been used by the church in years and needed a good workout. Liz qualified as the perfect person if she would agree.

In the midst of all this happening in Northern California, I was facing some daunting questions with this Calvary congregation. A group of sixty people, very lovely Christians, who were so enmeshed with each other that they couldn't function well as a corporate body. The vote which Council refers to above is their decision about bringing in a charter school at my pastoral direction, or keeping the elementary school, which had been their identity for over seventy years open, and die a quiet death within a year, as it was no longer a viable ministry.

This urban/inner city church had great potential to be many things for God, other than a school and day care center. I had come to know the congregation well enough in six months to expect them to make the best choice, but if I was wrong, then it was time for me to leave as interim as this choice could determine their survival as a church. I had begun meeting with some other pastors in the area about combining ministries to meet the growing needs of the community, as well as opening up our facilities for other Christian groups to use. Things were starting to get challenging and interesting, and the possibility of a Liz testimony…wow!"

Meeting regarding Liz being baptized:

Liz, do you want to be baptized?

Well…yeah but a Baptist church Jesus? Church and me don't mix. I mean… do I look Baptist?

What does a Baptist look like Liz?

You know Baptist! And I just ain't traditional. I hate those robes… makes me look like an angel or something. I ain't no angel!

I'll agree to that.

(Chuckle from Paladin.)

Shut up Paladin. You ain't no angel either.

Liz, I want to know why you want to be baptized.

You're God, don't you know?

Yes, I do, but I want to hear it from you. Why do you want to be baptized?

Cuz it's being real. If I am going to say I am a follower of Jesus then I gotta be willing to stand for what I say in front of people, but a church? It's the start of turning me into an Ann or a Ruth. I can just see it. No more beer. No more fun. Just work and more work...health food and rules. I'll die. I'll lose me!

Liz, I will not mold you into an Ann. I made you different from Ann. But as I told you before, a wild mustang is no good to his master if he is unwilling to be led by the master. Are you willing to be led by me, Liz?

Shit!

Is that a yes, or a no, Liz?

It's a yes, but I need help in the willing department.

Liz I want you to be baptized on April 4ᵗʰ at my church in Pasadena. I do not care if you wear a robe or not. I want to tell my people what I have done for you.

Are you nuts? I can't talk to church people. I mean they won't understand my language. How do you expect me to talk to Baptists?

With your mouth, Liz.

Real funny. You know what I mean. I don't have a church style.

Liz, tell them what I have done. And I want you to think about it ahead of time.

You mean I can't just do it. I gotta prepare.

I want you to prepare with me.

A Baptist church...can't you pick like a roller coaster ride or maybe a rock concert, or how about a bungy jumping baptism?

Are you ready to start being led? Liz we start preparing tomorrow.

I can't believe it...from a shady life on Broadway to baptism at Calvary. A Baptist church. Me, Liz, being baptized in a church. You are sure the big shits in that church are going to let somebody like me in to be baptized?

Liz we prepare starting tomorrow.

Liz walks away. Jesus tells council to inform Mike. Liz's verse will be Psalm 40:2.

E.R.

P.S. Per Dragonslayer. Baptismal song: Amazing Grace

> **"I waited patiently for the Lord;**
> **And He inclined to me, and**
> **heard my cry. He brought**
> **me up out of the pit of**
> **destruction, out of the**
> **miry clay; and He set**
> **my feet upon a rock**
> **making my footsteps firm."**
> **Psalm 40: 1-2**

I knew Liz's personal testimony would change their lives. She and I started talking about it in March to plan this once-in-a-lifetime event for her. I saw the irony of having her baptized in a Baptist church, even if nobody else did. It was going to be my privilege to do it, if the church could survive Liz's rough rhetoric. It was good that Jesus would prepare her with His plan on what to say.

As I made plans to hold the ceremony there over Easter, I wondered what was next on our journey to discover God's truth. Being able to baptize my buddy was sure to be a challenge for both of us. It would be a time of reflection as well, about all that the Lord had done in the last three years. The crescendo was building in the spiritual life of the System's symphony. More parts were believing in the hope of Jesus Christ and taking leaps of faith to know if God could be trusted. People were being changed around them and though most of it was ultimately good for God's purposes, some of it will cause more stress upon the System to trust their new leader, Dragonslayer.

I'm sure that most of my readers by now might be saying to themselves, "If Jesus was doing the things in my life that He has done in the System's lives…well, I would have no hesitation in following His every command." The factor which they discover is this; Once you gain the knowledge of truth that Jesus is alive and walking with us everyday to empower us to affect His changes in other people's lives today… the feeling of overwhelming responsibility can be disabling. However, this feeling does not come from Jesus, but from our enemy, who would like nothing better than to disable us with the fear of failure. Ask yourself this; Are the things which limit me from serving Him my understanding or His? Jesus tells us of two important realities about following and serving Him:

*"I have learned to be content in whatever circumstances
I am. I know how to get along with humble means, and
I know how to live in prosperity; in any and every
circumstance I have learned the secret of being filled and
going hungry, both of having abundance and suffering need.
I can do all things through Him who strengthens me."*
Philippians 4: 11-13

*"But if anyone suffers as a Christian, let him not feel
ashamed, but in that name let him glorify God. For it
is a time for judgment to begin with the household of
God; and if it begins with us first, what will be the outcome
for those who do not obey the gospel of God? And if it is
with difficulty that the righteous are saved, what will become
of the godless man and the sinner? Therefore, let those who
suffer according to the will of God entrust their souls to a
faithful Creator in doing what is right."*
1 Peter 4: 16-19

We are promised power to accomplish anything which is in the Lord's will for us to do for Him as His servants, anything! And He also makes it clear that we will suffer in this world for doing so.

These are some of the choices facing the System as we bring this leg of their journey to a close. They have witnessed the awesome power of Dragonslayer defeating their common enemies before their very eyes and felt the sting of a lack of faith on their part, when only their eight-year-old child Mariann has the strength to not only face several trials of physical pain, but the faith to face up to the powers of darkness. Her love for her Dragonslayer is only overmatched by His love for her.

For the first and only time in their lives, the believers outnumber those who have yet to believe, in His love being sufficient for them to overcome the challenges of being a multiple in this world. How does this alter their choices in the future? Soon, they will face the ultimate choice in obedience, that I began this book by discussing the ramifications of it for them. Will Maria's sharing before a group of Christians publicly about her 'differences' be a blessing, or their downfall as Ann expects? To some degree, both are right. Their trust and support of going with Pastor Bob to begin a new ministry to glorify Jesus will challenge the faith of all connected to this venture. What God teaches all of us in this endeavor will cause us to look with renewed hope at why and how we worship; why the Lord looks at how we treat each other as a measuring rod of faith in Him; and is there a limit to the amount of suffering which the Lord will ask us to endure for His name's sake?

Within two years time, evil will have numerous victories in battles, and be defeated in fewer, yet more important battles, that reveal even more clearly how it divides and seduces the present day church away from following Jesus. With every victory and every defeat, we are reminded that 'time is short' to grasp the full meaning of the power of Jesus in our lives. Just as our journey with the System will become more deeply embedded in the love of Christ, so will the challenges of joining with us in our journey, test the faith of many who choose to be a part of it.

As at the end of book one, I raised a number of questions that were left unanswered in it and offered new ones about what lies ahead in our journeys. This book raises even more questions and hopefully, it has put some readers on the path of finding answers to old ones. The adventure of discovering truth about God isn't so much of asking the right questions but learning the truth of more important questions that you didn't know how to ask. The next leg of the journey will be no different than what we have been growing accustomed to, drawing close to Easter 1999. The miracles of God's healing power in our lives begin to increase exponentially as our obedience and faith in Him grows.

Synopsis:

The System has no more parts to be revealed, and they are more aware of the demonic influences attempting to break up their newfound structure under Jesus. They are just beginning to understand the variety of ways that the enemy will attack new believers of Christ. They think they are ready to endure more pain and suffering that now has meaning, though not with the perception as martyrs, but as people of faith in a God who will carry them through it. None of them or I could imagine the places, the people, or the circumstances, that we would be encountering in His holy name over the next five years.

The question of how far Ann will go in teaching and the effect she will have on so many lives was one we didn't ask. What if she won more major awards, would the System survive the notoriety? Ann had witnessed the awesome power of God and was yet still in doubt about giving up control of her life to Jesus. What opportunity of ministry does Jesus use to open her heart to her fellow man? How does Jesus use a mathematical formula to open her eyes and mind to the possibility that He is who He says He is? How will Ann respond to the marriage with Sergio, as things get worse before they get better? What changes for her as she experiences the achievement of a major life goal?

Maria continues in her struggle to stay committed in her marriage. Hope that things will get better only seems to be getting more difficult to maintain, until God changes something through her pain and suffering. How will these events change the perceptions of the other parts who are getting stronger and able to survive outside of the marriage? What happens to Maria and also to Mariann, at an encounter in Sioux Falls, SD, with three bishops of the Catholic Church?

Mariann is growing stronger in her faith all of the time and in her ability to switch to the outside and control her world. How will Dragonslayer teach her the meaning of sharing; time, her daddy and mommy with other children in the System and outside, her faith and trust in Him, and her abilities through spiritual giftedness to reveal what is happening in two dimensions? How will she handle the loss of close friends and playmates? What does she do when given the choice to break free of the control of the Catholic Church from her past, through the love of Jesus? How does the impending sex scandal affect the entire System through her? What prompts her to write in her journal, "Today my daddy helped a man be deaded?" What is the meaning of her prophetic warning that one day the 'Rat People' will come and destroy? Why does she ask the question, "Dragonslayer, did you have a headache when you made this place?"

What happens to Mariann and Hopi as they enter the 'heart room'? How does Hopi respond to meeting his first real live cowboy, Wild Bill Hickok in Cody, WY? Does he ever get the respect he wants from Mariann?

How does Liz handle the responsibility of being a prophet for God to His church? Does she ever mellow out and find a 'Suburban Christian' church to fit her tough requirements, or is this effort futile? Does she ever make life easier for the rest of the System? Will she respond to anger management therapy?

What happens to the integrity of the System as they encounter three more near death experiences? How do they respond to the changes that come with the publishing of their stories? What does Council do when they learn the reality of how clergy abuse is a systemic disease that affects families for generations, including Maria's family? As more people of the System choose to blend personalities, how does this alter their position on individuality of the soul? How does one pastor bring them all to tears?

Then, there is Raquel and her prophecies and visions which continue to challenge everyone connected to her. Does any include me in their future revelation? What happens to the System in NV, at the Lost River Trading Post that changes the lives of everyone in a moment? How does everyone respond when prophecy touches home in a big way?

As Carol and I seek direction from the Lord for our future, why does He call us to "sell all that you have and come and follow Me" and we do it without a job, a home, or any security behind us except His promises? Why do we begin again at the 'bottom' by building house churches in order to build a community? What is the meaning behind, "Build an Isaiah 61 church and you will be sent?" What do I learn about forgiveness that is the hardest lesson of my life? Why does having worship on the top of a hill, lying in the tall grasses with eagles overhead, having communion with Cheerios and water, become one of the most significant worship services ever for all of us?

Final Revision Notes:

Book Three, _Living With Jesus Each Day_, will continue the journeys of the System and include the journeys of new clients of Shepherds Care Counseling Ministries. Most, but not all, will be survivors with DID/MPD & PTSD who will share their struggle to find and renew a relationship with God in Jesus Christ. All find the value of learning how they are not alone in their struggles with faith, fear, pain of suffering, hopelessness, wanting hope and trust in a God they think abandoned them... or at least couldn't love them.

It is because of these additional examples that I'm changing the chronological flow of the System's stories; to include these stories that affirm differing perspectives of the love of Jesus coming into their lives with grace and healing. He meets them where they are in life unconditionally ready to set the captives free from evil to choose an abundant life.

I begin these inclusions now because it is the first time this ministry has provided me time to finish the Shattered People Series Trilogy. After the end of Book Two in 2005 originally, He began revealing the scope of so many in need of these examples of what it means to "live in the Kingdom of God Daily" that we had to respond to pleas for help in the midst of life's struggles for all to find wholeness and purpose in **Spirit and Truth.**

> **"Come to me you who are weary and burdened,**
> **And I will give you rest. Take my yoke upon you and**
> **Learn from me, for I am gentle and humble in heart,**
> **And you will find rest for your souls." Matt. 11:28-29**

> **"For I know the plans I have for you,' declares the Lord,**
> **'plans for welfare and not for calamity to give you**
> **A future and a hope." Jeremiah 29:11**

Author Biography & SCPublishing Notes

Michael E. Chalberg is pastor and cofounder of Shepherd's Care Ministries in Gilbert, Arizona. He offers 3 primary areas of ministry; Pastoral Counseling & Mentoring over the Internet and privately; Christian Renewal as an Intentional-Interim Pastor & Consultant; and building Community Outreaches in and out of the church. He has been in ministry 44 years, working as an interim minister for 23 years offering renewal and healing to troubled communities of faith, using conflict resolution, leadership training, restoration of Biblical Disciplines, instruction in spiritual warfare & deliverance ministry and establishing prayer teams to support a laity-empowered church.

The past 26 years he has specialized in pastoral counseling to survivors of ritual abuses; Clergy Abuse; sexual abuse; Incest; Satanic Ritual Abuse; Human Trafficking of Minors; Pornography; Domestic Violence; Post Traumatic Stress Disorder; Dissociative Identity Disorder (MPD); and other trauma induced issues in adults and children. Several clients gave permission to publish their spiritual journeys of healing with him in this first published series Shattered People Series: Journeys to Joy (2003) & Love (2005) revised & updated to release in December 2020. Their stories include my commentary as counselor, pastor, friend and fellow traveler. SCPublishing started 23 years ago to publish books & educational and self-help information for survivors and caregivers who help them recover. Now 17 years later, SCP has added another Loved Back to Life Series in May 2020 with autobiographical books from various authors telling their stories of surviving severe abuse and trauma with Jesus' love & power to heal and redeem ... true stories as revealed to Pastor Mike since 2003.

He began the free counseling ministry in 1989 to include an Internet based chatroom reaching an international audience in need of counseling for ritual abuse and trauma. Here both survivors of abuse and their caregivers can come together for the soul purpose of learning about God's methods of healing in the midst of spiritual warfare, alongside of the SCM staff and fellow survivors on their healing journeys. He provides a 'virtual' church office atmosphere for topics discussed including personal histories and experiences in the healing process, spiritual warfare, deliverance ministry and the development of spiritual gifts for survival. Private counseling is given as well via emails, chat rooms, phone and video conferencing.

He moved his ministries to Arizona in 2010 to create Starbright Foundation Inc. with partners in ministry to focus on children/minors caught up in human sex trafficking by providing free support for rescues, protection, counseling and education to heal the traumas they have endured. SFI expanded to include training of law enforcement, first responders, school systems, childcare workers, foster parents, churches, families and social groups ... anyone who will listen about how to get involved in intervention and prevention of this criminal industry.

He and his wife, Carol (SCM cofounder), are graduates of Fuller Theological Seminary. He has a Master of Divinity in Pastoral Care & Counseling and Carol has a Master of Arts in Theology. He is a member of the Association of Traumatic Stress Specialists; American Association of Christian Counselors; International Critical Incident Stress Found. Inc; Christian Association for Psychological Studies; Titus Task Force Intern. - retired.

The Adventure Continues in Book Three!

Shattered People Series:

Living With Jesus Each Day

ISBN 97817349703-40 PB Pub. March 2021

ISBN 97817349703-57 PB Ebook March 2021

Living With Jesus Each Day completes the trilogy of the journeys for the people of the **System**. As you journey with them through the final ten years of their 16-year journey of healing with me, discover with them why they are at peace in the knowledge that the journey isn't finished.

Book Three joins their stories alongside many other survivor stories as they learn how to live with our Lord in His kingdom and in this surface world together. See how finding answers to the toughest questions of life can create more questions, as well as the joy of being certain that God will answer them, as soon as we are ready and able to hear them. Learn with us this truth:

"Jesus said to them, "With men
This is impossible, But with God
all things are possible."

You will learn with us the practical reality of the old excuse that says: ***"Be patient... God isn't finished with me yet."*** Read how the Age of Miracles isn't over until God is finished with us. Discover how evil can only control as much of our lives as we allow those spiritual forces to have dominion over us. See how these journeys of suffering, brokenness and heartache fulfill this endurance race to be crowned with Joy, Love & Faith... by our Lord Jesus Christ.

www.ingramcontent.com/pod-product-compliance
Lightning Source LLC
Chambersburg PA
CBHW031942090426
42739CB00006B/56